MARXISM AND THE
LINGUISTIC PHILOSOPHY

MARXISM AND THE LINGUISTIC PHILOSOPHY

by

MAURICE CORNFORTH

1971

LAWRENCE & WISHART
LONDON

PRINTED IN GREAT BRITAIN BY
LOWE AND BRYDONE (PRINTERS) LTD., LONDON

Contents

II

Linguistic Philosophy

4 LANGUAGE AND LOGIC

5 THE LANGUAGE OF MORALS

6 LIBERALISM AND INDIVIDUALISM

7 A PLACE IN THE ESTABLISHMENT

III

Marxism

1 THE DIALECTICAL MATERIALIST APPROACH

2 THE LAWS OF THOUGHT

3 SOCIALIST HUMANISM

4 COMMUNISM AND HUMAN VALUES

5 COMMUNISM AND MORALITY

6 COEXISTENCE AND CONTROVERSY

INDEX

Foreword to Second Edition

THIS book sets out to criticise one branch of contemporary philosophy from the point of view of Marxism. At the same time its aim is to discuss what can be learned from this philosophy. The Marxist standpoint which I try to maintain against all comers is not a stationary one, since Marxist ideas must always be developing and be formulated for our own times and problems. That is why as much as a third of this book deals with Marxism itself, and discusses Socialist Humanism, Marxist views on Ethics, the significance of the present-day scientific and technological revolution, and Materialist Dialectics. I have been criticised for putting all this in about Marxism, as irrelevant to the critical purpose of the book. But it was essential to my purpose. For I do not think one should separate criticism of other views from development of one's own.

There was once an idea among Marxists, which I shared, that there is an impassible gulf between "us" and "them". This is only a part-truth. One would not propose to water down Marxism by adopting ideas opposed to it. But that is no reason to condemn everything that is not Marxist as wholly reactionary and false. If something is false one must prove that it is false; that it is not Marxist does not constitute such a proof. And honest criticism of ideas one does not accept often shows that they are neither so reactionary nor so false as might have been originally suggested. In reviewing contemporary ideas there are factors to take into account. One is the growing influence of a scientific approach not only in natural science but in social and philosophical studies. Another is that individual thinkers of any originality are intelligent, well-educated and sincere; they see much wrong with the *status quo* and are seeking how to change it, so that to impute reactionary motivations to their work is often to mistake them greatly. These are all reasons why I finished this book with some observations about "Co-existence and Controversy". One must not compromise in ideas, but one must discuss, understand and learn.

As for the contemporary philosophy which is discussed and criticised in this book, Wittgenstein once said: "Philosophy is not a theory but an activity." I wanted to try to understand better the sort of activity now being done in the philosophy departments of British and some American universities—the so-called "Linguistic Philosophy". The name is in one respect misleading, for there exists no set doctrine or theory of "Linguistic Philosophy". As I have said in the course of this book, it is not so much a theory as a method of discussing and criticising theories. It is distinguished from other methods of discussion in philosophy by its concern with questions about uses of language.

For linguistic philosophy, every philosophical problem concerns the use of words, and is therefore to be solved by the method of inquiring into the uses of words. This is the "activity" Wittgenstein recommended to philosophers. Contrariwise, problems which cannot be reduced to questions about words are not philosophical problems at all, but some other sort of problem.

In this the linguistic philosophy emerges as the very antithesis of any philosophy, like Marxism, which seeks to find a perspective and purpose for human life by an inquiry into the foundations of human thought and action. It makes no such inquiry, but says it cannot be made. In this way it is representative of some very pervasive features of our day and age—namely, loss of perspective, lack of confidence in mankind and its future, scepticism as to the possibility of finding out any reasons why, disengagement from the big issues of human progress and, instead, narrow specialist concern with technical questions.

In order to try to understand this philosophy as a contemporary phenomenon—to criticise it and at the same time try to find what can be got out of it—I thought it best to study its background. Hence the long historical introduction to this book. In this I also wanted to correct some of what I had previously written about the same subject in my book *Science versus Idealism*. I have tried to show how the "empiricist" precursors of the contemporary philosophy created for themselves a series of problems and difficulties, and evolved by trying to find ways of getting round them. And I have tried to show, too, how these problems were not merely adventitious but came up out of the problems of the development of social life.

In this connection it was specially important to consider the development of Logic, and to try to disentangle the proper questions of Formal Logic, as a scientific discipline, from philosophical theories about them. Russell's *Principia Mathematica* was an immense contribution to science, but in it there was mixed up, to its detriment, some very dubious philosophical theory. This disentangling is important, not only because of the key role of discussion of logical problems in contemporary philosophy, but because Marxists need to rid ourselves once for all of the idea that materialist dialectics is in any way contradictory to, or supplants, formal logic.

Another important consideration is that modern philosophy has been concerned more and more with questions of the interpretation of the sciences. In this connection I have tried to point out the significance of Subjective Idealism, as a philosophical theory growing out of discussion about the sciences. But at the same time I have pointed out that, ever since George Berkeley, philosophers have been preoccupied with the criticism of Subjective Idealism. In contemporary philosophy it is more or less defunct. And so far from being a form of Subjective Idealism, the contemporary "Linguistic Philosophy" has contributed some of the most telling criticisms.

In the criticism of contemporary philosophy what seems to me of key importance is not so much criticism of Subjective Idealism as of the contrast and divergence which still holds between natural and social sciences. The former study processes and relations within them which lie hidden behind appearances. But the latter, as Marx said long ago when he criticised "bourgeois economics", deal "only with appearances". They deal with how capitalism *looks* to the trader, industrialist or businessman, but not with the processes of exploitation of labour on which it is based, nor with the social contradictions which presage its end. The thought I have tried to express in this book is that the most crucial thing in modern empiricist "bourgeois" philosophy has been the working out of a view of science, of scientific knowledge and the functions of science, which squares with and justifies the actual character of bourgeois *social* science and more especially economics. This question of what it is to study not only appearances but the underlying reality, in its real development, is the main question about which Marxists have to argue. The relation of appearance to reality is a very basic philosophy problem for Marxism.

In criticism of the "Linguistic Philosophy" I have entered into some discussion about the subject matter of philosophy, but without attempting to argue about any formal definition. It seems to me that to define "philosophy" is to define the problems of philosophy; and these change with the times. As to the problems of philosophy today, it seems to me that the "linguistic philosophers" go wrong by taking an extremely narrow and restricted view. But on one matter I agree with them, namely, that problems of philosophy must be distinguished from problems of empirical science and consist of problems remaining to be solved by other methods (if such methods can be found). I agree with them that philosophy, as compared with the sciences, does not deal with "what is the case", which we have to find out by empirical investigation, but with questions about "how to interpret what we find?", "how do we know what we know?", "what is the methodology?", and also with questions about "the meaning of life", "purpose", "values" and the like.

A basic thought of Wittgenstein, and in "Linguistic Philosophy", is that in such discussions a lot of nonsense is talked. And with this, too, one can hardly disagree. They want to clear away this nonsense, and for that purpose ask how it arises. Wittgenstein was responsible for the suggestion that it happens because people ask badly formulated questions, or "pseudo-questions"—and so we get "pseudo-theories" as the answers. This is what led to posing the investigation of uses of language as of basic importance in philosophy. We play various "language games", said Wittgenstein. Nonsense results from getting them mixed up. If then we are puzzled by some philosophical question we should ask: How is language being used here? If we can pin down and clarify the uses of language, philosophical puzzles vanish.

This book contains a lot of detailed criticism of the writings of several "linguistic philosophers", where it seems to me they have made false assumptions or reached unjustified conclusions in their general observations about language and its uses. I recommend these criticisms to anyone who is either puzzled by these writings or, on the other hand, inclined to accept them as contemporary gospel. But at the same time, I would like to emphasise, and have emphasised in the text, that whatever criticisms may be made of this or that book or article by this or that "linguistic philosopher", or of the overall point of view that results, the linguistic approach can be fruitful. Indeed, linguistic analysis is an indispensable tool for philosophical discussion even though not by itself the only thing needed.

In particular, I have tried to show that there is much to be learned from the work of Gilbert Ryle. His *Concept of Mind* has been attacked by some of his colleagues. But it is a materialist book and a useful book for Marxists; and possibly that is one reason why it has been criticised so much by people who are also opponents of materialism and Marxism.

Ryle introduced the conception of what he called "category mistakes", as the typical errors made in philosophy. This idea is a profound and fruitful one. He used it to criticise traditional conceptions about body and mind. He showed that to say the mind exists independent of the body is the same sort of absurdity as we find in *Alice in Wonderland* when the Cheshire Cat's smile exists independently of the Cheshire Cat. It is a "category mistake" in as much as it puts "mind" in the same category as "body", as though a mind were a ghostly body attached to the physical one. But minds and smiles are not thus related to bodies and cats. I have taken up this idea of "category mistake", and of studying "the logic of categories", and tried to show its materialist and dialectical content—which Ryle himself does not at all realise. In this connection I have also discussed some problems of the methods and subject matter of logic.

I have also devoted some attention to the work of the late J. L. Austin, not only in the criticism of Subjective Idealism but in the study of ways in which words are used for purposes other than making statements of fact. Very suggestive, in my opinion, is Austin's book *Doing Things with Words* in which he deals with what he called the "performative" use of language. The basic point is quite simple. To say "I will" when getting married, for example, is not simply a statement recording one's mental condition at the time. It is an act, a pledge. With those words one does not merely state a fact, but one performs an action—namely, one gets married. And without this sort of verbal "performance" there would be no marriage as a human institution. We do things with words. And I think it important to try to follow up Austin's analysis by seeing how this use of language enters into more or less the whole of human social activity. Thus I have suggested that such a basic human institution as *property* could not be established without the use of language. And similarly with all, or nearly all, human relations.

Marx and Engels maintained that the use of language is a product of social production. This is the materialist account of it. And language as a product of social production is needed for carrying on not only production but every form of human activity, human institution and human relation of which social production forms the basis.

This leads finally to considering the special use of language in what are called "value judgments". Some "linguistic philosophers", and notably R. M. Hare, have contributed interesting studies on this—in which, in my opinion, they have got quite a few bourgeois prejudices mixed up with their analysis. It seems to me that the distinction which these studies make between value judgments, on the one hand, and factual judgments, on the other, is of importance in the discussion of problems of Ethics; and I have accordingly applied it in the last part of this book in the discussion of Marxist views about Ethics. My main point is that we can find as good reasons for value judgments as for factual judgments (for example, as good reasons for saying that socialism is a better form of society than capitalism as for saying that Everest is a higher mountain than Ben Nevis); but that to argue the case we must distinguish the objective criteria of moral argument from those of factual argument.

To conclude, I am well aware that some of the propositions I have advanced in this book may not be very readily acceptable to many of my fellow-Marxists. For one thing, some of them are new; and whatever is new raises queries and needs to be scrutinised carefully. For another, some go contrary to traditionally accepted interpretations of Marxism. I do not believe for a moment that all I have put forward on these questions is yet correctly formulated in this book. A lot more work needs to be done. I think, however, that this discussion can contribute to the creative development of Marxist theory in its application to contemporary problems.

The only changes made in the new edition of this book are that some misprints have been corrected and the original Foreword is replaced by this new one. It is based on some remarks I made at a discussion on the book organised last year by the Cultural Committee of the Communist Party of Great Britain.

M. C.

London, June 1967

Acknowledgements

In discussing and criticising in this book the views of various philosophers, and the views about philosophy of various authors, I have aimed, on the most important points, to quote their own words. I do not think quotation for this purpose requires the formal permission of contemporary authors or their publishers. But I would like to take the opportunity of expressing the appreciation and gratitude which I feel (along, I presume, with everyone else interested in discussing philosophy) to these authors and their publishers for writing, editing and publishing works so well worth discussing.

In dealing with contemporary philosophy I have referred only to those works which are easily available in volume form, and have not delved further into the very copious literature of articles and discussion contributions available only in the journals. Of great value here are three recently published volumes in which articles are collected together—*Logical Positivism*, edited by A. J. Ayer, and the two volumes *Logic and Language*, edited by A. G. N. Flew. As the world knows, these editors are very well equipped to select the most important and most interesting articles.

The following is the list of works quoted in this book—in the case of works first published in this century I have also noted their publishers:

J. L. Austin—*How to do Things with Words* (Oxford University Press); *Philosophical Papers*: "A Plea for Excuses", "Other Minds" (Oxford University Press).

A. J. Ayer—*Language, Truth and Logic* (Gollancz); *Philosophical Essays*: "On the Analysis of Moral Judgements" (Macmillan); *The Concept of a Person and Other Essays*: "Philosophy and Language" (Macmillan), edited by A. J. Ayer, *Logical Positivism*: "Sociology and Physicalism" by O. von Neurath, "Positivism and Realism" and "The Turning Point in Philosophy" by Moritz Schlick (Allen and Unwin).

Francis Bacon—*Novum Organum*.

Sir Leon Bagrit—*The Age of Automation* (Weidenfeld and Nicolson).

George Berkeley—*A Treatise concerning the Principles of Human Knowledge; The Analyst.*

Rudolf Carnap—*The Logical Syntax of Language* (Kegan Paul); *The Unity of Science* (Psyche Miniatures); *Introduction to Semantics* (Chicago University).

Friedrich Engels—*Speech at Marx's Graveside; Ludwig Feuerbach; Origin of the Family, Private Property and the State; Anti-Duhring; Socialism, Utopian and Scientific; The Dialectics of Nature.* (See also Marx.)

edited by A. G. N. Flew—*Logic and Language,* 2 vols; Introductions by A. G. N. Flew, "Categories" and "Systematically Misleading Expressions" by G. Ryle, "The Language of Political Theory" by Margaret Macdonald (Blackwell).

Ernest Gellner—*Words and Things* (Gollancz).

R. M. Hare—*The Language of Morals* (Oxford University Press); *Freedom and Reason* (Oxford University Press).

Thomas Hobbes—*Leviathan; Human Nature.*

E. J. Hobsbawm—Introduction to Marx's *Pre-capitalist Economic Formations* (Lawrence and Wishart).

David Hume—*Treatise of Human Nature; Inquiry concerning the Human Understanding; Dialogues concerning Natural Religion; Essays.*

William and Martha Kneale—*The Development of Logic* (Oxford University Press).

V. I. Lenin—*The Tasks of the Youth Leagues* (Lawrence and Wishart, included in *Lenin's Selected Works*).

John Locke—*Essay concerning the Human Understanding; Essay concerning Civil Government.*

Ernst Mach—*The Analysis of Sensations.*

Karl Marx—*Capital,* vols. I and III; *Theories of Surplus Value; Theses on Feuerbach; The Eighteenth Brumaire of Louis Bonaparte; Critique of Political Economy; Economic and Philosophical Manuscripts of 1844; Critique of Hegel's Philosophy of Law; Critique of The Gotha Programme.* And with F. Engels: *The Holy Family; The German Ideology; The Communist Manifesto; Correspondence.*

G. E. Moore—*Principia Ethica* (Cambridge University Press); *A*

Defence of Common Sense (in *Contemporary British Philosophy*, Second Series, Allen and Unwin).

William Morris—*Communism*.

P. H. Nowell-Smith—*Ethics* (Penguin).

K. R. Popper—*The Logic of Scientific Discovery* (Hutchinson); *The Poverty of Historicism* (Routledge); *Conjectures and Refutations* (Routledge).

Bertrand Russell—*Our Knowledge of the External World* (Allen and Unwin); *Mysticism and Logic* (W. W. Norton); *History of Western Philosophy* (Allen and Unwin); *My Philosophical Development* (Allen and Unwin).

Gilbert Ryle—*The Concept of Mind* (Hutchinson); *Dilemmas* (Cambridge University Press); *Philosophical Arguments* (Oxford University Press).

Adam Smith—*The Wealth of Nations*.

Alfred Tarski—*Logic, Semantics, Metamathematics*: "The Concept of Truth in Formalised Languages" (Oxford University Press).

F. M. Voltaire—*Philosophical Dictionary*.

Ludwig Wittgenstein—*Tractatus Logico-Philosophicus* (Kegan Paul); *Philosophical Investigations* (Blackwell).

I would like also to acknowledge a special debt to two works by Professor Adam Schaff, of Warsaw, recently translated into English —*A Philosophy of Man* (Lawrence and Wishart) and *Introduction to Semantics* (Pergamon Press); to Dr. John Lewis, whose *Life and Teaching of Karl Marx* (Lawrence and Wishart) I was able to read before its publication; and to the research workers of the Institute of Philosophy of the Academy of Sciences of the U.S.S.R. with whom I was able to discuss, a few years ago, some points about both the peculiarities of contemporary bourgeois philosophy and the logical character of the laws of dialectics. But in making this last acknowledgement I hasten to absolve them from complicity in such errors or misconceptions as may be found in the following pages.

I

Empiricism and Logic

CHAPTER ONE

Principles for Science
and Principles for Government

I. MAN THE INTERPRETER OF NATURE

"Man, as the minister and interpreter of nature, does and understands as much as his observations on the order of nature, with regard to things or the mind, permit him, and neither knows nor is capable of more." In this First Aphorism of the *Novum Organum* Francis Bacon stated a principle which has given the direction to the main stream of British philosophy ever since.

Bacon's main contention was the old one, that all knowledge is furnished through the senses. But he carried it to radical conclusions. Because we can know nothing except what we can learn through our senses, it follows that we can form no ideas that are not derived in one way or another from experience, and theories which cannot be experientially verified are worthless.

This was to set up the scientific view of nature as against the previous philosophy. It expressed the revolt against the categories (or rather, the category-mistakes) of feudal thought—first causes, substantial forms and the like—which stood in the way of understanding the real causes and laws of motion of natural phenomena.

Thus for instance Thomas Aquinas, who was a traditionally recognised philosophical authority, would agree that knowledge *begins* from observation, and that the senses provide the data for the system of human knowledge. But for him that system had to be constructed on the basis of principles laid down by authorities recognised by the Church, leading to orthodox theological conclusions. And by arguing from empirical data to "first causes" he constructed a body of theoretical propositions which could not possibly be submitted to any test of experience.

If science was ever to flourish this traditional philosophy had to be destroyed. Bacon's doctrine sought to replace dogmatic theology and speculation about God and nature by scientific investigation of nature. It did not formulate any all-embracing "system" but called for the experimental investigation of natural processes, whether these concerned "things or the mind".

Moreover, Bacon maintained that this experimental investigation of the order of nature was not required merely to find things out and satisfy human curiosity. "Knowledge and human power are synonymous," he wrote, "since the ignorance of the cause frustrates the effect; for nature is only subdued by submission, and that which in contemplative philosophy corresponds with the cause in practical science becomes the rule" (*Novum Organum*, I, 3).

By submitting ourselves to nature—that is to say, by finding out how things really are by observation and experiment, instead, of vainly trying to work out *a priori* how things "must" be—we can subdue and master nature; and the discovery of real causes is the discovery of the practical "rule" of how to produce the effect.

2. DISCOURSE ON METHOD

Seventeen years after the publication of *Novum Organum* (1620) there appeared René Descartes' *Discourse on Method* (1637), which marked out another starting point. Bacon was not a man of science, but a politician who had the imagination to see what experimental science might yet do and achieve. Descartes, on the other hand, was a working scientist, a great mathematician—but he had less imagination.

These two works, which together may be said to have laid the foundation of all subsequent scientific philosophy, were contradictory but yet significantly alike. Both proceeded from the conviction that the old feudal philosophy was futile—its categories had no application, and its proofs proved nothing—and worse than futile, a positive hindrance to any progress of knowledge. And both proceeded to state *a method* for the discovery of *demonstrable* truth.

Descartes' method has been called the method of "universal doubt". But that is an incomplete description of it. It is rather the method of "clear and distinct ideas".

According to Descartes, "clear and distinct" ideas are true. His pattern for clearness and distinctness was derived from geometry (he was himself the discoverer of co-ordinate geometry), and his contention was that when analysis and definition are made sufficiently rigorous the resulting propositions are always demonstrable, in just the same way as in geometry.

In pursuit of demonstrations in philosophy he took the course of doubting everything except that which was clearly indubitable. And this he found in the proposition *"cogito ergo sum"* ("I think therefore I exist"). For, he argued, to doubt is to think, and, if there is thinking, a thinking being must exist. From this (as he thought) indubitable existential premise he then proceeded "in the geometrical manner" to demonstrate the general order of the universe. First, from the mere postulate of existence it followed that God, an uncreated and infinitely perfect being, exists; therefore God must have created us; and as a perfect being could not intend to deceive, he must also have created the material objects of which he has caused us to have perceptions. Material and mental substances are distinct and independent creations, Descartes maintained. We know that they are independent because we have a clear idea of the essence of each—material substance is essentially extended, and mental substance is essentially perceiving and thinking; and as these ideas are distinct, so must the substances themselves be distinct.

Descartes' universal doubt cast doubt on the existence of everything except the thinking self—on the existence of bodies, and the existence of other minds. Thus he first raised the question which has harried philosophers ever since, of how we know that anything exists beyond our own awareness. His own answer has long since been abandoned (for it contains a good many very clear and distinct *non-sequiturs*); but the question has remained.

In one way Descartes went much further than Bacon in his sceptical questioning of ideas previously taken as unquestionable. Bacon never had a doubt that the use of the senses yielded knowledge of material reality independent of the mind and there to be explored by the investigator. Descartes squarely rejected this assumption, until it could be proved as rigorously as theorems in geometry were proved.

But in another and, indeed, far more revolutionary way, Bacon went much further than Descartes.

For Bacon maintained that the methods of the natural sciences were the *only* methods of obtaining knowledge of the real world, and that on the basis of natural science a sufficiently complete picture of the world (of nature and society) could be built up as to require no supplementation by any philosophy standing above the sciences. Descartes, on the other hand, considered that the sciences themselves must have as their foundation a philosophy independent of the sciences, worked out by *a priori* reasoning from first principles evident to the mind.

Bacon had little to say about mathematics; but his view implied that mathematical reasoning was essentially a tool of the sciences. Descartes, on the other hand, considered that such reasoning was autonomous and was the way to systematic knowledge of final or ultimate truth independent of the natural sciences, by reference to which any and all conclusions of the sciences must be interpreted and judged.

3. BODY AND SENSE

While Descartes was deducing God and the coexistence of distinct material and mental substances, Bacon's certainty that observation and experiment yielded knowledge of material reality, and that this was the one and only road to knowledge, led his pupil, Thomas Hobbes, to the only consistent conclusion: that all knowledge is knowledge of the material world and that to assert the existence of anything other than the material world, transcending it, creating it or acting on it, was to engage in fantasy.

Hobbes took as his starting point Bacon's principle that all knowledge is furnished through the senses. But he did not follow this up by further expounding the principles of scientific method and leaving it to the future development of science to elaborate the theory of the constitution of the universe and the nature of man. Rather, he followed it up by deducing straight away a materialist metaphysics which stated of what the real world consisted.

As his successors in materialism, Marx and Engels, afterwards commented: "In Bacon, its first creator, (modern) materialism contained latent and still in a naive way the germs of all-round development. In its further development materialism became one-sided. Hobbes was the one who turned Bacon's materialism into a system" (*The Holy Family*, VI, 3(d)).

According to Hobbes, that which really exists, and which appears to us through our senses as clothed in the appearance of sensible qualities, is *matter*, or *body*. Nothing else exists. The world consists of bodies, which are always in motion. What we call "mind" is only a specific motion of bodies.

And he reached this conclusion by considering how "the thoughts of man" originate.

"Concerning the thoughts of man," he wrote, ". . . the original of them all is that which we call sense; for there is no conception in a man's mind which hath not at first, totally or by parts, been begotten upon the organs of sense. The rest are derived from that original.

". . . The cause of sense," he continued, "is the external body, or object, which presseth the organ proper to each sense, either immediately, as in the taste and touch, or mediately, as in hearing, seeing and smelling" (*Leviathan*, I, 1).

The action of external objects upon the sense organs produces in the mind what Hobbes variously called "seemings" or "apparitions" or "fancies"—the sensations of light, colour, sound, odour, hardness, softness, etc.—"all which qualities called *sensible* are in the object that causeth them but so many several motions of the matter by which it presseth our organs diversely. Neither in us that are pressed are they anything else but diverse motions, for motion produceth nothing but motion. But their appearance to us is fancy, the same waking as dreaming."

Thus: "Whatsoever accidents or qualities our senses make us think there be in the world, they be *not* there, but are *seeming* and *apparitions* only; the things that really *are* in the world without us are those motions by which these seemings are caused" (*Human Nature*, 2).

Hobbes defined body, or matter, by the property of existing objectively in space, external to and independent of our consciousness of it. Our consciousness was for him only an "appearance" or "apparition" arising from the interactions of other bodies with human bodies.

"The word body," he wrote, "signifieth that which filleth or occupieth some certain room or . . . place; and dependeth not on the imagination, but is a real part of that we call the universe. For the universe, being the aggregate of all bodies, there is no real part thereof that is not also body; nor anything properly a body, that is not also part of that aggregate of all bodies, the universe" (*Leviathan*, II, 34).

From this standpoint, Hobbes went on to develop some theories about the nature of knowledge and thought (or reasoning).

All knowledge must relate to the properties and motions of bodies, derived from what we can learn about them through the medium of the senses.

Thought is impossible without a body that has sensations, and it consists in a train of ideas derived from sense-impressions. But the train of ideas itself is nothing but a process of the stringing together of *words*. We attach different words to bodies and to the various motions of bodies, according as we have become aware of them by sensation; and so by joining words together we affirm or deny facts concerning the bodies that surround us.

"Reason", said Hobbes, "is nothing but the reckoning of the consequences of general names agreed upon" (*ibid*, I, 4).

It follows from this that various kinds of error are possible. There are errors in fact, errors in reckoning, and also *absurdities*, to which philosophers are peculiarly prone.

"Seeing that truth consisteth in the right ordering of names in our affirmations," Hobbes wrote, "a man that seeketh precise truth had need to remember what every name he uses stands for; and to place it accordingly; or else he will find himself entangled in words, as a bird in lime-twigs" (*ibid*, I, 4).

General words, that is, those which do not (like proper names) stand for particular bodies, but signify properties or relations of bodies, must have their use and application *defined* in order that reckoning or reasoning may be performed with them. But when such words are used *without* definition, or when they are combined in ways *repugnant* with their definitions, the result is "absurdity or senseless speech".

"And therefore," said Hobbes, "if a man should talk to me of a *round quadrangle*, . . . or *immaterial substances*, . . . a *free will*, or any *free* but free from being hindered by opposition, I should not say that he were in an error; but that his words were without meaning; that is to say, absurd" (*ibid*, I, 5).

Most philosophies, he concluded, consist of nothing but such absurdities. And indeed, any philosophy must always be senseless that deals with anything other than bodies and the words we use for speaking of bodies and their various motions.

"Substance and body," he wrote, "signify the same thing; and therefore substance incorporeal are words which when they are joined together destroy one another, as if a man should say an incorporeal body" (*ibid*, II, 34).

These views about thought and reason, and about the absurdity of any but a strictly materialist philosophy, brought Hobbes, the successor of Bacon, into a very direct clash with Descartes.

Hobbes ridiculed Descartes' interpretation of *cogito ergo sum* as implying the existence of an immaterial substance which thinks. "That which thinks is corporeal," he objected. For since "we cannot separate thought from a matter that thinks, the proper inference seems to be that that which thinks is material rather than immaterial." Furthermore: "Reasoning depends on names, names on the imagination, and imagination on the motion of the corporeal organs. Thus mind is nothing but the motion in certain parts of an organic body."

Against Descartes' "geometrical" proofs derived from "clear and distinct ideas" about the nature or essences of things, Hobbes objected: "Reason gives us no conclusion about the nature of things, but only about the terms that designate them . . . Essence as distinguished from existence is nothing else but a union of names by means of the verb 'is'. And thus essence without existence is a fiction of our mind."

The very curt and indignant replies which Descartes addressed to Hobbes indicated clearly enough his abhorrence of Hobbes' evident atheism and of the whole tendency of his conclusions. (See Descartes, *Objections urged by certain Men of Learning against the preceding Meditations, with the Author's Replies: the Third Set of Objections, with the Author's Reply*).

4. THE OBJECT OF KNOWLEDGE

Was there a middle path between Hobbes' uncompromising materialism and Descartes' deductive method? Did Bacon's conception of "man the interpreter of nature" have to lead to Hobbes' conclusions? This path was discovered by John Locke, the philosopher of the "glorious" bourgeois revolution of 1688 and the father of "British Empiricism".

Locke began his *Essay concerning the Human Understanding* with an onslaught against "innate ideas"—the doctrine that certain ideas, such as God, substance, cause, etc., are innate in the human mind, not derived from experiential sources, and self-evidently true. Thus he began with an implied attack on Descartes and justification of Bacon and Hobbes. As against the doctrine of innate ideas, he tried to show in elaborate detail how the whole of human knowledge is built up through the action of external material objects on the bodily sense organs.

"Let us suppose," Locke wrote, "the mind to be, as we say, white paper, void of all characters, without any ideas; how comes it to be

furnished? . . . To this I answer in one word, from experience . . .
Our observation employed either about external sensible objects, or
about the internal operations of our minds, perceived and reflected
upon by ourselves, is that which supplies our understanding with all
the materials of thinking. These two are the fountains of knowledge,
from whence all the ideas we have, or can naturally have, do spring"
(*Essay*, II, 1, 2).

According to Locke, the action of external objects upon our sense
organs produces, in the first place, "simple ideas", the elementary
sense-data supplied by each of the senses. These simple ideas are the
atoms, so to speak, from which the whole complex of our thoughts
is built. They form "the materials of all our knowledge".

"When the understanding is once stored with these simple ideas,"
Locke maintained, "it has the power to repeat, compare and unite
them, and so can make at pleasure new complex ideas. But it is not
in the power of the most exalted wit, or enlarged understanding . . .
to invent or frame one new simple idea in the mind" (II, 2, 2).

Locke then distinguished simple ideas which, as he asserted, were
exact resemblances of qualities inhering in the bodies which evoked
them, and simple ideas which nothing in the external world resem-
bled. The former he called ideas of "primary qualities", the latter
ideas of "secondary qualities".

Thus our ideas of solidity, extension, figure, motion or rest, and
number, were ideas of primary qualities, corresponding exactly to
the real solidity, extension, figure, motion or rest, and number, of
the objects of the material world. But our ideas of colour, taste, smell,
sound were ideas of secondary qualities only, not corresponding to
any real colour, taste, smell or sound inhering in material objects.

"The ideas of primary qualities of bodies," Locke wrote, "are
resemblances of them, and their patterns do really exist in the bodies
themselves; but the ideas produced in us by these secondary qualities,
have no resemblances to them at all. There is nothing like our ideas
existing in the bodies themselves. They are in the bodies we
denominate by them, only a power to produce those sensations in us;
and what is sweet, blue, warm in idea, is but the certain bulk, figure,
and motion, of the insensible parts in the bodies themselves, which
we call so" (II, 8, 15).

In this theorising about "ideas" Locke made an assumption which
proved of the greatest importance for his successors, in as much as
none of them ever questioned it until recently. Namely, he main-

tained that when we perceive, think, understand, judge, know, in other words, when we carry out any act of cognition from the simplest sort of sense-perception to the most complicated or abstract thought, then the *objects* of our cognition are not external material object themselves, but are rather *our own ideas* which are called up in our minds by the action of external objects.

This assumption is made in his initial definition of the term "idea", which he defined as "that term which, I think, serves best to stand for whatsoever is the *object* of understanding when a man thinks" (I, 1, 8).

In dealing with the development of knowledge, Locke proceeded to say: "Since the mind, in all its thoughts and reasonings, hath no other immediate object but its own ideas, which it alone does or can contemplate, it is evident that our knowledge is only conversant about them. Knowledge, then, seems to me to be nothing but the perception of the connexion and agreement, or disagreement and repugnancy, of any of our ideas. In this alone it consists" (IV, 1, 1–2).

The perceptions, thoughts and knowledge of man, therefore, are confined within the circle of his own "ideas". It is ideas, not things, that we "contemplate" or are "conversant about".

In order to grasp what Locke was saying, we should note that he was using the word "idea" in an extended sense, wider than that in which the word is generally used. For him, "idea" included sensation and perception. When we perceive something, then (according to Locke) the action of that thing on our sense organs has evoked an "idea", which is the object we are sensibly aware of. If afterwards we think about that thing in circumstances when we are not actually perceiving it, then the object of our thought, still called the "idea", is a kind of replica or image of the original "idea" which was implanted upon the senses. Whether we are perceiving things or only thinking about them, the *object* of our cognition is always the "idea", whether this be the actual sense-datum (as in the case of perception) or its replica (as in the case of thought).

5. THE APPEARANCE BECOMES THE OBJECT

If one compares Hobbes' earlier account of perception and thought with the alleged improvement made upon it by Locke, it is doubtful whether the latter was really an improvement at all.

According to Hobbes, when we perceive something there occurs a "seeming" or "apparition" of it. These words do not (for him) denote the objects of perception, but are used in the description or statement of the process in which a sensitive organism interacts with other bodies, those bodies being then the objects perceived. But Locke made the "apparition" or "appearance" into an object. It became (for him) the object and the only object of cognition.

Again, according to Hobbes, to think is to use words. But according to Locke, when we think we are contemplating, combining and recombining the replicas or images of the alleged objects of perception. And (for him) these replicas, or ideas, are the objects of thought.

Certainly, the texts cited from both these philosophers lack the definition of terms and precision of language very properly demanded by professional philosophers today. But Hobbes' account has the advantage of postulating nothing except the existence of human sensitive organisms which have acquired the use of language; whereas Locke postulates also "the mind" and all sorts of "objects" which exist solely in the mind—"its own ideas, which it alone does or can contemplate"—without offering any evidence at all for such postulates, or demonstrating any advantage to be gained from them. We shall see later that the rather acute analyses of questions connected with perception published by contemporary linguistic philosophers in effect demolish the assumption of Locke and lead to conclusions much more like those of Hobbes.

Having announced that "its own ideas" are the objects of all the mind's thoughts and reasonings, Locke nevertheless concluded that human knowledge does relate to the objective material world, because ideas are caused by the action on us of external material objects and are "copies" of them. "It is evident," he wrote, "that mind knows not things immediately, but only by the intervention of the ideas it has of them. Our knowledge therefore is real only so far as there is conformity between our ideas and the reality of things" (IV, 4, 3).

But this means that our knowledge of things is necessarily very limited. Thus because we can be "conversant" only with our ideas of bodies, and not with bodies themselves, "therefore I am apt to doubt, that how far soever human industry may advance useful and experimental philosophy in physical things, scientifical will still be out of our reach; because we want perfect and adequate ideas of those very bodies which are nearest to us, and most under our command" (IV, 3, 26).

In particular, we must remain for ever ignorant of "the substance" of things.

According to Locke, when we repeatedly find a group of "simple ideas" associated together, then "we accustom ourselves to suppose some substratum wherein they do subsist, and from which they do result; which therefore we call substance" (II, 23, 1). But what the nature of this substance is, our ideas do not inform us. They only indicate to us that substances exist, which are the ultimate cause of our ideas. "The secret, abstract nature of substance" is unknown. "The idea of corporal substance or matter is as remote from our conceptions and apprehensions, as that of spiritual substance or spirit" (II, 23, 5).

Thus with Locke a position was reached, which he derived from the original Baconian principle that all knowledge is based on experience, according to which the object of our knowledge is not the objective world but the subjective world of our own ideas. The scope of knowledge is limited to the perception of the order and arrangement, agreement and disagreement, of our own ideas. Behind our ideas, so to speak, and causing them is the objective world. But of the nature of the objects which constitute this world we can know nothing. They are, to use a phrase coined a hundred years after Locke, unknowable "things in themselves"

Thus both Hobbes' assurance of the materiality of the universe, and Descartes' assurance of the existence of distinct material and spiritual substances, alike vanish.

At the same time, and certainly inconsistently, Locke maintained that, to a certain extent, our ideas are true copies of real things, and that to that extent we do know what things in themselves are like; namely, our ideas of solidity, extension, figure, motion and number are true copies of the real solidity, extension, figure, motion and number of objective things.

How did Locke's theory come to involve such inconsistencies? It happened because he turned certain distinctions into hard oppositions, which it would nevertheless be difficult to justify by any appeal to experience.

He opposed the sensation or idea produced in the mind to the external object, on the one hand, and to the act of cognition, on the other hand; so that (for him) "ideas" existed as a set of sensible or mental objects standing between the knowing mind and the objective world.

He opposed the substance of a thing to the totality of its properties, so that while the properties might be known, the substance remained as the unknown "support" of such properties. The substance or being was abstracted from the thing's becoming, and set up as a separate and unknowable entity distinct from the totality of happenings, relationships and properties.

And he opposed theory to practice, knowing to doing, so that it appeared that while a man might in his practical life be engaged with material things, in his theoretical activity he was not engaged with them at all, but with his own ideas.

It was from such abstract oppositions that the difficulties and inconsistencies arose.

6. THE SOCIAL CONTRACT

It was by no accident that the kind of discussion engaged in by Hobbes and Locke, about the sources and objects of knowledge, was started in seventeenth-century England. The early rise of capitalism, and the break-up of every form of feudal institution and ideology through the growth of capitalist relationships within the old system, caused these problems to be posed. Old scholastic ways of thinking had to be overcome if the spirit of science, invention and discovery, so necessary for the development of capital, was to hold sway. Such developments as navigation, mining, and the use of artillery in warfare were demanding the aid of scientific research; and the new philosophy sought, above all, to explain and justify the methods of the natural sciences.

But it also sought to show how new, scientific methods of thought could be extended beyond the phenomena of nature to the comprehension of human relations and, in particular, to the comprehension of government—what government is and how it should best be conducted.

It was natural enough that questions about government should have loomed large, since at that time the right of the old rulers to rule was being called in question and efforts were being made to establish forms of representative government. Hobbes and Locke both considered that their new philosophy completely refuted the old idea that government rested on divine decree. Where was the evidence for such a view? It had been put forward and believed on no basis of evidence whatsoever. They considered, on the contrary, that an empirical examination of the actual circumstances of human social life would show up both the origins and functions of government.

Hobbes' *Leviathan* was concerned with "that great Leviathan called a Common-wealth, or State". The "natural" condition of mankind, he considered, is one of war of all against all, in which each would try to get what he could at the expense of all the rest, and in which human life would be in consequence "solitary, poor, nasty, brutish and short" (I, 13). The only way of avoiding the inconveniences of this state of nature is for men to enter into a compact with one another "to confer all their power and strength upon one Man, or upon one Assembly of men, that may reduce all their Wills, by plurality of voices, unto one Will"; thus constituting an Authority, or "Mortal God", which "hath the use of so much Power and Strength conferred on him, that by terror thereof, he is enabled to form the wills of them all, to Peace at home, and mutual aid against their enemies abroad" (I, 17).

Once such an authority is set up, people have to obey it—simply because it has the material power to force them to; for "Covenants, without the Sword, are but words" (II, 17); and if it weakens and loses its terror, then its subjects cannot but relapse into the miseries of the state of nature.

Hobbes had no doubt at all that government rests on the exercise of physical force. But he also stressed that various other means are brought into play to subdue the governed—and notably the teachings of religion. (This view of the functions of religion was not, with him, an argument for the abolition of religion. Very much to the contrary; it was an argument to show that, although religion rests on no evidence, it is politically necessary to uphold it.)

Hobbes was careful to point out that this theory of government was not put forward as an historical one. He did not maintain that in any historical period everyone had lived in "condition of war", nor that on any historical occasion they had actually entered into a compact to end it. What he did maintain was that, without government, such would be people's condition; that the origin of government is the need to avoid such a condition; and that the function of government is to secure people against it (I, 13).

Leviathan was published in 1651—three years after the execution of Charles I—and found favour with no-one. It was obviously unacceptable to the defeated Royalists, and the Parliamentary Army wanted to claim some other foundation than naked force as the justification of the Commonwealth. Parliament condemned it officially in 1666. Hobbes, who had been non-partisan during the civil wars, and had lived in retirement overseas, afterwards found favour at the Court of Charles II, though probably more because he was good company and Parliament had condemned his book, than for any more politic reason.

Locke's *Essay Concerning the True Original, Extent and End of Civil Government* (the second of his *Two Treatises of Government*, the first of which contained an elaborate refutation of the doctrine of "divine right of kings") came in 1690, and was in effect a theoretical justification of the settlement made by the "glorious revolution" of 1688. Locke started from the same premise as Hobbes, that government has no divine sanction but arises simply because men could not maintain their social intercourse without it. But when it came to the actual origins and functions of government, he took another stand.

According to Locke, government originates from property, and its function is to preserve and protect property.

He did not accept Hobbes' idea of man in a state of nature being a kind of wild beast. He considered that men were naturally industrious—and had to be so, in order to live. Property originated naturally from the claims which men make on the products of their own labours. And to protect property, government became necessary. Submission to government represented, as Hobbes had stated, a kind of compact. But this compact was made for the sake of protecting the products of men's labours, or preserving property. And that (according to Locke) was the same thing as preserving liberty, namely, each man's "liberty to dispose and order freely as he lists his person, actions, possessions, and his whole property . . . and therein not to be subject to the arbitrary will of another" (6). Locke considered that the property of improving landowners, merchants and manufacturers (unlike that of bad feudal barons, which was got by pillage) was theirs by virtue of their industry.

"The great and chief aim of men uniting into commonwealths and putting themselves under government," he wrote, "is the preservation of their property" (9). The power of government "is limited to the public good of society. It is a power that hath no other end but preservation, and therefore can never have a right to destroy, enslave, or designedly to impoverish the subjects . . . It cannot assume to itself a power to rule by extemporary arbitrary decree . . . The supreme power cannot take from any man any part of his property without his own consent" (11). And therefore "there remains still in the people a supreme power to remove or alter the legislative, when they find the legislative act contrary to the trust reposed in them" (13).

According to Locke, to acquire property is natural to men; and therefore the right to property is a natural, inborn or inherent right of human beings. Governments, instituted to protect and preserve property, are therefore the guardians of the rights of man; and are well or ill constituted and conducted to the extent that they fulfill this obligation.

7. APPEARANCE AND REALITY

With his insistence on the role played by social production and by property, Locke was certainly far more realistic and less doctrinaire than Hobbes, with his myth of "the state of nature". At the same time, Locke did succeed in obscuring the central and key fact which emerged in the theory of Hobbes, that far from men possessing inborn inalienable "rights", all "rights", like "covenants", are "but words" save in so far as they can be enforced, and that governments or states represent an organisation of physical force and coercion employed for compelling people, by "terror", to act in one way rather than another.

Convinced of this central fact, Hobbes asked why such an organisation should have come into being. And he answered, that the only reason could be that without it human existence would be impossible, since in that case the conflicts between people would rage unchecked.

This idea that the state came into existence to moderate human conflicts reappeared two hundred years later in the political philosophy of Marx and Engels. In their case it was based, however, on an analysis of the actual development of historical *class* struggles, which resulted from the improvement of primitive forces of production, division of labour and the emergence of private property. In order that class antagonisms "should not consume society . . . a power apparently standing above society became necessary to moderate the conflict," wrote Engels (*Origin of the Family, Private Property and the State*, 9). Marx and Engels likewise showed that the rights men claim are expressions of class interests, and that the struggle for the enforcement of claimed rights is the struggle of one class against another.

But unlike the later materialist theory of Marx and Engels, Hobbes' theory of the state was not historical, and it included no conception

of the historical development of state power. Hobbes maintained
that men are individually so constituted by nature that each must
always seek only his own satisfaction, so that all must always be at
each other's throats unless some armed authority exists to control
them. Men must therefore always be subject to a state, which must
always assume some more or less tyrannical and arbitrary form. Marx
and Engels, on the other hand, seeing the state as the product of
class struggles, were able to show that it generally functions as an
organ of class rule and that, with the eventual disappearance of class
antagonisms in communist society, the state, as an organisation of
coercion, must eventually "wither away". "The society which
organises production on the basis of free and equal association of the
producers," wrote Engels, "will put the whole state machinery
where it will then belong—into the museum of antiquities, next the
spinning wheel and the bronze axe" (*ibid*).

Hobbes' conception of human nature, with each man the natural
enemy of every other, was almost a caricature of bourgeois
individualism. He was undoubtedly a bourgeois thinker. But his
peculiarity was that he insisted on carrying things to their logical
conclusions in a way that was unacceptable to the bourgeoisie of his
own or any subsequent date. For this reason he was, and has
remained, the odd man out of bourgeois philosophy.

He carried Bacon's conception of "man the interpreter of nature"
to its logical conclusion in atheistical materialism. And he carried the
refutation of the idea of the divine sanction of government to its
logical conclusion in the doctrine that the authority of the state rests
on its possessing the material means of coercion.

Locke, on the other hand, was a thinker who well succeeded in
formulating the ideas of the progressive bourgeoisie of his time, in
such a way as to define and justify the system of liberties within
which that class was able to rule. His theories, which soon assumed
a rather conservative tone in Britain, were, when exported to America
and, later, to France, highly revolutionary. He insisted that good
government must be placed on a representative basis; and he urged
the adoption of that system of constitutional "checks and balances"
which was, at the time, intended, and did actually serve, as a guarantee against despotism, but which later came to serve so well as the
means whereby men of property could obstruct legislation which
might not be in their interests.

But in pulling off these not mean achievements, Locke's theory of government did, at the same time, disguise the reality of the state. The state existed, according to this theory, for "the public good of society", namely, "the preservation of property". And property, entitlement to which was founded on each man's honest productive labours, was sacrosanct and inviolable. So far, therefore, from being an organ of coercion, the state was the effective guarantee of each man's liberty in the enjoyment and use of his property.

Propounded at the time of the primitive accumulation of capital, when fortunes were being made from the slave trade and overseas plunder, when landowners were enriching themselves by improving estates got by enclosing common lands, and when a few grandees were directing everything while the majority of people touched their forelocks, this theory of the state was a staggering example of deception and humbug—however sincere Locke may have been, and however brightly the flame of liberty burned in his breast.

Thanks to the analysis made by Marx, it is now a well known fact of capitalist society that appearances belie reality.

The employment of wage-labour looks like a fair contract between employer and employed; in reality, it is the means by which the former gets the product of the unpaid labour of the latter. The laws look as though they protect everyone's right to the use of his own property; in reality, they protect the right of a few to own all the means of production while the majority have no property apart from personal belongings (and those they may forfeit if they are unlucky enough to fall out of work). The state looks like an organisation representing everyone and acting for the public good; in reality, it represents the interests of the capitalist class and acts on behalf of that class.

The link between Locke's *Essay concerning the Human Understanding* and *Essay concerning Civil Government*, his theory of ideas and his theory of government, his general philosophy and his political philosophy, lies precisely in this—that in the former he maintained that knowledge has for its object only the appearances of things presented to us in the ideas formed of them in our minds, while in the latter he treated only of the appearances which the bourgeois state presents in the minds of the progressive bourgeoisie.

8. THE BOURGEOIS DILEMMA

In the contrast between the theories of Hobbes and Locke there appeared for the first time that dilemma which has troubled bourgeois philosophy ever since—how to follow the paths of science without abandoning bourgeois illusions.

The great intellectual and social impact of the writings of Hobbes did not consist in their founding any new school of thought, still less in their serving any political or class interests, revolutionary or counter-revolutionary. There have never been any Hobbists or Hobbesites. Hobbes' power lay in repulsion rather than attraction. His writings served as a warning, a red light signalling danger ahead.

The promotion of the sciences is part of the very life-blood of the bourgeois social order. The dilemma presented to all bourgeois thinkers consists of this—that either you take your stand by the sciences and sacrifice your illusions, or else you take your stand by your illusions and sacrifice the sciences. But they are prepared to do neither the one thing nor the other. And so some third way has to be found.

The method proposed by Descartes, of constructing a philosophy standing above the sciences but not contradicting them, by means of deductions from allegedly self-evident axioms or first principles, represented one attempt at finding the way—though Descartes himself, due to the conditions under which he had to work, seemed more concerned with avoiding being condemned by the Catholic Church than with squaring the sciences with more properly bourgeois ideas. And in the centuries since, a variety of such supra-scientific philosophies have been proposed. (It may be remarked, incidentally, that the so-called "deductive system", often supposed to be the typical scholastic or feudal mode of philosophy, is in fact a bourgeois product. It was invented by Descartes.) Such philosophies, however, have always been vulnerable. The more the sciences have advanced, the less plausible have such philosophies become—for their first principles are never self-evident, their deductions always contain fallacies, and their conclusions are always found to contradict later scientific discoveries.

The most fruitful, the most plausible, and at once the simplest and most flexible way was that discovered by Locke.

This interpretation of Locke is confirmed by what he himself put on record about the origins and motives of his philosophy. In 1670 (when he was confidential secretary to Lord Ashley, subsequently Lord Shaftesbury, Chancellor under Charles II) he used, as he relates, to meet regularly with a few friends to discuss "the principles of morality and religion". But "they found themselves quickly at a stand by the difficulties that arose on every side". In other words, they found those principles hard to justify by current conceptions of scientific analysis. It seemed to him then that before reaching any conclusions they ought first to inquire more deeply into the processes of reasoning and understanding themselves. "Before we set ourselves upon inquiries of that nature, it was necessary to examine our own abilities, and see what objects our understandings were or were not fitted to deal with." This examination occupied him for the next twenty years, and its final results were published in his *Essay concerning Human Understanding*.

The essence of Locke's approach was to find how understanding could be extended by first examining its limitations. And he laid it down that the human understanding is "fitted to deal" with no more than the ideas, impressions or appearances of things implanted in the mind. With these alone we are "conversant", and no science can ever make us conversant with anything else. The scientific approach, whether in the natural sciences or in matters of morality and government, must always be content to argue about things only as they affect us, its object being not the things but the ideas of them in our minds.

Locke thus limited the sphere of possible scientific inquiry, and denied that it could penetrate to "the substance" of things. To try to do that meant pushing inquiry beyond our capacities, and could only result in difficulty and error.

This "way of ideas" has, as we shall see, been persistently explored from the time of Locke right up to the present day. Its virtue is that it enables the explorers at one and the same time to accept the empirical approach and the discoveries of the natural sciences, and to reject all materialism (such as that of Hobbes or, more to the point later, of Marx) and keep the discussion of social and moral problems on a plane where the real contradictions and motive forces operating in society, behind the facade of social consciousness, remain hidden and are never allowed to intrude.

CHAPTER TWO

Scepticism and Conservatism

I. THE ABOLITION OF MATTER

LOCKE was a political philosopher, whose main concern was to establish and justify bourgeois political liberties and the rights of bourgeois property. In pursuit of these objects, he never concerned himself much with allied questions of religion. However, such questions remained. And some of those who professed themselves impressed by Locke's theory of "the human understanding" were inclined to deduce from it sceptical conclusions about our knowledge of God and the human soul.

Yet the bourgeois revolution, which demanded a scientific culture and led to the triumph of science over church authority, at the same time clung to religion and to the authority of a reformed church. Anything savouring of atheism was abhorrent. And while the new bourgeoisie, in the most revolutionary way, set out to destroy feudal forms of ownership and feudal institutions and ideas, they took great care that the social position of privileged classes should remain secure. Church and State, they realised, must remain the pillars of society. For the new capitalist society, then in process of formation, could no more do without religion than it could without science.

Locke's successor, George Berkeley (a theological student at Trinity College, Dublin, who afterwards became a Bishop of the Church of England in Ireland), made it his concern to refute the view that the acceptance of the principles and methods of science must lead to a view of the world in which religious beliefs have no place.

The full title of Berkeley's principal philosophical work was: *A Treatise concerning the Principles of Human Knowledge, wherein the chief causes of error and difficulty in the sciences, with the grounds of scepticism, atheism and irreligion, are inquired into.* In the very title of his work Berkeley proclaimed that his purpose was to deal with the relations of science and religion, and to remove those "errors" in the concept of science which appeared to involve anti-religious consequences. The reconciliation of science and religion was his first avowed aim.

Locke had maintained that the "immediate objects" of knowledge are our own ideas; but that these ideas are produced by the action upon us of external material things, and that at least our ideas of "primary qualities" are copies of the qualities of external bodies.

It is easy to see the inconsistency in this doctrine. For if *only* our own ideas are the objects of knowledge, how can we possibly know which ideas "resemble" external objects and which do not?

This inconsistency permits two opposite lines of criticism of Locke's doctrine of ideas.

On the one hand, he could be criticised in that, having said that ideas are the products of the action of external objects and are copies of such objects, he nevertheless maintained that knowledge is limited to the relations between ideas and that the substance of objective things is unknowable. This line of criticism was afterwards taken up by the revolutionary wing of the French enlightenment—by Holbach, Helvetius and, above all, Diderot—and led to openly materialist conclusions.

On the other hand, he could be criticised in that, having said that knowledge is limited to the world of our own ideas, he nevertheless maintained that these ideas afford us some knowledge of the external material world. And this line of criticism was that adopted by Berkeley.

When we perceive any sensible object, what we are aware of is nothing but the existence in our consciousness of certain combinations of sensations. What can be meant, then, Berkeley asked, by the existence of a material object, external to the perceiving mind, corresponding to our sensations?

"The table I write on exists; that is, I see and feel it; and if I were out of my study, I should say it existed; meaning thereby that if I was in my study I might perceive it, or that some other spirit actually does perceive it. There was an odour, that is, it was smelt; there was a sound, that is, it was heard; a colour or figure, and it was perceived by sight or touch. That is all I can understand by these and the like expressions" (*Principles of Human Knowledge*, 3).

"It is indeed an opinion strangely prevailing amongst men," Berkeley continued, "that houses, mountains, rivers, and in a word all sensible objects, have an existence, natural or real, distinct from their being perceived by our understanding . . . For what are the forementioned objects but the things we perceive by sense? and what do we perceive besides our own ideas or sensations? and is it not plainly repugnant that any one of these, or any combination of them, should exist unperceived?" (4).

He went on to argue against Locke's contention that our ideas are copies of the qualities of external material things.

"I answer, an idea can be like nothing but an idea; a colour or figure can be like nothing but another colour or figure . . . Again, I ask whether these supposed originals, or external things, of which our ideas are the pictures or representations, be themselves perceivable or no? If they are, then *they* are ideas, and we have gained our point; but if you say they are not, I appeal to anyone whether it be sense to assert a colour is like something which is invisible; hard or soft like something that is intangible; and so of the rest" (8).

Berkeley was able very soon to dispose of Locke's distinction between "primary qualities", which allegedly inhere in material objects independent of the mind, and "secondary qualities" which are merely subjective.

"I desire anyone to reflect, and try whether he can, by any abstraction of thought, conceive the extension and motion of a body without all other sensible qualities . . . extension, figure and motion, abstracted from all other qualities, are inconceivable. Where therefore the other sensible qualities are, there these must be also, to wit, in the mind, and nowhere else" (10).

As for Locke's conception of "substance" as the "substratum" which "supports" the various qualities of material things, Berkeley asserted that this was a completely meaningless and incomprehensible abstraction.

"If we inquire into what the most accurate philosophers declare themselves to mean by material substance, we shall find them acknowledge they have no other meaning annexed to those sounds but the idea of Being in general . . . The general idea of Being appeareth to me the most abstract and incomprehensible of all other . . . So that when I consider the two parts or branches which make the signification of the words material substance, I am convinced there is no distinct meaning annexed to them" (17).

Here Berkeley turned the tables on Hobbes' assertion that "substance incorporeal" is a meaningless expression. It is "material substance" that is now asserted to be a meaningless combination of words. In this assertion Berkeley first formulated the contention, which has been repeated many times since, that "matter" is a meaningless abstraction. Materialism is condemned as a doctrine based on unintelligible abstraction—confused, meaningless, nonsensical.

Finally, Berkeley asserted: "If there were external bodies, it is impossible we should ever come to know it; and if there were not, we might have the very same reasons to think there were as we have now" (20).

And so his conclusion was demonstrated: "Some truths there are so near and obvious to the mind that a man need only open his eyes to see them. Such I take this important one to be, viz. that all the choir of heaven and furniture of earth, in a word, all those bodies which compose the mighty frame of the world, have not any subsistence without a mind; that consequently so long as they are not actually perceived by me, or do not exist in my mind, or that of any other created spirit, they must either have no existence at all, or else subsist in the mind of some Eternal Spirit; it being perfectly unintelligible, and involving all the absurdity of abstraction, to attribute to any single part of them an existence independent of a spirit" (6).

Berkeley hastened to defend himself against the imputation that there was anything paradoxical, or contrary to common sense and experience, about this conclusion.

"It were a mistake to think that what is here said derogates in the least from the reality of things . . . we detract nothing from the received opinion of their reality, and are guilty of no innovation in this respect . . . the difference is that, according to us, the unthinking things perceived by sense have no existence distinct from being perceived" (91).

But while the concept of matter has no basis in experience, its chief use is as an aid to the enemies of religion.

"How great a friend Material Substance has been to Atheists in all ages it were needless to relate. All their monstrous systems have so visible and necessary a dependence on it, that when this corner-stone is removed, the whole fabric cannot choose but fall to the ground; insomuch as it is no longer worth while to bestow a particular consideration on the absurdities of every wretched sect of Atheists" (92).

On the other hand, the articles of the Christian faith can be much more readily accepted, once the prejudice of the existence of matter is removed. Many objections have been raised against Christian dogmas, from the creation to the resurrection of the dead, on the grounds that they assert impossibilities. But: "Take away this material substance . . . and mean by body that which every plain ordinary person means by the word, to wit, that which is immediately seen and felt, which is only a combination of sensible qualities and ideas: and then their most unanswerable objections come to nothing" (95).

Indeed, "Matter being once expelled out of nature drags with it so many sceptical and impious notions, such an incredible number of disputes and puzzling questions, which have been thorns in the sides of divines as well as philosophers, and made so much fruitless work for mankind, that if the arguments which we have produced against it are not found equal to demonstration (as to me they evidently seem) yet I am sure all friends of knowledge, peace and religion have reason to wish they were" (96).

In this way, then, Berkeley refuted all those who were trying to draw anti-religious conclusions from what they supposed to be a scientific attitude. Such "wretched Atheists" supposed that science was about the objective material world, its constitution and laws, which are independent of human thought, will and sensation. When so interpreted, it is true that science is materialistic and may seem to be irreconcilable with any idealist or religious doctrines. But such an interpretation is absurd. Scientific results are, indeed, valid and useful —but we must interpret them correctly. They deal only with sensations, which come to us in certain orders and combinations, the rules and laws of which the sciences discover. Science has no other object—and therefore nothing it can establish can ever possibly contradict the main tenets of religion and idealism.

2. THE ROAD TO SOLIPSISM

Berkeley's circumscription of science and reconciliation of science and religion was not, however, entirely consistent—any more than Locke's doctrine had been consistent. For not content with showing that science could not overthrow religion, Berkeley tried to develop his philosophical principles as a *justification* of the fundamental tenets of religious faith.

Having made out that matter does not exist, and that our sensations are therefore not caused by the action upon us of external material objects, Berkeley was led to speculate upon the real origin of our sensations and of the order and combination which is observable amongst them. We must distinguish, he declared, between sensible objects, the existence of which "consists only in being perceived", and the "soul or spirit", which is "an active being, whose existence consists, not in being perceived, but in perceiving ideas and thinking" (140).

"It is evident," he continued, "that . . . the far greater part of the ideas or sensations perceived by us, are not produced by, or dependent on, the wills of men. There is therefore some other Spirit that causes them; since it is repugnant that they should subsist by themselves" (146). Therefore "nothing can be more evident . . . than the existence of God, or a Spirit who is intimately present to our minds, producing in them all that variety of ideas or sensations which continually affect us . . ." (149).

Following up this line of speculation, Berkeley was led to postulate another mode of cognition, additional to that derived from the senses. And this he called cognition through "notions", as distinct from "ideas". "We may not, I think strictly be said to have an *idea* of an active being, or of an action; although we may be said to have a *notion* of them" (142). The world is spiritual; but we do not know spirit—either our own souls, or God—through ideas implanted on the senses, but through "notions".

Now in this Berkeley was obviously inconsistent. For if it is illegitimate to infer the existence of the material world as the ground of our experience, it must be equally illegitimate to infer the existence of God. If all knowledge is derived from sense, how can knowledge of God and the soul be allowed? Or if we are allowed a "notion" of spirit, why is it absurd to have a "notion" of matter? If the words "material substance" are meaningless, surely the same must go for "infinite spirit"?

David Hume, in his *Treatise of Human Nature*, set about the removal of these inconsistencies of Berkeley.

"We may observe, that 'tis universally allowed by philosophers, and is besides pretty obvious of itself, that nothing is really present to the mind but its perceptions or impressions and ideas, and that external objects become known to us only by those perceptions they occasion . . .

"Now, since nothing is ever present to the mind but perceptions, and since all ideas are derived from something antecedently present to the mind; it follows, that 'tis impossible for us so much as to conceive or form an idea of any thing specifically different from ideas or impressions. Let us fix our attention out of ourselves as much as possible; let us chase our imagination to the heavens, or to the utmost limits of the universe; we never really advance a step beyond ourselves, nor can we conceive any kind of existence, but those perceptions, which have appeared in that narrow compass" (I, II, 6).

By "impressions" Hume meant the objects of sense; and by "ideas", "the faint images of these in thinking and reasoning" (I, I, 1). The objects of the mind being thus strictly limited to our own impressions and ideas, any external reality "beyond" the "narrow compass" of impressions and ideas is absolutely inconceivable.

In other passages Hume tried to show in some detail how the belief that external material things exist arises solely from the persistence and recurrence of certain groupings of impressions. Such experiences dispose us to believe that corresponding permanent external things exist. But we have no evidence that anything exists beyond impressions and ideas. When submitted to strict analysis, the supposition of such existence turns out to be logically baseless.

So far Hume agreed with Berkeley. But he went on to point out that, on the same principles, not only do external material objects disappear, but the knowing mind, or the soul, disappears as well.

"Self or person," Hume wrote, "is not any one impression, but that to which our several impressions and ideas are supposed to have reference." And so he asked:

"After what manner therefore do they belong to self, and how are they connected with it? For my part, when I enter most intimately into what I call *myself*, I always stumble on some particular perception or other . . . I never catch *myself* at any time without a perception, and never can observe anything but the perception . . . If anyone, upon serious and unprejudiced reflection, thinks he has a different notion of *himself*, I must confess I can reason no longer with him . . . But setting aside some metaphysicians of this kind, I may venture to affirm of the rest of mankind, that they are nothing but a bundle or collection of different perceptions . . ." (I, IV, 6).

And so just as permanent external material objects are reduced to collections of fleeting impressions, the same applies to the permanent self, or soul, or mind. "We may observe, that what we call a *mind*, is nothing but a heap or collection of different perceptions, united together by certain relations, and supposed, though falsely, to be endowed with a perfect simplicity and identity" (I, IV, 2).

So much, therefore, for Berkeley's "notion" of spirit. It has gone the same way as matter—and nothing remains but the series of fleeting impressions.

The train of thought which led from Locke, through Berkeley, to Hume, was a train of thought which relentlessly reduced the scope of what was asserted to exist. Thus Locke allowed three circles of being, so to speak: impressions and ideas; the self, to which these belong; and material objects, which they represent. Berkeley reduced these three circles to two: impressions and ideas; and the self or soul. Hume left standing only impressions and ideas, which belong to nothing and represent nothing.

Having arrived at this conclusion, Hume went on to develop it further, with the same relentless consistency. He next attacked the idea of causality.

He pointed out—as, indeed, Berkeley had pointed out before—that sense-impressions are quite "inert",· and do not contain any element of "power" or "efficacy" or "necessary connection", whereby one can produce or cause another. They simply follow one another, and enter into combinations, without any causal connection.

From this Berkeley concluded that they must be caused by God. But Hume concluded that, since our knowledge is limited to whatever is presented to us by the senses, the idea of causality as some kind of necessary objective connection between events independent of our consciousness of them, must be an illusion. "All events seem entirely loose and separate. One event follows another, but we never can observe any tie between them. They seem *conjoined* but never *connected*" (*Inquiry concerning Human Understanding*, 7).

Finally, Hume went on to conclude that, the objects of knowledge being limited to fleeting impressions, the knowledge of any one person at any moment is limited to the existence of his own impressions at that moment. There are no principles of reason which would allow us to infer from the impressions of the moment the existence of anything else—past, present, or future.

If, therefore, the philosopher is determined to admit nothing except what can with certainty be demonstrated, he can admit nothing whatever—neither the external world, nor other people, nor even his own continuous existence as presented by his memory—beyond "those perceptions which are immediately present to consciousness" (*Treatise of Human Nature*, I, IV, 7).

Here, therefore, there appeared the logical consequence of consistently following up Locke's original doctrine of "ideas". That consequence is solipsism.

It is a disturbing consequence, and has disturbed followers of the empiricist tradition of philosophy ever since. "I am at first affrighted and confounded with that forlorn solitude in which I am placed in my philosophy," Hume exclaimed (I, IV, 7).

3. KNOWLEDGE, BELIEF AND SUPERSTITION

Hume did not, however, *believe* that nothing existed except the momentary impressions in his own mind. "I dine, I play a game of backgammon, I converse, and am merry with my friends; and when, after three of four hours' amusement, I would return to these speculations, they appear so cold, and strained, and ridiculous, that I cannot find it in my heart to enter into them any further. Here, then, I find myself absolutely and necessarily determined to live, and talk, and act like other people in the common affairs of life" (I, IV, 7).

His conclusion was, therefore, that what can be known with certainty, and what one must believe, are two different things; and that it is in practice impossible to base beliefs exclusively on what can with certainty be known. The whole point of Hume's philosophy consists in this.

What is the nature of belief? Hume asked. What is the difference between believing or assenting to an idea, and not believing it? He answered: "An idea assented to *feels* different . . . and this different feeling I endeavour to explain by calling it a superior *force*, or *vivacity*, or *solidity*, or *firmness*, or *steadiness*." Belief is a matter of feeling, rather than reason. It is "something *felt* by the mind, which distinguishes the ideas of the judgment from the fictions of the imagination. It gives them more force and influence; makes them appear of greater importance; infixes them in the mind; and renders them the governing principles of all our action" (*ibid*).

As to why some ideas attain such "vivacity" as to become beliefs, Hume considered that this circumstance ultimately derives from their association with sense-impressions.

It is the repeated occurrence of certain combinations of impressions which engenders the firm belief in the existence of stable external objects; and similarly, the recurrence of certain sequences of impressions leads to the belief in causal connection.

Of course, social custom and education enforce certain beliefs— such as religious beliefs. But these beliefs, too, owe their vivacity, in the last analysis, to association with sense-impressions. Thus religious beliefs are kept alive by association with the lively impressions produced by religious ceremonies, and are apt to fade away without rituals to induce and reinforce them (I, III, 8-9).

In this connection, Hume was the first to draw a sharp distinction between propositions which are demonstrated in a logical or mathematical way, and beliefs in matters of fact, which cannot be so demonstrated. It is impossible, he said, "for the imagination to conceive any thing contrary to a demonstration"; but "in reasonings from causation, and concerning matters of fact, this absolute necessity cannot take place" (I, III, 7).

As regards "matters of fact", therefore, we can have no demonstrations or proof. And all that Hume claimed to have proved, was to have proved this necessary truth. If you demand conclusive proof of matters of fact, then *all* you can say with certainty is that your impressions of the moment exist at the moment you are aware of them.

Hume's object, then (as he made very clear), was not to tell us to stop believing in the existence of material objects, of other people, of past history, and so on. For he insisted, on the contrary, that we cannot help but assent to those ideas, which are enlivened by the whole content and sequence of our experience. His object was rather to destroy the false idea that certain beliefs are *demonstrable*, when they are demonstrably not so, and to puncture the fanaticism so often associated with unfounded pretensions to infallible knowledge.

He proceeded to stress the distinction between what he called "philosophy", meaning in this context "natural philosophy" or "science", and "superstition".

"Superstition is much more bold in its hypotheses than philosophy", he said; "and while the latter contents itself with assigning new causes and principles to the phenomena which appear in the visible world, the former opens a world of its own, and presents us with scenes, and beings, and objects, which are altogether new. Since, therefore, 'tis almost impossible for the mind of man to rest, like those of beasts, in the narrow circle of objects, which are the subject of daily conversation and action, we ought only to deliberate concerning the choice of our guide, and ought to prefer that which is safest and most agreeable" (I, IV, 7).

The methods of science are the safest guide, for they allow us to assent only to that which is substantiated by actual experience—and with regard to that, too, they renounce dogmatism, and are prepared to alter or modify whatever is concluded, in the light of further experience. We should always be cautious, Hume declared, in the "use of such terms as these, *'tis evident, 'tis certain, 'tis undeniable*; which a due deference to the public ought, perhaps, to prevent" (*ibid*). On the other hand, such expressions are freely used to recommend speculations which have no other basis than "a warm imagination".

"While a warm imagination is allowed to enter into philosophy," he said, "and hypotheses embraced merely for being specious and agreeable, we can never have any steady principles, nor any sentiments, which will suit with common practice and experience. But were these hypotheses once removed, we might hope to establish a system of opinions, which if not true (for that, perhaps, is too much to be hoped for), might at least be satisfactory to the human mind, and might stand the test of the most critical examination ... For my part, my only hope is, that I may contribute a little to the advancement of knowledge, by giving in some particulars a different turn to the speculations of philosophers, and pointing out to them more distinctly those subjects, where alone they can expect assurance and conviction" (*ibid*).

In his *Inquiry concerning Human Understanding*, Hume finished with a more forceful statement of this same conclusion:

"When we run over libraries, persuaded of these principles, what havoc must we make? If we take in our hand any volume, of divinity or school metaphysics, for instance, let us ask, Does it contain any abstract reasoning concerning quantity or number? No. Does it contain any experimental reasoning concerning matter of fact and existence? No. Commit it then to the flames; for it can contain nothing but sophistry and illusion" (12).

4. JUSTIFICATION BY FAITH

Whatever Hume may have had to say about the fallibility of demonstrations, it is evident from the record that his own conclusions were reached only by accepting and following up Locke's contention that the mind has no other object than its own perceptions, and Berkeley's that there is no way of comparing these with external objects existing independently of what is present in the mind. If this premise is disallowed, then the whole of Hume's argument is disallowed with it. Yet the premise itself hardly falls under the headings of either "abstract reasoning concerning quantity or number" or "experimental reasoning". Despite his apparent consistency, therefore, there was still inconsistency at the heart of Hume's philospohy.

But leaving this point aside for discussion later on, it is equally evident that, with Hume, Berkeley's pious endeavour to justify belief in God had come to grief. Hume did quite conclusively show, that from Berkeley's premises no demonstration of the existence of God followed. But nor did any demonstration of God's nonexistence. And certainly, according to Hume, a materialist view of the world was as lacking foundation as a theological view. Hume was, in fact, the first (as well as by far the greatest) of the agnostics.

Hume's own attitude to religion was negative. He regarded it as "superstition", and as socially injurious in as much as it encouraged intolerant zeal. "Generally speaking," he said, "the errors in religion are dangerous; those in philosophy only ridiculous" (*Treatise of Human Nature*, I, IV, 7). But he was opposed to "zeal" of any description; and he deprecated that of the materialists equally with that of religious enthusiasts.

His writings on "miracles", on "immortality", and on "natural religion", were much applauded by all the anti-clerical zealots of his own and subsequent times. Yet they were disappointed that, even though in an ironical tone, he always inserted small saving clauses into his demonstrations of the lack of evidence for any religious beliefs. At the end of the *Inquiry concerning Human Understanding* he remarked of religious belief that "its best and most solid foundation is faith and divine revelation". At the end of his essay on *Immortality* he remarked: "Nothing could set in a fuller light the infinite obligations which mankind have to Divine revelation, since we find that no other medium could ascertain this great and important truth." And at the end of his *Dialogues concerning Natural Religion* he made the principal speaker conclude: "A person seasoned with a just sense of the imperfections of natural reason, will fly to revealed truth with the greatest avidity . . . To be a philosophical sceptic is, in a man of letters, the first and most essential step towards being a sound believing Christian."

Hume's intention in making these remarks was, perhaps, mainly to provoke. But at the same time he was sticking to his brief by showing that, while he could find no matter-of-fact evidence to justify religious belief, he could find none to contradict it either; and that while proofs of the existence of God were impossible, refutations were impossible too.

He might have been surprised had he known that later on a whole school of Protestant theologians would take his polite sarcasms quite seriously, and proclaim faith and faith alone as the foundation of religion; and that dozens of the most eminent men of science would justify their faith in all kinds of religious hocus-pocus by his sceptical doctrine, that the unavoidable limitations of scientific knowledge left all questions of the meaning or purpose of life to be decided in the light of faith alone, because science had no bearing upon them.

Though this was not his intention, Hume in fact continued and completed the work of Berkeley in the matter of the reconciliation of science and religion. He agreed that the object of scientific knowledge is nothing but our own sense-impressions. He corrected the extravagance of Berkeley, who had tried to make out that the observable order in our sense-impressions was proof of the existence of God. But equally, he reinforced Berkeley's own refutation of extravagant claims made on behalf of science. Men of science were deluded if they supposed that their investigations led to the discovery of material causes which were "the ultimate and operating principle as something which resides in the external object" (*Treatise of Human Nature*, I, IV, 7).

Science, therefore, can discover nothing that can possibly conflict with religion. A scientist can be religious or not, as he chooses—his researches simply throw no light at all on the truth or otherwise of religious faith. On the other hand, the religious man has no cause to fear or quarrel with science.

In the first period of the development of modern natural science, it took up arms against religious obscurantism. The philosophy which Hume developed from Berkeley meant that science was now to be disarmed. It was to lay aside any claim to represent a true and expanding picture of the real nature of things, of natural history, the forces at work in the world, and the explanation of events.

5. MORALS AND REASON

The main upshot of Hume's work was the production of a lay philosophy, scientific in outlook, entirely free from any theological trappings, but equally free from making any claim that the sciences could discover the objective causes or "operating principle" of events. The "external object" lay quite outside the possible sphere of human knowledge. At the same time, Hume thought that by observation, unprejudiced by preconceived opinions, we could find out enough about "human nature" as "will suit with common practice and experience". "Human Nature is the only science of man," he said, "and yet has been hitherto most neglected" (*Treatise of Human Nature*, I, IV, 7).

Hume was one of the principal architects of that characteristic form of humanism which, while considering that "the proper study of mankind is man", refusing to see man as subject to any extra-human purposes, and judging everything as it affects human interests, at the same time considers human beings only as they exist within the confines of bourgeois society, taking this mode of existence as the one naturally conformable to human nature.

From this standpoint, Hume turned his attention to questions of morality, and government.

He considered it evident that men are moved to action not by "reason" but by "passion"—and considering his own demonstrations of the limitations of "reason", this conclusion was not unreasonable. From this he immediately deduced that "the rules of morality are not conclusions of our reason". For "morals have an influence on the actions and affections", whereas "reason alone, as we have already proved, can never have any such influence" (III, I, 1).

From this he went on to a second conclusion: "Morality consists not in any relations that are the objects of science . . . It consists not in any *matter of fact* . . ." (*ibid*).

"Take any action allowed to be vicious," Hume argued. "Examine it in all lights, and see if you can find that matter of fact, or real existence, which you call *vice*. In whichever way you take it, you find only certain passions, motives, volitions and thoughts. There is no other matter of fact in the case. The vice entirely escapes you, as long as you consider the object. You can never find it, till you turn your reflection into your own breast, and find a sentiment of disapprobation, which arises in you, towards this action . . . So that when you pronounce any action to be vicious, you mean nothing, but that from the constitution of your nature you have a feeling or sentiment of blame from the contemplation of it."

And so he concluded: "Morality, therefore, is more properly felt than judged of" (III, I, 2).

It is, therefore, entirely impossible that any moral conclusions —or any "value judgments", as philosophers say nowadays—should be validly derived from matters of fact. There can be no valid conclusion from "fact" to "value".

"In every system of morality that I have hitherto met with," said Hume, "I have always remarked, that the author proceeds for some time in the ordinary way of reasoning . . . when of a sudden I am surprised to find, that instead of the usual copulations of propositions, *is*, and *is not*, I meet with no proposition that is not connected with an *ought*, or an *ought not*." But as this "expresses some new relation or affirmation", it "seems altogether inconceivable, how this new relation can be a deduction from others, which are entirely different from it" (III, I, 1).

Why are some things judged "good" and others "bad"? Why do we say that some actions "ought" to be done and others "ought not"? Hume considered that this was simply due to the pleasure or pain which they afford us "by the mere view and contemplation" (III, I, 2). At the same time, moral judgments are not based on purely individual or selfish considerations. A concurrence of moral judgment occurs in society, because of human "sympathy", which renders the contemplation of the pain or pleasure of others painful or pleasant to oneself. "Sympathy is a very powerful principle in human nature" which "has force sufficient to give us the strongest sentiments of approbation . . . as in the case of justice, allegiance, chastity, and good manners" (III, III, 6).

Of course, these views of Hume about morality were taken by many to be extremely immoral, in as much as they contradicted traditional dogmas to the effect that morality was founded on the commands of God, or on certainties guaranteed by reason, or on infallible moral intuitions. Yet they were very far indeed from having any tendency to overthrow accepted moral standards.

By saying that "ought" could not be deduced from "is", Hume certainly did not imply that we ought not to say "ought". On the contrary, moral judgments are practical ones, which people living in society cannot in practice avoid or ignore. Hume simply sought to correct the "warm imagination" of partisans and fanatics, of sectaries of all sorts, whether these were people over-zealous for established authority or, on the other hand, people seeking to subvert the establishment in the name of new principles and "reasons" which they supposed to have been revealed to them. The whole force of his argument was in favour of those standards of "justice, allegiance, chastity and good manners" which had come to be generally accepted in his society, and which had won approbation (as he supposed) as a result of experience and of their being conformable to human nature.

6. IMPROVING THE ANCIENT FABRIC

What Hume had to say about political questions was said in his *Essays*; and it was short, and very much to the point.

He was a Tory in politics, of that moderate variety inspired more by a conviction that it is best to let well alone than by any conviction of the sanctity of established institutions; and served for some years with distinction as Secretary to the British Embassy in France. His principal aversion was to any kind of "enthusiasm" or excess, whether of the left or of the right.

Locke had deduced how government ought to be constituted from the alleged fact that governments were instituted to protect property. Hume doubted whether this was even a fact. "Government," he said, "commences more casually and more imperfectly" (*Of the Origin of Government*). But in any case, such inferences from "is" to "ought" are without foundation. "It is," he said, "on opinion only that government is founded" (*Of the First Principles of Government*). All governments have their conveniences and inconveniences. And "in all governments, there is a perpetual intestine struggle, open or secret, between Authority and Liberty; and neither of them can ever absolutely prevail in the contest" (*Of the Origin of Government*). The only wise course is, therefore, to seek to preserve that government which has been in practice found most convenient. We should avoid reforms and innovations which claim to be founded on "reason" but are in reality merely doctrinaire.

"Let us cherish and improve our ancient government as much as possible," Hume concluded, "without encouraging a passion for dangerous novelties" (*Of the First Principles of Government*). "An established government has an infinite advantage, by that very circumstance, of its being established . . . To tamper, therefore, in this affair merely upon the credit of supposed argument and philosophy, can never be the part of a wise magistrate . . . and though he may attempt some improvement for the public good, yet he will adjust his innovations as much as possible to the ancient fabric, and preserve entire the chief pillars and supports of the constitution" (*Idea of a Perfect Commonwealth*).

This is exactly the same argument as Burke afterwards produced, with more prolixity, against the French Revolution, and as still serves today as the foundation-stone of British Conservatism.

When Hume was with the British Embassy in Paris, he came into close contact with the revolutionary thinkers of the French Enlightenment. They were attracted by his sceptical attitude to religion, but repelled by the same attitude applied to social questions (including his readiness to tolerate clerics while still believing them peddlers of superstition). For his part, he deplored their evident desire to turn society upside down in the name of "truth" and of "the rights of man" deduced from a materialist philosophy. He deplored their theories of the perfectibility of men and of the power of "reason".

Those who are conscious of wrong and oppression must always try to penetrate in their thoughts to its causes, and to justify their revolutionary proposals by an appeal to objective truth. Hume contended that we could never possess any cogent demonstration of such truth, and condemned revolutionaries as enthusiasts carried away by their own brand of superstition. Like Locke, he deprecated any pretensions to be able to discover the objective causes behind the appearances. But he carried forward this deprecation with far greater force and consistency than Locke. Locke was still concerned with the completion of a bourgeois revolution. With Hume there emerged an attitude very well content with the existing social order.

The whole record shows that this philosophy, as it was developed from Locke's doctrine of "ideas", is socially conservative, well suited to the defence of an established bourgeois order. For when revolutionaries proclaim that a scientific method of thinking points the way to social innovation, including in their programmes derivations of "ought" from "is", this philosophy claims to show conclusively that no method of scientific thought can ever possibly justify such pretensions. It can never possibly justify the undermining of either state or church. And if it seems to do so, that is only the irrational delusion of dogmatic enthusiasts.

CHAPTER THREE

The Philosophy of Science

I. FRANCIS BACON WAS RIGHT

THE present-day linguistic philosophy is essentially a continuation, though in changed circumstances, of the tradition of British Empiricism founded by Locke, Berkeley and Hume. And indeed, these philosophers all acknowledge their debt, to Hume in particular. But in the two hundred years since Hume a great deal has happened. The sequence of thought which has been reviewed, from Bacon to Hume, took place on the basis of the bourgeois revolution in Britain and the primitive accumulation of capital. Then came the great social transformation wrought by the industrial revolution, which was made possible by, and carried along in its train, the tremendous development of the natural sciences. Germane to our present theme are those philosophers who directly adapted the heritage of Locke, Berkeley and Hume to the new conditions of industrial capitalism and the new discoveries of the sciences.

These discoveries amply bore out what Francis Bacon asserted at the beginning of his *Novum Organum*—"man does and understands as much as his observations permit him, and neither knows nor is capable of more". What with Bacon had been a bold stroke of imagination became almost a truism, born out by the most abundant experience. While philosophers sat speculating and deducing from first principles how the universe was and must be constituted, and what laws all things in it must obey, scientists got to work with their techniques of experiment and observation, and began to find out what processes really take place in nature, how they work and how they can be used. The whole epoch of great foundation discoveries by the natural sciences during the nineteenth century was prolific of philosophical speculations and philosophical systems of all sorts. But the advance of the sciences was putting these in the shade, and furnishing an ever more effective demonstration that what men cannot know about nature and society by following the empirical methods of science, they cannot know at all.

The science of the seventeenth and eighteenth centuries had been mainly mechanistic. That is to say, it had assumed that nature was rather like a machine, made of fixed parts which moved and interacted according to unchangeable laws, continually repeating the same movements and producing the same results. The great discoveries of the industrial revolution, on the other hand, were mostly concerned with the transformations and processes of evolution and development which take place in nature. As a result, the conception of nature was revolutionised. Instead of the same motions endlessly repeated, there emerged the picture of one form of motion being transformed into another, and of change, development and evolution taking place everywhere.

Discoveries in thermodynamics, for example, showed how different energies are transformed into one another—as in the steam engine heat is transformed into mechanical motion. Faraday showed how electrical forces are generated by a moving magnet. The investigation of living organisms showed how all forms of life are developed from cells. The Darwinian theory showed how all living species had evolved by natural selection from more primitive forms. Geology showed how the earth itself changed, and astronomy that the stars are not unchanging.

2. DIALECTICAL MATERIALISM

In this way the sciences began to present a picture of the material world in which everything could be explained from the material world itself, in terms of processes of the transformation and development of material systems. A living cell is a chemical system, and the original forms of life themselves came into being by the formation of complex molecules. Man himself evolved by natural selection from among the primates. It remained to work out how human society and human consciousness could have evolved from natural rather than from supernatural causes—and this was done by the hypothesis of historical materialism, put forward by Marx at about the same time as Darwin was working out the theory of evolution by natural selection. This was a hypothesis comparable with those advanced in other fields of fundamental theory in the sciences. Marx showed that what differentiated man from other animals was his way of using tools to produce his means of life; men thus created social forces of production, corresponding to the development of which they entered into relations of production, and corresponding to those relations of production they created social institutions and the whole complex of conscious social life. As Engels put it: "Just as Darwin discovered the law of development of organic nature, so Marx discovered the law of development of human history" (*Speech at Marx's Graveside*).

The philosophy of dialectical materialism, put forward by Marx and Engels, was based on accepting the fundamental principle that we can know only so much as we can discover by empirical procedures. All *a priori* principles, all alleged certainties founded on anything other than observation and the verification of theories by practice, were ruled out. But this was far from meaning that our knowledge is limited to our own sense-impressions. On the contrary, human knowledge is capable of penetrating further and further into the constitution, causes and laws of material processes which take place independently of our perceiving or knowing them. Being is prior to thinking. The object exists independently of its being perceived or thought about; and all the phenomena of consciousness are to be explained as the reflection and result of material processes, not the other way about.

Adopting this strictly materialist standpoint, Marx and Engels at the same time rejected the mechanistic assumptions of earlier materialist philosophies. The world was to be understood, not as a complex of things, but as a complex of processes, in which apparently stable things, together with their reflections in our consciousness, go through an unending succession of coming into being and ceasing to be, of change and development. Motion is the mode of existence of matter. But the motion of matter cannot be reduced to one fundamental mode of mechanical interaction. Simple spatial displacement and mechanical interaction, chemical change, life, and human conscious activity, are so many evolving forms of material motion, in which the higher always presupposes the lower, but cannot be reduced to it. The task of scientific inquiry is always to discover the laws of motion in terms of which particular phenomena can be explained and brought within the scope of human prediction or control. This means understanding things always in their motion and change, and in their complex interconnections; understanding the ways in which purely quantitative changes result in qualitative changes; and unravelling the tangle of contradictory relationships between and within processes by the working out of which all real change and development takes place.

This philosophy represented a summary and generalisation of the methods and discoveries of the natural sciences. As Engels insisted, it was not a philosophy which attempted to impose itself on the sciences, but it was drawn from them. As such, its tendency was to liberate the sciences from pre-scientific philosophical or theological doctrines, as well as from the hangover of the earlier purely mechanistic assumptions of the sciences themselves. And it served as the guiding light for the further application of scientific methods in formulating the fundamental theory of the development of human society and human consciousness.

3. THE ANALYSIS OF SENSATIONS

By contrast, right throughout the nineteenth and well into the twentieth centuries there continued to be asserted what had by then become the classical doctrine of empiricism, namely, that sense-impressions are the objects of knowledge, and that knowledge cannot be concerned with an external material world. A succession of philosophers—not noted individually for any special originality, verve or consistency, but taken all together producing a quite impressive body of theory—took it upon themselves to philosophise about and interpret the natural sciences in this fashion. They all tried to assimilate the great scientific discoveries of the age of industrial capitalism, while maintaining that scientific knowledge extends no further than the limits of one's own sense-impressions.

The emphasis which Hume had formerly placed on the sceptical implications of this doctrine came to be changed. Hume's whole emphasis, as we have seen, was laid on the lack of any positive foundation for human knowledge. But the subsequent development of scientific discovery and technology was so impressive, that the bland scepticism of Hume seemed out of place. His successors sought to interpret the methods of the empirical sciences as methods of acquiring positive knowledge, and the chief problem which engaged their attention was that of interpreting scientific discovery. The resulting philosophy of science, in all its variations, may be conveniently labelled "positivism".

In Britain, J. S. Mill elaborated what was called "inductive" logic, and formulated what he considered to be the reliable scientific methods for inferring from particular data of observation universal conclusions about the order and sequence of events. According to him—and to Karl Pearson, of T. H. Huxley and others, who adopted the same point of view—what the sciences achieve is the methodical prediction of the ordering of sense-impressions. They explained that when science refers to material objects and material causes, what it actually does is predict what groupings and sequences of sensations to expect. A material object, as J. S. Mill put it, is a "permanent possibility of sensation".

This contention proved capable of elaboration in two divergent ways.

One way (which I need not discuss further, since it has little relevance to my theme) was proposed in the United States by Charles Peirce, and led to the peculiarly American brand of positivist philosophy known as "pragmatism", "instrumentalism" or "operationalism". Peirce suggested that what we mean when we talk about objects should not be construed as simply a prediction of sensations, but rather as a prediction of the results of action. For sensations are not merely passively received, but are obtained in the course of human activity. Significant statements are like programmes of action, and those which serve no such practical purpose are virtually meaningless. This led to a new definition of "truth". What makes a statement true is not the fact that objects are actually related in the way the statement says they are. What makes it true is the success of the action which we take in conformity with it.

The other way consisted in trying to state explicitly what is really the case, or what really exists, corresponding to statements vouched for by scientific methods of inquiry. Taking it for granted that knowledge is limited to sense-impressions, it was concluded that the real "elements" of the world—the constitutive atoms out of which all things are built up, as in the ancient atomic philosophy of Democritus and Epicurus—are nothing but sensations. Perhaps the simplest and least ambiguous statement of this conclusion was that contained in Ernst Mach's book, *The Analysis of Sensations*.

"Bodies do not produce sensations, but complexes of elements (complexes of sensations) make up bodies," Mach announced. "If to the physicist, bodies appear the real, abiding existences, whilst the 'elements' are regarded merely as their evanescent, transitory appearance, the physicist forgets, in the assumption of such a view, that all bodies are but thought-symbols for complexes of elements (complexes of sensations)" (I, 13).

Having said that, Mach proceeded to dispose of the view (first foreshadowed by Locke, and afterwards stated by Kant) that causing our sensations there exist "things in themselves", the nature of which cannot be known.

"For us," he said, "the world does not consist of mysterious entities, which by their interaction with another, equally mysterious entity, the ego, produce sensations, which alone are accessible. For us colours, sounds, spaces, times, are provisionally the ultimate elements, whose given condition it is our business to investigate. It is precisely in this that the exploration of reality consists" (*ibid*).

Although Mach stuck in the word "provisionally" in deference to scientific caution—as a physicist might have said that "provisionally" atoms were to be regarded as the ultimate constituents of matter, until such time as later techniques might succeed in splitting the atom—it is pretty obvious that he saw no prospects of ever reducing sensations to anything other than sensations. The word "provisionally" was, indeed, quite out of place in his exposition.

Mach proceeded to argue that his "analysis" in no way represented a subjectivist or idealist point of view. He was not saying (as Berkeley had done) that reality was in essence mental or spiritual, as opposed to material. On the contrary: "The antithesis between ego and world, between sensation (appearance) and thing, vanishes, and we have simply to deal with the connection of the elements" (I, 7).

The "elements", he explained, are not mental, but neither are they material. They are, as he put it, "neutral". And in this way he ingeniously explained the connection between the physical sciences and psychology. When we deal with one sort of "order" of the "elements", that is the science of psychology, and we call them "mental". When we deal with another sort of "order", that is the science of physics, and we call them "physical" or "material". But really they are "neutral"—just "elements"; and all our knowledge and all science has the same objects, namely, the "elements" with which we are acquainted in experience, and which in one order make up a mind, and in another order a body.

4. A MISFIT

All the various positivist schemes for justifying the methods of science and interpreting its discoveries assumed that what science achieves is the prediction of experience, and that the method of science is the method of reaching universal conclusions from particular data. The scientist, in other words, observes certain connections within his experience (whether these are termed combinations of sensation or experienced consequences of activity) and then formulates his scientific conclusion in the form of a law. This law is, in effect, a formula for predicting future experience—namely, that the elements of experience will always be connected in accordance with the law. So long as experience continues to verify the prediction, the law is all right; but if future experience contains anything which does not accord with the prediction, then the formulation of the law must be altered so as to accord with experience.

Of course, the laws formulated by the sciences need not all be of the same form. And a good deal of attention was given by the philosophers of science to sorting out the various different forms of scientific law. For example, there are laws of the simplest form, which simply say that A is invariably combined with or followed by B; there are more complicated laws (of the sort which J. S. Mill called "concomitant variation"), which say that A varies with B, or express A as a function of B; and there are also statistical laws, which do not say that a certain sequence invariably occurs but state the frequencies with which different sequences occur.

This study of the form of laws lent to the positivist philosophy of science a certain plausibility. Physics has often been held to be, in some sense, the most fundamental or universal of the natural sciences; and as physics advanced, especially at and after the turn of the century, this philosophy was able to supply a very simple interpretation of physical laws. Physics came to be regarded as the model science, and other sciences as scientific in so far as they approximated to standards set by physics. The fundamental laws of physics express the dependence of one quantity on another, where these are measurable by readings from physical apparatus. The laws of physics, then, were represented simply as generalisations, largely statistical, and expressed as mathematical formulas, co-ordinating such readings. As A. S. Eddington later put it, the subject matter of physics consists of "pointer readings", "flashes on screens" and "similar indications" (*The Nature of the Physical World*). These elements of experience, and nothing else, were said to be the subject matter of physical science. When the physicist talks of "atoms", "electrons", and so on, he is merely using convenient (though somewhat misleading) expressions for the formulation of complicated laws co-ordinating data given in experience. He is not discovering anything about the constitution of the material world which exists independent of his experience.

The plausibility of this interpretation of the procedures and findings of the physical sciences depends on two conditions—first, that attention is confined to how the sciences draw conclusions from observational data, and no attention paid to how the observational data themselves are obtained; and second, that the conclusions of the sciences are taken to consist of laws which enable future events to be predicted.

The work of the theoretical physicist, it is true, begins with the data which are presented to him; his job is to devise formulas which will fit all the data. But where do these data come from? They are readings off various kinds of apparatus, and the apparatus must first be devised and constructed in order to get the data. The science of physics does not in fact start from "pointer-readings and similar indications". On the contrary, such data are a product of scientific work and not its commencing point. Modern natural science, whether one considers physics or any other of its branches, is not an undertaking for devising formulas to fit given data, but is a major co-operative undertaking for devising research techniques.

The theoretical physicist may be content to accept the data that are given to him and use them as the starting point for his theories. But that is only because he knows and is satisfied with the techniques by which they were obtained. And if he did not know those techniques, he would not know how to construct his theories or formulate the laws of physics. Thus, for instance, there are various sorts of "pointer-readings", taken from scales, clocks, galvanometers, etc. The pointer is, of course, a part of a physical object, namely, a scientific instrument, which was very carefully constructed and tested according to certain established rules in order to register certain changes by measurement on a scale. The "pointer-reading" is not a "datum" but something obtained by definite means for a definite purpose, namely, the purpose of finding out more about physical processes than is revealed by crude observation unaided by special techniques.

All natural sciences depend on specialised research techniques, adapted to the particular subject matter. The techniques consist of co-operative activity, interposed between the senses and the object, with the purpose of more thoroughly exploring the properties of the object. People devise means of acting on external objects, and making those objects produce their effects, in order by that means (as Francis Bacon explained long ago) to know more about those objects and to be able to do more with them.

And that being so, it does not fit the facts to interpret physics, or any other of the natural sciences, as though the subject matter were confined to the observational data given in experience (such as the pointer-readings, in the case of physics). Nor did the pragmatists or operationalists improve the fit by making the subject matter the "operations" performed by experimenters. On the contrary, scientific theory is founded, not just on given data, or records of operations, but on the co-operative purposive activity of producing changes in external objects, together with the construction of means to register and record those changes; and the subject matter of scientific research is, accordingly, not just the observational data (the end-record) but the constitution, properties and laws of the objects of the research activity.

If, then, we consider the content of the conclusions of the sciences, or of scientific theories, it is also evident that these cannot be interpreted simply as formulas for predicting future experiences. On the contrary, since the sciences engage in practical exploration of the objective material world, their discoveries concern the constituents of that world, the forms of motion and inter-connection, the interdependencies of material structures, the emergence of more complex structures with novel properties from simpler ones, and the processes of transformation and development by which what exists at one time came into being out of what existed at an earlier time. And the outcome is not only ability to predict experience, but a practical mastery over those processes themselves.

According to Mill's inductive logic, the sciences are based on procedures of arguing from the particular to the general, from particular connections, several times observed, to a universal law. Although it came to be recognised that "Mill's methods" were far from affording a satisfactory account of the processes of scientific reasoning, nevertheless it continued to be assumed that the sciences proceed by induction, that is, by extrapolating laws from observed instances. Hume had pointed out that there are no known principles of logic to justify any such procedure; nor have any such principles been discovered since. And yet it continued to be assumed that this is the basic or essential procedure of the sciences.

The fact is, that if one takes into consideration the whole social activity in which science consists, instead of confining attention to the logical relationship between formulas and their instances, it appears that the problem of understanding and justifying the procedures of the sciences is not at all the so-called problem of induction. Scientific work devises powerful techniques of research by the use of which people are able to make discoveries about processes hidden in the absence of such techniques, so that, having discovered such things, they can use them for their own purposes. The problem of understanding how this is done is not primarily a logical problem—though, of course, any problem concerning knowledge does involve logical considerations; it is a part of the more general problem of understanding how in conscious purposive social activity men develop the human capacity of mastery over their environment.

The positivist philosophy of science which maintains that the sciences are concerned only with the order, combination and sequence of events within the field of sense experience, and that the conclusions of the sciences consist of laws enabling us to predict such experience, does not fit the sciences. Any survey of the whole field of activity which constitutes scientific research shows that that is not what the natural sciences in fact do. This philosophy results in a total misapprehension of what the natural sciences do and of the real problem of how they do it. It did not arise from the development of the natural sciences themselves, but was foisted on them as an interpretation of their methods and findings, deduced from the philosophical doctrine that the object of knowledge is one's own sense-impressions. From that doctrine, this philosophy of science followed. But on the other hand, the fact that this philosophy of science does not fit the natural sciences is one very good reason for questioning the philosophical doctrine from which it was derived.

5. SCIENCE AND SOCIETY

The big point which positivists always made in favour of their views is that they refused to entertain the existence of anything not immediately open to observation. Everything that is supposedly hidden behind our sensations, as their real cause, as the objective reality not immediately open to inspection but which takes on a sensuous appearance, was ruled out, as "mysterious" and "unknowable". They persistently laboured Berkeley's contention that the concept of the external material object, or "matter", is "the most abstract and incomprehensible of all other", with "no distinct meaning annexed".

As Mach forcibly expressed it: "For us the world does not consist of mysterious entities." For the positivists, the world was just as it seemed. Everything they admitted to exist was always above board and open to view.

The account which such a philosophy gave of the methods and achievements of the scientific investigation of nature did not fit the actual methods and achievements, though it could claim a specious plausibility for its account of the laws of nature. But it fitted in far better with the methods and postulates which were at the same time being adopted for the investigation of society.

The development of the sciences, which came as an integral part of capitalist development as a whole, could not but lead to the conclusion that a scientific outlook must apply to society as well as to nature. Those who followed in the footsteps of Locke hoped to understand the workings of society in the same way as nature, by drawing conclusions from observation and experience. And they hoped to derive reliable principles for regulating social affairs— principles of ethics, of political economy, and of government—as conclusions from a naturalistic view of society. However, in the investigation of society the desideratum was rather to take the phenomena of bourgeois society at their face value, as given facts of human nature, than to seek—as in the natural sciences—to penetrate behind the appearances to the operative causes which bring them into being and lead to their dissolution or transformation. As we have seen, Locke's contention that the object of our knowledge is our own sense impressions had already begun to suggest and to justify such an approach.

From the very start of the bourgeois epoch the study of economics was recognised as of fundamental importance for the practical understanding and government of human affairs, since material welfare and the accumulation of wealth depend on the proper workings of the economy. With the great increase of wealth in the forms of rent, interest and profit the need was felt, as early as the middle of the seventeenth century, for understanding the mode of its production and distribution. And it was taken for granted that all wealth comes from labour. As Adam Smith put it at the beginning of *The Wealth of Nations* (1776): "The annual labour of every nation is the fund which originally supplies it with all the necessaries and conveniences of life which it annually consumes." How the values produced by labour are maximised, and some returned to the labourers as wages and some appropriated by owners of land and capital, was the problem posed.

Marx observed that "with Adam Smith, political economy had developed into a single great aggregate, and to a certain extent the ground it covered had been delimited." But "Adam Smith himself moves with great naivete in a continuous contradiction. On the one hand he traces the inner connection between the economic categories —or the hidden structure of the bourgeois economic system. On the other hand, alongside this inner connection he sets up also the connection as it is manifested in the phenomena of competition, and therefore as it presents itself to the unscientific observer as well as to the man who is preoccupied and interested from a practical point of view in the process of bourgeois production. These two modes of approach in Adam Smith's work not only run unconstrainedly side by side, but are interwoven and continuously contradict each other: the one penetrating to the inner relations, the physiology, as it were, of the bourgeois system; the other only describing, cataloguing, expounding and bringing under classifying definitions the external phenomena of the process of everyday life in their outward manifestation and appearance" (*Theories of Surplus Value*, section on "Adam Smith").

Marx went on to say that this happened because Adam Smith's "task was in fact a double one: on the one hand, to attempt to penetrate to the inner physiology of bourgeois society: on the other, . . . to describe the living forms in which this inner physiology manifests itself outwardly, to show its relations as they appear on the surface . . . The one task interests him as much as the other, and as both proceed independently of the other, the result is a completely contradictory way of looking at things—one that . . . expresses their intrinsic relations, the other . . . expressing the relations in their outward appearance."

Marx himself was primarily interested—and in this his interest was analogous to that which inspired the great contemporary discoveries in the natural sciences—in what he here calls "the hidden structure of the bourgeois economic system", or its "physiology". The clue to this was provided by Ricardo's contention that (in Marx's words, *loc-cit.*) "the foundation, the starting point for the physiology of the bourgeois system—for the understanding of its internal organic coherence, and life process—is the determination of value by labour time".

In *Capital* Marx took over Ricardo's contention that since what commodities have in common is that they are produced by expenditure of human labour, the objective standard for the comparison of economic values consists of the quantity of labour. And working from this starting point, he was able to uncover the secret of the capitalist appropriation of surplus values and of the accumulation of capital. The capitalist mode of production was revealed as a historically constituted method of the exploitation of labour. And from this Marx was able to demonstrate how in capitalist conditions surplus value is appropriated in the various forms of rent, interest and profit; how wages, costs of production, prices, rates of profit and interest, etc., etc., are determined; how forms of government reflect economic conditions; how the organisation and class struggle of the working people develops.

Writing to Engels (April 30, 1868), Marx said that thus "we have arrived at the forms of appearance which serve as the starting point in the vulgar conception : ground rent from the earth, profit (interest) from capital, wages from labour. But from our point of view the thing is now seen differently. The apparent movement is explained."

Of course, as Marx pointed out in the Preface to *Capital*, the kind of techniques employed in the natural sciences are inapplicable in the scientific investigation of society, which requires to develop its own special methods. "Neither microscopes nor chemical reagents are of use. The force of abstraction must replace both." The method is not experimental but analytic. By means of his method of analysis Marx succeeding in achieving in social science what the natural sciences achieve, namely, explaining the immediately observed or "apparent" phenomena (in economic life—wages, rents, profits, rates of interest, price variations, etc., etc.) from the more fundamental, but nevertheless empirically discoverable and verifiable, processes and relationships by which they are determined. By this means he demonstrated, not that the capitalist system can be made to work well and to last for ever, but that it is essentially an unstable and temporary social formation. His scientific theory became a practical programme of action for the working-class struggle against capital and for socialism.

6. POSITIVISM: METHODOLOGY FOR SOCIAL SCIENCE

Marx had observed (*Theories of Surplus Value*) that Ricardo was already, as early as 1848, being repudiated by other economists. "Ricardo discovers and proclaims the economic contradiction between the classes—as shown by the intrinsic relations—and hence the historical struggle and process of development is grasped at its roots and disclosed in economic science." The American economist H. Carey already "therefore denounces him as the father of communism: 'Mr Ricardo's system is one of discords . . . its whole tendency is to the production of hostility among classes and nations . . . His book is the true manual of the demagogue.'"

The consequences of the labour theory of value and of Marx's ensuing investigation of "the physiology" of the bourgeois economic system proved quite unacceptable. And that theory, with all its works and consequences, was and has continued to be repudiated, on the grounds—directly taken from the positivist philosophy—that the whole idea of real value and its objective measurement is a metaphysical invention. Instead, it was asserted that science should stick to the observed facts. And so what Marx had called the second side of Adam Smith's field of interest became, and has continued to be, the exclusive field of recognised bourgeois economic and social theory—"describing, cataloguing, expounding and bringing under classifying definitions the external phenomena of the process of everyday life in their outward manifestation and appearance".

Bourgeois economic theory studied to formulate laws connecting such observational variables as supply and demand, costs of production, wages, prices, rents, rates of interest, etc. This conception of "law" was precisely that formulated in the positivist philosophy; and the task which bourgeois economic theory set itself was precisely the task allotted to science by the positivist philosophy.

In the nineteenth century, bourgeois economic theory was closely associated with the practical doctrine of *laissez faire*. While economic theory formulated the laws, the practical doctrine proclaimed that these laws should be let operate without interference, and that the result would be the maximum benefit all round. At the same time, other elements of the positivist philosophy were employed for formulating the naturalistic doctrine of ethics known as "utilitarianism", which might be described as the morals of *laissez faire* economics.

The premise of utilitarianism was the supposed fact that people always seek pleasure and avoid pain. From this Jeremy Bentham concluded that pleasure is the only good, and that what people ought to do is always that action which will contribute to the greatest possible sum of pleasures—or, as it was expressed, to "the greatest happiness of the greatest number". He concluded, secondly, that the duty of government is to promote the greatest good by regulating people's actions by rewards and punishments. However, people should be left to their own devices as much as possible, and be regulated and restrained only when strictly necessary to prevent them from injuring others. The actual conduct recommended by these conclusions might have been in doubt, but for Bentham's tacit assumption that the free development of private profit-making contributes most to the public good by promoting the greatest attainable sum of satisfactions—so that private trade and industry should always be allowed full rein, and whatever hinders them severely discouraged.

By means of this doctrine of ethics there was worked out by Bentham a most active system of doing exactly what Hume had said could not be done—deducing what people *ought* to do from alleged empirical facts (above all, facts of economics). The whole stress was laid on that side only of Hume's contention, which declared that ethics could not be derived from knowledge of the will of God, or from any transcendental principles. Instead, morality was made a matter of empirical calculation of the supposed effects of actions, allegedly on the sum of pleasures, in practice on the pursuit of private profit.

Laissez faire became a thing of the past in the twentieth century, with the development (foreshadowed by Marx) of competitive into monopoly capitalism. Government became the tool of the great monopolies, and government intervention in economic affairs became more and more expedient for them. At the same time, the former theory of what Marx called "vulgar bourgeois political economy", that the free operation of economic laws would produce full employment and continuous expansion, could not stand up in the face of experience to the contrary. Government intervention in economic affairs became imperative, social services had to be instituted, economic levers had to be manipulated, and economic theories reformulated accordingly. However, the basic procedure of bourgeois economic science remained the same—ignoring "the hidden structure", studying "the external phenomena".

Very elaborate methods of fact-finding, statistical correlation, etc., were developed in the course of this study—and these methods have been very widely extended outside the narrow field of economic processes, to embrace sociological phenomena generally. The result is a very impressive body of descriptive knowledge. But it is social science only in the sense defined by the positivist philosophy of science, not in the sense that it reveals the objective structure and movement of human society in its historical development. Accordingly, it serves the turn of those who—as Marx said long ago of Adam Smith—are "preoccupied and interested from a practical point of view in the process of bourgeois production", who accept the system and do not wish to see beyond it; but not of those who want to understand how to change it, and to emancipate mankind from exploitation. For that purpose more than merely descriptive science is required, just as more than merely descriptive science is required for the mastery of nature.

The positivist philosophy of science was, then, in its actual development the philosophy which enunciated the principles of the methodology of bourgeois social science. That science confines itself to "describing, cataloguing, expounding and bringing under classifying definitions the external phenomena of the process of everyday life", and to formulating laws correlating the data of observation. The positivist philosophy proclaimed that this is exactly what all science is called upon to do, and that it cannot do more. And so it also provided canons of criticism of the Marxist science of society, as a metaphysical invention; and of communism, as a dangerous conspiracy of deluded underdogs seeking to disrupt the social order and establish themselves in power in the name of mere doctrinaire schemes and utopian imaginings.

Most of the effort of positivist philosophers went into the interpretation of the natural sciences—and especially of physics. It was presented as a philosophy of natural rather than of social science. This meant, in effect, that what was being done was to misrepresent the methods and findings of the natural sciences in such a way as to represent the officially recognised social sciences as practising the same scientific method, and to represent scientific socialism as unscientific.

It does not seem likely that the misinterpretation of the natural sciences could have become so persistent, or gained so much social prestige, had it not been for this evident, but never stated, service which positivist philosophy performed for bourgeois social ideology.

At the same time, the positivist philosophy continued—as with its precursors in eighteenth-century British Empiricism—to serve wider ends as well. In so far as the stress was laid on the positive functions of scientific investigation, the effect was to bolster up bourgeois views about the social system and its workings. But in so far as stress could be laid, on the contrary, on the limitations of scientific knowledge—which, after all, revealed nothing but laws of combination and sequence of sense-impressions—the effect was to stress the inadequacy of mere scientific modes of knowledge, and to leave scope for religious dogma, faith and, indeed, every kind of obscurantist authority, to stake a claim for recognition as essential elements in human consciousness, which supplement but do not conflict with the findings of the sciences.

CHAPTER FOUR

"Principia Mathematica"

I. MATHEMATICAL ANALYSIS

THE great development of mathematics in the nineteenth century was an essential part of the development of the natural sciences, especially mechanics and physics. And the way from nineteenth-century positivism to its successor-philosophies in the twentieth century goes through the discoveries of mathematics and mathematical logic.

Mathematics is written down and elaborated as a system of definitions and theorems concerning spatial elements and numbers, so that it looks as if it could ideally be worked out in its entirety independent of every other technical accomplishment or scientific investigation. Just as there is controversy about the subject matter of the empirical sciences, so there is controversy about the subject matter of mathematics. What is it all about? Way back at the beginnings of Western philosophy, the Pythagoreans and Platonists were engrossed with problems about the nature of mathematics, and put forward the view that it brings knowledge of pure forms or ideas which are self-subsisting and eternal, and are, somehow or other, materialised in the world of sense. This view had a considerable appeal for some of the modern philosophers of mathematics too. However, if we consider how mathematical theory actually develops and how it is used, it becomes pretty evident that people do not make discoveries about space and number until they are practically engaged in measuring and counting, and that the concepts of pure spatial forms and of numbers are reached by a process of abstraction from comparing, measuring, counting and dividing material objects. Mathematical theory develops along with technology and the associated empirical sciences, and serves the purpose of providing techniques for stating quantitative relations within material processes, and making calculations about them.

The differential and integral calculus, as first formulated by

Newton and Leibniz, was a mathematical technique devised for use in mechanics, for calculations concerning mechanical motions (as well as for the solution of analogous geometrical problems). For example, if a body is accelerating under the influence of forces continuously acting on it, that means that from instant to instant its velocity is increasing. How to calculate its velocity at an instant, and the increase from instant to instant? The calculus was devised to solve this kind of problem. For this purpose it treated of infinitely small increments occuring in infinitely short periods of time—the ratios of infinitely small quantities, and the summation of such "infinitesimals". Originally formulated in such terms, it did yield the practical results required of it. But it lacked rigorous definitions of its terms and proofs of its theorems, so that it was impossible to see just how the results were arrived at. In this respect it was an efficient but still imperfect instrument. And as mechanical and physical science and technology advanced, a better constructed mathematical tool was required than Newton and Leibniz had provided. This led to the later and very brilliant development of mathematical analysis.

Some credit is due here to the philosopher George Berkeley, who as early as 1734 attacked the fundamental concepts of mathematical analysis, as they were then formulated, in a pamphlet called *The Analyst, or a Discourse addressed to an Infidel Mathematician*. As usual, Berkeley was chasing "infidels"; and his aim was to examine "whether the object, principles, and inferences of the modern analysis are more distinctly conceived, or more evidently deduced, than religious mysteries and points of faith". He concluded that they were not, and that mathematicians should clear up their own "mysteries" before they presumed to question those of the theologians. The first part of this advice was well founded, and mathematicians did take it about a century later.

Berkeley drew attention to the fact that the concept of the "infinitesimal" was undefined. "Now to conceive a quantity infinitely small . . . is, I confess, above my capacity. But to conceive a part of such infinitely small quantity that shall be infinitely less than it . . . is, I suspect, an infinite difficulty to any man whatsoever; and will be allowed such by those who candidly say what they think; provided they really think and reflect, and do not take things upon trust."

And he also drew attention to the consequent defectiveness of the proofs of the calculus. If the theorems nevertheless worked, he said, they must be based on other principles than those alleged by their authors. "When the conclusion is evident and the premises obscure, or the conclusion accurate and the premises inaccurate, we may safely pronounce that such conclusion is neither evident nor accurate, in virtue of those obscure inaccurate premises or principles; but in virtue of some other principles, which the demonstrator himself never knew or thought of."

These "other principles", which Berkeley demanded, were worked out by the great mathematicians of the nineteenth century, who introduced exact definition and rigorous proof into mathematical theory.

The rigorous proof of theorems in mathematics depends on exact definitions. The procedure of analysis involved: first, taking certain terms and relations between them as primitive or undefined (such as points, lines and planes, in plane geometry, or, in arithmetic, zero and the operation plus-one, leading to the series of "natural" numbers); second, formulating axioms concerning the terms and their relations (the axioms must be independent and consistent, i.e. no axiom may follow from or be incompatible with the others); third, defining other terms and other relations so as to show their construction from the primitive terms and relations. That being done, theorems can be proved from the axioms and definitions.

This analytic procedure was very successful indeed in the theory of numbers.

Calculation and reckoning, as required in geometry and mechanics, operates with various different sorts or types of numbers. To begin with, there are the whole numbers, or *cardinal numbers*: 0, 1, 2, 3, ... n, n + 1, ... These are used for counting, and may be added and subtracted, multiplied and divided. If you subtract from a number a number greater than itself, the result is a *negative number*. For example, $2 - 3 = -1$. For reckoning relations and proportions, what are called fractions, ratios or *rational numbers* are used: $\frac{1}{2}$, $\frac{1}{4}$, etc. Then, however, complications turn up in the form of the so-called *irrational numbers*. Thus there is no rational number equal to the square root of two, or equal to the ratio between the circumference and the diameter of a circle, denoted by the Greek letter π. However, $\sqrt{2}$, π and other irrational numbers are needed for calculation, so these irrational numbers have to be used along with the rational numbers, the whole lot together being called *real numbers*. And then further complications arise, involving so-called *imaginary numbers*. Since the multiplication of a negative by a negative is always positive, it follows that there can be no real number equal to the square-root of a negative number. However, for some purposes of calculation multiplication by the square-root of minus-one is required. Such a number is called "imaginary", because no real number can possess such a property.

A basic achievement of analysis was, then, the definition of all these various kinds or types of numbers in terms of the cardinal numbers, using for this purpose only the concepts of order, set (or class) and limit.

Starting from the "natural" numbers, positive and negative cardinals were defined, and then rational numbers were defined as ordered pairs of cardinal numbers. If, then, the rational numbers are considered in order of magnitude, it can be shown that any rational number divides them into two sets, such that it is the upper limit of the one set and the lower limit of the other. For instance, the rational number $\frac{1}{2}$ is the upper limit of the rational numbers less than $\frac{1}{2}$, if they are considered in ascending order of magnitude, and the lower limit of those greater than $\frac{1}{2}$, considered in descending order of magnitude. This simple consideration provided the clue for defining irrational numbers. If you consider, for example, the set of rational numbers less than $\sqrt{2}$, and the set greater than $\sqrt{2}$, there is no rational number which is the upper limit of the one and the lower limit of the other. In this way, what Dedikind called "gaps" appear in the series of rational numbers, corresponding to the irrationals; and this circumstance was used to define irrational numbers themselves. The irrational numbers corresponding to the gaps could be defined as the sets of rational numbers below the gap. Thus, for example, $\sqrt{2}$ is the set of rational numbers in order of magnitude the squares of which approach nearer and nearer to 2 without ever equalling 2. The real numbers could then all be defined as ordered sets of rational numbers, and were divided into rational real numbers and irrational ones (according as they had or had not a rational number as upper limit).

Having got so far, the theory of the *functions of a real variable* was worked out. An expression "$x = f(y)$" is called a *function* of a real variable when the variables x and y take real numbers as their values, and when f expresses a rule whereby to every value of y there is assigned a corresponding value of x. It is then possible to define functions such that when y varies continuously towards a defined limit, so does x. And these definitions then permitted all the theorems of the old calculus, and a lot more besides, to be rigorously formulated and proved, in terms of functions of real variables, without any recourse to such obscure concepts as "infinitesimal quantity".

Further successes for analysis were scored when it was shown that the so-called imaginary numbers could be defined as ordered pairs of real numbers. In this way theorems concerning the imaginaries could be as rigorously proved as any others, and the principles of calculation with imaginaries were put on a firm basis. The "imaginary" numbers were renamed "complex numbers", and a very high degree of generality in the formulation of mathematical theory was achieved in the theory of the functions of a complex variable.

Subsequently, other operations have been defined—such as those employing matrices, introduced into calculations of quantum physics, which do not obey the commutative rule (i.e. $a.b$ is not equal to $b.a$).

2. MATHEMATICS AND LOGIC

The success of mathematical analysis suggested that something of the sort should be done for the theory of formal logic, the aim of which was to formulate the general principles employed in reasoning, i.e. in deducing one proposition from another.

The foundations of formal logic had been established for more than two thousand years by Aristotle, whose greatest achievement was the technical one of introducing a notation using variables. Since Aristotle, it has been taken for granted that general formulas should be expressed by the use of letters (or other symbols employed as variables), and that meaningful expressions to which these formulas apply should be obtained from them by substituting meaningful symbols for the variables. Thus Aristotle's formula for the syllogism, employing the variable terms "A" and "B"—"if all A is B, and all B is C, than all A is C"—gives a rule of inference applicable when meaningful terms are substituted for the variables: for example, "if all men are mortal, and all Greeks are men, then all Greeks are mortal". The subsequent development of mathematics and of mechanics would not have been possible without a notation employing variables, as first demonstrated in Aristotle's *Analytics*. Although Aristotle has been much decried, the sciences owe him a great deal.

However, while mathematics forged ahead, formal logic remained in a very imperfect condition. Its chief defect was that in its formulas the same variables, A, B, etc., were used indifferently to stand for individuals, properties of individuals, and classes, and that no formulas at all had been devised for expressing relations. As a consequence, the traditional logical theory lacked formal rigour, and was virtually inapplicable to the processes of reasoning involved in the modern sciences.

The starting point for the reformulation of formal logical theory was made in the "algebra of logic" worked out by Boole and others in the middle of the nineteenth century. Boole used a notation in which all the variables stood for *classes*—a class being understood to consist of all the individuals possessing some common property. And by this restriction he was able to construct a system of formulas applicable to classes and the relations of classes, which could be rigorously proved. Then De Morgan, Peirce and others extended this to the general logical theory of relations.

The key contribution to the advance of logical theory was made by Frege, in the last quarter of the century. Frege's aim was not, however, to present logic as a branch of mathematics, by working out an "algebra of logic". He rather saw mathematics as a continuation of logic. What he set out to do was to take the definition of number a stage further back, by defining cardinal number in terms of the nonmathematical and purely logical conception of *class*.

Cardinal numbers express the results of counting, and are used for saying how many members belong to a given class—a cardinal number is always the number of a class. Classes have the same number of members when to each member of the one there corresponds a member of the other. And classes between which there exists such a one-to-one correlation may be called "similar". It is, then, possible to define classes of similar classes, which all have the same number of members. What Frege did was to define cardinal numbers as classes of similar classes. In terms of this definition the series of cardinal numbers, from zero (the number of "the null class") onwards, could be defined. And the operations of addition, subtraction, multiplication and division could be defined so as to give all the right answers. Two plus two was proved equal to four.

This method of defining cardinal number meant that mathematics should be derived from logic. But to carry out this derivation evidently required a reformulation of the principles of logic. An analysis was required which would deduce the recognised principles or theorems of formal logic from a minimum set of axioms, and do so in such a way that there could be constructed from it the definitions required to pass from such logical concepts as class and relation to the mathematical concepts of number and quantity.

Frege himself employed for this purpose a clumsy and very complicated notation, which was a barrier to the development of his programme. Others, however, invented a more workable notation. And these efforts culminated in the production of *Principia Mathematica* by Bertrand Russell and A. N. Whitehead (the first edition of the first part was published by Cambridge University Press in 1910).

3. THE SYSTEM OF "PRINCIPIA MATHEMATICA"

In *Principia Mathematica* the basic conception, taken as "primitive", i.e. as self-understood and not to be defined in terms of anything else, was that of the "elementary" or "atomic" proposition. Such a proposition, which says that a certain individual has a certain property, or that certain individuals are related by a certain relation, is the simplest possible form of statement. Such propositions are unanalysable into simpler propositions; but from them, on the other hand, all other forms of proposition can be derived.

Denoting elementary propositions by the letters "p", "q", it was shown that from every elementary proposition, "p", can be constructed its negation, "not-p"; and that from elementary propositions and their negations can be constructed "molecular" propositions. *Principia Mathematica* took as the basic, or undefined, operation for constructing molecular propositions the operation commonly expressed by the word "or"—"p or q". "Implies" (or "if . . . then") was defined in terms of "or": "p implies q" means, by definition, "not-p or q". (For example, "If you move I will shoot you" was represented as meaning the same as "Don't move or I shoot"—which quite accords with common usage).

The most important logical device of *Principia Mathematica* was that employed for the construction of *general* propositions, i.e. propositions which refer, not to specified individuals, but to all or some unspecified individuals which possess some common property or stand in some relation. This involved the introduction of what were called "propositional functions", and operational symbols called "quantifiers", which applied to propositional functions. Propositional functions and their quantifiers were due to Frege, and represented his most important and abiding contribution to formal logical theory.

A propositional function was defined as an expression containing a variable, such that, when a value is given to that variable, the result is a proposition. Thus where "F" and "G" stand for properties belonging to individuals, the expressions "F(x)", "G(x)" are elementary propositional functions—and elementary propositions are obtained from them when the variable "x" is replaced by references to specific individuals. Thus, for example, "x is red" is a propositional function, which has as values "This is red", "That is red", etc.

Suppose, then, we construct a compound propositional function "F(x) implies G(x)". A general proposition may be obtained from this by saying (i) that this function yields true propositions for every value of x, or (ii) that it yields true propositions for some values of x. The first operation was represented symbolically as follows:

$$\text{(i) "(x). F(x) implies G(x)"}$$

which, in ordinary language, may be read as "For every x, F(x) implies G(x)". The second operation was represented by:

$$\text{(ii) "}\exists x. F(x) \text{ implies } G(x)\text{"}$$

which, in ordinary language, may be read as "For some x's F(x) implies G(x)", or (what comes to the same thing) "There is an x, such that F(x) implies G(x)". The operational signs "(x)" and "∃" used for these purposes are known as "quantifiers", and the operation is known as "the quantification" of a propositional function. All general propositions could then be represented as constructed by the quantification of propositional functions.

Though it looks difficult when first encountered, this technique achieved an extraordinary simplification and clarification of traditional logical theory. It enables all the principles of logic whereby one proposition is validly inferable from another to be exactly formulated and rigorously proved. Formal logic became an exact calculus.

The principal use made of quantification technique in *Principia Mathematica* was for the analysis of propositions about classes. Consider, for example, a proposition "Class-A is included in class-B" (say, "The class of all Frenchmen is included in the class of all Europeans"). This looks like a proposition asserting a relation between certain entities, namely, classes. And that is how it had been treated in Boole's "algebra of logic". However, a class is defined as consisting of all the individuals possessing a certain property. Let *F* be the defining property of class-*A*, and *G* of class-*B*. Then the proposition "Class-A is included in class-B" can, by the quantification technique, be represented as saying: "(x).F(x) implies G(x)". In our verbal example, "The class of all Frenchmen is included in the class of all Europeans" simply says "For every x, 'x is French' implies 'x is European' "—or still more simply, "Everyone who is French is European". Thus by means of the quantification technique, propositions about classes could be constructed from propositions about individuals—and there was shown to be no need to postulate such entities as classes existing additionally to the individuals which are the members of classes. The authors of *Principia Mathematica* expressed this by saying that "classes" are "incomplete symbols" or "logical constructions", which "disappear in analysis".

An important application of this technique of analysis was made in what was called "the theory of descriptions". As well as such class expressions as "The class of all Frenchmen", such descriptive expressions as "The present King of France" had occasioned much debate amongst logicians and philosophers. The expression "The present King of France" looks as if it "stands for" some object, namely, the present King of France. But since France is a republic, what is this object, and where is it to be found? And if the expression does not stand for anything, how can it have any meaning? Some philosophers went so far as to say that the present King of France enjoys an immaterial existence in the realm of ideas, even though deprived of material existence in France. However, by means of the quantification technique a very simple and convincing analysis was offered of propositions containing such descriptive phrases. Suppose, for example, that it is asserted that "The present King of France is bald" This simply says: "There is an individual, such that he is at present King of France and he is bald". Since there is in fact no such individual, the proposition is false; but there is no real puzzle as to the "reference" of the descriptive phrase. Such expressions as "the so-and-so" are, like "the class of so-and-so", incomplete symbols which disappear in analysis.

To get from here to the definition of cardinal number required a series of further operations employing quantification technique. First, relations were dealt with, so that statements of the similarity and dissimilarity of classes could be constructed. Similar classes have the same cardinal number; and so propositions about cardinal number— the elementary propositions of arithmetic—could be constructed as propositions about similar classes; and these in turn were constructed as more complicated statements about the one-to-one correlation of individual members of such classes. Cardinal numbers were thus defined, following Frege, as "classes of classes" (to say something about the number two, for example, is to say something about all classes with two members); but "classes of classes", like "classes", were shown to be incomplete symbols disappearing in analysis. These constructions, as might be expected, turned out very complicated indeed. In particular, they were found to involve what in *Principia Mathematica* was called the "theory of logical types" (individuals, classes, classes of classes, etc., are of different logical types, and rules had to be formulated to forbid confusion of types). However, axioms and definitions were worked out so that the arithmetical properties of cardinal numbers could be deduced from the logic of classes and relations.

4. THE FLAWS IN THE SYSTEM

How successful was *Principia Mathematica*'s deduction of mathematics from logic? Could the claim that this had been achieved be substantiated? Further examination of the system has revealed flaws in it—and two in particular which show that the conceptions employed need some drastic revision.

Apart from some technical difficulties connected with the theory of types, the first objection concerns the method of defining cardinal numbers.

A number, n, was taken to be the class of all classes with n members. And the definitions supposed that there actually exist as many as n individuals—otherwise there would be no classes with n members. Hence to define (as was required) an infinite series of cardinal numbers (in which every number is followed by the number one greater, and so on without end) there had to be introduced a special, and quite arbitrary, axiom—the so-called "Axiom of Infinity", which says that for any number, however great, there exist at least that number of individuals. This axiom made the whole system of mathematical truths, supposedly independent of any matter of fact, dependent on an alleged matter of fact, namely, that the number of existing individuals is infinite.

Thus *Principia Mathematica* postulated that an infinite number of individuals exist. And from this was deduced the existence of an infinite series of cardinal numbers, and an even greater number (of a higher order of infinity) of real and complex numbers. It was thus a system for deducing necessary truths—expressing formal properties of propositions, of classes, and of numbers—consequent upon the

existence of an infinite number of individuals. But that the existence
of an infinity of individuals is a necessary truth is far from evident.
How can this be known? Indeed, what precisely does it mean? That
for every cardinal number there is a rule for constructing a number
one greater, so that there is no greatest cardinal number, and so that
however many individuals may be counted the numerical system
always provides for counting some more, is undoubtedly a necessary
truth. But in *Principia Mathematica* this necessary truth was made
dependent on a postulate of empirical fact, which cannot be deduced
from any purely logical considerations, and which can never be
verified empirically either. Such a postulate, put forward as an axiom,
is quite arbitrary in relation to the construction of a working logical-
mathematical calculus. But without it, the calculus would not yield
the results required.

The second objection is even graver, and more decisive. It arose
out of problems presented by so-called unprovable theorems in
mathematics. And it, too, is concerned, in another way, with infinity.
There is an infinite series of numbers, and no limit to the theorems
which, theoretically, may or may not be true of them. Is it, then,
possible to establish a set of axioms such that it can be proved that
all true theorems about numbers follow from them, i.e. that they
enable it to be decided whether or not any proposed theorem is true?

Mathematicians have been able to formulate theorems about numbers, which are true of all numbers that anyone has ever calculated
with, but which they have found themselves quite unable to prove.
An example is the theorem that every even number is the sum of two
primes. Take any even number you can think of, and this theorem
is true of it. Thus $2 = 1 + 1$, $4 = 3 + 1$, $6 = 5 + 1$, $8 = 5 + 3$, $10 = 7 + 3$,
$12 = 7 + 5$, and so on. But no one has succeeded in proving that being
the sum of two primes is necessarily true of every even number in the
entire infinite series of even numbers.

Now, of course, it cannot be proved that any given theorem is
unprovable. All that can be said is that a given theorem has defied all
efforts to prove it. And so it might still have been hoped that one day
any unproved theorem would be proved, so that everything connected
with number would be provable and its eternal necessity demonstrated, had it not happened that the opposite was proved in a paper
by Kurt Gödel, published in 1931—*On Formally Undecidable
Propositions of Principia Mathematica and Related Systems*. With
great technical ingenuity, Gödel furnished a proof that no set of

axioms can ever be capable of deciding or proving all theorems about numbers.

It is important to be clear as to just what Gödel did and did not establish. Gödel's proof did not impugn the axioms, definitions and theorems of *Principia Mathematica* (though the objection remains that the theorems would not follow without the arbitrary Axiom of Infinity). It certainly did not demonstrate (as some enthusiasts for unreason have tried to make out) that logic and mathematics provide only fallible instruments of human calculation and that reason must always break down. Rather, it demonstrated that no technical development of logic and mathematics can ever represent the final end, the ultimate achievement of universality and formal perfection. There is no system of necessary truth such that we have only to discover the foundation principles and all of it without end comes within our grasp.

Briefly, these two objections, or major difficulties involved in the working out of the system of *Principia Mathematica*, add up to the following:

First, while formally numbers exhibit the properties of classes of classes, the definition of cardinal numbers in terms of classes of classes does not enable arithmetic, and then the rest of mathematics, to be deduced from formal logic. For with mathematics there enters the definition and deduction of the properties of infinite aggregates and infinite series, which cannot be derived from the elementary logic of propositions and classes.

Second, no set of primitive concepts and axioms is feasible by means of which all questions of the properties of numbers and the results of mathematical operations could be decided. The development of mathematics must therefore be like that of the empirical sciences which mathematics serves, in the sense of being an endless quest of technical invention and discovery. It does not consist of the unfolding of the formal consequences of any set of necessary principles established and finalised once and for all.

That is what these objections add up to. And so, of course, they do not invalidate the elementary calculus of propositions, or the quantification technique and its applications, or the logical theory of classes and relations, or the foundations of arithmetic, or the definitions of real and complex numbers, or the theories of the functions of real and complex variables, or any other of the great technical achievements of modern logic and mathematics. But what they do show is that the idea of demonstrating the principles of logic and mathematics as a self-contained system of necessary truth deducible from axioms of formal logic is one which necessarily cannot succeed; and that the conceptions employed in *Principia Mathematica* therefore need revision.

5. THE INTERPRETATION OF LOGICAL AND MATHEMATICAL ANALYSIS

When people achieve something they often misunderstand it and represent it as other than it is. To do something, and to know just what you are doing, are not the same thing. In some aspects, philosophy, as a critical reflection on nature and human life, is a product of this circumstance—it is an effort to get to know what we are doing. And its value and practical importance stem from this. For it is not enough just to do something: we need to know what we are doing, or what we do is apt to land us in difficulties we did not expect.

The achievements of logical and mathematical analysis were impressive. But Frege, and afterwards Russell, worked with a conception of what analysis does which led to difficulties.

The conception of analysis due to Frege, and developed in *Principia Mathematica*, represented analysis as the reformulation of propositions in such a way as to make explicit exactly what they refer to. Thus Frege's definition of cardinal number was represented as demonstrating that the objects which mathematical propositions about cardinal number refer to are—classes of classes. The *Principia Mathematica* theory of incomplete symbols and logical constructions was a generalised theory about how such analysis is done. Thus the analysis of objects, A, was to be accomplished by reformulating propositions "F(A)" in the form "G(x,y,z . . .)", where x,y,z . . . are the objects referred to in propositions nominally about A. The sign "A" was thus shown to be an incomplete symbol, and A was shown to be a logical construction out of the elements x,y,z . . . Such analysis could, then, be carried on until it arrived at the ultimate or irreducible elements to which propositions nominally about other things refer. All these other things were then revealed by analysis as logical constructions out of the ultimate unanalysable elements.

From this it was (rather rashly) concluded by Russell that logical analysis had at last revealed what philosophers had often wanted to know—the ultimate structure of reality. The simplest form of proposition, the atomic proposition of *Principia Mathematica*, referred to the ultimate unanalysable elements of reality: atomic individuals, with their simple qualities and relations. The fact expressed by an atomic proposition (namely, that a certain individual has a certain property, or that certain individuals stand in a certain relation) was called an "atomic fact"—and the real world was revealed by analysis as a kind of granular structure of atomic facts. This conclusion was given the name "Logical Atomism".

This conclusion by itself is enough to make suspect the conception of analysis from which it was derived. For it seems extraordinary that a definitive conclusion about the metaphysical structure of the universe should be deducible from the discovery of a technique for making a logical calculus.

That atomic or elementary propositions, which say what properties individual things have or how they are related, are the simplest kind of propositions that can be constructed, and that more complex forms are to be derived from these elementary forms, as demonstrated in *Principia Mathematica*, is, indeed, indubitable. But it simply does not follow from this that the world consists of atomic facts. That such a statement as "This is red" is the simplest sort of statement does not entail that such simple statements must refer to unanalysable individuals with their unanalysable qualities and relations. For the fact is that statements such as these, though formally simple, are at the same time extremely abstract. If, then, one wishes to say more concretely what is the case, one has always to make more complex and generalised statements. For the individual things about which we make statements are never simple, ultimate or unanalysable. If I point to something and say "This is red", which is logically the simplest form of statement I can make, I am not thereby getting down to metaphysical bedrock and stating a simple and irreducible atomic fact. On the contrary, my statement is very abstract. And the more I try to say what exactly is the case which renders my statement a true one, the more complicated in logical form will my statements become.

That in logical analysis more complex statements are constructed out of simpler ones does not demonstrate, therefore, that the simplest statements reveal the irreducible elements to which the more complex ones refer. For the logical analysis of how statements are to be constructed is not at all the same thing as an analysis of the objects to which the statements refer.

However, it was precisely on the assumption that analysis consists of the revelation of what statements refer to, that the achievements of analysis in logic and mathematics were interpreted. They were interpreted as demonstrating that propositions about complex numbers refer to real numbers, about real numbers to rational numbers, about rational numbers to cardinal numbers, about cardinal numbers to classes—and that propositions about classes refer, finally, to the irreducible individuals which are members of first-order classes, with their irreducible qualities and relations by virtue of which they are classified.

6. LOGICAL AND MATHEMATICAL NECESSITY

Now obviously, the propositions of logic and mathematics differ from commonplace factual statements and from the generalisations of the empirical sciences, in as much as their truth is necessary and demonstrable. The concept of analysis had, therefore, to explain and make manifest the distinction, stressed earlier by Hume, between knowledge of matter of fact and of necessity, or between what is conjecture based on observation and what is self-evidently necessary or can be formally proved. And this it proceeded to do in terms of the distinction between the content or meaning, and the *form*, of propositions.

Thus, for example, the propositions "This is red" and "That is green" differ in meaning but are identical in form. Propositions, whether singular or general, which state that certain things have certain qualities or stand in certain relations, are true or false. But we cannot tell whether they are true or false simply from their analysis. Their truth or falsity depends on whether what they state is a fact or not; and this we can only get to know (if we can know it at all) by observation of facts. We cannot discover independently of observation whether such propositions are true or false. All the propositions asserted by empirical sciences are of this kind. On the other hand (so the theory continued), logic, and likewise mathematics, are concerned purely with form. And it is for this reason that the propositions of logic and mathematics express necessary truths. Their necessary truth is made manifest by analysis.

A proposition of logic, Russell explained (*Our Knowledge of the External World*, chapter 2) "is absolutely general: it applies to all things and all properties". As an example he cited the proposition :

"If anything has a certain property, and whatever has this property has a certain other property, then the thing in question has the other property."

Such a proposition "is purely formal . . . Since it does not mention any particular thing, or even any particular quality or relation, it is wholly independent of the accidental facts of the existent world, and can be known, theoretically, without any experience of particular things or their qualities and relations."

He went on to say that in the formal calculus of logic there are formulated "supremely general propositions, which assert the truth of all propositions of certain forms". And this "merges into pure mathematics, whose propositions all turn out, on analysis, to be such general formal truths".

Thus logic and mathematics consist of "formal" or "absolutely (or supremely) general" truths, which can be known independently of all particular experience, and are necessarily true. Since such necessary truths are true by virtue of their form, their truth can always be made evident by formal analysis, starting from "primitive" or "self-evident" formal truths and using methods of formal construction and proof to build up from that basis.

Thus starting with formal generalisations of elementary logic (like the one cited above), which are the simplest of formal generalisations, we can proceed to the logical construction of more and more complicated generalisations, expressed not in terms of "any individual", but of "any class", "any relation", "any class of classes", and so on. And in this way, starting from elementary logic, we may construct and prove the whole of mathematics.

7. THE OBJECT OF ANALYSIS

THE programme of *Principia Mathematica*, for deducing mathematics from logic, thus followed from the conception of analysis. Conversely, the success of the programme would demonstrate the soundness of the conception of analysis on which it was based.

But as we have seen, in the end the programme turned out not to be an unqualified success after all. In the first place, mathematics could not be made to follow from logic without introducing the Axiom of Infinity, which is certainly not an absolutely general formal truth of the sort required. In the second place, Gödel's proof proved that theorems of mathematics, which according to the programme ought to be absolutely general and formal propositions the necessary truth of which can be proved and made manifest by analysis, are not all capable of formal proof. This outcome of the programme is quite fatal to the whole conception of analysis which inspired it.

So a negative conclusion about the stated conception of analysis seems inescapable. Whatever the analysis undertaken in modern logic and mathematics does (and there can be no doubt at all that it does do something, and does represent a technique capable of producing undeniable results), it does *not* proceed by revealing exactly what all propositions refer to. The conception of analysis as doing that leads, on the other hand, to the arbitrary metaphysical conclusions of logical atomism (which are empirically unverifiable and formally uncertifiable), and, on the other hand, to a programme for deducing mathematics from logic which will not work.

The view, associated with this conception of analysis, that logic and mathematics consist of "formal and supremely general" truths, led Russell to a combination of logical atomism with a version of platonic idealism. In an essay on "The Study of Mathematics", contained in his book *Mysticism and Logic*, he wrote:

"Philosophers have commonly held that the laws of logic, which underlie mathematics, are laws of thought, laws regulating the operations of our minds. By this opinion the true dignity of reason is very greatly lowered; it ceases to be an investigation into the very heart and immutable essence of things actual and possible, becoming, instead, an inquiry into something more or less human and subject to our limitations . . . But mathematics takes us still further from what is human, into the region of absolute necessity, to which not only the actual world, but every possible world, must conform." And here, he went on, it "finds a habitation eternally standing . . . It is only when we understand the entire independence of ourselves, which belongs to this world that reason finds, that we can adequately realise the profound importance of its beauty."

It is this view that logical and mathematical analysis are not concerned with anything "human and subject to our limitations", but discover formal truths "eternally standing" in "entire independence of ourselves", which the actual development and uses of analysis compel us to question.

Logic and mathematics are concerned with operations involved in human statement, reasoning, counting and measuring, locating things in space and time and specifying their motions. These are the objects of their analysis. The distinction between logical and mathematical procedures (the analysis of which demonstrates the necessity attaching to their results) and what Hume called "reasonings from causation and concerning matters of fact" (in which, as he said, "this absolute necessity cannot take place") is not to be questioned. But what *is* to be questioned is that what logic and mathematics demonstrate are "supremely general" propositions stating "the immutable essence of things actual and possible".

What are called "propositions" of logic and mathematics are not propositions at all, in the sense of the word applicable to observational statements and to the hypotheses of empirical science. They are not propositions true of all things without qualification, as distinguished from propositions of empirical science which are true of particular classes of things having particular properties. The distinction between what is matter of fact and what is logically or mathematically necessary is not one between general propositions, which require empirical verification, and absolutely general propositions which are certified by virtue of their form alone. The distinction lies rather between the conclusions of investigating *things* (conclusions which require to be empirically verified, and for the derivation and formulation of which techniques of reasoning and calculation are used) and the elaboration and certification, for use in such investigations, of those techniques themselves.

8. ANALYSIS AND PHILOSOPHY

The employment of methods of analysis, first to construct rigorous proofs in mathematics, and then to reformulate principles of formal logic, suggested to some philosophers, and to Bertrand Russell in particular, that the same methods could be extended to philosophy. Could not philosophy be made analytic, on the model of mathematics and logic, so that the dubious and often ambiguous generalisations of philosophy should be replaced by the exact analysis of concepts, demonstrating with clarity and precision their true and indubitable foundation?

The fact that Russell, co-author of *Principia Mathematica*, was the principal founder of the analytic philosophy has led to the belief that this philosophy, along with the nineteenth-century positivism which it in fact continued, was what inspired and was responsible for the successes of analysis in formal logic and mathematics. Those successes are therefore cited as evidence in favour of the philosophy.

This is not, however, the first time that philosophy has tried to imitate and model itself upon the methods of the exact sciences. Descartes thought that the methods which had served him so well in geometry should provide the model for philosophy. We do not therefore conclude that his philosophy had the merit of inspiring discoveries in geometry, but rather that he had misunderstood the methods of geometry in supposing them to be applicable in philosophy.

The introduction in the nineteenth century of exact definition and rigorous proof into mathematics, and then into formal logic, was primarily the result of needing more effective logical and mathematical techniques for the purposes of science. The introduction of these methods was not a consequence of any particular philosophical doctrine, and was not inspired by any particular philosophy. On the other hand, it inspired some philosophers with the desire to introduce comparable standards of precision and rigour into philosophy.

We have already seen that a misunderstanding existed as to the nature of logical and mathematical analysis. It was only on the basis of this misunderstanding that the application of these methods to philosophy was proposed.

The proposal was, in the circumstances, a natural one enough. For positivist philosophers were already describing the methods they employed for interpreting the findings of the sciences as "analytic". These findings were interpreted and substantiated by making them out to consist of statements of laws regulating the combination and sequence of sensations, and this, the philosophers claimed, was an analysis of the main concepts used in science. Thus Mach, for example, claimed to have shown that bodies, and all the constituents of bodies discovered by scientific research—such as atoms, molecules, cells, tissues, etc., etc.—were revealed by his "analysis of sensations" to consist of sensations. Sensations were the ultimate individual elements to which all knowledge referred; and all propositions about bodies and their elements were, in his analysis, represented as propositions about sensations.

This meant, in the terminology of *Principia Mathematica*, that "external material things"—and the same would go, as Mach also suggested, for "minds"—were incomplete symbols, which disappear in analysis, the corresponding objects being thereby shown to be logical constructions out of the elements of sensation.

The proposal to extend the application of analytic methods from logic and mathematics to philosophy was, then, a proposal whereby positivist philosophers could state their ideas rather more systematically and in a new terminology.

It meant that the questions philosophers asked were to be posed in a new way. Instead of asking questions like "How do we gain knowledge?", "What do we know?" or "Do external material things exist independent of being perceived?", all questions were to be put in the form: "What is the analysis of such-and-such propositions?"

The introduction of what was supposed to be the tried method of logical-mathematical analysis into philosophy was widely advertised as effecting the regeneration of philosophy. It did give positivism a new lease of life, and enable it to develop its doctrines in some new ways to meet new circumstances in the twentieth century. But it soon led to greater difficulties than any it could claim to have solved; and it is out of these difficulties that the linguistic philosophy eventually emerged.

CHAPTER FIVE

In Search of the Right Analysis

I. OUR KNOWLEDGE OF THE EXTERNAL WORLD

PROCLAIMING the logical-analytic method for philosophy in lectures at Boston, Mass., in the spring of 1914 (see his book, *Our Knowledge of the External World*), Russell declared that "genuinely philosophical" problems "all reduce themselves to problems of logic".

He rejected what he called "the classical tradition" in philosophy, which consisted (so he said) in the belief "that *a priori* reasoning could reveal otherwise undiscoverable secrets about the universe". Instead, he declared that such "secrets", if discoverable at all, could be discovered only by the methods of the empirical sciences. Matter of fact can become known only through the senses, plus the more refined techniques of empirical science. The task of philosophy cannot be to discover facts or generalise about facts, but is to subject statements and generalisations of fact, established by everyday observation and by science, to logical analysis. Such analysis cannot establish any new truths. But by making an analysis of truths already known it can impart to positive knowledge a new clarity, and overcome the confusion and intellectual bewilderment which results from the lack of such analysis. In short, our knowledge derives from perception and is enlarged by the methods of science, and the task of philosophy is to provide, by logical analysis, a clarification of our knowledge.

Set out like that, the programme announced in these lectures sounded new and attractive. Let us turn from programme to performance.

"I wish to apply the logical-analytic method," said Russell, "to one of the oldest problems of philosophy, namely, the problem of our knowledge of the external world. What I have to say on this problem does not amount to an answer of a definite and dogmatic kind. But although not yet a definite solution, what can be said at present seems to me to throw a completely new light on the problem."

"In every philosophical problem," he continued, "an investigation starts from what may be called 'data', by which I mean matters of common knowledge . . . commanding our assent as on the whole and in some interpretation pretty certainly true." He went on to say that "data" are of three main kinds—facts known through current experience, facts known through memory and the testimony of others, and the generalisations vouched for by scientific research. "In the main, we may accept this mass of common knowledge as affording data for our philosophical analysis."

Here is demonstrated the essence of the logical-analytic method in action. All the philosophers who ever followed this method made such a beginning as this. They claim to accept the "mass of common knowledge", vouched for by common sense or common observation, and science, as the data of philosophy. They claim to take it for granted that all this is "on the whole and in some interpretation pretty certainly true". And they then submit this knowledge to logical analysis. In carrying out this analysis, they try to discover the ultimate irreducible elements to which the whole "mass of common knowledge" refers, and then to show how all statements are translatable or analysable into statements about these elements (just as the ultimate elements of mathematics were found to be the cardinal numbers, which themselves could be analysed as classes of classes).

But how to discover and decide upon these ultimate elements of the analysis? To do that is the crucial step, evidently; and Russell took it as follows. He pointed out that the various data mentioned vary in respect of certainty. Some of the data, when submitted to criticism, can very well be doubted. But the degree of legitimate doubt must vary; and some cannot be doubted at all. The latter Russell called "hard data". "Let us confine ourselves to the hard data," he said, "with a view to discovering what sort of world can be constructed by their means alone." But what are these "hard data"? Russell had no doubt about that at all. "Our data now are primarily the facts of sense, i.e. our own sense-data."

At this point we may well ask where the "completely new light on the problem" has come from. For such lights as have shone so far were all wired up some time before: first of all by Descartes, who said that philosophy should begin by accepting only that which cannot possibly be doubted; secondly by Hume, who said that the only things we can be certain of are our own sense-impressions; thirdly by Mach, who said that the elements out of which the world is constructed are sensations. Instead of speaking of "impressions" or "sensations", Russell employed the new-fangled (twentieth-century) word "sense-data". But apart from that there is, so far, nothing new at all.

Russell went on to analyse "our knowledge of the external world" in terms of sense-data. "I think it can be laid down quite generally," he said, "that, in so far as physics or common-sense is verifiable, it must be capable of interpretation in terms of actual sense-data alone." A sense-datum which might otherwise be called a sense-datum "of" a thing, perceived by a certain person from a certain point of view, he then called an "aspect" of a thing. For example, if you look sideways at a penny you experience or receive (according to this terminology) an elliptically-shaped visual sense-datum: Russell then calls this visual sense-datum an "aspect" of the penny. And there would be many other aspects, corresponding to all the appearances which the penny would have when looked at from different angles and from different distances.

He then proposed "the task of reconstructing the conception of matter without the *a priori* beliefs which historically gave rise to it . . . For this purpose it is only necessary to take our ordinary commonsense statements and re-word them without the assumption of permanent substance . . . A 'thing' will be defined as a certain series of aspects, namely, those which would commonly be said to be *of* the thing. To say that a certain aspect is an aspect *of* a certain thing will merely mean that it is one of those which, taken serially, *are* the thing."

Now according to the definitions of *Principia Mathematica*, a *series* consists of all those elements which are related together by a certain relation (that is, by a relation with certain formal properties defined as "serial"). Thus Russell's analysis says, that a "thing" is the totality of sense-data which are related together in series in such a way that we call them "aspects" of a thing. A body is the class of all its aspects.

This analysis was later worked out in considerable detail in two large works by Russell, *The Analysis of Matter* and *The Analysis of Mind*. Here he sought to accomplish three main objects. First, he tried to show how the spatial-temporal relations between bodies could be constructed out of the relations between sense-data, as "aspects" of those bodies—in other words, how "public" or "objective" space and time could be constructed out of the spatial and temporal arrangements of individuals' "private perceptual fields". Second, he tried to define with exactitude those serial relationships between sense-data which are used for the definition of material objects in public space and time, and likewise to define those relations which are used to define causality and "causal chains" of events. Third, he tried to show that as well as those relations between sense-data which permit the logical construction of material objects out of them, there are also other relations between them which lead us to say that certain sense-data belong to and constitute the subjective experience of different sentient individuals. In other words, the *same* sense-data, or elements, which in some relations constitute bodies, in other relations constitute minds. Accordingly, he concluded that what from my own subjective point of view is my own private experience is, from a public point of view, located in public space and time "inside my head". True, a brain surgeon would find only brains inside my head; but then, my brains themselves are only a collection of sense-data, some of which, if he opens up *my* head, would then be, regarded in certain of their relationships, inside *his* head.

If Russell has earned a lasting place in the halls of fame, as a great and original thinker, it is on account of his immense contributions to formal logic and mathematics, and not on account of his contribution of analysis to philosophy. That will have to be forgiven him, like Newton's deduction of the date of the creation, with which it deserves to rank.

As well as saying (in his lectures at Boston), that his method of logical analysis opposed the "classical" tradition "that *a priori* reasoning could reveal otherwise undiscoverable secrets about the universe", and threw "a completely new light" on the problems of philosophy, Russell declared that "it represents, I believe, the same kind of advance as was introduced into physics by Galileo; the substitution of piecemeal, detailed and verifiable results for large untested generalities, recommended only by a certain appeal to the imagination".

Russell's conclusions, as we can see, were in no sense "new". Although he nowhere refers to Mach, all that the analytic method accomplished, in his hands, was to find a new terminology for setting forth the conclusions of Mach's *Analysis of Sensations*. Nor did he even find new grounds for these conclusions. The grounds were the old ones: all that we know with certainty to exist is our own sense-impressions, and all knowledge is therefore to be interpreted as referring to these sense-impressions.

More to the point is Russell's claim to have opposed what he called "the classical tradition" and to have introduced into philosophy advances comparable with those which Galileo brought into physics. His analysis may have been "piecemeal" and "detailed", but it was certainly not "verifiable". According to him, as to Mach, the whole universe is built up out of the elements of sensation, the complex inter-relations of which constitute both bodies and minds. But how is it proposed to verify the existence of all the sensations inside people's heads? How is it proposed to verify the existence of myriads of other sensations, most of which nobody ever senses, which in their totality constitute what Berkeley called "the mighty frame of the world"? How is it to be verified that the same objects which constitute a mind also constitute a body? —This entire theory is the product of "*a priori* reasoning*", and of nothing else.

2. THE USES OF A RAZOR

Russell claimed that his analysis of material things into classes of sense-data was based on what he took to be one of the fundamental principles of all scientific method—namely, the "principle of economy", which had been first formulated by one of the medieval precursors of scientific materialism, William of Occam, and was often known, after him, as "Occam's Razor".

"The above extrusion of permanent things," said Russell, in his Boston lectures, "affords an example of the maxim which inspires all scientific philosophising, namely, Occam's razor: *Entities are not to be multiplied beyond necessity*. In other words, find out what entities are indubitably involved, and state everything in terms of those entities."

The "principle of economy" is undoubtedly employed in formulating scientific theory, in as much as the most "economical" hypothesis is always the one to be preferred. But let us ask what are the grounds for this preference, and whether "Occam's razor", which shaves scientific hypotheses clean of "unnecessary entities", will do the work for which Russell tried to employ it.

The principle of economy, as a maxim of the empirical sciences, is a corollary of the definitive principle that the sciences proceed by the empirical verification of their hypotheses. Of course, all conclusions of the sciences are provisional—in as much as investigations continue, and it cannot be known how far subsequent investigations may necessitate the revision of earlier conclusions. But provisionally, the sciences conclude on the existence of things (or "entities") so far, and only so far, as their existence is verified. Hypotheses have to be tested. If, therefore, hypotheses postulating the existence of various entities are put forward to account for observed phenomena, the task of science is to devise empirical tests for deciding (provisionally) whether these entities exist. In the end, therefore, that hypothesis will be (provisionally) preferred, which postulates entities the existence of which is pretty well verified by the investigations to date; and other hypotheses, which may have been put forward to cover the original observations, which were lavish of entities the existence of which could not be verified, will then be convicted of "multiplying entities beyond necessity" and will be (provisionally) given up.

The sciences regularly adopt this kind of procedure. Take, for example, Maxwell's original hypothesis to account for observed electro-magnetic phenomena. He postulated a most complicated system of stresses and strains in the ether. All this has been given up, because the existence of the things he postulated could not be verified. And so generally, scientific method always involves the search for, and provisional acceptance of, the most "economical" hypothesis.

Does this "principle of economy", as used in the sciences, bear the philosophical use for which Russell wanted to employ it? The methods of the empirical sciences can no more be imported into philosophy than the methods of the mathematical sciences. As Hegel said, philosophy must devise, and justify if it can, its own methods. It cannot borrow them from somewhere else.

The use of "Occam's razor" by the empirical sciences is in the testing and verification of hypotheses. But the method of "logical analysis" which Russell practised, the products of which he sought to shave clean of unnecessary entities by Occam's razor, was in no sense a method of framing hypotheses comparable with those of empirical sciences. His use of the razor was unconnected with any procedure of empirical test or verification. It amounted rather to a very simple example of circular argument. He began by taking it for granted that the only things we can know to exist are sense-data, and the only facts we can know are facts about how sense-data are related. From this he concluded that the most "economical" way we can state whatever we know is by stating it in terms of sense-data and their relations. The consequent "extrusion of permanent things" was not, then, an example of applying any scientific maxim, but an example of the typical fallacy of circularity in "*a priori* argument".

3. COMMON SENSE GETS INTO DIFFICULTIES

Russell's attempted use of the logical-analytic method to show that things are classes of sense-data may well be described as fallacious, impetuous and rash. The incapability of this method for deciding any questions of philosophy was shown even more convincingly in the more canny and cautious applications of it attempted by Russell's colleague, G. E. Moore.

In his lectures at Cambridge University, Moore used to hold up his hand before the class, and exclaim: "This is a human hand! Whatever can I mean by that?" He knew perfectly well, as a matter of common sense, that it *was* a hand he was looking at, and not something else. But what he was doubtful about, and what he wanted to find out, was the correct *analysis* of what he knew—that is to say, to what elements he was referring, and what facts about them were the case, when he truly judged "This is a human hand".

Accordingly, in an article entitled *A Defence of Common Sense* (his contribution to the second of two volumes of personal statements on *Contemporary British Philosophy*, edited by J. H. Muirhead, 1925), he remarked: "I am not at all sceptical as to the truth of . . . propositions which assert the existence of material things: on the contrary, I hold that we all know, with certainty, many such propositions to be true. But I am very sceptical as to what, in certain respects, the correct analysis of such propositions is."

About one thing, he proceeded to explain, he could have no doubt, and that was that such a proposition as "This is a human hand" refers, in some way, to a sense-datum. When you look at your hand, you are aware of the existence of a sense-datum; and the proposition "This is a hand" states that that sense-datum exists—and then something more about it. But what? This is the problem of analysis, of which Moore went on to say: "There seem to me to be three, and only three, alternative types of answer possible; and to any answer yet suggested, of any of these types, there seem to me to be very grave objections."

The first type of possible analysis of "This is a hand" would make that proposition state that the sense-datum to which reference is made is one of a class of sense-data which in their totality constitute a hand.

The second type of analysis would state that the sense-datum in question is related to something else, which is a material object and not itself a sense-datum, by a relation such that we call the sense-datum a sense-datum "of" that object.

The third type of analysis does not state categorically that anything else exists besides the sense-datum actually perceived, but states a whole set of hypothetical propositions, covering how what is perceived would have varied under different conditions of perceiving it.

Of these three types of analysis, the third roughly corresponds to the philosophy of Berkeley; the second to the philosophy of Locke; and the first to the philosophy of Mach. The first was the type of analysis worked out by Russell. Moore quite correctly pointed out that several other analyses were equally possible; "but as to what is the correct analysis . . . there seems to me to be the gravest doubt." And there he left the matter. Nor could he ever suggest any way of resolving this doubt.

Moore never demonstrated "the analysis" of any proposition whatsoever. What he did demonstrate was, that when an analytic philosopher sits down to do a philosophical analysis, all sorts of different analyses, each more complicated and far-fetched than the last, present themselves; but the method gives no means of deciding which of them, if any, is the right one, that is, the one which actually corresponds to the facts.

Such a negative result is not surprising. The quest for "the elements" to which all propositions refer is essentially a vain speculation. It is the old and naive search for the ultimate elements of reality, the irreducible atoms out of which all things are made.

To know the constitution of things—as Russell, like other positivists, said; but then contradicted it—requires the kind of analytic investigation done by the techniques of the empirical sciences. This yields provisional conclusions about the processes which produce familiar appearances. It shows that organic bodies are chemical systems, that chemical systems are atomic structures, and so on. It finds relationships which control other relationships—as is done in one way in sciences like physics and chemistry, and in another way in social sciences, which by analysis find relations between people in society which determine the particular and variable forms of their social life. But such investigations, by their very character of empirical investigation, never arrive at anything certifiably final, never dig down to metaphysical bedrock and demonstrate the "ultimate elements". To try to do that is to give up analysis the conclusions of which are verifiable and controlled by empirical tests, and embark upon uncontrolled speculations.

The technical analysis made by formal logic of how propositions are constructed is certainly of the greatest use for securing the clear unambiguous formulation of scientific conclusions, and for enabling them to be set out systematically, their interconnections shown and their consequences deduced and calculated. In this sense, logical analysis is an essential tool of scientific analysis. It is essential for computation. But the techniques and uses of formal logic are misunderstood if it is supposed (as the logical-analytic philosophy of Russell and Moore supposed) that they enable us to impose on the propositions of the sciences, and on empirical or matter-of-fact propositions generally, an interpretation which leaps from the empirical analysis of objects and processes to the revelation of ultimate elements and ultimate structure.

4. "PRINCIPIA ETHICA"

The most noteworthy product of logical-analytic philosophy was also its earliest—Moore's *Principia Ethica*, published in 1903, while Russell and Whitehead were still labouring over the preliminary work for *Principia Mathematica*. Here Moore directed his analysis to judgments of value rather than of fact.

This has proved a most influential work. But its importance did not lie in the "analysis" Moore proposed of value judgments (an analysis which even most of his own followers have been unable to swallow). Its importance lay rather in Moore's reformulation of the main problem of ethics, or of moral philosophy. Hitherto moral philosophers had tried to decide what things are good, and what actions we ought to perform. Moore proposed to ask, instead: What do we *mean* by "good"? He asked "not what thing or things are good, but how 'good' is to be defined" (5). For he considered it futile to try to decide what things are good until we had decided what we *mean* by "good", that is, until an analysis had been made of propositions of the form "x is good". As for propositions expressing moral obligation ("You ought to do this", "I ought to do that", etc.), he thought it evident that these must be subordinate to propositions of the form "x is good", since what one ought or ought not to do depends on what is good and what is bad.

The result of this twist which Moore gave to the problem of moral philosophy was well expressed later by A. J. Ayer, in an essay "On the Analysis of Moral Judgments" (*Philosophical Essays*, 1954): "The theory is entirely on the level of analysis; it is an attempt to show what people are doing when they make moral judgments; it is not a set of suggestions as to what moral judgments they are to make."

The analysis of propositions saying "This is good" seemed to Moore much easier than that of propositions like "This is a human hand", to which he devoted his attention later—for the simple reason that he found it evident that "good" is not a complex but a simple predicate.

"My business," he wrote, "is solely with that object or idea, which . . . the word is generally used to stand for . . . But, if we understand the question in this sense, my answer to it may seem a very disappointing one. If I am asked 'What is good?' my answer is that good is good, and that is the end of the matter. Or if I am asked 'How is good to be defined?' my answer is that it cannot be defined, and that is all I have to say about it . . . My point is that 'good' is a simple notion, just as 'yellow' is a simple notion; that, just as you cannot, by any manner of means, explain to anyone who does not already know it, what yellow is, so you cannot explain what good is." (6–7).

Since "good", like "yellow", is a simple, undefinable or unanalysable quality, Moore's analysis concluded that a proposition "This is good" asserts that a simple or unanalysable quality, "good", belongs to something, just as "This is yellow" asserts that a simple unanalysable quality, "yellow", belongs to something.

The essential point which Moore borrowed from logical technique for use in this analysis was the point that any system of definitions must employ terms which are not defined in the system, but taken as simple and undefined. And "good" he asserted to be such a term. Of course, things or states of affairs which are good are not simple. On the contrary, they are complex. And Moore explained at some length that a combination of objects none of which is good may be a good combination; and, bearing in mind that "good" is a quality which, while simple, admits of degree (just like "yellow" or, say, "soft" or "smelly"), that a combination of objects can possess a degree of goodness greater (or less) than the sum of the various degrees of goodness of its constituents. But while good things are complex, their quality of being good is simple and unanalysable.

Moore then distinguished "good" from sensible qualities like "yellow" by saying that the latter are "natural" properties of objects, while "good" is "non-natural". He had some difficulty in defining this distinction, but the upshot is that a "natural" property is one that can be known by the senses, whereas a "non-natural" property cannot. Thus we know that something is yellow by looking at it, but mere sense-data do not suffice to make it known whether it is good.

Taking a moral look round the universe in the last chapter of the book, Moore reported that two things above all are supremely good, or better than anything else, namely, "personal affection" and "aesthetic enjoyment". These he reported good, just as buttercups and cowslips are reported yellow.

The objections to this analysis of moral judgments are so obvious that, as mentioned above, it eventually proved unacceptable even to Moore's keenest admirers. If "good" is a simple quality not made known by the senses, how, by what means, by what moral sense or intuition, is it made known? And if people should disagree (as they do disagree) about the objects which possess this unique quality, how is a decision to be made, how is the judgment of the one party to be verified and of the other party to be falsified? It turns out that this first exercise of logical analysis merely announced a "non-natural" quality supposed to be known by an unexplained faculty of intuition, just as the later exercises announced the discovery of ultimate elements and structures of elements, equally incapable of empirical verification.

However, if Moore made little lasting impact by his *answer* to the question "how 'good' is to be defined", he made a very great and lasting impact by *asking* this question. The significance of *Principia Ethica* is not that it contained an "intuitionist" theory of value (which few take seriously), but that it directed attention to the difference between "moral judgments" and "statements of fact", and thereby reasserted—but in the language of modern logic—the old but forgotten principle of Hume, that ethical or moral qualities are not "matter of fact", and that it is impossible to conclude from fact to value.

True, Moore treated moral judgments as if they *were* statements of fact, in as much as he treated "This is good" as stating a fact, like "This is yellow", and so put ethical and factual propositions logically on a par. That is what led to the "intuitionist" conclusion of his analysis. But when he proceeded to distinguish non-natural, or ethical, from natural qualities, he in effect drew a sharp and impassable line between ethical and factual propositions, and so invited his successors to concentrate all their attention (as they duly did) on the logical definition and consequences of this division.

Having drawn this line, Moore denounced what he considered to be the most widespread fallacy in ethical argument, which he called "the naturalistic fallacy".

As originally defined in *Principia Ethica*, the fallacy is that of confusing non-natural with natural qualities. It consists in identifying the non-natural quality "good" with some natural quality or combination of qualities—for example, with being pleasant, or with being the object of desire, or with being the latest and highest product of evolution. In other words, it consists in seeking to define "good", and explain what it means, in terms of observable properties of objects (10).

As a consequence of the naturalistic fallacy, people argue from matters of fact (or what they take to be matters of fact) to conclusions about values—for example, from the fact that everyone desires something to the conclusion that it is good; or from the fact that something is the latest and highest product of evolution to the conclusion that it is good. If, then, Moore's contention that the word "good" stands for a simple undefinable non-natural quality is given up, the naturalistic fallacy still remains and turns out to be simply the fallacy denounced by Hume, of arguing from fact to value. It consists of confusing judgments of value with judgments of fact, and supposing that the former can follow logically from the latter.

Although Moore called "good" a "non-natural" quality, and so sharply distinguished judgments of value from statements of empirical fact, his line of argument enabled him to denounce not only what he called "naturalistic ethics", but also "metaphysical ethics". By this he meant any view which holds that "ethical truths" are to be deduced from alleged truths about "supersensible reality" (66).

A typical doctrine of "metaphysical ethics" would be the traditional religious one, that ethical truths follow from knowledge of the will of God. Moore argued, in effect, that even if whatever God wills is good, and whatever is good is willed by God, being good and being willed by God would still not be the same thing. All the theologians and philosophers who imagined themselves to have knowledge of "supersensible reality", and to be able to deduce ethical conclusions from that knowledge, were in double error—first, in imagining themselves to have such knowledge at all; second, in supposing that such knowledge, even if they possessed it, could have any relevance to the certification of moral judgments.

The main polemic in *Principia Ethica* was directed, however, against "naturalistic ethics" and particularly against utilitarianism. It was against utilitarianism that Moore scored most heavily.

In effect, Moore convicted utilitarianism on two counts. First, the utilitarian principle that good is pleasure, and that what is best to do is to be calculated by working out how to secure the greatest sum of pleasure, rests on the naturalistic fallacy. Second, the alleged facts which utilitarians cited to justify their identification of good with pleasure are not facts anyway. The usual argument was that good is the object of desire, and that the object of all desire is pleasure. Even apart from the naturalistic fallacy involved in identifying "desirable" with "desired", it is not true that all desire is for pleasure. It may be true that satisfaction of desire is pleasant, but people desire all kinds of particular things and not merely the pleasure associated with getting them.

5. THE REFUTATION OF IDEALISM

Moore's opposition to utilitarianism coincided with the general discredit which had overtaken that kind of moral and political outlook. By the turn of the century, when *Principia Ethica* was written, it had come to smell very musty. Theoretically it was cracking up, under the strain of the disagreements and oppositions encountered in trying to base actions on a calculus of pleasures. J. S. Mill had in fact already dealt it a death blow when he began to support stringent labour legislation and even a measure of socialism on the grounds that human happiness demanded it, and when, in his *Utilitarianism*, he introduced the idea of a qualitative distinction between pleasures according to which the lower pleasures should be sacrificed to the higher; by introducing such considerations he upset the so-called calculus completely. At the same time the working class, the majority of the nation, had won the right to organise, won the franchise, and so come (as it used to be expressed, though the idea is now taken for granted) "within the pale of the constitution". They could no longer be regarded as servants, whose good was to be decided for them by their masters, or be written off as "the poor". They had won the right to negotiate the regulation of hours, wages and conditions, and to assert their point of view generally. The calculated benevolence of the utilitarian calculus was not what working people were looking for—and this philosophy could not disguise its association with the point of view of the individual capitalist master. Behind concern for "the greatest happiness of the greatest number" workers sensed sordid calculations of commercial gain, to which culture, welfare, happiness and everything else were sacrificed.

The scientific socialist outlook which developed with the working-class movement was from the start opposed to utilitarianism. Indeed, Marx reserved for it some of his most scathing remarks and footnotes in *Capital*. But from early in the nineteenth century a reaction against utilitarian ideas also set in amongst liberal-minded intellectuals. The more radical ones took up Jacobin theories of the rights of man and human perfectibility. But others began to look to German idealism for their inspiration.

The idealist philosophy developed after Kant by Fichte, Schelling, Hegel and others, was a peculiarly German product, arising from conditions very unlike those obtaining in Britain. It was not under-stood in Britain. Nevertheless, the news got around that in Germany spiritual ideals had been preached opposed to the sordid material calculations which had become associated with British empiricism, and so a very amorphous philosophy was concocted, which claimed to base itself "on Kant and Hegel", although it had none of the rigour and realism of Hegel's dialectic. The world of sense was said to be only an "appearance", a manifestation of the eternal, necessary and changeless spiritual unity on which was bestowed the name "The Absolute".

This kind of philosophy originally represented a liberal, humanist and romantic protest, not against capitalism itself, but against its grossest effects on men's lives and minds. Essentially, it was quietist, escapist, and ineffective. That is why other romantics, like Shelley and his circle, had no use for it. Indeed, Shelley's friend T. L. Peacock, in his novel *Melincourt*, satirised Coleridge (one of the first to try to translate German idealism into English) under the name of "Moley Mystic Esquire", representing him as living in a house called Cimmerian Lodge in the middle of a swamp, perpetually surrounded by a thick fog through which he sought to guide visitors with the aid of a "synthetic torch". Mr. Mystic's philosophy proclaimed that reality is not what it seems, and called for no struggle to change it. It was anti-socialist. And in a very profound sense, it was anti-science. "Transcendental" science was solemnly invoked; but "merely empirical" science, though admittedly useful for limited practical ends, was no guide to understanding reality. It was merely concerned with sensible appearances, irrelevant to the understanding of spirit, and quite beside the point in comparison with knowledge of The Absolute.

Towards the end of the nineteenth century this second-hand idealist philosophy became far more assertive in Britain, was systematised by professionals like Bernard Bosanquet, T. H. Green and F. H. Bradley, and gained rapidly in influence. This was due, no doubt, to the growing discredit of utilitarian ideas; but more positively, it was due to changing social conditions, which were leading to a new emphasis being put on the unity of the nation and the role of the state. A number of factors contributed to this result. The growth of the working-class movement itself led to the idea that all citizens were entitled to their share of education, and to a say in the common affairs of the nation, which were the common interest of all—but they must be educated to a proper sense of "spiritual values", and of their own personal subordination to higher things; the loss of Britain's position as "workshop of the world", with economic difficulty at home and formidable competition abroad, led to the assertion of a common interest in Britain's claims in face of other nations, and in imperialist foreign and colonial policy; and in these conditions the role assigned to the state began to change—it was no longer required to interfere as little as possible in affairs, but its powers and functions as general manager of the nation's business began to be enlarged. Responding to such circumstances, English absolute idealism made another borrowing from Hegel, and began to preach social responsibility and authoritarianism. It was above all Bosanquet who translated into English the Hegelian doctrine that the State is the manifestation in human life of the Moral Idea, that the individual exists only through the State and receives everything he needs through the State, that his good lies in obeying the State, and that the State is itself a spiritual entity, a spiritual unity more real than the fragmentary individual selves of its citizens. All this was put forward with a great show of moral fervour, of class reconciliation, and of contempt for mere science and empirical calculation.

This kind of idealist philosophy played upon its opposition to utilitarian calculations. Significantly, Moore's *Principia Ethica*, opposing utilitarianism, opposed equally this idealist philosophy with its "metaphysical ethics". Moore theoretically demolished utilitarian ethics to such effect that it never again became theoretically respectable. He proclaimed that ethical considerations differed from matter-of-fact calculations of gain or loss. But at the same time, he exposed the theoretical hollowness of the high-sounding claims of absolute idealism. The logical-analytic philosophy, adopting what was essentially a positivist outlook, freed that outlook from its former damaging association with utilitarianism, and then set out to reinstate positivism by the demolition of absolute idealism.

Both Russell and Moore worked out their ideas in continuous polemic against what then passed in Britain for Hegelian idealism. The so-called Hegelians had made out that the part has no existence save within the whole, and that objects exist only as parts, unreal in themselves, of the higher spiritual unity within which they are presented as objects of perception. Moore called one of his most important early papers "The Refutation of Idealism", and in it used the techniques of formal logic to demonstrate that the idealists' arguments had no validity. When Russell proclaimed his opposition to "the classical tradition", which sought by *a priori* arguments to prove that the world is different from what it seems, he was not, in fact, opposing any tradition which could justifiably rank as "classical", but only the foggy verbiage of the contemporary British absolute idealists.

These idealists had developed a special line of argument (only very remotely related to the Hegelian dialectic from which it was supposedly derived) to prove that material objects are unreal, that motion is unreal, that time is unreal, that we ourselves are unreal, and that only The Absolute is real, by finding "contradictions" in propositions stating facts about individuals or motion or the passage of time. Hence their contempt for mere facts, which they declared to be mere contradictory appearances: appearance was proved to be mere appearance by its contradictoriness. The "classical" statement of these arguments was in F. H. Bradley's *Appearance and Reality*; and their final parade, leading to their being finally shot down, was staged in Cambridge by J. M. E. McTaggart, who denied the reality of time on the grounds of its involving a logical contradiction. Logical-analytic philosophers had no real difficulty in showing that all these alleged contradictions were the products merely of imprecise statement and of ignorance of logical and mathematical techniques. As the fog of verbal confusions was dispersed, the doctrine of The Absolute perished—for as T. L. Peacock had remarked years before, it could live only in an environment of fog. And with it went the doctrine of the State as a higher spiritual being.

The great and wordy battle which logical-analytic philosophers fought with absolute idealists, and in which they won a famous victory, was of decisive importance for the development of ideas in modern Britain. It meant that the anti-empirical, anti-scientific, semi-mystical, authoritarian way of thinking which was growing up in the new conditions, out of the discrediting of positivist-utilitarian ideas, was halted, and was supplanted by new forms of positivist ideas. These emerged as the dominant, most pervasive ideology in Britain in the period of monopoly capitalism. Thenceforward the alternative to hard-faced nineteenth-century individualism and *laissez faire* no longer presented a choice between revolutionary socialism and a foggy idealism, which belittled the interests of individuals and despised science and technological progress. Instead, science was still to be regarded as the source of positive knowledge; the dogmas of *laissez faire* economics were to be corrected by more objective social studies, combining factual surveys with mathematical calculations; and the values of the good life were to be freed from subordination to both social utility and supernatural authority.

CHAPTER SIX

A Spot of Nonsense

I. THE VERIFICATION PRINCIPLE

THE chief difficulty involved in the method of logical analysis, as practised originally by Russell and Moore, lay in the lack of any criterion or principle for deciding what was the right analysis. The conclusions, therefore, appeared arbitrary and speculative. It was this difficulty, above all, that led to the theorisings of the philosophers known as logical positivists and, in particular, to the first or original philosophy of Wittgenstein.

The main innovation was the introduction of a new "principle"— one which would infallibly guide the analytic philosopher in his search for the true meaning of statements, and enable him to formulate his problems in a new way which would make their solution evident. This principle said that the meaning of a statement is given by its mode of verification in immediate experience, and is known as "the verification principle". It lay at the basis of Wittgenstein's *Tractatus Logico-Philosophicus* (1922) and of his teachings up to the 'thirties. Its formulation in print was due to Moritz Schlick, the principal founder of the so-called "Vienna Circle" of logical-positivist philosophers.

The proposed solution, then, of the problems posed by logical-analytic philosophy turned on the concept of verification. What is meant by "verification"?

In daily life we require information about the objects that surround us, and we obtain this by going around and using our senses. For example, if you want to know what is on the other side of the hill, you climb the hill and look—or you ask someone else, who has himself been there. As well as information about particular things, we also require general information, expressed in general propositions. Any such information may be said to be *verified* in so far as we have made contact with the objects concerned and investigated them with the aid of our senses. In general, it may be said that we find out and verify how things are by experience. As for the sciences, they do not represent any entirely new and different method of finding things out, compared with the methods employed in daily life. They rather represent a development, refinement and systematisation of methods that everybody knows and uses.

Questions can be asked such that experience provides no way of finding out and verifying the answer. Propositions suggesting answers to such questions are, then, *unverifiable*. But amongst them should be distinguished those which are unverifiable because of the limitations of existing techniques, and those which are absolutely or in principle unverifiable. What is on the other side of the moon? Until recently, there was no way of finding out; but new techniques solved the problem. Again, what did Julius Caesar have for breakfast on the morning he crossed the Rubicon? We have no means of finding out; nor is it likely that we ever shall find out; but nevertheless we *could* find out if there happened to turn up, say, documents of the Roman Army in which Caesar's breakfasts were recorded. On the other hand, such a question as the famous scholastic one: How many angels can stand on the point of a needle? is *in principle* unverifiable. For angels were so defined as to exclude observing and counting them. Similarly, the existence of God, or of disembodied spirits generally, is unverifiable; and so are such questions as that of the constitution of the Holy Trinity.

There has been a great deal of debate about such unverifiable questions. But so far as empirical science is concerned, they are by definition excluded from it. Questions are acceptable to the sciences only when some method can be proposed of verifying the answers, and propositions are accepted only in so far as they are verified.

But empirical verification is not at all the same thing as formal certification. It is never final, and however well verified a proposition may be, there is always the possibility of error. It is generally agreed that, as a matter of good sense, we should act, so far as we can, on verified information. At the same time, such information varies greatly in reliability, and is never absolutely reliable beyond every remote possibility of error. Renewed experience will very generally either add to the reliability of information, or lead to its being supplemented, qualified or otherwise modified, or, perhaps, rejected as entirely mistaken. Yet we have to act on such information as we can get. So we try to get as reliable information as we can, and scientific methods of inquiry and verification are designed for this purpose.

As outlined above, the verification of propositions is a human activity, a process; and, moreover, it is a social process, in as much as people generally have to co-operate to obtain and verify information. Of course, we do not continually seek each other's aid to verify facts which are obvious to our senses. But individual confidence in such facts rests on a basis of social agreement and confirmation; if an individual has doubts, he consults others; and information acquired by the practice of science is always acquired and verified co-operatively—for one man's results have to be checked by others, and very often the techniques employed are such as to require the co-operation of a number of people to work them. That being so, it would seem reasonable to say that in so far as information is verified, it is verified by, and only by, practical social activity.

However, Wittgenstein and Schlick took a quite different view of what constitutes the verification of a proposition; the peculiarity of the "verification principle" was that it gave its own definition of verification, and used this to define *meaning* and to solve the problem of how to find the right analysis of propositions. Verification is done by using the senses; and while neither Wittgenstein nor Schlick used the term "sense-data", but preferred synonyms (such as "the given", or "immediate experience"), they assumed that what verifies a proposition is not the activity, or the whole process, of verification, but simply the sense-data which result from it. In effect, they abstracted the content of individual sense-experience, and said that *that* is what constitutes the verification of a proposition. This, of course, at once contradicted the practical social character of the verification process; each individual had to find his own verification for himself, by contemplating what was presented or "given" to him in his own sensuous consciousness or "immediate experience". It also implied that, at least in some cases, final verification, or empirical certification, could be achieved.

The verification principle laid it down that what a proposition *means* is given by its verification in experience. Take any proposition —what would verify it? A certain kind of experience or sequence of experience. If you know what experience would verify it, if you can conjure up that experience in your imagination, then you know what a proposition means; and if you cannot do so, then you do not know what it means. To explain the meaning, therefore, you must always contrive to explain what experience would verify a proposition. The meaning, therefore, is given by the mode of verification in experience.

Thus the question of trying to state the right analysis of a proposition is solved by formulating the question in a different way: what experience would verify it?

Schlick summed up the verification principle in the following words:

"In order to find the meaning of a proposition we must transform it by successive definitions until finally only such words occur in it as can no longer be defined, but whose meanings can only be directly pointed out. The criterion of the truth or falsity of the proposition then lies in the fact that under definite conditions (given in the definition) certain data are present, or not present. If this is determined, then everything asserted by the proposition is determined, and I know its meaning . . . The statement of the conditions under which a proposition is true is *the same* as the statement of its meaning . . . And these conditions . . . must finally be discoverable in the given. Different conditions mean differences in the given. The *meaning* of every proposition is finally to be determined by the given, and by nothing else." ("Positivism and Realism", *Erkenntnis*, 1932/33).

2. THE PICTORIAL THEORY OF PROPOSITIONS

In *Tractatus Logico-Philosophicus* Wittgenstein, on the assumption of the verification principle, announced a theory of the nature of the representation of reality effected by propositions. This may be called "the pictorial theory" of propositions.

The idea was a very simple one. The simplest statements, or "atomic propositions", are pictures of corresponding facts—the structure of the picture mirroring the structure of the facts. They are true when the elements of the facts are arranged as in the picture; otherwise they are false. The verification of such propositions consists, then, of a direct comparison of pictures with facts—and these facts are given in immediate experience.

More complicated statements are, then, verified by the verification of the simplest or atomic statements from which they are constructed. Thus if "p" and "q" are atomic propositions, the molecular proposition "p and q" is verified by verifying (by direct comparison with immediate experience) both "p" and "q". If they both turn out to be true, the proposition "p and q" is true; but otherwise (i.e. if "p" is false, or "q" is false, or both are false) it is false. Similarly with molecular propositions such as "p or q" and "p implies q"; "p or q" is false when "p" and "q" are both false, otherwise it is true; and "p implies q" is false when "p" is true and "q" is false, otherwise it is true. Molecular propositions were then called "truth functions" of atomic propositions, because their truth or falsity depends solely and entirely on the truth or falsity of the atomic propositions from which they are constructed.

Similarly, generalisations are verified by the verification of atomic propositions. Thus "(x).F(x)" is verified by verifying one by one atomic propositions which are values of "F(x)". If I say, for example, "All swans are white", I verify this generalisation in a series of experiences consisting of continually checking up on the colour of swans. If I should undergo an experience pictured in the proposition "This swan is black", then the generalisation is falsified; but so long as I go on experiencing only the spectacle of white swans, it continues to be verified. It follows from this that whereas such universal generalisations can be decisively falsified, when a negative instance turns up, they can never be finally verified. For however many positive instances may turn up in experience, there is no guarantee that a negative instance may not turn up later.—This logical consequence, by the way, served as the basis for Karl Popper's "Logic of Scientific Discovery" (*Logik der Forschung*, 1934), in which he said that the criterion of a scientific generalisation was that it should be falsifiable.

The pictorial theory, then, claimed to show how all propositions are verified (and falsified) by means of direct comparison with facts of immediate experience. The simplest propositions picture such facts, and the more complicated propositions are verified, according to logical rules, by the verification of the simplest propositions. The mode of representation of reality in propositions is, then, pictorial. A statement of fact is a "logical picture". The form or structure of reality cannot itself be *stated*; but it is mirrored or, as Wittgenstein put it, *shown*, by the form or structure of the picture.

By means of the pictorial theory Wittgenstein was able to give an account of the distinction between empirical and necessary truth—namely, between those statements the truth or falsity of which has to be established through experience, and those, like the principles of logic, which are necessarily true independent of experience. For he was able to show that the rules of construction permit the construction of complex statements such that, whatever may be the result of comparison with experience, they are always true. These he called "tautologies". For example, if I address the reader of this book and say "You are not following the argument", that may be true or false. But if I say "Either you are following it or else you are not", that cannot but be true. So-called "necessary truths" are, Wittgenstein maintained, tautologies in this sense. Their peculiarity is that their rules of construction do not allow them to be falsified. Their necessity, therefore, does not consist in their stating eternal truth about pure form, as both Plato and Russell had once concluded, but is simply a consequence of the logical rules for making statements, of the manner in which statements picture facts.

3. NONSENSE

Wittgenstein's theory, derived from the logical researches of Frege and Russell plus the verification principle, claimed to have shown that statements of fact are pictures of experience, verifiable by comparison with experience, and that necessary statements or formal truths are tautologies. Schlick afterwards said that this did not represent so much a further development of the techniques of formal logic as an "insight into the nature of logic itself". "This simple insight," he said, "has consequences of the very greatest importance." For it marked "an altogether decisive turning point in philosophy". ("The Turning Point in Philosophy", *Erkenntnis*, 1930/31). Wittgenstein himself said, in the Preface to *Tractatus*, that the problems of philosophy had "in essentials been finally solved".

For if the *meaning* of a proposition is given by its mode of verification in experience, what becomes of all those statements, strewn around the writings of philosophers as well as of theologians, which are in principle unverifiable and are, at the same time, certainly not tautologies? Such statements are meaningless. They are simply nonsense. And so all those questions which philosophers have debated, the answers to which can be demonstrated neither by comparison with experience nor by formal procedures of logic, are nonsense-questions. As Schlick expressed it, they are "not genuine questions, but meaningless sequences of words. To be sure, they look like questions from the outside, since they seem to satisfy the customary rules of grammar, but in truth they consist of empty sounds, because they transgress the profound inner rules of logical syntax discovered by the new analysis" (*ibid*).

This conclusion repeated, two hundred years later, Hume's conclusion about what to do with the books in libraries. Those which contain statements neither empirically verifiable nor formally certifiable are to be thrown out. But whereas Hume declared that such statements were "nothing but sophistry and illusion", Wittgenstein and Schlick went further and declared them to be nothing but "nonsense". The "final solution" of problems of philosophy consisted, then, not in answering these problems, but in showing that there can be no answer because the problems themselves are "nonsense".

This insight and this solution marked a "turning point in philosophy" because, as Schlick put it, it brings to an end "the fruitless conflict of systems" (*ibid*). Every *genuine* question can, in principle, be decided either by empirical methods of inquiry, or by formal procedures of logic and mathematics. "There are no questions which are in principle unanswerable, no problems which are in principle insoluble. What have been considered such up to now are not genuine questions, but meaningless sequences of words" (*ibid*).

All questions about the nature of what exists, all questions of fact, can in principle be decided "through observation and empirical science". If the questions have been put in such a way that no method can be proposed for so deciding them—as has been done by philosophers—then they have been formulated wrongly and turned into nonsense-questions. Therefore "the totality of sciences, including the statements of daily life, is the system of cognitions. There is, in addition to it, no domain of 'philosophical' truths." What remains for philosophy is simply to clear up the meaning of meaningful statements. "By means of philosophy statements are explained, by means of science they are verified. The latter is concerned with the truth of statements, the former with what they actually mean . . . Then it will no longer be necessary to speak of 'philosophical problems', for one will speak philosophically concerning all problems, that is: clearly and meaningfully" (*ibid*).

Philosophy traditionally abounds with nonsense-questions, the attempts to answer which have led to "the fruitless conflict of systems". The long-standing conflict between materialism and idealism provides a good example.—Which is prior: matter or spirit? Is consciousness a product of material being, or are material things creations of mind or consciousness? Such questions cannot be decided by any method of verification in immediate experience, and so they are without meaning. Again : Do bodies exist independent of their being perceived? This, too, is a nonsense question. For whether they do or do not would make no difference to the actual content of sense-experience.

In a similar way, the questions posed by Russell and Moore in the first formulations of logical-analytic philosophy, as to the ultimate elements and structures of elements referred to by propositions stating facts, are nonsense-questions too. For there is no test of immediate experience by which they can be decided. The elements and structure of the world are (in Wittgenstein's phrase) *shown* by the structure of propositions and the way they are verified, but cannot be *stated*. "It was," wrote Schlick, "one of the most serious errors of former times to have believed that the actual meaning and ultimate content was in turn to be formulated in statements . . . This was the error of 'metaphysics' . . . Thus metaphysics collapses, not because the solving of its tasks is an enterprise to which the human reason is unequal . . . but because there is no such task" (*ibid*).

4. INSIGHT, THERAPY, ANALYSIS

From all this it emerges that Wittgenstein's *Tractatus*, together with the formulations of the verification principle by Schlick, proposed, in effect, three related tasks for contemporary philosophers. First, they should confirm themselves in and propagate the insight of which the *Tractatus* was the first communication. Secondly, and in the light of this insight, they should dispose of questions traditionally and currently debated by philosophers, by demonstrating them to be nonsense. Third, and likewise in the light of the insight, they should clarify and explain what statements of daily life and the sciences actually mean.

The dominant school of Western analytic philosophy has remained faithful to these tasks ever since.

The new insight, which supposedly solved the problems and led philosophy to a decisive turning point, was concerned with how propositions represent reality; and this they do by arrangements of signs, or in other words, by the employment of language (though all language is not necessarily word-language, since other things than words can be so arranged as to express a proposition). Thus this was by no means an insight into hidden depths of reality unrevealed to normal consciousness (such as various mystical religious teachers have claimed); it was an insight into how reality is represented in language, or, as Wittgenstein expressed it, "the form of representation", "the logic of our language". Thus in the Preface to *Tractatus* Wittgenstein stated: "The book deals with the problems of philosophy and shows, as I believe, that the method of formulating these prob-

lems rests on the misunderstanding of the logic of our language . . .
The book will, therefore, draw a limit to thinking, or rather—not to
thinking, but to the expression of thoughts; for, in order to draw a
limit to thinking we should have to be able to think both sides
of the limit (we should therefore have to be able to think what
cannot be thought). The limit can, therefore, only be drawn in
language and what lies on the other side of the limit will simply be
nonsense."

With this there began the doctrine that all properly philosophical
questions are concerned with *language*—not with the peculiarities of
particular languages, but with "the logic of language", observance
of which permits clear and significant statements, and non-observance
of which results in mere nonsense.

Every philosophy includes criticism of other philosophies. But the
criticism started up by Wittgenstein was different, in as much as its
object was not to show that other philosophies had made mistakes in
their answers to questions and, by criticism of wrong answers, to
substantiate the right ones. Its object was to show that the questions
other philosophies had sought to answer were nonsense, and that
therefore all the answers to them were nonsense too. And its method
of criticism was to demonstrate that the asking of the questions arose
from "misunderstanding the logic of language".

From this method of criticism there followed the conclusion that,
except in so far as they had been concerned with genuine problems
of logic, the inquiries made by all other philosophies had not been
genuine inquiries at all, but symptoms of an intellectual ailment.
This ailment was diagnosed as "misunderstanding the logic of language", as a result of which thinking people got confused and
puzzled, asked nonsense-questions and quarrelled about what kind of
nonsense to propound as the answers. Insight into the logic of language provided, then, a kind of therapy for the relief of this ailment.
For some of Wittgenstein's followers the chief value of his teachings
was regarded as "therapeutic", for they supplied a regimen for curing
people of a painful and sometimes socially harmful disorder.

Second, therefore, to the propagation of the insight afforded by
the doctrine of the logic of language (the verification principle and
the pictorial theory), the task proposed for philosophers was the
critical or therapeutic one of curing themselves and others of the
ailment of asking nonsense-questions.

But there also remained the third task, the task of analysis—of achieving with insight that clarification of the actual meaning of statements of daily life and of the sciences which the founders of the logical-analytic philosophy had demanded but been unable to accomplish. Such analysis, as Schlick had emphasised, is the positive task of philosophy. And Wittgenstein had already defined it in the *Tractatus*: "The object of philosophy is the logical clarification of thoughts. Philosophy is not a theory but an activity. A philosophical work consists essentially of elucidations. The result of philosophy is not a number of 'philosophical propositions', but to make propositions clear. Philosophy should make clear and delimit sharply the thoughts which otherwise are, as it were, opaque and blurred" (4. 112).

In his philosophical activity after completing the *Tractatus*—and especially in the early 'thirties, when he transferred the sphere of his operations to the University of Cambridge—Wittgenstein devoted much of his energies to such analytic elucidations, though the results were not written down.

5. THE RETURN TO SOLIPSISM

Wittgenstein's elucidations at that time had a startling effect on many who (like the present writer, when a student at Cambridge) had the advantage of hearing them and discussing them with him. For by the consistent application of the verification principle it turned out that many meaningful statements mean something quite different from what we ordinarily think they mean.

Take, for instance, statements about the past. These cannot be verified by going back into the past and re-experiencing it. If I say, for example, that I had breakfast this morning, the way I verify that statement is not by breakfasting but by remembering my breakfast —and additionally, if I mistrust and wish to check my memory, by other experiences, such as hearing my wife say "Yes, you did have breakfast" if I ask her. So if (as Schlick put it, and as Wittgenstein at that time agreed) "the statement of the conditions under which a proposition is true is the same as the statement of its meaning", what the statement "I had breakfast this morning" means is simply that, when I remember, I remember breakfast; when I ask my wife, I hear her reply . . . and so on. Similarly, if I say that William the Conqueror won the Battle of Hastings that means that history, starting with the Anglo-Saxon Chronicle, credits him with doing so, for I verify it by the sort of experiences described as looking it up in history books and consulting historical records.

Take again statements about other people. If I say you have tooth-ache, all I can mean is that I hear you complaining of toothache, that when I look in your mouth I see something which I describe as a decayed tooth, and so on. For one person cannot experience another person's sensation. Suppose I say that what I mean is that *you* have a sensation like *mine*? That is nonsense—for there is no way of my verifying that your experience is like mine, or, indeed, that you have any experience at all, in the sense that I have experience.

Wittgenstein's application of the verification principle thus led him slap into the very implausible philosophical position of "solipsism of the present moment". Nor could he get out of it, as Hume had done, by saying that he did not believe it. For any attempt to say what then he believed was, by the verification principle, condemned as non-sense. All statements are verified by experience—and for each of us, by his own present experience. Hence for each of us the world consists simply of his own present experience. Beyond that we not only know nothing, but we cannot even significantly state that anything else exists.

Solipsism is, as has often been pointed out, implausible, because if a philosopher declares himself a solipsist, who will credit him with meaning what he says? If he really thinks that the world consists only of his own sensations, why does he go to so much trouble to explain this truth to other people? Wittgenstein evaded this difficulty by saying that if to deny solipsism was nonsense, to assert it must be nonsense too. For the question "Do other experiences besides my own exist?" is a typical nonsense-question. His elucidations were solip-sistic—but solipsism was not a truth that could be stated: rather was it something shown in the making of the elucidations. This point was committed to writing by Wittgenstein in the *Tractatus*: "What solipsism *means* is quite correct, only it cannot be *said*, but it shows itself. That the world is *my* world, shows itself in the fact that the limits of language (the language which only I understand) mean the limits of *my* world" (5. 62).

6. A CROP OF DIFFICULTIES

The solipsistic character of Wittgenstein's elucidations constitutes a sufficient objection to the theory of the form of representation of reality by language which had dictated it. The verification principle and the pictorial theory of propositions were said to provide an insight which would guide philosophical analysis to the full elucidation of meanings. But yet they led to absurdity rather than to any such elucidation. Certainly, sense-experience is a necessary factor in any act of verification. But as certainly, when one talks of external objects and past events and other people's experiences, one's intention or meaning is not limited to expressing an expectation of personal private immediate experience. Even if it is wrong to think that other people exist, everyone thinks they do and tries to communicate with them concerning the common world which they all inhabit. In face of this fact of experience, Wittgenstein's insistence that we *cannot* so think, because it transgresses the limits of language, seems merely doctrinaire. His insight was evidently at fault.

But besides the general absurdity of the elucidations, the theories put forward by Witgenstein in the *Tractatus*, and which served as the basis for Schlick's formulations of the verification principle, became entangled in other—and more properly logical—difficulties.

The pictorial theory of propositions rested on the assumption that atomic propositions are verified by direct comparison with atomic facts of immediate experience, and that all other propositions are verified indirectly by verifying atomic propositions. But how are such atomic propositions to be *stated*? It turns out that they never are stated, and never could be. As a picture of immediate experience, an atomic proposition would have to be stated in words which would stand for objects "given" in immediate experience and, consequently, known only to the person having the experience at the time he was having it. It would be, therefore, a private and incommunicable proposition. The language for expressing atomic propositions would be (as Wittgenstein recognised in his statement about solipsism) a "language only I can understand". The logical theory thus postulates that the basic statements, by reference to which all other statements are verified, are statements which no one can understand except the person who makes them at the time he is making them. And furthermore, who can pin down an atomic fact in his immediate experience, in order to make a picture of it and then compare the picture with the fact? A painter in a studio can hire models to sit for him—but no one can stop the flux of his experience and get an atomic fact to sit for its picture.

Despite such difficulties involved in the very definition of atomic propositions (and Wittgenstein himself grew increasingly aware of them), the pictorial theory and the principle of verification were thought by many to have been signally successful in the definition of truth functions and tautologies. It was thought that the distinction between factual statement and tautology had successfully accounted for the distinction between empirical and formally necessary propositions, and that necessity had been shown to be equivalent to tautology. Yet difficulties crop up here as well.

In the first place, whatever may apply to principles of formal logic, theorems of mathematics cannot be regarded as tautologies. Nor did Wittgenstein himself suppose that they could. On the contrary, he drew in the *Tractatus* a sharp distinction between formal logic and mathematics, rejected the entire thesis that numbers are classes of classes and that mathematics is an extension of logic, and maintained that, whereas logic consists of tautologies, mathematics consists of equations. He sought to give an account of mathematics by treating it as essentially concerned with certain kinds of operations (involved in the techniques of counting and measuring, etc.) and with the demonstration of the equality and non-equality of the results of such operations. For example, counting two sets of two arrives at the same termination as counting one set of four. This was a fruitful approach to problems of the philosophy of mathematics. Wittgenstein continued throughout his life to work on it; and his *Remarks on the Foundations of Mathematics* (1956) contains, perhaps, his most positive and creative contributions to scientific philosophy. However, despite the incautious claim that in the *Tractatus* problems had been "finally solved", Wittgenstein could not claim to have finally solved problems of the nature of mathematics and of mathematical necessity (nor could anyone else, for that matter). And that being so, it is obvious that the theory of tautology does not suffice to define the distinction between matter of fact and necessity.

In the second place, while the theory of tautology thus fails to apply to the definition of mathematical necessity, it also breaks down in its application to formal logic. Wittgenstein's definition of tautology was derived from his conception of verification—a statement is tautological when the rules determining its truth-conditions do not allow it to be falsified. This implies a standard "decision procedure" by which it can always be decided whether or not a given form of statement is tautological. In other words, if all formulas of formal logic are tautologies (in the sense defined by Wittgenstein), there must exist a standard or routine decision procedure whereby their tautological character is certified. Sure enough, such tests have been devised for all the simpler formulas of formal logic (see W. van O. Quine,

Methods of Logic, 1950). But quantification technique can devise formulas of any order of complexity; and it was proved by Alonzo Church ("A Note on the Entscheidungsproblem", *Journal of Symbolic Logic*, 1936) that there can be no routine decision procedure applicable to all formulas of quantification theory. This does not mean that such formulas cannot, with sufficient ingenuity, be proved by the methods of deduction proper to a logical calculus. But it does mean that they do not satisfy the conditions of being "tautologies" in the precise sense required by Wittgenstein. His definition of tautology was worked out only for the elementary part of formal logic—the theory of the truth-functions of elementary propositions. When it comes to general quantification theory, it is no longer adequate.

What Schlick called "the insight into the nature of logic itself" provided by Wittgenstein's *Tractatus* sharply divided logic from mathematics. Yet while the totality of mathematics is not deducible from axioms of formal logic, it still holds good that logic and mathematics are closely related as sciences which discover formal necessities, as distinct from matters of fact. Wittgenstein defined the necessity of the formulas of logic as tautology; but he could not define the necessity of mathematics. Yet it appears that even in formal logic necessity is not reducible to tautology. Hence we are still a long way from having gained "insight into the nature of logic", let alone into the connection of logic and mathematics and the nature of formal necessity in general.

It appears, then, that the insight conveyed in the *Tractatus*, far from solving all problems, gave rise to a crop of difficulties. And finally, and worst of all, it suffers from that most fatal of all philosophical flaws, internal inconsistency. It destroys itself. For according to the theory, all statements which are neither tautologies nor verifiable in experience, are nonsense. By this criterion, the theory itself is nonsense. For it is not a tautology, nor is it itself verifiable by experience.

Wittgenstein realised this inconsistency from the start, but made a brave attempt to make out that it did not matter. He ended his *Tractatus* by saying that what he had written in it was all nonsense—but yet, he still claimed, an enlightening kind of nonsense. "My propositions are elucidatory . . ." he wrote. "He who understands me finally recognises them as nonsense, when he has climbed up through them, on them, over them. (He must so to speak throw away the

ladder after he has climbed upon it.) He must surmount these propositions, then he sees the world rightly" (6.54).

But that a theory which is self-confessed nonsense should at the
same time be elucidatory, takes a lot of swallowing—especially when
it turns out that the elucidations offered are themselves absurd. And
so does the method of criticism which condemns other theories as
nonsense on the basis of a theory which condemns itself as nonsense.

7. LOGICAL POSITIVISM

In the 'thirties there was a large output of philosophical writing,
generally known as "logical positivism", generated by the "Vienna
Circle" gathered around Schlick. These philosophers worked closely
together, and established their own journals. They were dispersed by
the Nazis, after which some went to the U.S.A. and carried on from
there. Their unifying characteristic was that they all started from an
acceptance of what Schlick had called Wittgenstein's "insight", and
devoted themselves to trying, in one way or another, to get round
the difficulties it involved. Wittgenstein held himself somewhat aloof
from the logical positivist school. He found his own methods of
coping with these difficulties, which were different from theirs. It
was the later philosophy of Wittgenstein which engendered the
contemporary linguistic school, whereas logical positivism proved a
dead end and petered out.

The chief proposal for getting out of Wittgenstein's difficulties was
made in the Vienna Circle by Otto von Neurath and Rudolf Carnap.
These difficulties were all concerned, in one way or another, with
trying to say how language represents reality. But the relation
between words and things, or between statement and fact, is only
another nonsense-question (or "pseudo-problem", as they called it in
the Vienna Circle). It is but a version of the time-honoured pseudo-
problem about the relation between thinking and being. Hence it
should be ignored, and the kind of analysis in which philosophers
are interested should be strictly confined to the analysis of language.
What had been vaguely called "the logic of language" was renamed
"the logical syntax of language", and was defined as being concerned
with the ways words are put together to make statements, and with
the way statements are put together to make theories, but not with
the ways statements represent objective reality.

In *The Logical Syntax of Language* (1934) Carnap began by saying
that in the consideration of logical syntax "no reference is made either

to the meaning of the symbols or to the sense of the expressions, but simply and solely to the kinds and order of the symbols from which the expressions are constructed" (1).

He accordingly distinguished "logical questions" from what he called "object questions". The latter "have to do with the objects of the domain under consideration, such as inquiries regarding their properties and relations. Logical questions, on the other hand, do not refer directly to objects, but to sentences, terms, theories, and so on, which themselves refer to objects" (72). The empirical sciences are concerned with object questions. But "the inextricable tangle of problems which is known as philosophy" results from trying to express questions which properly concern only the uses of words (logical questions) as questions concerning the properties and relations of things (object questions). For example, philosophers have been puzzled by the infinity and infinite divisibility of time. But questions which are very puzzling when asked about a supposed object, named "time", cease to be so puzzling when put merely as questions about how "real number expressions are used as time-coordinates" (79).

Accordingly, in the Foreword to *Logical Syntax of Language* Carnap stated:

"The aim of logical syntax is to provide a system of concepts, a language, by the help of which the results of logical analysis will be exactly formulable. *Philosophy is to be replaced by the logic of science* —that is to say, by the logical analysis of the concepts and sentences of the sciences, for *the logic of science is nothing other than the logical syntax of the language of science.*"

From this standpoint, the logical analysis of science was not concerned at all with trying to interpret or elucidate the meaning of statements of science. It did not seek to show that science is validated by its correspondence with given experience, with facts, with the objective world, etc. It was concerned solely with the logical rules for constructing scientific statements—not with their relationship with objective reality but only with their relationship with one another.

A new way was found of expressing the old positivist principle that scientific statements are tested or verified by reference to facts "given in experience". This had to be expressed, not in the traditional way in terms of the relationship of scientific statements to facts, but in terms of the inter-relationship of statements within the totality of statements which make up science. It was said that science proceeds by accepting a "protocol", consisting of a number of statements of the sort which would commonly be called observational, and then devising other statements, in the form of generalisations or laws, consistent with the protocol. In his paper "The Physical Language as the Universal Language of Science" (*Erkenntnis*, 1931/32— published later in English as a booklet entitled *The Unity of Science*) Carnap said that it is tempting to define "protocol statements" as statements which "refer to the given, and describe directly given experience". That is how Wittgenstein and afterwards Schlick had defined them, and got into all sorts of difficulties as a result, including Wittgenstein's solipsism. But the logically correct or accurate way of defining them is simply as follows: "statements needing no justification and serving as foundations for all the remaining statements of science."

Von Neurath put forward this analysis of science, and drew from it the logical conclusions, in the most explicit and uncompromising terms:

"It is always science as a system of statements which is at issue. *Statements are compared with statements*, not with 'experiences', 'the world', or anything else. All these meaningless *duplications* belong to a more or less refined metaphysics and are, for that reason, to be rejected. Each new statement is compared with the totality of existing statements previously co-ordinated. To say that a statement is correct, therefore, means that it can be incorporated in this totality. What cannot be incorporated is rejected as incorrect. The alternative to rejection is . . . the whole previous system of statements can be modified up to the point where it becomes possible to incorporate the new statement . . . The definition of 'correct' and 'incorrect' proposed here departs from that customary among the 'Vienna Circle', which appeals to 'meaning' and 'verification'. In our presentation we confine ourselves always to the sphere of linguistic thought" ("Sociology and Physicalism", *Erkenntnis*, 1931/32).

From this point of view, the different sciences are to be distinguished—not by their investigating different facets of the world, or different relationships given in experience—but by their employing different "languages". For example, said Carnap, the science of economics is distinguished "by the fact that its sentences are constructed from expressions 'supply and demand', 'wage', 'price', etc." (*The Unity of Science*). This way of distinguishing sciences simply as different scientific languages, with different protocols, led to what was regarded as the crowning achievement of logical positivist analysis—the demonstration of "the unity of science". All the different sciences could be made into a "unity" by translation into one common language. And this language was said to be "the physical language". It was characterised by the fact that its protocol statements "attach to a specific set of co-ordinates a definite value or range of values of physical state". *All* scientific protocol, it was asserted, is translatable into physicalistic protocol, and consequently "every scientific statement can be translated into physical language" (*ibid*).

This theory of "the logical syntax of language" certainly avoided the difficulties which had beset earlier attempts at logical analysis, including Wittgenstein's solipsistic elucidations. For of course, if the rule is laid down that you must never try to inquire how your thoughts correspond with reality, but must consider only the syn-tactical rules whereby the sentences expressing them are constructed then all difficulties connected with the relationship between though and reality are avoided. However, this was to avoid the difficultie. of philosophy in the same way as the ship's company in Lewis Car-roll's *Hunting of the Snark* avoided the difficulties of navigation:

> "Other maps are such shapes, with their islands and capes,
>   But we have our brave Captain to thank
> (So the crew would protest) that he's bought us the best—
>   A perfect and absolute blank!"

But just as that ship's company got into difficulties of their own ("the bowsprit got mixed with the rudder sometimes"), so did the logical positivists.

The central difficulty of the doctrine of Carnap and Neurath was obvious and insurmountable. Purporting to give an account of "the logic of science", and even of "the unity of science", that doctrine could give no account at all of how scientific conclusions are arrived at and how they are tested, but instead represented them as products of arbitrary choices and arbitrary decisions.

Science was treated simply as a system of statements. Of course, scientific textbooks and scientific papers do consist of statements. But there are no statements of science apart from the practice of science. It is their connection with practice which gives these statements their "scientific" status, and makes modern men, who have developed science and technology as their productive forces, take them so seriously. For these statements are not arrived at in any arbitrary way, do not depend on anyone's arbitrary claim to authority or arbitrary decision, but express the verified findings of systematic investigations. The credibility, the reliability, the scientific status of scientific statements depends, not on their relations with other statements, but on their connection with human practice. Hence the philosopher who insists that statements are to be "compared" only "with statements" is incapable of comparing scientific with non-scientific statements, or of giving any intelligible account of what science is and does and is all about. The control of scientific statement by scientific investigation and verification becomes the bringing of generalisations and laws into conformity with a protocol. But how is the protocol arrived at? This question goes outside what Neurath called "the sphere of linguistic thought", and is therefore disallowed. The laying down of the protocol therefore appears entirely arbitrary. (Neurath himself said that why scientists should agree to accept one set of statements rather than another is not a question for philosophy, but for that hitherto unexplored part of sociology which studies the social behaviour of scientists.)

In this connection, Carnap announced in the Foreword to *The Logical Syntax of Language* that we possess "complete liberty" regarding the language we choose to employ. Not merely are we at liberty to choose whether to speak in English or German or Russian, etc., but "both the rules for construction of sentences and the . . . 'postulates' and 'rules of inference' may be chosen quite arbitrarily". This charter of liberty he called "the Principle of Tolerance". Scientists, then, can choose their scientific languages quite arbitrarily —it just so happens that they tend to agree on a certain protocol and rules of procedure.

Coming on top of this "analysis of science", the crowning theory of "the unity of science"—the theory of so-called "physicalism"— appears merely as a crowning absurdity. Why should it be always possible to translate all the arbitrarily chosen languages of all the sciences into "the physical language"? To this question there is no answer. Moreover, it is one thing to say that this can be done, and quite another to find any way of doing it. For example, how can statements of economics, "constructed from expressions 'supply and demand', 'wage', 'price' etc.", be translated into statements which "attach to a specific set of co-ordinates a definite value or range of values of physical state"? This problem is so baffling that it was not long before the whole theory of "physicalism" and "the unity of science" was quietly dropped.

Logical positivism was supposed to lead the way out of "the inextricable tangle of problems which is known as philosophy". Yet never since the later middle ages had any school of philosophy contrived a tangle of problems so remote from any kind of practical relevance and so incapable of resolution.

The attempted restriction of philosophy to "purely formal" analysis —that is, to analysis which ignored the meaning of statements and confined itself to "logical syntax"—did not survive the 'thirties. In 1942, in his *Introduction to Semantics*, Carnap announced that "the field of theoretical philosophy is no longer restricted to syntax, but is regarded as comprehending the whole analysis of language . . ." For "the earlier discussions and analyses . . . have to be supplemented by corresponding semantical analysis." This was to admit that philosophers not only can but must consider how statements represent reality, what they mean, how they are to be interpreted, what they refer to, how they function as vehicles of information, how they are verified, how meaning and verification are connected—instead of theorising only about how statements are related to other statements.

This admission meant a certain turn from doctrinaire absurdity towards more constructive inquiry. But it also meant the breakup of logical positivism as a distinctive school of philosophy. Apart from specialised inquiries into problems of formal logic and of semantics, what continued to pass muster as "logical positivism" consisted of exercises in and variants upon the traditional nineteenth-century positivist analysis of science.

Meanwhile Wittgenstein, working with a select band of disciples at Cambridge, had been looking for other ways of escape from the difficulties in which logical analysis and his own earlier theories had involved him.

II

Linguistic Philosophy

CHAPTER ONE

A Therapy for Theories

I. SECOND THOUGHTS ABOUT LANGUAGE

WITTGENSTEIN was not only an ingenious philosopher but also an honest man. As time passed, he became more and more dissatisfied with his own conclusions. For he saw that they did not fit with either language or experience, that even purely logical or formal problems remained unsolved by them, and that a theory which was self-confessed nonsense could not at the same time be elucidatory. It was the combination of the verification principle with the pictorial theory of language that led to these unsatisfactory results. So he proceeded to question both the pictorial theory and the verification principle. His later philosophy, and the contemporary linguistic philosophy, were the result of this questioning. Their foundation was a new view about language.

Language, Wittgenstein had said, makes pictures of facts which are to be compared with facts. But this account of language, he now declared, ignores the real function of language, which is communication between human beings. Language is in fact used for many other purposes of communication besides making statements. But even if we consider only the making of statements, we still cannot equate the making of statements with the making of pictures. Words cannot be regarded simply as the elements of a picture. They are more like tools or instruments, which are used for a variety of different purposes of communication.

And now comes the most important point of all. There is no limit to the variety of the uses of words. There is no common or basic function served by words in the making of human communications.

"Think of the tools in a tool box," Wittgenstein wrote in his *Philosophical Investigations* (1953). "There is a hammer, pliers, a saw, a screw-driver, a rule, a glue-pot, nails and screws. The functions of words are as diverse as the functions of these objects . . ." (11).

It might be objected that all tools *do* have something in common, since (as Marx put it) they are all "instruments of labour" designed to "effect an alteration in the material worked upon". But Wittgenstein refuted this objection. "Imagine someone's saying: 'All tools serve to modify something. Thus the hammer modifies the position of the nail, the saw the shape of the board, and so on.'—And what is modified by the rule, the glue-pot, the nails?" (14). And so, following up the analogy with tools, Wittgenstein continued:

"How many kinds of sentences are there? There are *countless* kinds, countless different kinds of uses of what we call 'symbols', 'words', 'sentences'. And this multiplicity is not something fixed, given once for all . . . (23).

"Instead of producing something common to all that we call language, I am saying that these phenomena have no one thing in common . . . but that they are related in many different ways" (65).

Every use of words has its rules. And in this respect, Wittgenstein compared using language to playing games, which likewise involves obeying rules. Cricket, for example, is a ball game played according to the rules of cricket. And there are many other ball games with other rules—such as hockey, baseball, netball, football, including both rugger and soccer, and so on. There are also card games, and board games like chess or draughts. And indeed, besides the many games that are actually played, it would be possible to invent still more games, and to go on inventing them indefinitely.

Wittgenstein pursued this analogy between language and games by maintaining that in every historically constituted language an endless variety of language games can be played corresponding to the countless variety of possible uses of words.

These language games, or uses of language, come into being naturally, he maintained, and their rules get established and modified corresponding to the actual requirements of human life. The more varied that life, the more varied the communications required for living it, and the more varied the consequent uses of language. "To imagine a language," wrote Wittgenstein, "means to imagine a form of life" (19). Our uses of language "are as much a part of our natural history as walking, eating, drinking, playing" (25).

When we understand one another, it does not occur to us to ask what language game we are playing—any more than it would occur to cricketers to ask one another whether they were playing cricket or football. Those who play games usually know how to play, and they get on with it. But we do not always understand one another. In speech, and especially in abstract speech, we often get confused and break the rules, or get different uses mixed up together, or misinterpret what other people are saying by supposing them to be playing some different language game. When that happens we find ourselves asking questions which cannot be answered, and drawing the queerest conclusions from attempting to answer them.

In fact, we then get into the kind of muddle that would arise from questioning cricketers on the assumption that they were playing football. It might then be asked, for example, "How many goals have been scored?" Such a question arises simply from a misunderstanding of the actual games, and so it has no answer. (If the cricketers tried to answer it by saying "none", queer conclusions could be inferred. It could be concluded that the match was a draw. And then the more philosophical might generalise this conclusion into the theory that, whatever the appearances in terms of runs, all cricket matches were really drawn—because the real score in goals was necessarily "0–0".)

This, Wittgenstein now maintained, is how philosophical puzzles and philosophical theories arise. Philosophers do not understand how many different uses language actually has, and so become confused between them. "A philosophical problem," Wittgenstein wrote, "has the form: I don't know my way about" (123). The fact is that in civilised society language has so many different uses that some people get them mixed up—and hence philosophy. "When we do philosophy we are like savages, primitive people, who hear the expressions of civilised men, put a false interpretation on them and then draw the queerest conclusions from it" (194).

So our aim in philosophy should be continually to clear up the uses of language, in order to put an end to problems arising from the misuse and misinterpretation of language. "The philosopher's treatment of a question is like the treatment of an illness" (255). Those who get mixed up in the uses of language fall into a kind of mental trap, in which they buzz about like flies in a fly-bottle. "What is your aim in philosophy?" Wittgenstein asked. "To show the fly the way out of the fly-bottle" (309). —He was a man with a passion for picturesque analogies. Beginning with pictures, he then substituted a tool box, then got on to games, and the treatment of illness, and finished up with flies in a fly-bottle.

In all this revision of his earlier theories Wittgenstein remained true to the earlier conception of the threefold task of philosophy. First, there remained the basic insight concerning language—in which the pictorial theory was replaced by the conception of language games. Second, there remained the task of therapy, "the treatment of an illness". The traditional problems of philosophy were still to be resolved by clearing away confusions in the use of language— but the former crude conception of "nonsense" was replaced by that of the mixing up of language games. What, then, of the task of elucidation? This, too, remained, but was conceived of in a new way. The task remained of interpreting or explaining the meaning of different sentences. But the verification principle, which said that the meaning of a proposition is given by its mode of verification in immediate experience, was discarded.

You make some statement—what do you mean by it?

According to the verification principle, you must explain what you mean by stating what immediate experience would verify your statement—that is, by producing a word-picture of that experience. This would imply that you can employ, for purposes of elucidation, some kind of perfect or pre-eminent language, in which what was meant by every statement could be stated clearly. But the uses of language are limitless, with "no one thing in common", so that it is impossible to find one pre-eminently correct use of language into which all can be translated.

The verification principle, that the meaning of a proposition is given by its mode of verification in immediate experience, has there-fore to be discarded along with the pictorial theory of propositions. And with it are discarded all its queer consequences—its queer interpretations of all statements in terms of personal experience, and the queer kind of solipsism which was "correct" but could not be "said".

What, then, is required to explain or make clear the meaning of statements?

The basic error of the former "logical analysis" lay in supposing that this was to be done by casting all statements into the mould of a perfect or ideally clear language. But that is impossible. All that is in fact required is simply to make evident the particular language game that is being played. And the way to do that is to produce other examples of the same language game, and contrasting examples of different language games. Such examples were given the technical name of "paradigm case". Where doubt or confusion exists as to meaning, it is cleared up by producing "the paradigm case".

In place of the verification principle, then, Wittgenstein in his *Philosophical Investigations* substituted the following: "The meaning of a word is its use in the language" (43).

How, then, can we say what is or what is not "the right" use of words?

Words are used rightly when they are used according to the rules, that is, when they do serve a particular use of communication. But there are no super-rules which will determine which particular uses are justifiable. There is no pre-eminent language by reference to which the justifiability or otherwise of particular uses can be decided, or in terms of which everything can be clearly and correctly stated. And so a very important conclusion follows. We cannot criticise or improve upon the actual uses of language. We cannot distinguish one use as justifiable in comparison with another, or invent some special use or set of uses to supplant all the others. We must simply accept the actual uses as all in order, but take care not to mix them up.

Philosophers have looked at tables, and asked "Do tables really exist?" That is to say, they have suspected something wrong with the way people actually use such sentences as "There is a table in this room". They have suspected that such sentences are in some way or other inadequate and misleading, and that in the situations where they are commonly used it would be more correct to say something else, such as "I am now experiencing a particular kind of sensation". But they themselves are wrong in trying to amend the actual uses of language in terms of some artificial standard of metaphysical correctness. As words are actually used, it is correct to say "There is a table in this room" when one enters the room and sees a table. Only in rather exceptional circumstances—if, say, the table were to disappear, or if one were to go up to it and walk right through it—would one say "There is not really a table there at all".

So Wittgenstein declared:

"Philosophy may in no way interfere with the actual use of language: it can in the end only describe it. For it cannot give it any foundation either. It leaves everything as it is . . . (124).

"We may not advance any kind of theory . . . We must do away with all explanation, and description alone must take its place. And this description gets its power of illumination—i.e. its purpose—from the philosophical problems. These are, of course, not empirical problems; they are solved, rather, by looking into the workings of our language, and that in such a way as to make us recognise those workings in despite of an urge to misunderstand them. The problems are solved, not by giving new information, but by arranging what we have always known . . ." (109).

Philosophers have been prone to draw conclusions about the nature of the universe, and to draw them by arguing that, in despite of appearances, the universe must necessarily be of such and such a kind, of such and such a structure. They have argued that "it *must* be like *this*". Such arguments and such conclusions, Wittgenstein said, are based only on misunderstanding the actual uses of language. "In philosophy we do not draw conclusions," he declared. " 'But it must be like this!' is not a philosophical proposition. Philosophy only states what everyone admits" (599).

So here we have the conclusion of Wittgenstein's second thoughts on language: "In philosophy we do not draw conclusions." Gone now is the solipsism, and the infallible method of explaining what we really mean. Instead, we are advised to state only "what everyone admits", and so long as we do no more than that we are assured that what we say will be all right. Perhaps we would like to know "the foundation" for what we say, to find whether everyone is right in what everyone admits? But such a quest is out of order. For it involves trying to "interfere with the actual use of language". The actual use of language is all right, and requires no interference. To interfere makes nothing clearer, but on the contrary, causes confusions by mixing different uses together.

It is from this position that linguistic philosophy now operates.

2. NO THEORY—BUT A CURE FOR THEORIES

The guiding idea of the linguistic philosophy, developed from Wittgenstein's second thoughts about language, is that we have only to describe the actual use of language associated with any question debated by philosophers, and all the puzzles vanish, leaving clarity. For example, questions about "the mind" are to be cleared up by investigating how words for mental activities are actually used. Questions about "universals" are to be cleared up by investigating how universal words are actually used. Questions about "determinism", "freedom" or "morals" are to be cleared up by investigating how words connected with causality, with choice, or with moral judgment are actually used.

The philosophical theories which are supposed to provide the answers to philosophical problems arise solely from mixing up different uses of words. How this comes about, and how both the puzzles and the associated theories may be removed, can be demonstrated by examples. Let us take a rather over-simplified one.

It could be said of two identical twins that "they have the same weight" and that "they have the same father". Philosophical puzzles about the so-called "ontological status" of universal qualities like weight, to which many particulars are related by the relation of "having it in common", and the various rival theories about universals which result from discussing such puzzles, arise only from such confusions as mixing up the way we use words when we say "have the same weight" with the way we use words when we say "have the same father". It is like getting puzzled by the question "what is a bad temper?" as a result of hearing someone say "the Colonel came along in a bad temper and a bath chair".

Such puzzles vanish if you patiently describe the different uses of words, so that each use is clearly exhibited and distinguished from other uses. The clarity which is then attained does not consist in your then possessing a clear statement of some general truth which was obscure before. It does not consist in your having discovered anything not known before, or in your having demonstrated the truth of any theory. It consists simply in the absence of confusion, in your having succeeded in overcoming puzzles resulting from mixing up different uses of words.

It is in this and this alone that the illumination or insight claimed by the linguistic philosophy consists. Wittgenstein's precept that "we may not advance any kind of theory" is to be taken as meaning what it says. Quite literally, the linguistic philosophy puts forward no theory, no theory whatever—and it can never be understood, still less sensibly discussed or criticised, unless this point is taken. It proposes no theory, either about language or anything else; but it demolishes bad theory, and cures you of *wanting* a philosophical theory. As Wittgenstein said, "the problems are solved, not by giving new information, but by arranging what we have always known". The linguistic philosophy professes to have nothing new to say, nothing new to tell anyone. Its claim is that it practises a technique for describing and distinguishing uses of words, and removes philosophical puzzles by doing so.

3. WORDS AND THEIR MEANING

The type of analytic investigation of the ways in which words are actually used in different cases and in different contexts, proposed by Wittgenstein and subsequently practised by the linguistic school of philosophy, certainly does avoid all those perplexities which befuddled the earlier practice of the logical-analytic method—from G. E. Moore and Russell right up to Wittgenstein's first philosophy.

Philosophical analysis was originally proposed for the purpose of stating clearly what we really mean when we make various statements the truth of which is generally agreed; the implication being that prior to such analysis we do not know what we mean, or what we are talking about. The perplexities arose from the difficulty of deciding what we do really mean, as distinct from what we confusedly think we mean; plus the difficulty that the proposed analyses were always absurd.

The new type of analysis done by linguistic philosophy avoids these perplexities, because it does not try to tell us anything we did not know already. It does not tell us that we are really talking about sense-data when we confusedly think we are talking about physical objects, or that we are really making pictures of our own immediate experience when we think we are talking about the objective material world. It recognises that normal language is a perfectly adequate instrument for human communication, so that normally we know very well what we mean and do not need to have it clarified by philosophers. Instead, by investigating the given uses of language it sets out to remove those purely philosophical puzzles which arise from misunderstanding them. It is not ordinary people who are confused and who need to have clarity brought to them by philosophers; it is philosophers who are confused, because they have got themselves muddled by the ordinary uses of language. (As Wittgenstein said, philosophers "are like savages who hear the expressions of civilised men, put a false interpretation on them and then draw the queerest conclusions from it".)

To this end, the linguistic philosophy works on one important (and undoubtedly correct) idea that was contained in the former analytic philosophy—that of the potential misleadingness of normally employed linguistic forms. Sentences of similar linguistic form are, in different contexts, used for such very different purposes of communication that incredible confusions and puzzles can result for philosophers if they fail to understand how similarity of verbal form may mask dissimilarity of meaning. This idea was central in Frege's criticism of the traditional Aristotelian logic and reform of formal logic. It was taken up by Russell and Moore for the purposes of making their philosophical analysis; Moore, indeed, remarked that language seemed to "have grown up just as if it were expressly designed to mislead philosophers" (*The Conception of Reality*, Proceedings of Aristotelian Society, 1917–18).

But Russell and Moore went wrong owing to their tacit assumption that the meaning of a sentence is made clear by discovering for what objects its terms really stand. It was the search for these alleged objects, for an analysis which would make clear to what objects propositions ultimately refer, which led them into perplexities. And Wittgenstein's way of escape from these perplexities involved a rather radical criticism of the whole traditional philosophical conception of the meaning of words.

Language is something we use to communicate with one another . . . It may be said that this was no great discovery. Yet to state the obvious is a merit rather than a demerit in philosophy. When philosophy denies or ignores the obvious it becomes absurd. But it becomes instructive when, after stating the obvious, it goes on to draw implications which are not so obvious. Wittgenstein certainly did bring out some instructive implications of the obvious truth that language is the human means of communication.

From the time of Plato (when it first began to be realised that words have meaning only by convention) the view was tacitly accepted by philosophers of all schools that words, phrases and sentences, or language-expressions generally, have a meaning when they *stand for* something, and that what they stand for is what they mean. So what do expressions stand for? This question has involved philosophers in a great tangle of difficulties and inconsistencies.

On the one hand, it could be said that expressions stand for the thoughts which they express. In that case, there are ideas, concepts, thoughts, propositions (a number of words, none very clearly defined, are available), which may be expressed in words but exist independently of any such expression. According to some philosophers, they have a timeless existence on their own, independent also of people's mental processes (such was the view of Plato and, in another version, of Hegel, and in yet another version, of Russell). According to other philosophers, they exist "in the mind". But whatever the account that may be given of the ideal or mental entities which expressions stand for, just where and how they exist, and how they are constituted and formed, remains a puzzle.

On the other hand, it is characteristic of *thought* that it is *about* something. It would seem, therefore, that words which express or stand for thoughts must also stand for whatever objects thoughts are about. True, some schools of modern idealism have denied this implication. According to these philosophers, thinking creates its own objects for itself. When you have said how words express thoughts, or express judgments, you have said all there is to say about them—and this view led to the modern idealist logic, opposed to formal or mathematical logic, which took as its subject matter the classification and laws of development of "judgments". But these philosophers are opposed by others who take what has been called a "realist" view and hold that words stand for the objects which thoughts are about. This view has always regarded *naming* as the basic or fundamental function of words. We have words which are the names of objects, and also names of qualities and relations of objects, and by combining those names together in various ways we express the thoughts of how the objects named are combined. This account of language goes right back to the medieval scholastics, and even earlier, to some of the Fathers of the Catholic Church. It figured prominently in the views about language put forward by Thomas Hobbes, and received its final *reductio ad absurdum* in Wittgenstein's own "pictorial" theory. It leads to the conclusion that the universe must possess a metaphysical structure corresponding to the grammatical structure of sentences—and consequently to interminable speculations and counter-speculations about the elements of that structure.

In general, then, the traditional view which equates "means" with "stands for" leads, first, to uncertainties and ambiguities as to whether expressions stand for thoughts or for objects or for both together; and second, to a kind of metaphysical stockpiling of independent entities which words stand for, the nature and status of which remains obscure—ideas, concepts. propositions, judgments, on the one hand; on the other hand, objects, complexes of objects, facts and elements.

All these perplexities were present in the analytic philosophy, from *Principia Mathematica* to *Tractatus Logico-Philosophicus*. Wittgenstein must be credited with having cut right through this ancient tangle of ambiguities and speculations with the simple formula which equates meaning with use.

He began his *Philosophical Investigations* by quoting from Augustine's *Confessions* the view that "the individual words in language name objects—sentences are combinations of names". And he continued: "In this picture of language we find the roots of the following idea: Every word has a meaning. This meaning is correlated with the word. It is the object for which the word stands. Augustine does not speak of there being any difference between kinds of word. If you describe the learning of language in this way you are, I believe, thinking primarily of nouns like 'table', 'chair', 'bread', and of people's names and only secondarily of the names of certain actions and properties; and of the remaining kinds of words as something that will take care of itself" (1).

He then had little difficulty in demonstrating, with the aid of examples, that while it is proper to speak of some words as being used to "stand for" something, other words are used in all kinds of other ways, and that to equate meaning with standing for something is to confuse the use of words in general with one particular use of words.

This criticism of the traditional view of meaning was directed especially against the idea that accompanying and attached to the expression is something else, a kind of double—the meaning of the expression. But to know the meaning of an expression is not to discover something else which accompanies it in its use, but is simply to know its use.

An important corollary of the equation of meaning with use was the demonstration that an expression has meaning only in the context of its use, so that in different contexts the same expressions may have different meanings, because they are differently used.

Take, for instance, the uses of the verb "to know" in the three sentences "I know Mr Smith", "I know the multiplication table", and "I know the height of the Post Office Tower". The uses are different, and the meaning of "to know" is different (though not unrelated) in the three cases, because the context is different. This difference can be demonstrated by pointing out that each of the three sentences is the answer to a different question: "Have you been introduced to Mr Smith and could you recognise him again?", "Can you repeat the multiplication table and use it for doing sums?", "Can you truthfully fill in the blank in the sentence 'The Post Office Tower is . . . feet high'?" Each question is appropriate to a different human situation, or to a different sphere of social practice. The context of use is the context of practice, for the purposes of which people require to speak. Thus the first case relates to the practice of recognising people, the second to the practice of calculations, and the third to the practice of measurement. (And of course, besides the three quoted, there are other related meanings of the verb "to know"). It is, then, futile to try to work out a "theory of knowledge", on the basis of supposing (as many philosophers have nevertheless done) that there is one activity, named "knowing", which the verb "to know" stands for, or one thing named "knowledge" which is the single product of knowing, and that we have to produce an analysis of that activity and that product. What is required is rather to investigate how we use the verb "to know" in the context of a variety of different, yet related, practical activities.

And there is a further interesting and instructive corollary, which can be demonstrated by following up the same examples.

The different uses of the verb "to know" may be contrasted with, say, the uses (in English) of the verb "to draw" in the contexts "to draw a picture", "to draw water", and "to draw a cart". We can easily recognise that the verb "to draw" has three quite different and unrelated (or at all events, only very remotely related) meanings in English. Obviously, when an artist draws a picture, a cottager draws water from a well, and a horse draws a cart, the word "draws" does not stand for different forms of a single activity named "drawing". Similarly, the different uses of the verb "to know" do not stand for different kinds of knowing—in the way that, say, "oak", "beech" and "chestnut" stand for different kinds of trees, or "trotting", "cantering" and "galloping" stand for different kinds of locomotion of a horse. Yet these uses of "to know" are related with an intimacy which does not hold for the contrasted uses of "to draw". For the contexts in which they are appropriate are similar in many ways. The uses of "to know" are not related by the fact that in each of them "to know" stands for a form of the same thing, but they have a kind of kinship, in rather the same way that the members of a family are akin. As Wittgenstein expressed it, they "form a family" and have "family resemblance" (67). So such an expression as the verb "to know" has no single meaning, in the sense of there being a single thing it stands for; nor does it take a variety of unrelated meanings;

but, as used in different contexts, its uses constitute "a family" of meanings.

Hence the equation of meaning with use, with its corollary that meaning depends on context, leads to the conclusion that, for many expressions, to elucidate their meaning does not involve discovering any one thing that they stand for, but the demonstration of a family of meanings or of kindred uses.

All this is very relevant to the practice of logical analysis. And while the linguistic philosophy does make the very large claim of having brought about the reformation of philosophy in its entirety, by providing a cure for all philosophical theories without exception, its effective result is to reform the logical-analytic philosophy. The main point of all its contentions and arguments is to remove the perplexities that beset the path of logical analysis. Instead of trying to express the exact meaning of various words, phrases and sentences, and to discover the ultimate unanalysable elements to which they refer, analysis is given the much more hopeful task of describing and distinguishing the varieties of the actual uses of words in the various different contexts of their use. And this suffices to cure the bewilderment which philosophers experience when they confound these uses together.

4. A PROGRAMME FOR PHILOSOPHICAL INVESTIGATIONS

We must not, says the linguistic philosopher, try to formulate any kind of general theory about what all statements have to refer to, and then try to interpret all statements in the light of it. Such a programme for philosophy is based simply on failure to take into account the endless variety of the actual uses of words, and on supposing instead that all uses of words can be reduced to forms of a single basic function (such as making pictures of facts) which all have in common. "There are countless different kinds of uses of what we call 'symbols', 'words', 'sentences'," said Wittgenstein. "Instead of producing something common to all that we call language, I am saying that these phenomena have no one thing in common." That is, indeed, the fundamental text for the linguistic philosophy.

To have a general theory about what all statements refer to, and then to interpret all statements in the light of it, was the procedure of the positivist philosophy of the nineteenth century, and of the logical-analytic philosophy which continued it. The linguistic philosophy was, then, specially directed against this fundamental procedure of positivism in general and the logical-analytic philosophy in particular.

However, linguistic philosophers have a marked tendency to interpret *all* past philosophy as a kind of "analysis", as though what *all* philosophers had always done (from the earliest times to the conclusion of the second world war) was to try to analyse what statements mean, and to get into muddles through misunderstanding the uses of language in so doing. Thus, for example, Gilbert Ryle (who began to lay the foundations of the linguistic philosophy before ever Wittgenstein took a hand in it) began his paper on *Systematically Misleading Expressions*, presented to the Aristotelian Society in 1931–32, by saying: "Philosophical arguments have always largely, if not entirely, consisted in attempts to thrash out 'what it means to say so and so'."

Instead of trying to work out a general theory about what all statements mean, in the light of which they can all be interpreted, philosophy is presented with a programme in which no general theory is allowed, but only investigations of different uses of language, as they turn up and happen to interest philosophers, one by one.

Thus the claim of Russell, to conduct philosophical investigations which, like those of the sciences, are "piecemeal, detailed and verifiable", is at last realised. It is, by the way, this very renunciation of theory, and replacement of theory by piecemeal investigation, which proves so exasperating to many contemporary critics of linguistic philosophy. They want to have a theory to criticise—but they cannot find one and so (like Mr Ernest Gellner) have to invent one in order to refute it.

This programme of investigations continues to embody the basic idea which Wittgenstein expressed in the *Tractatus*, that the problems of philosophy can all be "finally solved" when once it is realised that the traditional "method of formulating these problems rests on the misunderstanding of the logic of our language". Wittgenstein never revised *that* idea, but sought only to purify it of misunderstandings. And it continues to be hailed as a great revolutionising insight. We saw how years ago Schlick celebrated it as a "turning point" for philosophy; but, along with Wittgenstein in those years, fell into absurdities thanks to the verification principle and the pictorial theory of propositions. Now, with such "principles" and "theories" disposed of, Professor Flew, writing an editorial introduction to the collection of linguistic essays *Logic and Language,* can say that "from this first fundamental insight" a "new sort of logical criticism of language has been developed". Professional philosophers are "engrossed in the exciting work of following up their fresh insights".

The field proposed for investigation is very wide, and rewarding in that positive results come of investigating it. The "uses of language" may or may not be "countless"; but certainly they are very various, and Wittgenstein and linguistic philosophers who follow him have devoted a great deal of careful work to describing and distinguishing them.

Not only are words used in a variety of ways for making informative statements (of the kind which can be practically verified or falsified), but they are also used for many other purposes, such as questioning, commanding or recommending. It is true that no one is very likely to confound a question or command with a factual statement—but many other uses of language may be distinguished, which it is easy to confound with statements and which have in fact often been so confounded.

As we shall see, Wittgenstein's injunction to study the differences between different kinds of uses of words, so as not to confound them together, was applied by linguistic philosophers in the field of ethics, where moral judgments and value judgments generally were distinguished from both ordinary statements of fact, on the one hand, and from ordinary commands or recommendations on the other.

Again, a whole course of lectures was given at Harvard University by Professor J. L. Austin, of Oxford, on what he called the "performative" use of words (*How to Do Things with Words,* 1962). Austin pointed out, and it is both true and interesting, that in the marriage ceremony, for example, the words "I will" are not used to make a factual statement of the sort which can be true or false. The use of these words is rather a performance or pledge, prescribed by the ceremony. Such expressions as "I bet you . . ." provide other examples. That such expressions do indeed differ from factual statements is shown by considering that the latter are verified or falsified by subsequent events, whereas this does not apply to performative expressions. When you utter the prescribed words at a registry or betting shop you have thereby become married or laid a bet, regardless of how subsequent events turn out or what you yourself may or may not subsequently do.

It has often been said that such distinctions drawn between

different uses of words are trivial. However, trivial or not, they exist. Moreover, from the point of view of philosophy many of these distinctions are not trivial, for confusions do result from overlooking them. Thus, as Hume pointed out before linguistic philosophy was ever thought of (but little notice was taken of him), confusions result from confounding ethical or moral judgments with statements of fact. Again, Austin's distinction of the performative use of words does throw light on some vexed philosophical problems. For example, it throws light on some problems concerning the "self" or "ego", associated with the uses of the word "I". Those uses of "I" which are only effective when made by myself, and which therefore cannot be construed as statements referring to an organic body to which anyone else can equally well refer, are performative uses and not statements at all—this is a point which is certainly not trivial, and especially not from the point of view of materialism. The distinction of the performative uses may also throw some light on the use of words in law and in politics, and so be relevant to political philosophy.

As Professor Flew said, such investigations of uses of language can become very "engrossing" and even "exciting". And in his presidential address to the Aristotelian Society in 1956, entitled *A Plea for Excuses*, Professor Austin began by rejoicing at the happy results of pursuing them. "Much, of course, of the amusement, and of the instruction, comes in drawing the coverts of the microglot, in hounding down the minutiae, and to this I can do no more here than incite you. But I owe it to the subject to say, that it has long afforded me what philosophy is so often thought, and made, barren of—the fun of discovery, the pleasures of co-operation, and the satisfaction of reaching agreement."

Austin may well be remembered as the John Peel of the Microglot Hunt. And at this and many another meet of the Aristotelian Society he hounded down the minutiae in a way it would be hard to rival. It is fun, no doubt. And as for agreement, he could have the satisfaction of knowing that not even Marxists (notorious as we are for disagreeing) could possibly disagree with most of his findings. But while Austin often seemed content to draw the coverts and enjoy the fun even when the eventual trophy was no more than the tail of a microglot, he and Ryle and their colleagues were at the same time after bigger game—nothing less than the solution of the traditional problems of philosophy.

5. STATING WHAT EVERYONE ADMITS

Since, according to linguistic philosophers, the traditional problems of philosophy only arise through misunderstanding and mixing up uses of language, as a result of which "the queerest conclusions" are drawn, it is natural that their discussion and solution of these problems should always take the form of criticism of other philosophers' theories. For outside the confusions perpetrated by other philosophers, there are no philosophical problems to discuss.

I cannot attempt here to set out, or even try to do justice to, the very subtle and elaborate argumentation which linguistic philosophers have to date devoted to the philosophers' problems connected with such themes as the objects of perception, the relation of mind and body, freedom and determinism, or the foundations of knowledge. I shall only try to indicate (and I hope not unfairly) the lines of argument adopted. In their numerous writings on these and other themes example is piled on example, analogy on analogy; and besides the published writings, the same thing is being done all the time by word of mouth, in lectures, seminars and discussions. The cumulative effect is impressive. And as Professor Flew said in his Introduction to the essays on *Logic and Language*, "it has gained momentum until now it dominates the philosophy faculties of Oxford, Cambridge, and London, is powerfully represented elsewhere in the United Kingdom, and even has outposts overseas, especially in Australasia and the United States". (To have made some impression "even in the United States" is indeed an achievement.) Perhaps this piling up of examples and analogies properly belongs to what Plato and Aristotle called "rhetoric", or the art of persuasion. But if that is so, it must at least be admitted that philosophers nurtured in one of the homes of classical scholarship are very good at it.

In all this argument, linguistic philosophers proceed on the basis that other philosophers have posed artificial and unanswerable questions by fancying, in the first place, that the ways in which words are actually used in situations of normal practical life involve "problems"; and that they have then adopted special philosophical means, special philosophical terms and theories, to answer these problems. Yet the problems exist only for the philosophers, whereas the actual uses of language, if only we examine them carefully enough, involve no such problems.

An outstanding example is afforded by the philosophical problems

about perception and the existence of material things independent of
their being perceived, which have dominated modern philosophy.
The whole of J. L. Austin's *Sense and Sensibilia* (1962) is devoted to
showing that these problems arise only out of misunderstanding the
actual uses of language. It is a familiar situation that things are not
what they seem. Fancying that there were problems concealed here,
philosophers began trying to improve on normal language by saying
that when we see something, what we see is a "sense-datum", and
that we do *not* see the material thing at all. After that, they began
to question whether the material thing existed. The only result of
this, says Austin, has been that philosophers have landed themselves
with unanswerable questions. And yet if we patiently examine the
various actual uses of language, each appropriate to its own context,
we shall find that they are perfectly adequate for the statement of all
the phenomena of perception. Actual uses of language enable us to
say when things exist and when they do not, when we see them and
when we do not, when they are what they seem and when they are
not. There are no problems. There is no need to invent theories about
sense-data and the non-existence, or merely problematic existence, of
material objects. A veritable avalanche of such argument, all set out
in meticulous detail, overwhelms the misguided believer in "sense-
datum theory" who reads Austin's lectures; and a great deal besides
had been let loose earlier in Ryle's books *The Concept of the Mind*
(1949) and *Dilemmas* (1954).

The effectiveness of this kind of argument is due above all to two
things. First, it shows that certain philosophical theories create their
own problems, which are then insoluble within the theories. Second,
it shows that the theories lack cogency, because the familiar facts
which they seek to interpret are stated with greater clarity and consistency without the aid of the theory than they are in terms of it.
The ghost of the "sense-datum" has been haunting philosophy for a
long time. Of course, it never troubled Marxists. But the others are
to be congratulated that, after the linguistic criticism, this particular
ghost has been laid.

Ryle continued his demolition of the theory that the objects of
perception consist of sense-data as distinct from material objects, by
disposing likewise of the theory that sensuous consciousness belongs
to a spiritual entity ("the mind") distinct from the body. In *The
Concept of Mind* he wrote that "to talk of a person's mind is not to
talk of a repository which is permitted to house objects that some-

thing called 'the physical world' is forbidden to house; it is to talk of the person's abilities, liabilities and inclinations to do and undergo certain sorts of things, and of the doing and undergoing of these things in the ordinary world". He disposed of philosophical theories about "the mind" as an independent entity animating the body ("the ghost in the machine"), and of the resulting philosophical problems about what sort of an entity this can be and its relations with the body, by a detailed examination of how words like "thinking", "judging", "seeing", "feeling" and "deciding" are actually used. In talking about people's minds "we are not making inferences to any ghostly processes, occurring in streams of consciousness which we are debarred from visiting; we are describing the ways in which those people conduct parts of their predominantly public behaviour."

Accordingly Ryle, Austin and others were able to dispose of the old puzzles about the evidence or lack of evidence for other people's minds and other people's sensations which had led a succession of philosophers, starting with Hume, into solipsism. The vexed question of what I can mean when I say that someone else has toothache was answered by pointing out that I simply mean what I say. Thus Austin concluded a paper on *Other Minds*, presented to the Aristotelian Society in 1946, by noting: "One speaker at Manchester said roundly that the real crux of the matter remains still that 'I ought not to say that I know Tom is angry, because I don't introspect his feelings': and this no doubt is just what many people do boggle at. The gist of what I have been trying to bring out is simply: (1) Of course I don't introspect Tom's feelings . . . (2) Of course I do sometimes know Tom is angry. Hence (3) to suppose that the question 'How do I know that Tom is angry?' is meant to mean 'How do I introspect Tom's feelings?' . . . is simply barking our way up the wrong gum tree." Ordinary language includes the phraseology for talking coherently about both our own and other people's feelings and sensations—and the only puzzles that arise are those adventitiously invented by philosophers who have created their own extraordinary language of "immediate experience", "sense fields" and "sense-data". As Ryle put it, "we have no employment for such expressions", and they can all "be returned to store".

Questions about determinism and freedom are connected with those about mind and body, in as much as philosophers have found it a problem to reconcile the causal determinism of material events with the freedom usually ascribed to conscious activity. Ryle dealt with these matters too, and in the same way.

In *Dilemmas* he cleared the ground with a discussion about "fatalism", in which he sought to show (and, indeed, did show) that the idea that nothing could possibly turn out otherwise than it actually does, so that any conception of our being free to alter the course of events by our own volition is illusory, is merely a consequence of misunderstanding the actual uses of such words as "it is true that . . ." For example, if a certain horse wins a race, then it is true that that horse won the race. But to suppose, as the theory of fatalistic determinism does, that this entails that it was true that that particular horse was going to win even before the race was run, is merely to misunderstand the uses of the words "it is true". Just as it is not correct to talk about "the deceased Mr X" until Mr X is dead, so it is not correct to talk about anything being true until it becomes true. Those who back a·horse that wins a race turn out to have backed the winner. But the fact that their prediction of the winner was correct is not incompatible with its also being true that the horse might not have won the race.

Turning then to questions about conscious voluntary behaviour, the linguistic analysis claims to show that, in a similar way, the idea that free choice is incompatible with causal determination is a consequence only of misunderstanding the actual uses of words. If we consider how words are actually used, there is no more a problem about freedom and determinism than there is a problem about fatalism. For in actual use, to talk about free choice goes along with talking about causes. We make our choices in the light of judgments about cause and effect, and unless we could say what effects different causes are expected to have we could never decide what to do. The philosophical problem about freedom and determinism disappears once we examine how words are actually used.

"The billiards player asks for no special indulgences from the laws of physics any more than he does from the rules of billiards," wrote Ryle in *The Concept of Mind*. "Why should he? They do not force his hand. The fears expressed by some moral philosophers that . . . there is some contradiction in saying that one and the same occurrence is governed both by mechanical laws and by moral principles" is "as baseless as the assumption that a golfer cannot at once conform to the laws of ballistics *and* obey the rules of golf *and* play with elegance and skill. Not only is there plenty of room for purpose where everything is governed by mechanical laws, but there would be no place for purpose if things were not so governed. Predictability is a necessary condition of planning."

A stock objection to linguistic philosophy is that it allows for no theory of knowledge. Yet as a criticism, this is like criticising vegetarians on the ground that they do not eat meat. Of course, the linguistic philosophy includes no theory of knowledge, because it maintains that the problems which such theory professes to answer only arise from misunderstanding uses of words. Instead of having a theory of knowledge, linguistic philosophers examine the many and various ways in which words are used when we talk about "knowing". All these are adequate for the contexts in which they are properly used, and philosophers who have thought there is some great problem connected with the nature and foundations of knowledge have merely got the uses of words mixed up.

There are in fact so *many* different uses of words associated in one way or another with "knowing", and they are so extremely diverse (the family is a prolific one, including younger sons and country cousins, and a host of illegitimate branches too) that linguistic philosophers have, to date, never been able to complete any systematic work covering them all. Indeed, they might well claim that that is neither necessary nor possible. But much has been written on particular points germane to the general theme.

For example, in his paper *Other Minds* Austin dealt with the procedures, and the corresponding uses of words, appropriate to answering such normal questions as "Is this really so-and-so?", "How do you know?", "Why do you believe it?" He showed that such questions may be asked in a variety of contexts, and that in different contexts the procedures and words proper for answering them may differ in various ways. But where the procedure proper to the context is adopted, it may thereby properly be answered either that "it really is so-and-so", "I do know it", or "I have good reason to believe it", or else that it is not really so-and-so, that one is mistaken in thinking one knows it, or that it is believed without good reason. Philosophers who have invented special philosophical problems associated with such questions have done so only because they have not paid enough attention to the minutiae of how words are actually used. As Austin told them at Harvard (*How to do things with words*), "We must at all costs avoid over-simplification, which one might be tempted to call the occupational disease of philosophers if it were not their occupation".

Again, in relation to another area of the uses of "know" words, Ryle in *Dilemmas* dealt with the relationship between scientific and everyday knowledge. He did this by considering the employment of "technical" words in the sciences in relation to that of "untechnical" words in everyday use. Philosophers have invented a number of problems in this connection. Is not the world of science different from the everyday world? Are not the things and relations which sciences study the real things, whereas everyday things are merely illusory? Since sciences rely on observations, is not the language of science merely an elaborate way of predicting observations? The philosophy of science has become hopelessly tied up with such questions, which vanish when we examine the actual uses of technical and other words in the various contexts of their uses.

Of course, Ryle, no more than Austin, ever claimed to have dissolved *all* the philosophical problems that have ever been raised about knowledge. Their claim is no more than to have demonstrated in a few separate instances the method for doing so.

These various linguistic investigations, or new-model philosophical or logical analyses, do seem to get philosophers out of the wood. They dispel the darkness of theory and—as G. E. Moore long before hoped could be done—let in the light of commonsense. And what is left, when the problems and theories have been dispersed? Only "what everyone admits". Language was made by men for practical communication—for the communication of information and, related to that, for questioning, recommending, enjoining, judging, and performing social acts. We may sometimes make mistakes in grammar, we may sometimes not be able to hit on the right word, we are often in doubt as to what to say—but there exists a standard by reference to which all philosophical perplexities may be resolved, and that is "the actual use of language". Let philosophers but realise this, and their special problems vanish and, with them, their philosophical theories.

CHAPTER TWO

Philosophy and Ordinary Language

I. THE USES OF PHILOSOPHY

THE linguistic criticism of philosophical theory always appeals to the standard of the normal sane ordinary sound and practical use of language. This (it is suggested) is the sum of usages which are familiar, which always serve their purpose, which can always be understood (or if there are misunderstandings, they can be cleared up), and which can always be described for any given language and translated from one language into another. Since these usages suffice for all practical purposes of communication, we need no others. And there is no need to question the actual uses, to try to give them a philosophical "foundation" or find for them a philosophical "explanation". The questions philosophers ask, such as "Do material objects really exist?", simply do not arise from the normal practical uses of speech, because we know perfectly well how to employ words for communication and do not need to ask such questions. We may sometimes need to ask, for example, whether a particular object really exists, as when Macbeth asked "Is this a dagger that I see before me?" But to ask, not whether this or that object really exists, but whether *any* object really exists, is merely silly or pointless. Such questions could not be asked at all unless one had become confused in the uses of language. And the philosophical theories which are built up in the attempt to answer them have to depart from normal language and to employ a jargon (or rather, a collection of rival jargons), the proper use of which is continually in doubt, and the meaning of which becomes the more obscure the more minutely one examines it.

The criticism of the linguistic philosophy may well begin by questioning this distinction between normal and philosophical language, and by asking, in the first place, whether the account rendered of the origin and nature of philosophical problems and theories is in fact, historically, correct. Is philosophy simply a theorising about pointless and unanswerable problems due to verbal confusion and misunderstanding the actual and normal uses of words?

It is no doubt true that many of the arguments which philosophers have advanced in support of this or that theory have depended on verbal confusions. But is it also true that the problems the theories have dealt with arise solely from mixing up "language games" and that the theories themselves consist of nothing but such mixing up? To substantiate such a generalisation would require a rather more comprehensive study of the history of philosophy than linguistic philosophers have yet devoted to it in their published writings. Indeed, they pay little attention to the history of philosophy, but only to selected philosophical statements (not even philosophical theories, but bits of philosophical theories) in isolation from their historical context. As a broad generalisation, they say with Wittgenstein that philosophy is due to "misunderstanding the logic of our language". But in particular cases it has to be admitted that there is more than that in philosophical theorising.

For example, Miss Margaret Macdonald discussed some theories of political philosophy in an interesting paper read to the Aristotelian Society (1940-41) on *The Language of Political Theory*. She remarked on the "very peculiar" uses of language in such theories as "the social contract" or "the general will", or in Hegel's theory "that the State is a very superior moral person". And she went on to say:

"No one will deny that in political affairs philosophical nonsense may have serious effects. Is this philosophically relevant, or not? . . . not to try to understand how this language has effects, even though it may give no information, is to miss half its philosophical point and so is bad philosophy. The philosophical 'point' of a remark (or the 'point' of a remark which is of philosophical interest) is, at least partly, connected with the cause or reason which induces people to go on making it, though it can neither be supported nor refuted by any empirical evidence . . . they feel it has some use. This does seem to be relevant to the understanding of some philosophical remarks, if not of all."

She then observed that political philosophy, however "peculiar" its language, tends to serve certain interests and aims, and to supply people with certain criteria or reasons for obeying or disobeying established authority. That, in fact, is the "use" of its language.

These are very deep waters, into which the Aristotelian Society generally allows no more than a cautious toe to be poked (for they are dangerously infested by Marxism). The interests and aims which a philosophical theory serves, and in connection with which it was engendered, are generally considered irrelevant to its philosophical criticism. In the case of certain political theories Miss Macdonald boldly asserted the opposite, saying that to consider such things irrelevant misses "half the point" and is "bad philosophy". And she was surely in the right, even from the purely linguistic point of view—except that it misses not half the point, but the whole point.

How is it possible to abstract what a theory *says* from what it *does*? If one merely examines its peculiar language, without considering what such language is used to do, then no wonder one cannot make any sense of it. In fact, whatever may be said of "the use of language", the orthodox method of linguistic criticism of philosophy (as distinct from what I will compliment Miss Macdonald by calling her more Marxist approach) consists of the absurdity of trying to criticise uses of words by philosophers without taking into account what the philosophers are using words to do; or to put it another way, to examine only the verbal shell without taking into account the meaning inside it.

Whatever part verbal confusion may play in philosophy, it is certainly not the case that the questions which have troubled philosophers originate *only* from verbal confusion, or that philosophical theories do *nothing* but mix up uses of words. For mere confusion and mixing up of uses would hardly serve the uses for human communication which philosophies serve, or serve them so effectively. A mixing up of uses is failure of communication; but philosophies do effect communication—at least while they are alive, however difficult academics with a defective sense of history may find them to understand afterwards. And on the same showing, it is certainly not the case that the statements of philosophers are of interest only to themselves, being quite pointless in relation to the normal communication of practical people engaged in the practical affairs of life.

As Wittgenstein said, meaning is not something separate from use. The meaning of a philosophical theory can only be understood in the light of what the theory was made to do. To understand it one must relate it to the kind of questions it was framed to answer, and the kinds of answers too that it was framed to refute, in the actual historical context.

For example, Plato's "theory of ideas", with its peculiar language according to which the qualities of things exist eternally independent of and prior to the material things which exemplify them, was connected (as he made clear in his published writings) with a theory about the divine creation of the world. Material things were created in accordance with an eternal and perfect model, but being subject to dissolution and decay they fall away from it. This in turn was connected with a view of human nature, expressed in the platonic metaphors about the soul—"the rider on the horse" and "the prisoner in the body". You cannot hope to understand what Plato meant if, like his linguistic critics, you suppose that he was only engaged in theorising about the meaning of statements ascribing universal qualities to particular things, and getting mixed up between the uses of language in doing so.

2. INFORMATIVE AND UNINFORMATIVE STATEMENTS

The linguistic analysis which Wittgenstein and his followers have advocated and practised consists of describing and distinguishing between different uses of words. And Wittgenstein pointed to *analogy* as one very fertile source of verbal confusion. "Misunderstandings concerning the use of words are caused, among other things, by certain analogies between the forms of expression in different regions of language" (*Investigations*, 90).

In accordance with this observation, one may criticise Hegel's theory of the State, for example, on the grounds that, in speaking of the State as "a very superior moral person", he confused the different uses of language as between, say, "The park-keeper tells you not to walk on the grass" and "The Parks Committee prohibits walking on the grass". Misled by analogy, he supposed that an institution was a kind of super-individual.

It is true that Hegelians, or at least some of the less intelligent of them (English Hegelians, unfortunately), have introduced such confusions into their arguments in support of the Hegelian theory. But it surely does Hegel rather less than justice to presume that he was mentally deranged to the extent of confusing institutions and persons. He did indeed say that the State was some sort of an entity in its own right, though not a material one; and he did use analogies with individual persons in describing what he took to be the moral activities of the State; but he could not have supposed that the State was an individual like an individual person. As he would have said, and as everyone must agree, institutions and individuals are of different *category*, and so what is predicated of the one cannot sensibly be predicated of the other.

There is of course, as is quite obvious, a difference between talking, for example, about "the State" and about "the Officers of the State". Without entering into refinements of analysis, it may be said that the difference consists in this—that the Officers of the State are individuals located in space and time and open to inspection by the senses, whereas the State has no such location and cannot be so inspected. For example, one can say that the Head of the British State is on a certain day located at Ascot, where she can be seen by those who get inside the enclosure, but not that the British State is located at Ascot or anywhere else, nor that anyone has ever seen it, though many have suffered by the authorised actions of its Officers.

Although Wittgenstein said we "must not" try to "explain" them or to give them "any foundation", theories of the State must and do, not only take such differences into account, but also try to explain them and give them a foundation. The Hegelian theory of the State did that (and so did the Marxist theory, in a different way). The peculiarity of the Hegelian theory of the State—and this is what made it what Miss Macdonald called a "very peculiar" theory— was that it treated an abstraction (the State) as a being endowed with its own properties independent of those of any concrete or observable objects.

Thus if, for example, it is prohibited to walk on the grass, that (according to the theory) is because the State, a being independent of any mere human individuals, prohibits walking on the grass. Hence, as Miss Macdonald observed, the effectiveness of this theory as a pillar of established authority. Those who walk on the grass are not merely defying the park-keeper, nor even the members of the Parks Committee, individuals they may know well and for whom they may have no great respect, but defying the State—an unseen and awesome power, which controls people but which people cannot control.

Such being the philosophical theory of the State, it is evident that those who expound it must use, in talking about the State, the same kind of phrases as are used in talking about individuals. They will talk about "the will" of the State, and so on. But they do not do that because they have got confused in the employment of words. They make use of analogies—and maybe the analogies are false—but they have not been confused by them. What they are doing is to use abstract words for a purpose which Miss Macdonald may call "very peculiar", but which is nevertheless as old as human speech itself, namely, to ascribe properties to ideal beings existing independent of and prior to anything material, that is, to anything located in space and time and open to inspection by the senses.

No doubt the abstract words have a primary use for talking about material things. For abstraction is made from fact. But once in use, abstract words are available for uses other than simply stating verifiable fact. As Marx and Engels rather neatly put it in *The German Ideology*, "First of all an abstraction is made from a fact; then it is declared that the fact is based on the abstraction" (Part III, "True Socialism"). It is just this use of abstraction which is characteristic of Hegel's theory of the State, of Plato's theory of Ideas, and in general of all philosophical theories which in Marxist terminology are classified as "idealist" (because they make "the ideal" independent of and prior to "the material").

What is produced by this procedure is statements and theories which are in principle unverifiable. And for that very reason, objection may well be taken to them. Miss Macdonald said of such statements that "they give no information". Evidently she is using the word "information" in a sense in which "information in principle unverifiable" is a contradiction in terms. This is a useful sense of the word, and I shall join her in using it. The idealist-type theories, then, are non-informative. But the only conclusion to draw from that is that there are actually non-informative as well as informative uses of language for making statements.

It may be objected that a non-informative statement must be a very peculiar sort of statement. But this is a peculiar use of "peculiar", for it is a very common sort. The differences between statements, questions, commands, and so on, are easily to be understood (though they may be rather difficult to describe with exactitude) in terms of human practice. The distinctive feature of a *statement* as distinct from, for example, a question or a command, is that it is a communication of what to take into practical account. The use of non-informative statements, therefore, is to say that information we can check or verify empirically is insufficient for our practical needs. We need not only information but also revelation.

The informative uses of language for making statements are, then, connected with various procedures of empirical verification. The non-informative uses are not. But that does not entail that they have no meaning, or are a mere illogical or non-communicative mixing up of informative uses. On the contrary, it is well known that they do effect communication, and play a very considerable role in social life as it has actually been lived to date. If, then, one really wants to describe the actual uses of language, its non-informative uses should not be overlooked.

The verification principle of Wittgenstein and Schlick was designed, amongst other purposes, for the criticism of non-informative uses of language. According to that principle, non-informative statements are simply meaningless nonsense. The principle was given up, because of the absurd consequences to which it led when applied to informative statements. But linguistic philosophers try to have it both ways. For they still regard a significant use of language for making statements as necessarily an informative use, and insist that non-informative statements are produced only by misunderstanding and mixing up informative uses, and so represent not a significant use of language but a nonsensical misuse.

Accordingly, they represent philosophical theories as based on puzzles resulting from mixing up different informative uses of language, and in particular from being misled by analogy. Such an account is, to say the least, an over-simplification.

3. SOME VERY PECULIAR USES OF LANGUAGE

We may now turn from the theories of philosophers to some equally peculiar uses of language by non-philosophers, or ordinary people.

The linguistic philosophers have said that there is no need for philosophical theory, because the actual and ordinary uses of language suffice for all purposes. They want to dispel philosophical misuse of language by appealing to the diversity of its actual uses.

But this "actual use of language", as something contrasted with the misuse of language by philosophers, and by appeal to which we can resolve all philosophical puzzles, is a myth. By setting it up in the first place, Wittgenstein was behaving not very differently from many of his illustrious predecessors, who set up various absolutes and indubitable certainties by reference to which all questions were to be decided once and for all. It is only the latest of a long succession of miraculous touchstones. And as we shall now see, it has led linguistic philosophers into a great deal of trouble.

Linguistic philosophy refers the positive decision on how we should talk and what we should say, once we have renounced philosophical bad language, to the standard of actual use.

For example, should we deny that there are material objects? No, certainly not. For the actual use of language permits us to say that there are tables and chairs and mountains—all of which are, as the words are actually used, material objects.

Again, should we deny that people have minds? Of course not. We should no more deny that minds exist than that bodies exist, for both are vouched for by the actual use of language. But should we say that minds exist and function independent of bodies? No, for that too departs from the actual use of language. According to such a theory we should, for instance, be able to say "Mr Smith's body goes for a walk and his mind admires the scenery". But then everyone (or at least, everyone outside a theological seminary or certain university lecture rooms) would laugh, for that does not accord with the actual use of language.

As Wittgenstein said, "philosophy may not interfere with the actual use of language". On the contrary, this "actual use" is, according to him, the standard, and the only one possible, by which we can decide the right way of talking, and clear up the confusions philosophers get into whenever they try to speak in a special philosophical way.

In the next chapter I shall discuss certain ambiguities in the expression "actual use of language". For linguistic philosophers are by no means immune from the common fault of using words in a variety of senses and mixing them all up together. For the present, however, let us assume that the actual use of language is something open for inspection in the way people actually talk, and is properly codified in the standard dictionaries and grammars. For such an assumption has to be made if any sense at all is to be given to Wittgenstein's original reference to the actual use of language as a standard.

On this assumption, then, it is certainly not true that the actual use of language carries its own assurances as to how in all circumstances we should speak. For human practice is no such uncomplicated affair as such a view would suggest. Human practice consists of more than sitting down at tables and recognising that they exist when you do so. It consists of economic activity, making the things we need and getting them distributed; it consists of magical and religious practices, politics, science and the arts; it is full of complications and contradictions; and it does not remain the same but develops and changes. Whatever is the actual use of language, it is the outcome and reflection of the whole social practice of those who use it. To do him justice, Wittgenstein said as much himself. But this entails that actual use is not fixed but extremely changeable and (like philosophy) may include some very peculiar uses.

If instead of being dons at Oxford University the linguistic philosophers were witch doctors in some primitive tribe, then they would not find the actual use of language in all respects like it is at Oxford. True, they would probably use the same sorts of expressions when talking of, say, tables and chairs (supposing their tribe sufficiently advanced economically to possess such things). But about many other matters they would talk very differently. For example, continual references to *spirits* would be part of their actual use of language. It would be just as obvious to them that the corn spirit existed as it is to Oxford dons that tables exist. When an Oxford don sees a table, he says "There is a table". When a primitive man sees the corn sprouting, he says "There is the corn spirit reviving again". While the don sits down to eat a meal with the master of the college, the primitive man gets out a knife and makes a meal of the corn king. But he has just as good a reason for being sure the corn spirit exists as the Oxford don claims he has for being sure the table exists. It is vouched for by the actual use of language.

The truth is that it is totally impossible to separate out any normal or standard use of language which is unmixed with the cultural attainments and current beliefs of the people speaking the language. The normally acceptable ways of talking embody culture and belief. When, therefore, Wittgenstein set up the actual use of language as a standard, that was equivalent to accepting a certain set-up of culture and belief as a standard. And so, when he said that philosophy "may not interfere", that came to saying that it may not interfere with currently accepted culture and belief. It is lucky no such philosophy was thought of until recently, or we should still be under the sway of witch doctors, and the decorous feasts of Oxford University would be transformed into ritual sacrifices.

The standard to which the appeal is made is inescapably a standard of time and place. The actual use of language is subject to change. Old uses get given up as new practice shows them to be misleading, delusory, false. They then appear as "peculiar". But why should we now accept without question, and be forbidden to interfere with, something so notoriously susceptible of improvement?

4. VERIFIABILITY

Of course, there is a reply ready for the type of objection just urged. The witch doctor has not the same good reason for asserting the existence of the corn spirit as the Oxford don has for asserting the existence of the table. For what actually happens when the corn sprouts can be stated by simply saying "The corn is sprouting", and to bring in the corn spirit as well as the corn is therefore to assert the existence of something extra for which there is no empirical evidence. The existence of tables is verifiable empirically, whereas the existence of spirits is not.

One may agree with this completely, and for that reason consider science superior to witch doctoring. But if that reply is made, then the entire basis which Wittgenstein proposed for the linguistic philosophy is given up. For then it is admitted that there is some standard other than the actual use of language itself by reference to which the actual uses of language are to be evaluated. Or at least, either that, or else the words "actual use of language" are being used in some special pickwickian sense for which we have so far been vouchsafed no definition.

The fact is, that simply to appeal to the ordinarily acceptable uses of language appropriate for this or that occasion and for this or that purpose, achieves nothing whatever, either by way of the dissolution of philosophical problems, or of the refutation of philosophical theories, or of establishing the right and proper uses of language. And if one looks again at the actual arguments used, for example, by Austin and Ryle in connection with the sense-datum theory, or by Ryle in connection with mind and body and what he called "the ghost in the machine", then it becomes apparent that the real point of what they were saying, and of all their criticism of certain philosophical pseudo-problems and theories, lay in the question of *verifiability*. The real point of their criticism was that the philosophical theories used unverifiable concepts. All those terms, such as "sense-data", "sense fields" and the like, which Ryle said could be "returned to store", were terms used by philosophers for talking about ideal objects the existence of which could not be verified by any distinctive empirical procedure. Therefore the sentences containing such terms could either be put just as well in the normal language of informative statement, or else, if they were intended to mean something more, they were non-informative and incapable of verification.

The use of words by a philosopher who, when he sees a table, says "Certain sense-data are present in a certain visual field", is, indeed, very like that of a medicine man who, when he sees the corn coming up, says "The corn spirit is born again". If they mean anything more than simply that they see a table, or that the corn is sprouting, then they may be criticised on the grounds that they make use of unverifiable concepts and so pose unanswerable puzzles about the relationship of the corn spirit to the corn and of the sense-datum to the table.

It is unfortunate that in the criticisms offered of philosophical theories a straightforward appeal to verifiability should have been buried beneath a load of ambiguous phrases about "the actual use of language". And still more unfortunate that, as a result, profound questions raised by the concept of verifiability should have been passed over. Anyway, so far as the philosophical criticisms go, they could have been effectively made far more briefly and simply. All the piling up of examples and analogies drawn from current colloquial English, though often entertaining, is largely irrelevant. The procedure of linguistic philosophers has been very like that of the Grand Old Duke of York.

5. UNANSWERED QUESTIONS

In the practice of philosophical discussion, linguistic philosophers do not, of course, make an uncritical appeal to the actual use of language. As we have seen, that would be impossible; and they do not attempt it. For whatever may be said in theory about the demarcation line between the misuse of language by philosophers and its actual use by ordinary people, in real life no such hard and fast division is to be found. The most far-fetched philosophical theories, peculiar as their specialised terminology may be, are generally only attempted rationalisations or systematisations of popular notions about unseen forces and spirits, the creation of the world, and so on. Ordinary people are not innocent of philosophical ideas, which they do not develop out of perversity but out of problems that trouble them in practical life; nor do philosophers spend all their time arguing about problems which have no connection with the affairs of ordinary people.

Faced with the actual use of language, linguistic philosophers cannot accept the whole of it as perfectly proper, but have to pick and choose. When it comes, therefore, to that residuum which is considered properly representative of "what everyone admits" we are bound to ask—on what grounds have these uses been found admissible? Wittgenstein said that we may not try to give the actual use of language "any foundation". Yet in practice his followers do have to accept some uses as having a foundation which others lack.

Accordingly, in his Presidential Address to the Aristotelian Society in 1956, Professor Austin explained that the investigation which linguistic philosophy makes of actual uses of language requires us to examine not only the ways we talk but also what we are talking about.

"In view of the prevalence of the slogan 'ordinary language', and of such names as 'linguistic' or 'analytic' philosophy or 'the analysis of language', one thing needs specially emphasising to counter misunderstandings. When we examine what we should say when, what words we should use in what situations, we are looking again not *merely* at words . . . but also at the realities we use the words to talk about: we are using a sharpened awareness of words to sharpen our perception of, though not as the final arbiter of, the phenomena."

Again, in *Freedom and Reason* (1963) Mr R. M. Hare declares that "most philosophical inquiries" are "at one and the same time about language and about what happens . . . One cannot study language, in a philosophical way, without studying the world that we are talking about" (5.6).

Austin went on to be even more explicit in his countering of misunderstandings.

"Certainly ordinary language has no claim to be the last word, if there is such a thing. It embodies, indeed, something better than the metaphysics of the Stone Age, namely . . . the inherited experience and acumen of many generations of men . . . yet this is likely enough to be not the best way of arranging things if our interests are more extensive or intellectual than the ordinary . . . And it must be added too, that superstition and error and fantasy of all kinds do become incorporated in ordinary language and even sometimes stand up to the survival test (only, when they do, why should we not detect it?). Certainly, then, ordinary language is *not* the last word: in principle it can everywhere be supplemented and improved upon and superseded."

No doubt all that is well said. But what are the implications? And what else does it counter, besides misunderstandings?

Uses of language, acceptable or normal turns of phrase, have a history like everything else, as Austin readily agreed. One consequence, as Austin also agreed, is that in customary conventional usages of the present are to be found embedded all kinds of traces of now dead superstitions of the past. For instance, our standard way of talking about the wind, as in "The North Wind doth blow", derives from a long dead superstition according to which natural forces were personified, so that the wind was a windy person who, on occasion, had a good blow.

Why should we not detect such incorporations? Why not indeed—except that to do so entails some standard for evaluating and giving a foundation to the actual uses of language other than by reference to those actual uses themselves? It involves reference to "the realities we use the words to talk about". And therefore, as both Austin and Hare agreed (and, indeed, proclaim), the practice of philosophy demands such reference. All the criticisms of, for example, philosophical theories associated with false analogies demand it. For how otherwise tell which analogies are false and which are not, or in what ways the false ones are false?

Let us suppose that some philosopher chooses to revive the ancient views of animism by saying that the wind is a person, and then poses the difficult problem of what sort of person this is and where he or she lives. He would be justly criticised on the grounds that the wind is not a person at all, that statements like "the wind blows the roof off" are not analogous with statements like "Miss Smith blows the candle out", and that he has got his "language games" mixed up.

But why are we so sure nowadays that these statements are not analogous? For this was far from evident to people in days gone by. Indeed, some of those philosophers, early precursors of the natural sciences, who first began to depersonify things like the wind, got into serious trouble for so doing and were had up for blasphemy, corrupting the youth, and similar offences. The reason why *we* can so readily detect the fallacy of animism is that we are the inheritors of many advances of human knowledge, in the conquest of which those same philosophers, who in their day refused to admit "what everyone admits", played no small part. Animism is in fact still embedded in our actual phraseology. But this seldom if ever deceives us. For we are quite well equipped with such knowledge of ourselves and of our environment as renders us immune from confusions which might otherwise result from our customary animistic modes of expression.

Naturally enough, linguistic philosophers, practising in an ancient seat of learning where (though later than anywhere else) science has also won its place, make use of all this knowledge. All their practice of linguistic analysis presupposes it. We can hardly reproach them for this—for, when you look at it, Wittgenstein's own conception of language games, with its insistence on examining the whole context in which words are used, presupposed it. But then, the founder's doctrine that philosophical problems arise only from getting uses of language mixed up and are to be therapeutically removed by the linguistic analysis of the uses of language, is being contradicted by the practice of that very linguistic analysis. "One cannot study language, in a philosophical way, without studying the world we are talking about . . ." Agreed; but that means that a philosophical inquiry involves problems concerning the relation of the use of words, on the one hand, and the realities we use them to talk about on the other— or, as Engels succinctly put it a long time ago, of "the relation of thinking and being".

But how is such an inquiry to be conducted? On what principles can it establish its conclusions? How exactly does that "inherited experience" to which Austin appeals enable us to distinguish truth from error, and rational belief from superstition and fantasy? What is this "acumen" we now lay claim to, and how can it be developed? What is it that distinguishes superstition and illusion from scientific enlightenment?

All these questions require an answer. And perhaps it is to the credit of the linguistic philosophy that it does bring us so sharply up against them. But it proposes no answer. To answer these questions requires a general theory of human life and thought, which linguistic philosophy renounces.

The supposed linguistic insight is in fact entirely negative—we can only "describe" the actual use of language, but "may not advance any kind of theory", "must do away with all explanation", and "cannot give it any foundation". But how you describe must depend on a theory, and what you regard as proper or improper use of language must depend on an explanation of its foundation.

CHAPTER THREE

The Actual Use of Language

I. LANGUAGE AND THOUGHT

CERTAIN expressions or phrases sometimes come to play a key role in the development of different trends of philosophy. Such a role was played, for example, in the development of British empiricism by the word "idea", as introduced by Locke. To a great extent, a philosophical school consists of those for whom such a word or phrase has become specially important. In the contemporary linguistic philosophy, then, this role is played by the word "language" and the phrases "use of language" or "actual use of language", as introduced by Wittgenstein.

These kinds of key expressions in philosophy are always very versatile. For they are many-purpose expressions. Or, in other words, they are ambiguous. They are generally first introduced in the midst of polemics, like Locke's argument against the doctrine of "innate ideas" or Wittgenstein's efforts to overcome the absurdities in the older teachings of "logical analysis"; and then many good points are made with their assistance. But once the adversary has been overcome, their very versatility leads to incoherence and inconsistency, and the need arises to sort out the ambiguities.

One part of the role of a philosophical key word is to indicate the main object or subject matter of a philosophy school's discussion or inquiry. For this purpose, "language" may be considered a great improvement on "ideas". For examples of it (or rather, of its uses) can be exhibited for public inspection, whereas ideas, which are presumed to hide themselves away inside people's minds, are extremely elusive. The linguistic philosophy is the successor of empiricism, and may be said, like its ancestor, to be preoccupied with some sort of inquiry about thought and the objects of thought. The character of this inquiry has now been pin-pointed to the extent of being called "logical", and its subject matter has been defined as language and the uses of language.

Whatever some critics may say about the triviality, narrowness and parochialism of the linguistic philosophy as practised by English-speaking philosophers, it is a fact that to have established that an inquiry about thought is an inquiry about the uses of language represents a considerable achievement. Locke used to talk about ideas as though first they were formed in people's minds and then were denoted by or expressed by words. Nor was he the only philosopher to do so. To insist that when we speak of thought and ideas we are not speaking of anything separable from the use of language, is to introduce a most useful clarification into both thought and the use of language.

"It is sometimes said that animals do not talk because they lack the mental capacity," wrote Wittgenstein. "And this means: 'they do not think, and that is why they do not talk.' But—they simply do not talk. Or to put it better: they do not use language—if we except the most primitive forms of language" (*Investigations*, 25).

People, as distinct from animals, live such a life that they need to communicate by means of language—that is what Wittgenstein was insisting on here; for, as he said, using language is a mode of life. Our thinking is embodied in our use of language, and is not something prior, to communicate which language was invented. To separate thought from language is just a symptom of the old confusion that expressions stand for thoughts. It is to suppose that the thought "accompanies" the speech in the same way as it was supposed that the meaning is distinct from but accompanies the expression.

"When I think in language, there aren't 'meanings' going through my mind in addition to the verbal expressions," Wittgenstein further wrote. "The language is itself the vehicle of thought" (329).

"Is thinking a kind of speaking?" he continued. "One would like to say it is what distinguishes speech with thought from talking without thinking. And so it seems to be an accompaniment of speech. A process, which may accompany something else, or can go on by itself" (330). But ". . . Say a sentence and think it . . . And now do not say it, but just do what you accompanied it with . . ." (332). This abortive experiment proves that "thinking is not an incorporeal process which lends life and sense to speaking, and which it would be possible to detach from speaking, rather as the Devil took the shadow of Schlemiehl from the ground" (339).

Of course, as Wittgenstein well realised, we are familiar with processes in which we arrive at conclusions without formulating everything in words; and also with cases in which words are repeated, as by a parrot, without the person repeating them meaning anything. But what is going on in such cases can be fully described in terms of the complex activities of a sensitive organism in relation to its environment, without having to suppose that thoughts and meanings exist apart from their verbal expressions. Similarly, it is a familiar fact that the same thought, or the same meaning, can be expressed in different words, and in different languages. That is not because the thought or meaning exists independently of its verbal expression, but because the different expressions have the same uses in similar contexts.

Roughly speaking, to talk either about the meaning of words, or about the thoughts or thought-processes expressed, does not refer to something else, separable from words, but to the ways people actually use words.

In point of fact, the inseparability of thought and language, which is so well argued by Wittgenstein, is a very old tenet of *materialist* philosophy, going right back to what is known as "nominalism". As we saw, Thomas Hobbes had already made a cardinal point of it. And doing so, he had already identified confusion of thought with confusion in the use of language, whereby people become "entangled in words, as a bird in lime-twigs"—though he himself needed disentangling from his own theory of how words acquire meaning.

The question of the relation between language and thought has, indeed, a very direct bearing on what Engels described as the central issue dividing philosophers—the question of the relation between the ideal and the material. This question still retains a very "metaphysical" complexion so long as it is confused by the postulate of disembodied "thoughts", "ideas", "concepts" and "meanings" as objects of study, the relations of which with material processes have to be determined. For any materialist philosophy that follows the prescription of Engels, an inquiry about "thought" or "thought processes" or "laws of thought" or "logic" must, as linguistic philosophers have said, be identified as an inquiry about the use of language.

It appears appropriate, then, to consider, at least in outline, and if only in a rough and ready way, some of the ways in which the phrase "use of language" may be applied—when we are considering, for example, the way a person writing a letter or a treatise uses words, as distinct from the way words might happen to be produced by a monkey strumming on a typewriter; or the way a person uses words to address another person, as distinct from the way a parrot uses words to address its visitors.

According to Wittgenstein, the person is playing language games, which monkeys and parrots do not play. Though the expression "language games" is now going out of currency, Wittgenstein's essential point about the multiplicity of the significant uses of language, and about their having "no one thing in common", remains with us. That is to say, there is no *one* essential thing which people do, in using language, to distinguish them from other animals.

2. USES OF WORDS AND WHAT THEY HAVE IN COMMON

The basis of the insight into language, by the aid of which Wittgenstein considered that philosophical puzzles could be resolved, consisted of the negative proposition that the "countless different kinds of uses of what we call 'symbols', 'words', 'sentences' . . . have no one thing in common".

Because they "have no one thing in common" he concluded that "we may not advance any kind of theory" about them—"we must do away with all explanation, and description alone must take its place." In other words, there can be no general theory applying to all the uses of language, but only separate descriptions of each of the different actual uses; just as you cannot lay down the law for all games from a general theory of games, but can only describe the different rules of different games. And because "we may not advance any kind of theory", he concluded that "philosophy may in no way interfere with the actual use of language"—no more than a referee could interfere with the way a particular game was played in the light of a general theory, or universal rule-book, of all games.

Of course, as Wittgenstein immediately agreed, all uses of language have it in common that they communicate or signify something. They are all in some way or another expressive of thought. But to say merely that, he contended, is still to say "nothing whatever" (*Investigations*, 13). For it is merely to say that uses of language are uses of language.

A negative proposition may be impossible to establish, but quite possible to refute. Let us see if we cannot, after all, say a bit more.

All uses of language are for communication. They all signify something. As Wittgenstein said, to say merely that says nothing. It merely says that communications communicate. But the uses of *language* are, more specifically, for communication between *people* —and to say that is to say something to the point. Lots of animals communicate (by squeaks or grunts or snarls, or, as in the case of bees, by dances) but only people speak. The unique character of language as the *human* means of communication is, evidently, a product of the unique character of the human mode of life, of the requirements of communication in social production and in the social practice of human productive communities.

Marx was the first to point out the obvious fact that everything in human social life depends on people co-operating to produce their material means of life. And, indeed, Marxism consists of nothing but taking this obvious fact, with all its implications, seriously. He devoted much attention to the labour process, as the basic process for the human mode of life. What distinguishes it from the constructive activities of other animals, he pointed out, is that "at the end of every labour process we get a result that already existed in the imagination of the labourer at its commencement . . . man's activity, with the help of the instruments of labour, effects an alteration, designed from the commencement, in the material worked upon" (*Capital*, I, 7, 1).

The development of *speech* is an essential part of the development of *labour*. For human labour, unlike the life activity of other animals (including social animals, and animals that build things for themselves or even use various objects in a crude way as tools), requires that people should communicate a design; and therefore that they should not merely grunt or cry (though people still do that on occasion, and use words for merely grunting or crying purposes), but should develop means to communicate not only how things are but how they may be changed. Articulate speech is essentially the means of such communication. What distinguishes it from other communication is that it is used not only to signal present perceptions and evoke responses, but to represent possible states of affairs and ways and means to bring them about or avoid them—in other words, to make them "exist in the imagination".

This distinguishing mark of language is conveniently denoted by saying (in the customary terminology of logic) that it serves "to express propositions".

Of course, this does not imply that all that any sentence is used to do can be accounted for simply by saying what proposition it expresses. On the contrary, the various diverse uses of language in communication are to assert or deny, to question, to recommend, to approve or disapprove, to perform, to admonish or command, and so on, with countless variations of possible use. By itself, the expression of a proposition is *not* a communication. And it is just because of all the variations of communication relative to a proposition that there neither exists nor could exist a single standardised system of linguistic expression, such as would be represented by the pre-eminent and logically perfect language which Wittgenstein rightly said was not feasible. But at the same time, all these uses derive from the primary power of language to express a proposition, or to represent imaginatively a possible state of affairs. Wittgenstein asked us to try to imagine the thought without the words. Try a similar experiment, and try to imagine yourself issuing a command but not able to represent what you want done, or approving something but not able to represent what you approve, and so on with other uses of language. What all uses have in common is that they all derive from and relate to the expression of propositions.

Incidentally, Wittgenstein was fond of illustrating and supporting his contentions by imaginary and simplified examples. Thus in the *Investigations* (19–21) he says: "It is easy to imagine a language consisting only of orders", and invents a language for use in giving orders for building operations with objects called, in German, *Platte*, and in English, *slabs*. The example is certainly instructive, for the purpose of gaining some insight into the "giving orders" functions of language. But if it proves anything, it proves the very opposite of what he was contending. For it becomes pretty obvious that even people whose technology consisted of nothing else than laying slabs could not confine their utterances to giving orders.

This same point was succinctly made in the historical work *The Development of Logic* (1962), by William and Martha Kneale, of Oxford. "Communication is essentially the deliberate manifestation of an attitude towards a proposition or thinkable state of affairs" (X, 1). It explains the fundamental bearing of formal logic, or the abstract study of the operations for constructing propositions, on every kind of human communication effected by language. For standards of consistency, logical standards derived from the formal properties of propositions, apply not only to statements but to every kind of language-communication. Questions, commands, expressions of approval, performances, and all the rest, may be consistent or inconsistent. This applies even in such a case as the poetic uses of language. Poetry does not consist of statements; but consistency belongs to poems as to statements, with which poetry shares the logical form of representation.

In this earlier theory Wittgenstein said that the fundamental feature of language is that it makes "pictures" of facts. His subsequent assertion that the uses of language "have no one thing in common" seems to have been dictated by his anxiety to repudiate this picture theory. It was a sad case of letting the baby go down the plughole with the bathwater. The power to represent possible states of affairs *is* the fundamental feature of language, and the representation or "picture" *does* possess logical form, just as Wittgenstein originally said. What was wrong with his former theory was not that he said language makes pictures, but that he said the logical form of the picture mirrors the metaphysical structure of the fact, and combined this with the verification principle—that the picture must be directly comparable with facts given in immediate experience.

Wittgenstein's entire philosophising about language was vitiated by the rather uncritical way in which he handled the various analogies he made use of—pictures, families, tools, and games.

When he gave up the pictures, he said that the uses of language form a family, in as much as the various phenomena we subsume under that heading do not come under it because they all possess some single recognisable quality (that of being pictures) but because they "are related to one another in many different ways" (65–67). The countless different kinds of uses of language form a family in that sense, he said, as distinct from being species of a genus or varieties of a single thing distinguished by a common mark of identification.

But let us agree that the uses of language do form a family, in the sense Wittgenstein intended. It simply does not follow that they "have no one thing in common". The members of a human family, with which the analogy is drawn, are, as Wittgenstein said, "related in many different ways". But these ways are all *family* ways. The members of a family may not be all identifiable by a single recognisable mark or quality, such as the family nose; but they are all related by marriage and descent, so that who does and who does not belong to the family can always be determined by reference to the family tree. In other words, they *do* have one thing in common, by virtue of which they form a family—even though it is not a common characteristic such as the shape of the nose, but a common relationship.

Wittgenstein's other quite good analogy, the one with tools, no more bears out his conclusion than the family one.

He pointed to the difference between a rule and a hammer as evidence that tools have "no one thing in common". For while a hammer is used to "modify" a nail (by banging it into wood), what is a rule used to "modify"? Of course, a merely superficial survey of tools and their uses fails to reveal any observable characteristic in common between them—but a more diligent inquiry cannot but discover the common relationship which makes tools of tools. Such an inquiry was made years ago by Karl Marx, whom Wittgenstein never studied. "An instrument of labour is a thing, or a complex of things, which the labourer interposes between himself and the subject of his labour, and which serves as the conductor of his activity" (*Capital, loc. cit.*). This definition takes in not only tools like hammers, by using which the labourer acts directly on the subject of his labour, but also tools like rules, which play a subsidiary but none the less necessary part in conducting the labourer's activity so as to modify the subject of labour according to his design. It permits us to do much more than merely make a list of tools and describe their different uses. It permits us to say what is "essential" for a tool, what condition a thing "must" satisfy to be a tool. It also shows us the "foundation" of our standards for judging tools.

Wittgenstein's recognition that language is used for communication would have sufficed to show how to correct his earlier picture theory, if he had paid closer attention to what is involved in human communication, instead of being misled by merely superficial considerations about families and tools, and then jumping to a different and far more misleading analogy, the one with games. Many philosophers have proclaimed that logical form is eternal, necessary and known *a priori*—and Wittgenstein's picture theory was only an offshoot of such views, with its doctrine that the metaphysical structure of the world "shows itself" in the structure of the picture. But if we consider how and why language is used for human communication, and that, as Wittgenstein himself well said, "to imagine a language is to imagine a form of life", then it may be concluded that the form of representation of reality in language is the product of nothing but our practical human relationship with the rest of nature.

And from this stem all the various significant (that is, communication-making) uses of words.

The doctrine announced at the beginning of the *Investigations*, that different kinds of uses of words "have no one thing in common", was fundamental for Wittgenstein's reconsidered views of language. It was the foundation of his conception of language games and all that followed from it. But this doctrine is demonstrably false.

3. CONVENTIONS OF LANGUAGE AND THEIR USES

In the light of the above considerations about what distinguishes the use of languages as a means of human communication, we may now further consider the application of the words "use" and "uses" of language.

Whoever sets out to investigate or describe the use or uses of language can hardly fail to note that there is not one human language, but there are many languages. Every language is characterised by its distinctive vocabulary, grammar and syntax, and these differ in all kinds of ways. To employ a few handy all-purpose words to describe these phenomena of language, it may be said that every language is characterised by its conventions, by means of which communication is effected, and so has its peculiar mannerisms and devices and idioms for effecting communications.

Conventions, mannerisms, idioms and devices may all be called, with perfect propriety, "uses" of the language in question.

In the English language, for example, the two words "it" and "is" are put together in one order to make a statement ("it is"), and in the reverse order to ask a question ("is it?"). In Chinese alterations of word-order perform other functions, and the question "is it?" is expressed by a juxtaposition of contradictories "it is, it is not?". The force of this Chinese usage is, of course, to invite the hearer to choose between the contradictories, which in juxtaposition cancel each other out, and to select one of them as the definitive statement of fact. These are different devices of language to ask a question about fact: in English it is done by reversal of word-order, and in Chinese by juxtaposition of contradictories.

The uses of language, in the sense of conventions, mannerisms and devices, are not only different in different languages, but sometimes change for the same language. For example, in Elizabethan English the device of the double negative was often used for the purpose of emphasising a negation. That use has now died out, and a double negative signifies a positive. If you want to emphasise a negation in modern English, you have to do so in a different way from that occasionally used by Shakespeare.

The conventions, mannerisms, idioms and devices of language, as they are actually used by different people for all kinds of different purposes, in all the variety of situations in which people experience the need to communicate, are, indeed, "countless". And it would be perfectly true to say of them that they "have no one thing in common" but "are related to one another in many different ways". It would further be true that it is no part of the business of philosophers to "advance any theory" about them, since that is the business of grammarians and philologists; and certainly, philosophers "may in no way interfere" with them, or try to give them "any foundation".

In short, all the conclusions Wittgenstein draws for the benefit of philosophers about "the actual use of language" make very good sense (and indeed, such good sense as to be merely trivial) if by "uses of language" is meant no more than "conventions, mannerisms, idioms and devices of language".

It does, perhaps, seem rather presumptuous to suppose that philosophers of such eminence as Wittgenstein and the linguistic experts who followed him may have fallen into such an elementary confusion as that of drawing conclusions proper to one use of a phrase and then covertly applying them to other uses; especially when these philosophers have made it their special mission to distinguish different uses of words and to rebuke others for confusing them. However, it is certainly the fact that Wittgenstein's principal conclusions make good sense for one use of the phrase "uses of language", but not for other uses of the same phrase, which are also to be found in his writings and in the writings of those who follow him.

With the exception of Wittgenstein himself, all the principal linguistic philosophers have written in English. There is perhaps no great difficulty in translating their works into other languages, if other than English-speaking people become interested in them; but the circumstance that they write and discuss in English does really seem to have misled them, incredible as it may seem, into confusing questions about English usage with more general questions about the uses of language. Thus in his Introduction to the first volume of *Logic and Language*, Professor Flew writes of "how easy it is to slip into nonsense by even apparently trivial deviations from standard English", and again of "unexplained and unnoticed distortions of standard English". But in the Introduction to the second volume he becomes uneasy about it, and writes: "It should be put on record that the absence of any study of the logical peculiarities of any language other than English has been noted and regretted: but extraordinarily little seems to have been done on this, at least by professional philosophers."

Some of the more facile critics of Wittgenstein and the linguistic philosophy seem to assume that the phrase "use of language" is employed by these philosophers only to denote conventions of the English language. So they taunt them with supposing that all philosophical problems are to be resolved by consulting *The Oxford English Dictionary*—a jibe especially unfair to Wittgenstein, who talked in English but wrote in German. But as such criticism is rightly regarded by the philosophers themselves as silly, there must evidently be some other sense in which the phrases "use" and "uses of language" are used. And, of course, there is such another sense. It is the sense in which we would say that *different* actual modes of expression, employing different conventions, mannerisms and devices in different languages or even in the same language, have *the same use*—that is to say, fulfil the same purpose in relation to the expression of propositions.

Examples of different use in sense-one may be examples of the same use in sense-two. Thus the different uses, in sense-one, of reversal of word-order and of juxtaposition of contradictories, in English and Chinese respectively, are examples of the same use of language in sense-two, namely, use for asking a question.

We may speak of the use (sense-two) of a use (sense-one). And it is pretty obvious that, for philosophers, the second sense is of more interest than the first. Generally speaking, those who are interested in "thought", or in "logic", are not primarily interested in the peculiar devices and conventions of a particular language, but rather in the common functions and purposes served by various modes of expression in all languages. Thus, for example, it would hardly be supposed that "the laws of thought" or "logic" are any different for Chinese-speaking people than for Russian-speaking people—or for people speaking English, Hebrew, French, Yoruba, Hindi, or any other language. It is for this reason that what people say or write can be translated from one language into another, and that rational discussions can be carried on through interpreters.

Now of course, the use of a convention or device of language for the purpose of communication for which that convention is standard use in a given language, requires neither criticism nor explanation nor justification. Those who use it use it properly and know what they mean; and there is no call on philosophers to interfere with the conventional use of their native tongue in any way, either to correct it or improve it, or to explain to people what they really mean when they use it. As for advice to tender to philosophers themselves, when they discourse on philosophical questions, it is well for them to write or speak standard English, or Russian, Hebrew or Hindi, as the case may be, and not try to alter or improve on it. For any kind of *Finnegans Wake* philosophy (Hegel perhaps provided some examples in German) is to be deprecated.

But this kind of practical wisdom does not yet solve the problems of philosophy, though it may be true that philosophers will make fools of themselves if they lack it. The purposes for which words are used cannot, it is true, be discussed except as they are exemplified in the employment of particular conventions of particular languages. But neither can those conventions be described or studied except in relation to the purposes which they serve. And it is with these purposes and with propositions expressed, rather than with the peculiarities of the conventions that serve them, that the problems of philosophy are concerned.

4. WORDS AND WHAT WE DO WITH THEM

If we consider the use of language in the sense of the purposes it is used for and the propositions it expresses, then its use coincides with more or less the whole of human social activity. People do give language countless uses, for its representational power is employed for everything we do that is distinctively human. But then, as we have seen, it is not true to say that the countless uses of language "have no one thing in common". It bespeaks a quite extraordinarily uncritical attitude towards human activities, to say that we "may not interfere" with uses of language in *this* sense, or try to give them "any foundation". And when we are told that "we may not advance any kind of theory" about uses of language, but "must do away with all explanation, and description alone must take its place", we may well ask why we should be forbidden to "explain" the uses to which people put language, and how we are possibly going to "describe" such uses in anything but a very slapdash and superficial way without having and testing out some "kind of theory" about human life.

Of course, Wittgenstein's disciples, and those who follow the trends of the linguistic philosophy, will say that he did not mean by "actual use of language" the actual social uses to which language is actually put. Nor did he mean the conventions and idioms of English or any other particular language. It becomes, indeed, very hard to determine just what he did mean. There seems to be required some new and hitherto uninvented metalanguage in which to say what Wittgenstein tried to write about language in German, and which his translators tried to put into English, but which neither German nor English can supply the words to express. The truth is, that his thoughts were obscure and his sentences confused and confusing.

If, however, we continue for the time being to mean by "uses of language" the uses to which people do actually put languages, when they make a proper employment for those purposes of the conventions, mannerisms and devices socially provided for them, then it is evident (as was already pointed out in the previous chapter) that these uses include many "very peculiar" ones. Language is actually used (as was pointed out) to make some "very peculiar" statements. If we turn for a moment from statements to performative uses, we shall find just the same peculiarities. For example, if people go on a deputation to the Ministry of Agriculture and ask the Minister to do something to relieve drought, in the presentation of their petition they make a performative use of language. Of course, they make statements to the Minister; but their use of words is not only to make statements. If, then, the same people go to church and pray for rain, they have made another performative use of words—but a "very peculiar" one.

We should ask what there is about the way words function which permits such peculiar uses to be made of them. In short, we need a theory which will enable us to explain such uses and in terms of which to describe them. The peculiarity consists of using words to make statements about and performances directed towards ideal objects for whose existence and properties there can be no sort of empirical test.

It is hard to see how to account for such common uses of words unless we are willing to recognise the fundamental feature of language, which is its power to express propositions.

Formal logicians have tended to be engrossed with questions about the "form" or "structure" of propositions, and their "formal relations", to the neglect of considering those essential functions or operations which words perform as vehicles of communication, by virtue of which alone they come to express propositions. If one considers, for example, the dances performed by bees, by which they communicate information about such matters as the location of sources of nectar, it must surely be admitted that the dance does express information about a fact, and that it does so by means of having a certain form or structure which, as Wittgenstein used to say, mirrors that of the fact. Nevertheless bee-dancing lacks the essential features of language. Bees do not dance a proposition. And why not? It is because a proposition always has its *negation*, but the functions performed by the dances of bees do not include negation. Neither do they include the other closely associated functions of words— abstraction and generalisation. (Bees cannot dance such communications as "There is no nectar over there, because it has been taken already, and, in general, if you want nectar you must look for it somewhere else".)

Negation, abstraction and generalisation are essential and interdependent functions of language. To be able to represent how things are not, and not only how they are, and to be able to abstract and generalise, are the powers which people possess thanks to language.

Hence we are not, like bees, restricted in our social communication to the communication only of particular bits of information. If we were, our social life would be like the life of bees, and lived unconsciously. Language is used to ask questions and propound answers, and these questions are not only of the "what" but of the "why" variety. For the question "why?" of course depends on the power of negation, since "why?" goes with "why not?".

People try to understand, so as to illumine their social practice by it. Such "peculiar" activities as magic, so characteristic of human societies (and the example given earlier of prayer is only a much more sophisticated if less well organised form of it), are associated with the attempt to understand matters of practical concern in terms of the activities and influence of unseen and intangible beings and forces. This way of understanding, or misunderstanding, things is very primitive, and is far more obvious, far more direct, far easier to learn and far more popular, than any other. It is achieved in a very straightforward way by means of the negating, abstracting and generalising power of language. Thanks to abstraction, we can speak of beings and forces; thanks to negation, we can deny that they are visible or tangible or located in any particular place; and thanks to generalisation, we can say that they exert all sorts of influences.

In what way is the performative use of words for magic or prayer, and the use of words for the associated statements and theories of what Austin called "the metaphysics of the Stone Age", or of theology and idealist philosophy, a wrong use of words? It is not wrong for magic or religion. In what way does it infringe upon "the logic of our language"? No doubt certain theologians and philosophers who have tried to work out systematic theories have fallen into purely logical errors by getting "entangled in words". But such errors are only secondary. For the employment of abstraction, negation and generalisation for the purpose of understanding the material in terms of the ideal, and the sensible in terms of the supersensible, does not consist of mixing up conventional uses of words, but of using words quite properly for the given purposes.

One may, of course, criticise the purpose for which words are used and, like Austin, say that magic and prayer are merely "superstition". In that sense, they may well be called misuses of language. But the "acumen" required to explode superstitions itself requires rather more than merely examining and comparing the conventional uses of some given language in various contexts. The peculiar superstitions and practices and theories do not arise because anyone has been misled by the conventions of language into mixing them up and talking nonsense. They arise because in given conditions of life people have adopted these ways of trying to understand and cope with the things that concern them.

It is related in the old myth that Adam and Eve brought trouble on themselves and their descendants when they ate of the tree of knowledge. And that is just what certain apelike animals did when they took to social production and to speaking to one another. They took the path towards human mastery over nature, and involved themselves, not only in labours and enjoyments, but in sufferings and errors such as no other animal could experience or commit. For of course, when there is humanity there is inhumanity, and when there is understanding there is misunderstanding. These things are involved with one another; but it is only the misunderstandings that concern us in the present context.

Bees may all fly off in vain on false information. People often run around in similar error, there is nothing specifically human about that. But when people engage in magical practices to make the crops grow, that is a human error of which they alone are capable. For they would not fall into it if they could not speak.

No other animal has technology, or, consequently, speech; so none has magic or religion or politics or philosophy, or, on the other hand, the arts and sciences. All these things are dependent on the imagination and the use of language. The examination and criticism and consequent development of all human activity does therefore involve examination and criticism of uses of language. But simply to say that the "actual use" of language must not be interfered with, and that to escape misunderstandings we need only take care not to muddle uses up together, is a precept inadequate to the actual task.

5. FACT AND FANCY

Wittgenstein's obscure and ambiguous phrase "actual use of language", and injunction to consider and investigate "actual uses", appears to rely on the conception that with regard to every use of every convention, mannerism or device of a language, we can always look to see what we are actually doing by its normal employment. Thus if you together with a chosen member of the opposite sex lined up under definite conditions in a legally prescribed place say "I will", you have got married. Or if, in the garden, you say "That rose is red", you have communicated information about an identifiable object. What you are actually doing can always be "described" in empirical terms—that is to say, in such terms that anyone can apply an observational test to tell whether you have done it or not. The idea of infringing "the logic of language" seems, then, to imply that certain statements or performances do not actually do anything at all, because they result simply from misapplying and mixing up conventions that *do* do something.

This conception that certain combinations of words do something whereas others fail to do anything can be illustrated by an analogy of the sort of which Wittgenstein was fond. Imagine people constructing apparatus out of pulleys, ropes, levers, cogs, and so on, which they rig up to move things about. Some of these constructions are effective—they do something, they actually move something. But others may be rigged up in such a way as to do nothing—the rope fails to pass over the pulley, or the lever does not engage the gear. The "actual uses of language" are like the effective pieces of apparatus; infringements of "the logic of language" are like the badly rigged constructions.

In the Introduction to the first volume of *Logic and Language*, Professor Flew cites cases of "grammatically similar expressions" where "nothing but nonsense and paradox will result if we ask questions about one assertion which are only appropriate and significant when asked about the other".

"It would be absurd, but it would also be easy, to be misled by the grammatical similarity of 'It goes on to London' to 'It goes on to Infinity' into the misconception that 'Infinity' like 'London' refers to a place, albeit a very queer and very inaccessible place. It is absurd, but to some people it is also easy, to be misled by the grammatical similarity of 'Somebody came' to 'Nobody came' into the misconception that 'Nobody' refers to a person just as does 'Somebody'." And Professor Flew continues:

"It was this misconception of the logic of the word 'Nobody' which Lewis Carroll exploited in *Through the Looking Glass*." In reply to the question, who she saw on the road, Alice replied, "I see nobody on the road". "I only wish *I* had such eyes," the White King said. "To be able to see Nobody! And at that distance too! Why, it's as much as *I* can do to see real people, by this light!"

It is, of course, quite true that such questions as "Where is Infinity?" or "Who is Nobody?" can be dealt with by expounding the ordinary normal use of such expressions as "it goes on to infinity" and "I see nobody on the road." And misunderstandings of such expressions are, regrettably, to be found in certain works of certain philosophers. For instance, the puzzles (mentioned earlier) about what sort of an object is "the present King of France" were in fact of this type. Such puzzles are, indeed, typical "philosopher's puzzles". They do not worry "ordinary people". But nor do they constitute the main problems of philosophy, about which philosophers have disputed. At the most they are stumbling blocks over which some philosophers have stumbled. To suppose that problems about the ideal and the material owe their origin simply to this type of misunderstanding of linguistic conventions is almost as absurd as to suppose that Infinity is a place or Nobody a person.

If one takes typical statements and questions about ideal and supersensible objects, and related performances, it would be simply not true to allege that they do or achieve nothing, in the way that, say, "*You* can see Nobody but *I* can't see him" does nothing. Equally, therefore, the philosophical problems derived from them are not pseudo-problems about nothing, derived merely from misunderstanding "the logic of language". They are genuine problems about how to understand the world we live in and the life we live in it.

To investigate "the actual use of language" involves nothing less than to try to make a critical survey of all human activity—and that requires more theory than the linguistic philosophy has been willing to allow. Certainly, such an inquiry is not likely to be completed, with all the loose ends neatly tied up together. But even to contemplate it shows that there is a real problem of how to think, of how to understand things, which emerges from the actual practice of trying to think and trying to understand. And this problem is not solved by simply advising that we should use words in the standard ways in which they are actually used, and "leave everything as it is". On the contrary, to tackle it involves a criticism and evaluation of actual uses of words—or, what comes to the same thing, ways of thinking—in order to try to find the method of understanding and of avoiding misunderstanding. Nor is this in practice altogether such a formidable undertaking as it sounds in theory. For, as Professor Austin very rightly said, "the inherited experience and acumen of many generations of men" does represent something to go on.

It was pointed out earlier that many statements of popular belief and of philosophical theory, while not senseless, are non-informative. People have in fact been trying to understand the world in terms of non-informative statements about it. And that means that they have been representing to themselves a dual world, a dualism of the ideal and the material. It is from this way of representation and of understanding that the basic divisions of philosophies have arisen. And that trend which in Marxist terminology has been called "materialism" (and here the word does not stand for any definite theory, but rather for a definite approach to the making of theories) is based on the contention that all representation must be made informative. We must try to understand the material world in terms of the material world itself.

In so far as the linguistic philosophy condemns non-informative statement as based on "misunderstanding the logic of our language", it lends its support to materialism—but support so confused and shaky as not to be worth much. Why should we look for materialist ways of understanding? Not because of "the actual use of language", for "the actual use of language" enjoins nothing of the kind. But not, either, because we can work out *a priori* an infallible philosophical theory which says, as Wittgenstein put it, that "it must be like this".

It is because, in the rather pregnant words of Marx's *Theses on Feuerbach*, "Social life is essentially practical. All mysteries which mislead theory to mysticism find their rational solution in human practice and in the comprehension of this practice." Human practice requires to be *informed*, and in practice people learn to discard fancies as they gain information.

Thus by a realistic consideration of uses of language we arrive at a very different philosophy and criticism of philosophies than is provided by the linguistic school. The outcome is not to abolish all philosophical theory and resolve to "state only what everyone admits". Rather, as Engels put it (*Ludwig Feuerbach*, IV), it is resolved "to comprehend the real world—nature and history—just as it presents itself to everyone who approaches it free from preconceived idealist fancies", and "relentlessly to sacrifice every idealist fancy which cannot be brought into harmony with the facts conceived in their own and not in a fantastic connection." As he said, "materialism means nothing more than this".

CHAPTER FOUR

Language and Logic

I. MEANING AND LOGICAL NECESSITY

THE view that all philosophical theory comes from "misunderstanding the logic of our language", and so is to be cured by demonstrating the logic of our language, evidently supposes some view of logic.

A peculiarity of logic (as has been remarked earlier) is the logical or formal necessity which characterises its findings—or which, at least, is sought after by formal logicians, and characterises their findings in so far as they are correct. This is the "logical necessity" which Hume long ago and very properly contrasted with "matter of fact", and which is established by "demonstration" as distinct from "experience".

The linguistic philosophy carries on the good tradition of logical analysis by trying to make the method of analysis give a watertight account of the distinction of matter of fact and necessity in human thought. This is done by trying to show how the actual use of language gives rise to logical necessity—to relations of formal implication or entailment between sentences, and to logical principles of valid inference.

Logic is not an empirical science. But yet it is treated by linguistic philosophers as in some way or other *descriptive*—descriptive of the use of language. For as Wittgenstein said, we cannot "explain" or "give a foundation" to the use of language, but only "describe" it. How logic, though not an empirical science, can still be regarded as descriptive, is explained by Wittgenstein's analogy of language games.

To *describe* a game we use such words as "must"—"You must do this" and "You must not do that". In cricket, for example, the bowler must not throw, and he must pitch the ball so that it lands up somewhere within the batsman's crease. So far as physical possibilities go, balls may be discharged in all sorts of ways; but knocking a ball about is not cricket unless the rules of cricket are enforced. The force of the words "must" and "must not" as used in describing a game is very evident. It is not merely that the bowler never or seldom throws the ball—the history of Test Matches shows that he does in fact sometimes do so, whereupon the umpire signals "No ball!". Cricket cannot be described by saying "The bowler *does* not throw the ball", but only by saying "He *must* not throw the ball". Similar considerations apply to "offside" in football. And so too with language.

If you are using words in a certain way or a certain sense (a use of language, or language game), then, the linguistic philosophy maintains, that use may be described by saying that you must not say certain other things, and with regard to yet other things, that you must be prepared to assent to them—for this is required by the language game you are playing. If you nevertheless do say or, in the other case, deny those other things, then you are simply playing another game, making a different use of language, using words in another sense. You have another meaning from the ordinary or, maybe, you are in a muddle and what you say means nothing at all.

For example, if you say "I am going for a walk" you must not combine that with saying "I am not going to move my legs". If nevertheless you do say "I am going for a walk without moving my legs", your interlocutors can only conclude, either that you are a follower of Humpty Dumpty who employs the normal expressions of the English language in abnormal ways invented by yourself, or that you are posing a riddle of the sort that used to be popular with young ladies in the nineteenth century, or else that you don't mean anything at all.

Similarly, if you say "All men are mortal" you must be prepared to say "Socrates is mortal"; and in general, if you say "All A is B" you must be prepared to say that any particular "A" is "B". Otherwise your statements are meaningless, or you are not using words in the normally prescribed ways, or are using the same words in different ways in each sentence. (You are, of course, allowed to say "All men are mortal but Socrates is immortal", if by "immortal" you do not mean that Socrates does not die but that people will always revere his memory.)

Logical necessity, the linguistic philosophy suggests, consists of just this sort of "must" and "must not" which is involved in the use of language. In other words, the use of language involves formal implication, or entailment, as between different sentences. If, for a given use of words, "P" entails "Q", then to say so is to say something at once formally or logically necessary and descriptive of that use of words. But it is not a statement of matter of fact, which has to be tested by looking at anything other than the use of words; it is rather a way of describing or expounding or bringing out the particular way words are used or, in short, their *meaning*. And if there were not such "musts" or "entailments" or "logical principles" or "rules" governing the uses of words, then, of course, words could not be used with meaning—or would not be words at all. It is because words have meaning that sentences entail other sentences. The use of language is subject to its own laws of logic—"the logic of our language".

This account of entailment, or logical necessity, was summed up very neatly by Mr R. M. Hare: "A full discussion (of entailment), especially in mathematical contexts, would occupy many pages; but for my present purpose it may be defined accurately enough as follows: A sentence P entails a sentence Q if and only if the fact that a person assents to P but dissents from Q is a sufficient criterion for saying that he has misunderstood one or other of the sentences. 'Sentence' here is an abbreviation for 'sentence as used by a particular speaker on a particular occasion'; for speakers may on different occasions use words with different meanings, and this means that what is entailed by what they say will also differ. We elicit their meaning by asking them what they regard their remarks as entailing" (*The Language of Morals*, 2.4).

This is a generalised account of logical necessity which takes in Wittgenstein's "tautology" as a particular case. It makes clear the sense in which logical principles and statements of logical necessity may be said to be "analytic" as opposed to "synthetic". But the antiquated account of an "analytic proposition" as one in which "the predicate is contained in the subject", and likewise Wittgenstein's account of such propositions in terms of "tautology", may, in Ryle's phrase, be "returned to store".

2. PRINCIPLES OF FORMAL LOGIC

Professor Ryle, who has a happy gift for coining apt phrases, has introduced the term "logical behaviour" for the object of logical studies. A use of words is characterised by a certain mode of logical behaviour of those words.

Obviously, the description of logical behaviour goes far beyond the conventional bounds of formal logic. We shall see presently how Ryle himself carries it beyond those bounds. But he had no great difficulty in bringing formal logic, as a discipline with a distinct circumscribed subject matter, under the umbrella of the description of logical behaviour and defining the conditions of its shelter there. He pointed out that languages employ a variety of expressions which he called "topic-neutral"; that is to say, they are employed in very much the same ways in all contexts. Examples are afforded in the English language by such words as "all", "some", "not", "and", "or" and "if". Such words are used in *all* contexts, whatever the topic. And so, said Ryle, the "rules governing the employment" of such words are "perfectly general, anyhow in this sense, that differences of concrete subject matter make no difference" (*Dilemmas*, VIII). Formal logic describes the logical behaviour of certain topic-neutral expressions.

For example, "All A is B and all B is C" necessarily implies or entails "All A is C", so long as words are being used in the normal way, because to affirm the premise and deny the conclusion would be to break the actual rule of the game governing the use of the topic-neutral word "all". Thus formulas of formal logic such as "If all A is B and all B is C, then all A is C" are items from the rule-book for the use of the topic-neutral word "all". And so with other formulas in relation to the use of other topic-neutral words or expressions. They formulate the logical behaviour of these expressions.

Let us now follow up some of the implications of this conception of logical behaviour, as applied to principles of formal logic.

We could, if we liked, propose different rules for the use of "all", "some" and other topic-neutral words. If we were to do that, however, the games played with these words would be different games, their uses would be different from their actual uses, and so their meaning would be different. Thus if someone who objected to Aristotle were to say that, for him, "All A is B and all B is C" did not necessarily imply or entail "All A is C", then he would simply be proposing to use the word "all" in a different way from Aristotle. If he were then to add, however, that "All A is B" entails that " All B is A", we would begin to get a clue as to the actual way he was proposing to use the word "all". We could conclude then that he was proposing to use the word "all" in the same way as Aristotle (or rather, to be exact, in the same way as the English translators of Aristotle) used the word "some". Indeed, you can always tell, as Mr Hare has pointed out, what a person means by the topic-neutral (or by any other) words he uses by eliciting from him what he takes statements in which those words are used to entail. On the other hand, if he cannot say what they entail, then he is just making noises and does not mean anything. Anyone who uses language, that is, who utters sentences and means something by them, accepts logical formulas as logically necessary. For they are formulas of the actual uses, the rules of the language game. However, with regard to the actual expressions, "all", "some", "if", and so on, different formulas can be prescribed at will for their use. As Humpty Dumpty would have said, "all" need not mean—all. We could make words mean whatever we like by altering the rules.

The strength of the analogy between uses of language and games lies, of course, in the fact that both languages and games have rules. To that extent, the "insight" into logical necessity afforded by exhibiting the regulative character of logical formulas is a very useful one, and it does help to distinguish formulas of logic from statements of matter of fact. It is perfectly true that if you want to elicit people's meaning you may do so by cross-questioning them about "what they regard their remarks as entailing". And it does help to show that the different analogy employed by those who have said that logic obtains information about necessary connections between objects whereas matter-of-fact inquiries obtain information about contingent connections is misleading. But all the same, the games analogy is misleading too.

The bowler must not throw in the actual game of cricket, any more than, in the actual language game played in the actual use of the word "all", you may say "All A is B and all B is C but not all A is C". If you say that, it is a logical contradiction and you have said nothing, conveyed no information—just as if the bowler throws, it is a no-ball. However, although throwing is not allowed in cricket, there is no reason why a ball game should not be played in which it is allowed. In fact, baseball is such a game (the Americans being not so pernickety in their summer sports as the English). Similarly, rugger was evolved by breaking the rule of soccer that forbade picking up the ball. Does the same hold for language, in respect of logical rules?

Evidently, if different rules were to be used, then, whatever we might say by using them, we would *not* be able to say what, as things are, we actually do say. For example, people who rejected the logic of the word "all" would not be able to say what Aristotle said when he used the expression "All men are mortal". They might be able to say what we (the followers of Aristotle's rules) say when we say "Some men are mortal", but they could *not* say "*All* men are mortal". For if they wish to say that, they *must* use Aristotle's rules for saying it.

This example at once shows where the analogy between uses of language and games becomes misleading. As for the rules of games, you can "only describe" them, but you cannot "explain" them, you cannot give any reason for them beyond the fact that those are the actual rules; and, in that sense, you cannot "give them any foundation". This does not apply to the principles of logic. The rules of cricket are as the Committee of the Marylebone Cricket Club happens to have made them; and they can be altered if the members so desire (in fact, they are often altered—in the very summer I am writing the "no ball" rules were altered, to the discomfiture of Freddy Trueman). But the principles of formal logic are not just as Aristotle happens to have made them (indeed, he did not in fact get them all quite right). Nor can they ever be altered by anyone. Those rules stand wherever language is used, and whatever language is used. For they are necessary rules for all communication which reflects "the reality of the world we are talking about".

The task of formal logic is, then, by no means only to formulate actual rules appertaining to the logical behaviour of topic-neutral words in any particular language. Even if it were, the task of generalising these rules so as to be translatable into any other language would be a rather intractable one. Logic does more than produce formulas of the actual logical behaviour of topic-neutral expressions. Of course, the findings of logic are, as translated into different languages, expressible in just such formulas (though even this is subject to some awkward reservations which we will presently find that Ryle had to introduce). But the logician does not arrive at them by doing no more than describe how words are actually used. By considering the formulas as only descriptive of the actual logical behaviour of certain regions of our actual language, Ryle and other linguistic philosophers who followed Wittgenstein have simply evaded the problem of explaining how and why the principles of logic are arrived at. They have derived necessary implications, such as are followed up in valid reasoning, from actual rules regulative of actual uses of language: it is because using language involves rules that, using language, we find necessary implications, and are able not merely to state contingent facts but to deduce by logically valid reasoning the necessary consequences of such statements. This is to stand things on their heads. For all the actual rules are founded on necessary principles of logic. Actual uses of any particular language can be used to illustrate principles of logic, but are irrelevant to their demonstration. In investigating those principles we are not describing the actual use of any language but doing what Wittgenstein said was impossible—giving it its foundation.

3. THE FORMALISM OF LOGIC

The above considerations explain why the linguistic philosopher finds himself having to jump some awkward hurdles before he can reach the winning post and show how the actual symbolic procedures or devices of formal logic coincide with rules prescribed for any actual language.

Aristotle laid the foundations of formal logic by introducing the technique of using variables—a special symbolic device. For certain purposes of popularisation it may be said that the Aristotelian variables, "A", "B", take as values words like "men" and "mortal". However—and this becomes much more obvious if one looks at a modern textbook of symbolic logic, as compared with Aristotle's *Analytics*—the logical formulas cannot be interpreted simply as generalisations about the ways certain classes of words are used in "ordinary language". Formal logic, like mathematics, operates with a special symbolism of its own. Its formulas are not sentences, and have no meaning in the way sentences have meaning. Its symbolism is not merely a kind of shorthand which can be transcribed into ordinary words and sentences, and could therefore, in theory, be dispensed with. It may well be called a special language, an artificial language, a formalism, painstakingly devised for a special job. It is not so much "the logic of our language" as our language of logic. Of course, logical textbooks contain explanatory passages in ordinary language, just like mathematics textbooks. But the function of these is not to explain what the symbols mean, so that their use can be learned in the same way as, say, an English-speaking student learns to use French. Their function is much more like that of the words used by a technical instructor.

Consequently we find Professor Ryle taking some nasty tumbles.

He had to point out "that formal logic operates (1) only with some, and not with all topic-neutral expressions, and (2) only with artificial extracts from the selected few topic-neutral expressions of ordinary discourse" (*ibid*). There are ranges of topic-neutral expressions which formal logic ignores, some of these being dealt with by mathematics. And as for those that it does deal with, it does not describe how they are in fact used in ordinary language, but treats of them in an "artificial" way. He never can explain how or why formal logic makes its selection of topic-neutral expressions and then makes do so well with these few. Nor can he explain in what consists the artificiality of the extraction, or what is the point of such artifice.

To account for the artificiality of formal logic, Ryle can only appeal to the linguistic philosopher's favourite resort—analogy. He likens the ordinary use of language to a battle, and formal logic to the drill by which soldiers are trained. "Fighting in battles is markedly unlike parade-ground drill. The best conducted drill evolutions would be the worst possible battle-movements, and the most favourable terrain for a rearguard action would entirely forbid what the barrack-square is made for. None the less the efficient and resourceful fighter is also the well-drilled soldier . . . To know how to go through completely stereotyped movements in artificial parade-ground conditions with perfect correctness is to have learned not indeed how to conduct oneself in battle but how rigorously to apply standards of soldierly efficiency even to unrehearsed actions and decisions in novel and nasty situations and in irregular and unfamiliar country" (*ibid*). But this is, to say the least, a rather sergeant-majorly view of the science of formal logic.

In the same chapter Ryle very clearly points out how the drill in the use of words under the orders of the sergeant-majors of formal logic fails to conform to the ways words are actually and correctly used—not in battle this time, but in civilian life (for metaphors do have a way of getting mixed). "The logicians' 'and', 'not', 'all', 'some' and the rest are not our familiar civilian terms; they are conscript terms, in uniform and under military discipline, with memories, indeed, of their previous more free and easy civilian lives, though they are not living those lives now."

For example, the symbol of formal logic which is usually in verbal explanations equated with the word "and" obeys the commutative law. In the notation of *Principia Mathematica* this is expressed in the formula

$$p.q \equiv q.p$$

which is verbally represented as saying "*'p and q'* is equivalent to *'q and p'* ". But this formula often fails to apply to the use of the word "and" by civilians speaking ordinary language. "If you hear on good authority that she took arsenic and fell ill you will reject the rumour that she fell ill and took arsenic."

Commenting on this example, Ryle observes that "the logicians' conscript 'and' " is allowed to exert only what "might be called the minimal force of 'and' ". To this the "familiar use" adds "the temporal notion expressed by 'and subsequently' and even the causal notion expressed by 'and in consequence'." Though he does not realise it, this observation provides the clue to what formal logic is actually all about, and what it does.

The object of formal logic is *not* to *describe* how any particular words are actually used. Its object is rather to separate out and isolate the operations or functions which all uses of words perform in so far, and only in so far, as they achieve the expression of propositions; and to demonstrate the powers and results of these operations.

There is an obvious difference between making something happen and making the representation of what may possibly happen, and between bringing something into existence and making the representation of what may exist. It is the difference between doing and merely thinking. The use of words always involves representation, or expression of propositions. And it is with the operations for this, and the results of such operations, that formal logic is concerned. Its special symbolic devices serve the purpose of defining and demonstrating such operations.

The logical necessity which belongs to logical demonstration is what distinguishes logical (or proposition-making) operations and their results from material operations. For example, if you stir up various ingredients in a pot experience alone will discover the result; results of logical operations are demonstrated by exhibiting the logical operations themselves, in abstraction from whatever else words are actually used to say or effect. To effect this exhibition and demonstration is the function of the specialised symbolic devices of formal logic. (Similar considerations apply to mathematics, when we consider operations involved in counting and measuring.)

This is why what Ryle calls "the logicians' 'and' " behaves with such military precision as compared with the ordinary civilian "and". Sentences are used for a variety of jobs connected with asserting, questioning, recommending, commanding or performing. In any actual language there are a variety of different words and turns of phrase, including a wide range of so-called topic-neutral expressions, which serve all kinds of varied purposes. But although there are large clutters of topic-neutral expressions to be found in employment in actual language, and some languages are richer in them than others, formal logic ignores all their multifarious uses, abuses and ambiguities, and simply seeks to demonstrate the "selected few" logical operations by which propositions are constructed.

This being so, all uses of words, in every language, no matter what their peculiarities, are subject to logical norms of consistency. For example, we have in English the words "some" and "all" available for use whenever we wish to generalise. But in English, and also in other languages, there are, besides these two words, many others, many other expressions and turns of phrase, available for the same purpose. The consistent use of all such expressions is governed by the formal logic of generalisation. This has been generalised and systematised by the technique of quantification invented by research workers in symbolic logic. Is that technique simply a way of describing the logical behaviour of the English words "all" and "some"? On the contrary, it exhibits logical operations which all generalising uses of words in all languages must be able to express. Whatever the language, whatever the conventions, it must be able to generalise, and its generalisations are subject to the formal logic of generalisation.

4. THE LOGICAL BEHAVIOUR OF CATEGORIES

Ryle's account of formal logic leads him on to explaining how properly "philosophical" inquiries are essentially "logical". Having equated logic with the study of logical behaviour, he went on to say that "there remains a very important way in which the adjective 'logical' is properly used to characterise both the inquiries which belong to formal logic and the inquiries which belong to philosophy" (*ibid*). While the formal logician investigates the logical behaviour of topic-neutral words, the philosopher also investigates the logical behaviour of words—but not of topic-neutral but more "full blooded" ones. There is less difficulty, however, in discovering the principle of selection of words for philosophical investigation. The philosopher is interested in those which express "concepts which, in one way or another, generate genuine perplexities. He investigates the concept, say, of *seeing* and not that of, say, *perspiring*, since the former is charged with paradoxes where the latter is not" (*ibid*). The use of the word "seeing" is "charged with paradoxes" connected with questions about what does the seeing and what is seen; on the other hand, no one is puzzled with similar questions about "perspiring" (no one has been puzzled over identifying "the perspiring subject" or "the ontological status" of perspiration, though perhaps some may be now that Ryle has suggested the possibility of a philosophy of perspiration).

Ryle diagnosed the "perplexities" and "paradoxes" which are generated from the uses of certain words, and the cure of which is the business of philosophy, as due to what he called "category-mistakes". A category-mistake, as he expounds it, is essentially the same as Wittgenstein's mixing up of language games. It gives rise to what Ryle called a "philosopher's myth", and is to be cured by the investigation of the logical behaviour of categories.

"A myth," he wrote, in the Introduction to *The Concept of Mind*, ". . . is the presentation of facts belonging to one category in the idioms appropriate to another. To explode a myth is accordingly not to deny the facts but to reallocate them . . . The logical type or category to which a concept belongs is the set of ways in which it is logically legitimate to operate with it."

In the first chapter of *The Concept of Mind* he went on to "indicate what is meant by the phrase 'category-mistake'. This I do by a series of illustrations." Thus a foreigner visiting Oxford or Cambridge is shown a number of colleges, offices, laboratories, playing fields, and so on, and then asks "But where is the University?" Again, a child witnessing the march-past of a division sees the battalions, batteries and squadrons go by and asks "when the division is going to appear". Again, a foreigner taken to watch a cricket match sees how the bowlers bowl, the batsmen bat and the fielders field; but he has heard a lot about "the team spirit", and asks when he is going to be shown it.

"These illustrations of category-mistakes," says Ryle, "have a common feature which must be noticed. The mistakes were made by people who did not know how to wield the concepts *university*, *division* and *team-spirit*. Their puzzles arose from inability to use certain items in the English vocabulary."

He went on to define how the technical term "category" is used. "When two terms belong to the same category, it is proper to construct conjunctive propositions embodying them. Thus a purchaser may say that he bought a left-hand glove and a right-hand glove, but not that he bought a left-hand glove, a right-hand glove and a pair of gloves." Similarly, one does not see the university in addition to all its component institutions, the division in addition to all its sections, or the team spirit in addition to the play of the team.

The description of the logical behaviour of categories is the description of the ways in which different terms may and may not be combined and conjoined. And just as philosophical theories, or "philosophers' myths", arise from category-mistakes, so the whole constructive business of philosophy consists of correcting such mistakes by investigating the logical behaviour of categories. Thus the dualistic body-mind theory—the myth of "the ghost in the machine" which Ryle devoted *The Concept of Mind* to exploding—consists simply of a category-mistake. "It is not merely an assemblage of particular mistakes. It is one big mistake and a mistake of a special kind. It is, namely, a category-mistake. It represents the facts of mental life as if they belonged to one logical type or category (or range of types and categories), when they actually belong to another."

One may well agree with Ryle that this theory is a category-mistake, in that sense. Any *materialist* is indeed bound to agree that to present mental activities as activities of a mind which go alongside physical activities which are activities of a body, is precisely "to represent the facts of mental life as if they belonged to one category when they actually belong to another". A person may be said to have a mind because his members are so organised and so function that he perceives and thinks, and not because his body has attached to it somehow an unobservable perceiver and thinker in addition to its observable parts and organs. Similarly a cricket team may be said to have a team-spirit because its members play well together, and not because it has an unobservable team-spirit attached to it; and a person wearing matching gloves on each hand may be said to be wearing a pair of gloves, not because he has a pair as well as the right- and left-hand gloves, but because the two gloves match.

But while agreeing so far, one may well question Ryle's statement that the puzzles troubling those who have made such category-mistakes "arose from inability to use certain items in the English vocabulary".

If one considers, for example, the category-mistakes made by foreigners who ask silly questions about the university and the team-spirit in cricket, it is evident that they have nothing specially to do with English idiom. They could make the same mistakes in German or Dutch or Hebrew or Greek or whatever is their native tongue. The same goes for those who make a category-mistake in speaking of bodies and minds (that mistake was being made at a time when the English language did not yet exist). Their trouble is not inability to speak correct English—and therefore, by parity of reasoning, neither is it their inability to speak any other particular language. It is rather, as Ryle also said (but seemed to think it the same thing) not knowing "how to wield concepts" correctly.

The sort of category-mistakes that interest philosophers are those that can be made indifferently in any language, and concern categories in a sense in which the *same* categories receive expression in all manner of different ways in the idiom of all languages. And indeed, Ryle himself says so. In a paper on *Categories* for the Aristotelian Society, 1938-39, he states: "There are not English category-propositions as opposed to German ones, or Occidental as opposed to Oriental."

In dealing with the so-called logical behaviour of categories, Ryle is in fact involved in an analogous confusion to that in which he and other linguistic philosophers are involved in dealing with formal logic. Questions about categories are no more answerable by simply describing the multiform idiomatic uses of particular languages than questions about formal logic are answerable by the same method.

To sort this out we may begin by looking more closely at his definition of "category".

5. CATEGORY OF WORD AND CATEGORY OF CONCEPT

The definition of "category" used by Ryle in connection with the logical behaviour of categories is derived from the definition of "semantical category" given by Alfred Tarski in his famous paper *The Concept of Truth in Formalised Languages*, presented to the Warsaw Scientific Society in 1931. There Tarski explained that "two

expressions belong to the same semantical category" when no
sentence containing one of them ceases to be a sentence if it is
replaced by the other. Thus differences of category may be detected
by substituting one expression for another in a given sentence; if
the result is not a sentence, then there is a difference of category.
Accordingly Ryle maintained that whenever philosophers make the
mistake of treating expressions of different category as if they were
of the same category (as those philosophers allegedly do who treat
"body" and "mind" as two distinct components of the human
person), their category-mistake can be detected and exposed by
showing that this would lead to absurd consequences, i.e. to pseudo-
sentences containing "breaches of logical rules" (*Concept of Mind*,
Introduction).

Now certain disclaimers made by Tarski should be noted. First,
he was careful to use the expression "semantical" category, so as to
make it clear that he was referring to the way sentences are constructed out of expressions in a particular language. Second, all he
did was to offer a criterion for telling whether two expressions in a
given language were of different semantical category in that language.
Third, and most important, he was dealing "exclusively" with what
he called "the formalised languages of the deductive sciences", and
never supposed that what he said could be consistently applied to
ordinary everyday language. In a "formalised" language it is of
course possible to apply Tarski's definition of category and determine
precisely whether expressions are or are not of the same category—
but it is quite another matter in a living "everyday" language.
(In the same way, Tarski demonstrated in this paper that a definition
of "truth" could be given for certain—but not all—formalised
languages, such that it would determine when expressions were or
were not true in those languages. But as for "everyday language",
he said, "the very possibility . . . seems to be very questionable".)

As for the definition or criterion for "when two terms (expressions
in a language) belong to the same category", it is practically useless
in application to ordinary language, as Tarski realised. For ordinary
language is not "formalised" in such a way as to let the criterion
work. Applied to English, say, it will turn out that there are almost
as many categories as expressions. For example, one might suppose
that "arm" and "leg" belong to the same category. But they do not,
for whereas it is correct to say "He kicks with his right leg" it is
incorrect to say "He kicks with his right arm". Again, lions become

a special category of animal, at least in English, because one can speak of "a pride of lions" but not "a pride" of anything else. Further, it is perfectly allowable in English (and so with other languages) to construct sentences such as "His body is in Glasgow and his mind in the Highlands" (compare "My heart's in the Highlands a-chasing the deer"), which suggest that "body" and "mind" are of the same category, in that each has an independent location. True, such sentences are figurative ones—but how tell this? Again, it makes sense to say that when the body dies the mind (or soul) goes on thinking and knowing and communicating with other minds. Appeal to significant uses of words does not prove that it is a category-mistake to assert the independent existence of mind, but quite the contrary.

Evidently, therefore, a definition of "semantical category", in terms of how expressions may be substituted for each other in sentences, or of how conjunctions may be constructed embodying them, in a formalised language in which ambiguity, metaphor, non-informative uses, and so on, are precluded, is inapplicable when it comes to considering "the logical category to which a concept belongs" and "myths" which "represent facts as if they belonged to one category when they actually belong to another". For to decide the semantical category of expressions in a formalised language is not at all the same thing as to decide the categories of facts and concepts.

True, if we have sorted out questions about the latter, for a certain range of facts or concepts, then it is possible to effect a certain formalisation of language so that category-mistakes are precluded in the language so formalised. In a rough and ready way, this is what is done in the languages of the special sciences. The kind of inquiries Tarski and others have made about the principles of construction of formalised languages are most practical in relation to technology and the sciences—and the more so the more methods of computation are introduced, since a computing machine must be provided with a formalised language to work with if it is to produce answers which are unambiguous, consistent and informative. But before we can get formalised and specialised languages in which category-mistakes are precluded by the rules, we have to consider the concepts expressed rather than simply their expressions in everyday language. Or as Austin put it, we must "look not merely at words but at the realities we use the words to talk about".

6. DILEMMAS OF THE CATEGORY LIST

The confusion resulting from double use of the word "category" has landed linguistic philosophers in some irresolvable "dilemmas", quite on a par with the "dilemmas" they have found in other philosophies. These arise from problems about whether we might not if we chose employ other categories from those we in fact do employ, and associated problems about whether or not it is possible to compile a complete list of categories.

Wittgenstein's way of investigating the *differences* between different uses of language, and denying them any common derivation—which was followed by Ryle and other linguistic philosophers—certainly suggests that the categories employed in the representation of reality are, in a sense, accidental or arbitrary. There is no "have to" or "must" about them. We do not, for example, "have to" represent the world in terms of individual things with their properties and relations. That is just the way in which, for certain purposes, we speak. For other purposes we could speak in other ways. Thus Carnap's "Principle of Tolerance" has emerged once more.

Some pertinent questions about this were raised by Professor A. J. Ayer, at the conclusion of his inaugural lecture at Oxford in 1960 on *Philosophy and Language*. Having said that it is important "to examine the architectonic features of our conceptual system, to apply analytical techniques to the investigation of categories", and that this "to some extent marks a return to Kant", he continued:

"There is, however, a danger in following Kant too closely. It consists in succumbing to a kind of *a priori* anthropology, in assuming that certain fundamental features of our own conceptual system are necessities of language, which is the modern equivalent for necessities of thought. Thus it may be maintained that it is impossible for there to be a language which does not recognise the distinction between particulars and universals . . . (But) I see no *a priori* reason why even such an important concept as that of a physical object should be regarded as indispensable. Might not substantially the same facts be expressed in a language reflecting a universe of discourse in which the basic particulars were momentary events? And there are other possibilites. One which is worthy of consideration is that regions of space-time be treated as the only individuals. Neither is it certain that there need be any reference to individuals at all."

There is, however (as Austin had reminded philosophers earlier), a danger of forgetting what you are talking about. There is a danger of talking of language in the abstract, forgetting that its use is a part of practical life. Certainly there is no *a priori* reason why language should be used to refer to physical objects, individuals, or anything else. Categories cannot be "deduced *a priori*", in the way that Kant attempted. And equipped with the symbolic apparatus of formal logic, we can certainly invent all manner of logical calculuses and formalised languages—for example, one which would have no application to physical objects, but only to momentary events or to regions of space-time. But the alternative to *a priori* deduction is not freedom of choice. For there is a cogent practical reason why language employs the categories it does. What can be done by way of inventing specialised languages does not conflict with the basic practical necessities of language. People simply could not use a language every day which made no "distinction between particulars and universals", or in which the basic particulars were "momentary events" or "regions of space-time". Given language which has the basic function of expressing propositions assigning properties and relations to individuals, we can and do proceed by abstraction to talk about momentary events, regions of space-time—and also about disembodied spirits and all kinds of other things. But we could not possibly talk about all these other things unless, to begin with, our language served the basic functions required for the expression of elementary propositions.

Ayer's danger-warning appears to have referred especially to the speculations of Mr P. F. Strawson, whose *Individuals, an Essay in Descriptive Metaphysics* was published in 1959. In that work Mr Strawson conducted some very complicated linguistic investigations which led him to the conclusion that the actual use of language for informative statement always involves reference to individuals, and that there are two and only two categories of individual, namely, bodies and persons. A person has a body; but since predicates such as knowing, willing, and so on, apply only to persons and not to bodies, persons do constitute a separate category of individual. Since these are the only categories of individual revealed by investigation of the actual use of language, and since it would be absurd to talk of other categories of individual when we lack the use of words to talk about them, it can be concluded that in the universe there are these two quite different kinds of things—bodies and persons. This is what Strawson calls "descriptive metaphysics", an unviable hybrid begotten by grafting Kant on Descartes and feeding with Wittgenstein and water.

In a subsequent essay, *The Concept of a Person* (the centrepiece of a volume of essays of that title published in 1963), Professor Ayer picked some holes in Mr Strawson's linguistic argument. But if it is not possible to arrive at categories as "necessities of thought" by a method of "descriptive metaphysics" relying on investigation of the actual use of language, it does not follow, as Ayer suggested in his inaugural lecture, that there are no "necessities of thought" at all.

Ryle was involved in a similar dilemma at an earlier stage. In his paper on *Categories* he expressed his disagreement with what he called the "scholasticism" of philosophers like Aristotle and Kant, who tried to make a list or catalogue of categories.

"We should notice one presupposition which Aristotle and Kant share, which is, I believe, unreflectingly shared by a number of contemporary philosophers. Namely, it was supposed that there exists a finite catalogue of categories . . . This seems to be a pure myth . . . there are various grammatical constructions of English sentences, but there can be no complete table of those varieties.

"Scholasticism is the belief in some decalogue of categories, but I know no grounds for this belief.

"It follows that I do not think that we can ever say of a given code-symbolism in formal logic that its symbols are now adequate for the symbolisation of all possible differences of type or form. It may, of course, be adequate for the exhibition of all the type-differences that concern us in the course of some particular inquiry."

What Ryle opposes to the scholasticism of a "decalogue of categories" is simply the description one by one of the logical behaviour of various expressions as they happen to attract attention by their propensity to give rise to paradoxes and perplexities. What he opposes to scholastic systematisation is only complete lack of system. One or the other. As Wittgenstein said, we can "only describe" the "actual use of language"; its uses are "countless", and we cannot "give it any foundation". If you abandon the scholasticism of trying to deduce the list of categories *a priori*, then the only alternative is to describe, piecemeal, interesting facts about how expressions are normally used in your native language.

But this opposition is a false one. We are not in fact thus placed between the devil and the deep sea. If one considers category-differences not as "various grammatical constructions of English (or any other) sentences", but as differences in the concepts applicable to "the realities we use words to talk about", then it will indeed be found, as Ryle said, impossible to construct "a finite catalogue" or "decalogue of categories", or a "code-symbolism in formal logic adequate for the symbolisation of all possible differences of type or form". But that does not entail that it is impossible systematically to show how category-differences are derived, and how different categories are logically connected. What is most interesting about categories is their logical connection and derivation—something which Hegel very well realised, though he set about demonstrating it in a peculiar and fallacious manner.

7. CATEGORIES, CATEGORY-MISTAKES AND INFORMATIVENESS

Language serves to express propositions. And while propositions expressed may be compared in respect of logical form, or of the logical operations of their construction, they may further be compared in respect of category. The philosophically most interesting sense of "category", the sense in which we speak of categories of facts and concepts, has to do with the formation of propositions expressible in any language rather than with sentences in particular languages. The basic operations of the construction of propositions permit many modes of abstraction—and it is in the investigation of these that the philosopher may hope to find the most rewarding use of the word "category". Thus, for example, to speak of perceived objects and their sensible qualities, of processes and their courses, of things and their properties, of structures and their elements, of interactions, causes and effects, of qualitative states and quantitative relations, of number and measure, of the actions and properties of things individually and of things taken together, and so on and so on, is to assert or speculate or make hypotheses or ask questions relative to propositions exemplifying category-differences. These receive many and various modes of expression in the conventions and idioms of different languages.

Ryle's objection to the scholasticism of Aristotle's "decalogue of categories" hardly goes to the root of the matter. Aristotle was responsible for introducing a terminology for the logical-philosophical investigation of categories which has led logicians and philosophers into the paths of scholasticism ever since. He equated the study of categories with the study of "terms", so that the job was to find out what different categories of terms there are, and to make a list. Ryle now says that no list can be made, and that all we can do is to examine piecemeal the logical behaviour of particular terms when we run into paradox and perplexity in trying to use them. But the point is not to begin by studying terms but to begin by studying the formation of propositions, and to find the foundations for the ways terms should be used in the category-differences of the propositions they are used to express. Of course, a *sentence* is a structure of terms; but to think of a *proposition* in such a way is itself a category-mistake.

The investigation of the categories of propositions is essentially an investigation of their ways of formation, and this requires not the separate consideration of different formations but the consideration of the ways in which they are connected with and derived from each other. That there is such connection and derivation is evident from even a superficial glance at the examples of category-differences mentioned above. But to study it and work it out is a matter of considerable complexity and labour, which has been but sporadically undertaken by philosophers hitherto. And there are no grounds to presume that any classification formula can be discovered which would enable us to produce a complete table of category-differences and to prove that it was complete.

The category-mistakes which Ryle tries (and not without some success) to correct are mistakes in generalisation of a kind which make generalisations uninformative. Consider, for example, the category-mistakes in the theory of what he calls "the ghost in the machine" (the dualistic body-mind theory). This theory consists of generalisations according to which all physical happenings are represented as mechanical interactions and all mental happenings as activities of an independent and indissoluble subject. As has been argued earlier, the real point of Ryle's elaborate arguments against these generalisations is that they are uninformative—and so they are. They make generalised representations of physical and mental phenomena—that is, generalisations for use in those familiar contexts in which we are concerned about intention, judgment or feeling in relation to bodily activity and bodily environment. And they make these representations in such a way that the generalisations are uninformative. That is, as Ryle said, "a mistake of a special kind . . . a category-mistake". It represents the facts in a way that does not fit, it brings to given contexts of use propositions whose category-formation is ill tailored to those contexts—and this shows itself in uninformativeness. Thus if I say that Ryle is a professor at Cambridge, that is a mistake of fact; if I say that Ryle is a machine with a ghost in it, that is a category-mistake. The same goes for sense-datum theory, and other "philosophers' myths" which linguistic philosophers have criticised.

Such category-mistakes can be illustrated by examples where the mistake is so easily recognisable that people would never actually use the sentence in which it is expressed, except possibly as a joke or else because they really are foreigners or children who have not yet learned the use of some of the expressions of the language they are trying to speak. But these examples, which do serve very well for expository purposes, as illustrations, as well as for entertainment, appear to have helped mislead linguistic philosophers into thinking that category-mistakes arise only from not knowing the idiom or "actual use" of the language. But we have seen already that that is not true.

And now we can try to reformulate the point which Austin and Hare made when they said that "we are looking not *merely* at words but also at the realities we use the words to talk about", and that "philosophical inquiries are at one and the same time about language and about what happens". Such remarks as these are, to say the least, obscurely expressed, and if carefully examined will be found themselves to contain the germs of many philosophers' myths, dilemmas and perplexities. For how exactly does one "look" at "the realities" and at "what happens", so as to see what category "the facts belong to"? The point is to examine the informativeness of generalisations in the contexts of their use. This is what linguistic philosophers have in fact spent much of their time doing—so that Austin very properly protested when accused of "looking *merely* at words". But theirs is a curious and melancholy case: even when they have done well, they have failed to grasp the point of it.

We may likewise propose a reformulation of the point made by Ryle when he said that "the category to which a concept belongs is the set of ways in which it is logically legitimate to operate with it".

What is "a concept"? As has already been suggested, it would be a mistake—and one which we may now characterise as precisely a category-mistake—to say that concepts are ideal or mental entities which words express or stand for but which have form and being prior to and independent of the use of words. The word "concept" is in fact an ambiguous and many-purpose one—and such words have often drawn philosophers into confusion as they have confounded together the many purposes for which the same word is legitimately used. The relevant sense of "concept" when we are speaking of categories and category-mistakes is the sense in which we would speak of the formation, clarification, working out, and so on, of a concept.

Thus, for example, to expound "the concept of a person", as Ayer does, is not at all the same as *describing*, say, the physiognomy of some given person. The latter task involves looking at something already there and accurately recording and analysing its outstanding features. The former task is quite different, and involves working out how to generalise informatively about persons. To do this is difficult, and the questions involved may be called category-questions, and the mistakes liable to be made, category-mistakes.

But Ryle and other linguistic philosophers still speak about "concepts" as though a concept were something there to be descriptively analysed, rather than something to be made (if not from scratch, at all events put into shape and got into better working order). Of course, they do not think of a concept as Hegel did, as something ideal and pre-existing independent of men and their words. But they still think of it as in some way consisting of an "actual use of words" —as there, predetermined, to be described, with its rules of logical legitimacy all firmly embedded in it. However, the job of philosophy with regard to, say, "the concept of a person" or "the concept of mind", is not to describe the actual use of words with all its rules as something already given in particular languages (some of these uses are, as we have noted, "very peculiar"), but is to work out how to generalise informatively—and that means, sorting out the right categories for such generalisation.

This brings us back again to the self-same conclusion as was reached at the end of the two previous chapters. On the linguistic philosophers' own showing, the task of philosophy cannot be to abolish all philosophical theory and stick to describing the actual use of language and stating only what everyone admits. On the contrary, the proposals of Engels continue to fit the bill—"to comprehend the real world as it presents itself to everyone who approaches it free from preconceived idealist fancies" and "relentlessly to sacrifice every idealist fancy which cannot be brought into harmony with the facts conceived in their own and not in a fantastic connection."

CHAPTER FIVE

The Language of Morals

I. MORALS AND REASON

LIKE the former logical-analytic philosophy, which it continued and corrected, the linguistic philosophy has been applied to questions of ethics. The approach made derives directly from that of *Principia Ethica*, in that the first and fundamental question posed is that of the logical analysis of value judgments.

As we saw earlier, the key point about ethics made by Moore was his diagnosis of "the naturalistic fallacy" which consists of confusing judgments of value with judgments of fact. There is a distinction between saying "This *is* done" and "This *ought* to be done", and as Hume had originally argued, no statement of the second kind can be entailed by or logically deduced from one of the first kind.

Moore, working with the idea that the task of logical analysis was to make clear exactly what statements refer to, concluded that the word "good" stands for a "non-natural" or moral quality of things, known to us by some inexplicable kind of intuition, but at all events not in the way empirical facts are known. The main point against this conclusion was made originally by some of the logical positivists. Moore had simply been misled by grammatical form. He had been misled by the grammatical similarity of "This is good" and "This is yellow" into supposing that the former assigns a "non-natural" quality in the same manner as the latter assigns a "natural" one. But "non-natural" qualities are unverifiable. Appealing to the verification principle, the logical positivists pointed out that moral statements, taken as assignments of moral quality, are unverifiable and therefore meaningless. In other words, although they have the grammatical form of statements, they are not statements at all. And since they are not statements, what are they? They are simply expressions of sentiment or preference, or, when expressed in such terms as "You ought to do this", injunctions or "imperatives".

This view about value judgments, with its consequences, was

stated, in terms strikingly similar to those Hume had used two hundred years before, by A. J. Ayer, in Chapter 6 of his *Language, Truth and Logic* (published in 1936, when he was still a logical positivist).

". . . exhortations to moral virtue are not propositions at all, but ejaculations or commands, which are designed to provoke . . . to action of a certain sort . . . The presence of an ethical symbol in a proposition adds nothing to its factual content. Thus if I say to some-one, 'You acted wrongly in stealing that money', I am not stating anything more than if I had simply said, 'You stole that money'. In adding that this action is wrong . . . I am simply evincing my moral disapproval of it. It is as if I had said, 'You stole that money', in a peculiar tone of horror . . ."

So Ayer concluded that "moral judgments . . . are pure expressions of feeling and as such do not come under the category of truth and falsehood. They are unverifiable for the same reason as a cry of pain or a word of command is unverifiable—because they do not express genuine propositions." And accordingly, however strong our moral convictions, "we cannot bring forward any arguments . . . It is be-cause argument fails us when we come to deal with pure questions of value, as distinct from questions of fact, that we finally resort to mere abuse."

However cogent the demonstration that value judgments are not empirically verifiable and so do not state facts, the conclusion that on questions of value "argument fails us" remains hard to accept. It means that we can find no *reasons* for our valuations. Ayer and other analytic philosophers who put forward this conclusion were, one and all, what is loosely called "liberal-minded" people (like Hume him-self—for of course, a Humean Tory is very liberal-minded). They believed very strongly indeed in what are called "liberal values". But their conclusion about value judgments meant that they could have no more reason for their liberal views than, say, fascists or racialists could have for their totally contrary views. A liberal is as irrational as a fascist. Such a conclusion must be hard for liberal-minded people to accept. In fact, it would represent for them a kind of moral as well as intellectual and political suicide.

It is in this difficulty that the linguistic philosophy has come to the rescue. It had already thrown a life-line to rescue empiricists from subjective idealism and solipsism. Now it throws another to save them from irrationalism and nihilism in ethics. In this matter the principal lifeguard is Mr R. M. Hare.

The distinction of fact and value, the diagnosis of the naturalistic fallacy, the principle that statements of value are not empirically verifiable or entailed by statements of fact—these are all points of substance which need to be taken into account in any discussion about ethics. And no doubt to have made these points was a definite achievement of the empiricist analytic philosophy. But does it follow that statements of value are meaningless expressions and cannot be justified by reason? That consequence was drawn thanks only to the doctrinaire application of the verification principle. A more careful linguistic analysis of the actual use of language throws a new light on the nature of moral judgments and the reasons for them.

Carnap, Ayer and other logical positivists described expressions of moral judgments as "ejaculations" or "commands" or "expressions of feeling". So Ayer likened them to "a cry of pain or a word of command". It is true that an expression of moral judgment differs from a statement of fact in the same way as a cry or a word of command does, namely, that it does not function as expressing any verifiable statement, but as an expression of feeling or sentiment, or as a directive for behaviour. But having established that point, the next thing to do is to investigate how a moral judgment differs from a cry or a command.

In *The Language of Morals* (1952) Mr Hare starts by saying that it is "part of the function of a moral judgment to prescribe or guide choices" (2.5). For this reason he calls a moral judgment "prescriptive", and the use of words in it a "prescriptive" use of words, as distinguished from the use of words for "pure statement of fact". Moral words, he repeats (10.3), "are used primarily for giving advice or instruction, or in general for guiding choices".

How, then, does a moral judgment differ from an ordinary command or "imperative"? The short answer is that a moral judgment, one in which such words as "ought" are used in a moral or evaluative way (of course, they are sometimes used in other ways), "always refers to some general principle" (11.5). Thus, for example, a notice saying "No Smoking" stuck up in a railway compartment prescribes what to do (or rather, what not to do) in that compartment, but "does not refer to a universal principle of which this compartment is an instance". On the other hand, if you make a moral judgment, "You ought not to smoke in this compartment", then your use of the word "ought" commits you, not merely to the deprecation of smoking in this compartment, but also to some general or "completely universal" principle governing the choice of when to smoke and not to smoke— such as the principle of not smoking in any compartment in which there is a "No Smoking" notice.

Moral judgments have, then, the logical characteristic of being "universalisable". What this means was briefly defined by Mr Hare in *Freedom and Reason* (1963). A judgment is universalisable when "it logically commits the speaker to making a similar judgment about anything which is either exactly like the subject of the original judgment or like it in the relevant aspects" (8.2).

In this respect, moral judgments turn out to be just like factual judgments—and this accounts for our feeling that they express, or are intended to express, objective truths. For example, a factual judgment "This is red" commits the speaker to saying that anything else like this in the relevant aspect is also red. Similarly, the moral judgment "One ought not to smoke in this compartment" commits the speaker to advocating a ban on smoking in any compartment like this one in the relevant aspect—namely, in the aspect of having a "No Smoking" notice displayed in it.

Accordingly Mr Hare concludes (*Freedom and Reason*, 1.3) "that moral judgments are a kind of *prescriptive* judgments, and that they differ from other judgments of this class by being *universalisable*".

Now of course Mr Hare and other linguistic philosophers have embellished and refined this analysis by many well-made points, and continue to do so, for they are nothing if not meticulous in the description and distinction of the uses of words. But the essential point of it consists in distinguishing moral from other prescriptive uses of words by the logical characteristic of universalisability. How, then, does this rescue those who distinguish fact and value, and who insist that value judgments are prescriptive rather than factual, from the unacceptable doctrine of irrationalism in ethics?

"It is, most fundamentally," says Mr Hare, "because moral judgments are universalisable that we can speak of moral thought as rational (to universalise is to give the reason)" (*Freedom and Reason*, 1.3).

Moral principles, he states, "have to be universal, and . . . have to be prescriptive". The latter requirement "compels us to look for principles that we can sincerely adhere to, the former insists that these should really be moral principles and not the *ad hoc* decisions of an opportunist . . . these two features taken together supply us with a most powerful lever in moral arguments. And this is the sort of principle that we all actually use in our moral thinking, the more so as we gain experience" (3.7).

And further: "Just as science, seriously pursued, is the search for hypotheses and the testing of them by the attempt to falsify their particular consequences, so morals, as a serious endeavour, consists in the search for principles and the testing of them against particular cases. Any rational activity has its discipline, and this is the discipline of moral thought: to test the moral principles that suggest themselves to us by following out their consequences and seeing whether we can accept them" (6.3).

These observations suggest that moral thought is rational in a double sense. First, it is rational in that moral principles serve to guide actions, not by issuing arbitrary imperatives ("I say do this!"), but by giving reasons in the sense of referring the choice of action to a universal principle. But second, it is rational in that moral principles are themselves amenable to reason in the sense that they can be tested by experience.

This last consideration shows that the rationality of moral judgments does not imply (as so many moralists have thought it must, and so discredited the idea of the rationality of morals) that there are absolute indefeasible principles of morality which can admit of no exception and by reference to which the morality of every particular act can be unambiguously decided. No one who knows anything about science supposes that any scientific principle is unalterable or admits of no exceptions, or that science can ever guarantee the right answer to every question. But the pursuit of science is none the less rational; and the same goes for morality. Moral reasoning, like science, takes the form of "a kind of exploration" (10.4), in the course of which principles get modified and their exceptions become recognised. Absolute finality and certainty in moral judgment is not a claim of rational moral thinking.

2. THE NATURE OF MORAL REASONING

Mr Hare's basic assumption about the function of moral judgments is that they serve for "guiding choices". Why is such a service needed? It is because "circumstances continually recur which force us to answer . . . the question 'What shall I do?'; . . . these circumstances are classifiable into kinds, the members of which are sufficiently like one another for a similar answer to be appropriate in all circumstances of the same kind; and . . . we have to learn (from others or by ourselves) principles for answering these questions" (*The Language of Morals*, 10.4).

A choice is always an individual act, and what Mr Hare does is discuss the kind of reasoning that can have weight with the individual in deciding principles to guide his choices. In this he accepts the general account of "free choice" given by other linguistic philosophers. That is to say, situations do occur in which it is correct to say to an individual "You can do this or you can do that and the decision is yours". Unless such situations occurred there would be no sense in moral judgment—for such judgments as "One ought to do this" are not applicable in circumstances where one has no choice.

Now in choosing, everyone must decide for himself. For though a man can be guided, and even allow himself to be dictated to, by other people, his *decision* is and always must be his own, just as his sight or hearing is his own. So as to the principles he may adopt to guide his choices, here too the decision to adopt or not to adopt them is his own. Each man is therefore free to adopt whatever moral principles he sees fit; or equally, to refuse to adopt any at all. "We are free to form our own moral opinions" (*Freedom and Reason*, 1.2).

This last point was rather heavily stressed by Professor Nowell-Smith in his *Ethics*, published by Penguin for mass consumption in 1954. He ended it by saying: "The questions 'What shall I do?' and 'What moral principles should I adopt?' must be answered by each man for himself; that at least is part of the connotation of the word 'moral'."

In *The Language of Morals* Mr Hare pits the necessity of each deciding for himself against what he calls "conventionalist" morals, which consists of unthinkingly accepting whatever is handed down by tradition. "To become morally adult," he says, means "learning to make decisions of principle"—for yourself, without merely taking them from others. "It is to learn to use 'ought' sentences in the realisation that they can only be verified by reference to a standard or set of principles which we have by our own decision accepted and made our own. This is what our present generation is so painfully trying to do" (4.7). He tries to assist the present generation in its moral problems by discussing on what principles principles may be recommended.

It might be supposed that the insistence on each deciding for himself implies that we may as well agree to differ about moral principles. But that, Mr Hare insists, would not be practical. We cannot contract out of moral argument because "we cannot get out of being men" and "moral principles . . . are principles for the conduct of men as men" (10.5). Hence "in the case of differences about morals it is very difficult, and, in cases where the effect on our own life is profound, impossible, to say 'It's all a matter of taste; let's agree to differ'; for to agree to differ is only possible when we can be sure that we shall not be forced to make choices which will radically affect the choices of other people" (9.2).

In *Freedom and Reason* Mr Hare points out that there is no problem connected with moral argument between those who agree on moral principles. Indeed, Ayer himself had said that much in *Language, Truth and Logic*. If a certain moral principle is accepted as a premise there can of course be rational argument as to how it applies in a specific case—and such argument turns simply upon the facts of the case. Where Ayer said that "argument fails us" is where there is dispute about moral principles themselves. If a principle is disputed, how can it be substantiated? In such cases, said Ayer, "we finally resort to mere abuse". But Mr Hare maintains that "once the logical character of the moral concepts is understood, there can be useful and compelling moral argument even between people who have, before it begins, no substantive moral principles in common" (10.1).

This argument, as expounded by him, depends upon the *universalisable* character of moral judgments. The reasons which can be assigned for accepting or rejecting a proposed moral principle arise from imaginatively exploring whether it is a principle "which we can both accept for our own conduct and universalise to cover the conduct of other . . . people" (10.4).

Here it is of key importance to stress that *moral* principles are "principles for the conduct of men as men". The same words as are used for stating moral principles are often used in other than moral contexts. For example, successful poisoners may be guided by such a principle as "One ought to choose a poison which is not easily detected at the post mortem". Although "the logic of the word 'ought' is not markedly different in the two cases", this principle for poisoners differs from a *moral* principle, such as "One ought to tell the truth", in that it is intended only for poisoners, whereas the moral principle is intended for everyone (*The Language of Morals*, 10.5).

It is just that that makes it moral, and that permits us consistently to say both that poisoners ought to choose poisons difficult to detect and that one ought not to poison people. To take a less lurid example, a motorist may be told "You ought to make sure there is petrol in the tank" and "You ought to drive carefully". The moral flavour of the second piece of advice derives from its being an application to motorists of a general principle of consideration for human life which is applicable to everyone.

Bearing in mind, then, that a moral principle is for everyone, "for men as men", the way to reason about or test moral principles is evidently to inquire whether or not the results of applying them would be universally acceptable to "men as men". A moral principle, which is a universal prescription for everyone, has as logical consequences "singular prescriptions" for particular people in particular situations. Hence "what prevents us from accepting certain moral judgments . . . is . . . the fact that they have certain logical consequences which we cannot accept—namely, certain singular prescriptions for other people in hypothetical situations" (*Freedom and Reason*, 10.4). To reason about a moral principle one explores its consequences, just as one does with a scientific principle. If it has consequences "in hypothetical situations" which "we cannot accept", then the principle must be modified or scrapped; otherwise, we can continue to make do with it. And what determines its acceptability? Not, of course, any purely logical considerations, but rather "the desires and inclinations of the human race" (10.4).

Those versed in the history of moral philosophy cannot fail to remark on the similarity at this point of Mr Hare's view of ethics and Kant's theory of "the categorical imperative": "So act that the maxim of your action might by your will become a universal law". Linguistic ethics leads back to something like Kant, though it is still much more like Hume. Mr Hare duly acknowledges "a very great debt to Kant", but adds, with some justification, that "it is a difficult enough task to make my own views clear to the reader, without trying to do the same for Kant's" (3.3). The chief respect in which his account of the matter seems to differ from Kant's is that whereas Kant wrote as if "the categorical imperative" always prescribed with absolute certainty what ought to be done, Mr Hare insists that moral reasoning is always "a kind of exploration", that finality and certainty are no more to be expected in morals than in science, and that the final test for a moral principle lies in people's "desires and inclinations". Moral argument depends not simply on people's rationality—their being able to appreciate points of logic—but on their common humanity, their common desires and inclinations.

3. THE PROBLEM OF CONFLICTING INTERESTS AND IDEALS

It is at once obvious that a difficulty arises for moral reasoning in view of the differences between people. There are undoubtedly desires and inclinations common to "men as men". But at the same time there are differences between men which lead to disagreements and conflicts. Mr Hare regards these differences as diversities of "interests" and of "ideals", and considers that it is actual conflicts of interests and ideals which set the principal problems for moral reasoning. If what is acceptable to one person is not acceptable to another, in view of their divergent interests, and if what seems perfectly satisfying to one is not satisfying or is even hateful to another, in view of their divergent ideals, how on earth can we ever arrive at moral principles whose consequences would be acceptable to everyone? The principal conclusion of Mr Hare's moral reasoning emerges as the answer to this difficulty. Rational moral judgments are those that promote the reconciliation of interests and mutual tolerance of ideals.

So far as interests are concerned, he concludes that morality is "a way of arbitrating between conflicting interests. Put as briefly as possible, to think morally is . . . to subject one's own interests, where they conflict with those of other people, to a principle which one can accept as governing anyone's conduct in like circumstances" (9.1).

Of course, it is not denied that in many cases moral precepts are in fact enunciated only because they suit the interests of those who propose them. Professor Nowell-Smith made a point of this in his *Ethics* (Chapter 16). Referring to what he called the "pro-attitude" which people adopt towards moral rules, he wrote that to account for it "in many cases we need look no further than to the fact that a sufficiently powerful or influential set of people have a pro-attitude towards the inclusion of a particular moral rule in the moral code of their society . . . And their power enables them to provide an indirect pro-attitude to their subjects in the form of penalties for disobedience . . . laws are made in the interests of rulers . . . rules are promulgated and enforced because they are believed to be in the interests . . . of some class."

Mr Hare maintains, however, that the cause of a particular moral code being enforced at a particular time and place is one thing, and the rational justification of moral principles another. For items of a moral code which merely express sectional interests in conflict with others cannot be upheld by the sort of completely impartial moral argument which he expounds. Rational morality arbitrates. "Conflicts between interests," he says, ". . . admit of reconciliation by means of the forms of argument which the logic of the moral words generates" (8.7). He does not say that such reconciliation is easy, but that moral argument consists of exploring its possibilities.

But difficult as the reconciliation of interests may be, the difficulty is greatly increased where conflicts between ideals, and between ideals and interests, are involved. "In the broadest sense," says Mr Hare, "morality includes the pursuit of ideals as well as the reconciliation of interests" (9.1). Troublesome situations accordingly develop when people extol certain ideals to the point of maintaining that other people's interests should be sacrificed to them.

Such situations are only too familiar, not only in relations between individuals, but in international politics. "If two nations, or their governments, have conflicting interests, the conflict may be more or less easily resoluble"—in the short term by simple "bargaining", in the long term "by the introduction of moral considerations . . . But where ideals are introduced into international politics, neither of these methods is so easy of application, and conflicts become much more intractable. The chief cause of the Second World War, for example, was the conflict of ideals between Nazism and democracy; and the chief cause of the next World War, if there is one, will be a conflict of ideals between communism and Western liberalism" (9.1).

"If we are to understand these tensions," Mr Hare continues, "it is most important for us to see . . . wherein such conflicts differ from mere conflicts between the interests of two parties. The chief difference, and the source of all the rest, lies in the universalisability of ideals."

Judgments affirming ideals are, like all moral judgments, prescriptive and universalisable. But "good" differs from "ought" in having a comparative, "better". Hence "whereas the judgment that I ought in a certain situation to do a certain thing commits me to the view that no similar person in a precisely similar situation ought to fail to do the same thing, this is not the case with a judgment framed in terms of 'good' . . . For it is not inconsistent to admit that there may be different ways of life, both of which are good" (8.6). For this reason Mr Hare concludes that there are differences about ideals, that is, about what is the *best* way of life, which are not susceptible to settlement by moral argument, and concerning which we may well be content to "agree to differ".

But although "there are some conflicts of ideal with ideal which are not amenable to argument . . . it would indeed be a scandal if no arguments could be brought against a person who, in pursuit of his own ideals, trampled ruthlessly on other people's interests, including that interest which consists in the freedom to pursue various ideals" (9.1). Such a person he calls a "fanatic", and he evidently considers the argument against fanaticism to be the most vital of all moral arguments in the contemporary world.

As examples of fanaticism he cites the Nazis, who ruthlessly pursued an ideal of German supremacy, and contemporary racists, who ruthlessly pursue an ideal of white supremacy. In such cases it is obviously impossible to "agree to differ", since the victims cannot very well coexist with their oppressors in mutual tolerance. But there *is* a rational argument against such "fanatical" ideals, and Mr Hare expounds it in the last chapter of *Freedom and Reason*. Such ideals as German supremacy or white supremacy, and in general ideals which lead to some people ruthlessly trampling on others, are always (he suggests) based on certain judgments of fact which make out that the tramplers are different from those trampled on in some way that justifies the trampling. Demonstrate that the alleged facts are not facts, and the fanatic's case falls to the ground. The racist, for example, claims that black people are different from white in a way that makes it necessary for the white people to kick them around. But there is no such difference. And "it *is* morally relevant that blacks are people" (11.9).

Hence the essence of rational morality is this—to prescribe arbitration and reconciliation between interests, mutual tolerance of ideals, and rejection of fanatical ideals which do not allow such tolerance. And this conclusion is reached simply by examining, in the context of its uses, the language of morals, and finding that the moral use of words is distinguished by its logical peculiarity of being prescriptive and universalisable. In this department of inquiry the description of the actual uses of words and of their logical behaviour suddenly drags the linguistic philosopher from his academic seclusion, and lands him in the middle of the disputes and conflicts of life outside.

In undertaking to describe how language is used for prescribing choices and principles for social practice, the linguistic philosophy, like others, lays itself open to the test of how well or badly it can succeeed in providing its contemporaries with "a practical philosophy of life".

CHAPTER SIX

Liberalism and Individualism

I. THE ARGUMENT FROM UNIVERSALISABILITY

IN the Preface to *Freedom and Reason* Mr Hare states: "The function of moral philosophy . . . is that of helping us to think better about moral questions by exposing the logical structure of the language in which this thought is expressed."

The linguistic approach to ethics thus sets a double task: first, to investigate the use of "the chief moral words"; second, in the light of that investigation to clear up confusion in the use of those words and so "help us to think better about moral questions". To afford this help has been the traditional aim of moral philosophy. Hence linguistic philosophy has reinstated that traditional aim, its special contribution being that the way to achieve it is by investigating "the logical structure" of the language of morals.

Mr Hare rather disarmingly continued: "When I wrote my first book, which was a study of the chief moral words, I had no more than a dim notion of what account of moral reasoning would develop out of this study . . . although I am still far from clear on many matters, I think it worth while to publish this progress report, if only to enlist the help of others in becoming clearer." Nothing could be fairer than that, and this chapter represents an effort to help.

On the logical structure of moral language, or actual use of moral words, the conclusion of the linguistic investigation is, in Mr Hare's terminology, that moral judgments differ from factual judgments in being prescriptive but agree with them in being universalisable.

There is no more need to dispute this purely logical conclusion than to dispute, say, Austin's astute linguistic analysis which distinguished certain statements as performative. On the contrary, this account of the agreements and differences between moral and factual judgments is equally perspicacious. And far from being trivial, it does help dispose of three major confusions in the moral philosophy of the past—namely, the naturalistic view that moral judgments are simply statements of fact, the intuitionist view that they deal with "non-natural" characteristics of human affairs, and the theological or transcendentalist view that they express prescriptions emanating from some higher authority (such as God or Pure Reason). But yet how far does that get us? To have noted the performative character of the words uttered in the marriage ceremony is still far from providing a system of marriage guidance, and to have noted the prescriptive and universalisable character of moral judgments is still far from telling us how to reason about moral questions.

Endeavouring to jump from the logical structure of the language of morals to the validation of specific moral principles, Mr Hare's taking off point could only be the logical characteristic of universalisability, and his criterion of validation the logical characteristic of consistency. Moral principles are validated by passing a consistency test, and this consistency test in turn is a test of whether or not their consistent application ·could become universally acceptable taking into account the actual "desires and inclinations of the human race". Here, naturally enough, Mr Hare at once gets tangled up in questions arising from actual conflicts of "interests" and "ideals"; and his final conclusion about morals emerges with a certain logical inevitability. Rational or valid moral judgments are those that promote reconciliation of interests and mutual tolerance of ideals.

This conclusion accords with what Mr Hare himself calls "liberalism" (*Freedom and Reason*, 9), so that the whole analysis of the validation of the moral judgments, the whole argument from universalisability, turns out to be an argument for liberalism. The word "liberal" is one that, as Wittgenstein would have said, bears a whole family of meanings rather than one definite meaning. We may apply to Mr Hare's particular member of the family his own test of following up its logical consequences and seeing how acceptable they really are.

2. PRINCIPLES AND INTERESTS

The account of "interests" and "ideals" presented in *Freedom and Reason* is a singularly oversimplified one, for it pays only the scantiest attention to the very complicated social phenomena which in fact come under this heading. The examples cited by Mr Hare are mostly of individuals' interests in the possession of particular objects or freedom to perform particular activities which give them satisfaction; and similarly of the conceptions which individuals form, in accordance with their individual predilections, of the ideal way of life. For example, smokers have an interest in being able to smoke, and non-smokers in breathing an atmosphere free from tobacco fumes. Again, a sportsman may be inspired by an ideal of all-round sportsmanship, and a businessman by an ideal of business success. As Mr Hare very justly concludes, the interests of smokers and non-smokers can be reconciled by the one occupying "smoking" and the other "no smoking" compartments on railway journeys. And similarly, the sportsman and businessman can each pursue his ideal without either trampling on the other. But can the conclusions from such cases be generalised to cover all cases of "interests" and "ideals"? Mr Hare does not devote the same close attention to cases where not merely individual but class interests are involved, or to "ideals" in the sense of political or economic aims.

That morality reconciles interests supposes that interests are reconcilable. But this is true only within certain limits of individual interests. Certainly, it is part of the duty of a nursery school teacher to train the children to share their toys without squabbling over them. Nearly everyone would agree that this is an important item in moral education, inculcating rational principles essential for the subsequent conduct of the adult. But the rational principles of the nursery school have their limitations.

The moralist who tells the workers that they ought always to accommodate their class interests to those of their employers and accept arbitration is in effect upholding the class interests of the employers. He may also tell the employers that they ought to make such concessions as they can afford to the workers; but that is effectively in the interests of the employers too. The moralist may claim that the proposed arbitration is equally in the interests of both classes. For working-class interests, too, require that the wheels of industry should be kept turning, for which purpose reconciliation of capital and labour is required on the basis of mutual concessions. This moral argument is, indeed, a stock one—and not only on the employers' side, for it has been a contention of Labour ever since Keir Hardie sought to base the conduct of the Labour movement on moral principles. If the capitalist mode of production were susceptible of continuous adjustment and reform so that both workers and employers would go on benefiting from it equally, then the case for continuous reconciliation would be made. But if (as Marxists contend) that proposition is not in fact true of capitalism, then the moral reasoning is in fact biased in the interests of the one class against the other. The universalised prescriptions of the liberal moralist turn out to depend upon covert and highly questionable assumptions about the economics of capitalism.

And now let us turn to "ideals". Once again, there is a good argument for tolerance where it concerns only divergent conceptions of individual excellence. Why argue which is "best", to be good at sport or good at business? People should not try to impose their individual ideals on each other, and the businessman who insists on buying up sportsgrounds for property development may well be reprobated in the same way as a smoker who insists on smoking in "no smoking" compartments. Let him do his property development somewhere else, and let him smoke somewhere else! But when Mr Hare begins to talk of such "ideals" as "German supremacy" or "white supremacy" he changes the context and with it the sense of the words; and so he does when he talks of his own (far more attractive) liberal ideal of everyone tolerating everyone else. For then he is talking not of individual but of social ideals—of social aims, what sort of society we should aim at.

Ideals in the sense of social aims are always, if they count for anything, reflections of social interests, and primarily of class interests. Thus, for example, an individual believer in apartheid may be what Mr Hare calls "an idealist", in that he passionately believes that apartheid is best for everyone. But it puts a strain on one's credulity to say that apartheid owes its origin primarily to the occurrence of such idealism amongst individuals. Apartheid is a trampling of some interests by other interests, and the so-called ideal is a cover for doing that. Similarly, when Mr Hare says that "the conflict of ideals" was "the chief cause of the Second World War", he is proposing a crude idealist theory of historical causation which ignores the rival interests which found expression in the conflict of ideals. This may still pass muster with philosophers, but, since Marx, provokes raised eyebrows amongst historians even in the University of Oxford.

According to the moral argument, the pursuit of ideals is morally justified only in so far as it does not infringe on existing interests. But if social ideals are in fact tied with interests, it follows once again that the moral reasoning is rather heavily biased on the side of the social *status quo*.

Let us then consider an "ideal" which counts for much in the modern world, the revolutionary social aim of communism. Mr Hare evades discussing it (perhaps for the very creditable reason that he does not want to get involved in cold war polemics). He does say, however, that if there is a Third World War it will be due to the "conflict of ideals between communism and Western liberalism". This statement is as questionable as the one about the Second World War. Communists do not propose fanatically to impose one ideal in opposition to rival ideals, but to follow up the interests of the working majority of society to secure the social ownership and social planning without which modern means of production cannot be fully developed and used. And this is the only way in which the conflicts of interests (and consequently of "ideals") can be resolved, and a general human interest be established.

On the other hand, what are the logical consequences of Mr Hare's moral arguments about reconciliation and tolerance when applied to the questions communism raises? Evidently, his principles imply agreement with Mr Khrushchov, and with his successors, in advocating the peaceful coexistence of capitalist and communist states in the current conditions of international politics. The Russians had a revolution with which certain social aims are associated; and that being so, they and people in "the West" who have other "ideals" ought to coexist peacefully and settle any conflicts of interest by negotiation. But if we project the same moral argument some years into the past, it equally evidently follows that the Russians ought never to have had a revolution at all, for it certainly involved trampling on some people's interests for the sake of those of other people, and for the sake, too, of other people's "ideals". The Russians made a moral error; and though we ought to make the best of things now they have got away with it, they still stand condemned at the bar of moral reason. The same moral argument applied within capitalist countries today, and within colonial countries too, and countries where neo-colonialism is practised, implies that nothing revolutionary, that seriously damages capitalist interests for the sake of instituting what some people would consider an order of society that better accords with their own interests, ought ever to be attempted. So far as "socialist ideals" are concerned, the argument leaves us at liberty to believe in them as fervently as we like, but not to take any steps to realise them at the expense of capitalist interests.

In linguistic philosophy, then, the same study of the chief moral words which leads to the justification of the principle of not smoking in "no smoking" compartments on railway journeys leads to moral principles for the conduct of political affairs identical with those enunciated by Hume at the very beginning of this kind of moral argument. We should study to preserve and improve "the ancient fabric", while the "wise magistrate" continues to prevent fanatics from disrupting it for the sake of their various ideals. It is remarkable how conservative liberal principles always turn out to be.

The fact is that the prescriptions of liberal morality universalise admirably for the sphere of what may be called private life, and likewise for the purely administrative sphere of public life. Mr Hare's example of the ethics of smoking on railway journeys illustrates this fact. The argument from universalisability prescribes mutual consideration, fairness, kindness, understanding of other people's points of view, all the virtues of domestic life and of good administration. One should not belittle these principles; for it is *true* that if everyone practised them, everyone would find them very acceptable. But when it comes to public policies and social aims, then (to quote from *The Thousand and One Nights*) the liberal moralist is "carried into the mill of complication". How, in a class-divided society in which the profits of one class are derived from the labour of another, can public policies and social aims be judged by a criterion of universal acceptability? Under cover of that criterion, the principle of arbitration and reconciliation inevitably comes down in favour of preserving the profit-system.

3. MEN AS MEN

The argument from universalisability depends on evading any close examination of the actual social condition of mankind, and instead trying to prescribe universal principles of human conduct on the basis of an abstract conception of what Mr Hare calls "men as men". It is postulated that there exist certain "desires and inclinations of the human race", characteristic of men as men, which moral precepts must be made to fit and by reference to which they must be tested.

Indeed, all the liberal-humanist moral philosophies, as opposed to those which appeal to supernatural or transcendental moral sanctions, or to mysterious intuitions, have depended on this same postulate. Hume's conception of pleasure and pain, Kant's categorical imperative, the utilitarian principle of the greatest happiness of the greatest number, and the new linguistic analysis of moral reasoning, all alike depend on it. It states that human individuals as such are basically identical in desires and inclinations, and that therefore there can be worked out a morality for men as men, prescribing ways of living together, which is absolutely impartial as between particular interests and ideologies and adjusts and reconciles them all. Such a morality is truly universalisable, and stands right above all merely personal or class interests.

But what is characteristic of men as men is their social life, based on the social production of their means of livelihood. And this evolves, and presents very different formations from place to place and from time to time. There exist human individuals, identical in their anatomy and physiology and in basic material needs. But in order to satisfy these needs they have to live and work together in human society; and their desires and inclinations, like their capabilities, their interests and their ideals, are all determined not simply in accordance with their genetical attributes as human individuals, but in accordance with the forces of production possessed by their society and the relations of production within which they are used. To say anything to the point about "men as men" requires not only the abstract comparison of human individuals to find what desires and inclinations they have in common, but also the investigation of social relations and of the development of men in society.

This objection to the abstract liberal method of moralising was first lodged by Marx. "The human essence," he wrote "is no abstraction inherent in each single individual. In its reality it is the ensemble of social relations" (*Theses on Feuerbach*). Though he wrote that about Feuerbach in 1845, to apply it to what Mr Hare wrote in 1963 one need only substitute for "the human essence" the more or less synonymous phrase "men as men".

When the modern bourgeois social formation began to take shape, old ideas of status and hierarchy, according to which some people were slaves who belonged to their masters, or serfs who were tied to the land and owed corresponding duties to their lords, were challenged, and it was proclaimed that all men are equal and have the same human rights. This idea of human equality which, like the authors of the Declaration of Independence, all liberal moralists regard as "self-evident", reflected in the most obvious way the actual changes which were taking place in the economic organisation of society. But to justify it there came, not the critical analysis of economic changes (which shows that the changes need to go a lot further), but the abstract theory of "men as men". And from this theory the conclusion emerges that practical moral principles for regulating men's conduct in living together are to be tested and established by considering how far, if everyone applied them, everyone's basic claims as a human individual would be met.

This conclusion, now reargued and reformulated by linguistic philosophy in terms of "the logic of language", has been urged in one form or another for a long time. For example, analytic philosophers recently discovered that Bishop Butler, who preached a series of sermons on "self-love" and "benevolence" to a fashionable congregation in London in 1726, was the greatest of British moralists. The Bishop said that everyone should take care of his own interests with due regard to those of other people, and that conscience would guide him in finding the right balance. Though Mr Hare's exposition lacks his predecessor's episcopal decorum, his conclusions are not essentially different. Look after your own interests, respect other people's, and don't have ideals which interfere with interests—it is still the liberal Bishop addressing his well-fed bourgeois congregation.

The fallacy in this comfortable and comforting view is a simple one. Since at any given time and place the desires and inclinations, the interests and requirements of people in society depend not simply on the human nature of each individual, but also on the totality of historically determined social relations between individuals, it follows that the interests and claims of individuals which morality has to respect are determined in conformity with the established social order. Consequently the morality for "men as men" turns out to be in reality the morality for living within the social order, with all its contradictions and class divisions, in which the conception of "men as men" was born. As Marx said, "the abstract individual" of the liberal moralist "belongs in reality to a particular form of society" (*ibid*). He belongs, in fact, to the bourgeois form of society, and his moral nature will never permit him to infringe upon bourgeois interests or to pursue other than bourgeois ideals.

4. "I" QUESTIONS AND "WE" QUESTIONS

The idea of "men as men" which Mr Hare, like all liberal moralists, finds essential for moral reasoning, is bound up with what may be described as an essentially individualistic outlook. This should not be confused with selfishness or egotism. Some of the earlier bourgeois moralists did indeed fall into this confusion, and could find no moral reason why any individual ought to respect any interests but his own. But moral philosophy has long extricated itself from that position, and Mr Hare's moral arguments depend entirely on the idea that each individual ought to respect the interests of every other individual.

The individualism of Mr Hare and of other liberal and linguistic moral philosophers goes deep, for it resides not only in the answers they give but in the very questions they ask. They arrive at individualistic answers because they ask individualistic questions.

The "moral questions" which Mr Hare tries to help us "to think better about" are questions of the form: "What shall *I* do?" He never seems to doubt that "moral questions" must take this personal individualistic form, since the function of prescriptive judgments is to guide choices and choices are made by individuals. Hence each individual must decide for himself, and moral philosophy is the logical exposition of the moral reasons for individual decisions. It is in order to work out the answers to such questions that Mr Hare deploys the concept of "men as men". Individual people are endowed by God or Nature with common desires and inclinations, and so they can reason about and test universalisable prescriptive judgments adopted to guide their choices by exploring how far they are all able to accept their universalisation. But in order to account for how such questions come to be asked, he deploys another and more ancient concept, namely, that each individual is endowed with free choice or free will.

That people are often presented by choices and do make them, is indubitable. In a sense, to be in a situation of choosing is something that continually happens to all animals, whenever the relation of organism to environment permits them alternative modes of behaviour. What is unique about the *human* capacity of choosing, and makes us claim that *we* are able to choose what to do freely or deliberately or rationally or morally in a way not open to other species of animal, is that human individuals put the alternatives before themselves in a way not open to other animals. This is not due to our being endowed with something called "free will" which other animals lack, but to our having acquired the use of language in which alternatives may be presented. Language is a social acquisition. And so evidently human individuals possess their human capacity of deliberate choice because they are members of human society. Outside their relations with each other they would lack free

will, and could not indeed possess that kind of individuality or
personality that is specifically human and makes the human individual a moral agent. (It may be objected that Robinson Crusoe
presented an outstanding example of a person exercising free will
in a highly moral manner. But had he been stranded on an island
as an infant, his behaviour would have been different. His whole
story makes it very clear that the initial factor in forming his
character was, as he tells us, that "I was born in the year 1632, in
the city of York, of a good family".)

Such considerations about human choice seem fairly obvious—
but it is only by ignoring them that Mr Hare can consider "moral
questions" exclusively from the point of view of what each individual
should do and how each individual should decide for himself. He
argues as if to think out moral principles were to think out the
principles which I shall prescribe for myself, as an individual possessing free will, and thereby also by implication prescribe for other
people. He calls his conclusions not only "liberal" but "protestant"—
and rightly so, for they echo the protestant individualism which
sees moral questions as personal questions, and duty as obedience to
"the monitor within". But yet, the consideration that individuality
is a social product suggests that the individual puts moral questions
to himself because of his membership of society rather than because
of his individual attribute of free will.

The outstanding fact about people is their mode of dependence
on each other. It is not only that each is rather helpless alone and
that we can do things together which none of us can do separately;
it is that no one becomes a person except in human relations with
other people. Outside such relations there can be individuals of the
species, but not people. Hence the concept of "a person" is a concept
of human social relationship, of doing things together with other
people. And hence, when people are looking for principles to guide
choices, they are not only concerned with questions of the form
"What shall I do?" but also of the form "What shall we do?" And
indeed, whether judged by the effect of their answers on the fate of
the social organisation or on the fate of each individual, the latter
questions must rank as more important. But not only are they
more important, they are also logically prior to the individualistic
questions.

It is rash to presume, as individualists evidently do, that because
acts of choice are individual, and a collective decision can only be

carried out by individual actions, answers to "we" questions must follow logically from answers to "I" questions—that is to say, that what a number of people together ought to do follows from what in the circumstances each of them individually ought to do. The contrary is true. People can do together what they cannot do individually, and moral questions would not arise at all about what they do individually unless they did things together.

For example, if the question is mooted by members of a trade union "Should we come out on strike?", what each individual has to decide is "Should I vote for or against a strike?" But his answer to this question about what he individually should do is logically dependent on his answer to the question about what the members collectively should do. Again, the answer to the collective question is not arrived at by each considering for himself "Should *I* come out on strike?" As regards that question, most trade unionists would act on the principle that when it is decided to strike each individual should strike, and when it is decided to remain at work each individual should remain at work. In this instance, then, the answer, for each person concerned, to the question "What should I do?" is dependent on the answer to the question "What should we do?" And this same order of dependence is not unusual with questions about what individuals ought to do, though it is often overlooked. Thus in many socially controversial questions the answer to what individuals should do depends on the answer to whether we should preserve the existing social system or try to change it. Even the principle that one ought not to smoke in "no smoking" compartments on railways depends on the principle that we ought to run the railways so as to satisfy both smoking and non-smoking passengers.

The reason why moral questions are in fact posed is not because individuals are faced with choices and have individually to work out principles to guide their choices, but because individuals depend on each other in society in such a way that they need principles to regulate the way they live together. Naturally enough, the latter do serve as principles to guide what individuals should do. But it is the same social mode of life that makes individuals free to choose that makes their voluntary actions subject to moral principles. People in society cannot but regulate their affairs by judgments answering the question "What should we do?", and the answers to questions "What should I do?" are consequent on these.

5. CHOOSING THE WORSE

That Mr Hare and other linguistic philosophers have posed their questions wrongly when they conclude that moral principles are adopted simply to cope with the individual's predicament whenever he is faced with a choice, is shown by the fact that this leads them into an odd "dilemma"—one of those artificial puzzles which, as they themselves have observed in other contexts, are an infallible sign of something wrong somewhere in a theoretical exposition.

How can an individual ever deliberately act against a moral principle which he himself recognises? Mr Hare and others have tied themselves up in knots over this question, as their predecessors did over such questions as "How can anyone know that anyone else has toothache?" For though an individual may choose to act against the principles guiding someone else's choice, he cannot choose to act against the principles guiding his own choice; for if he did, the principles would not be the principles guiding his choice. Hence to say "I ought to do this, but I won't" is a contradiction in terms, and it is logically impossible deliberately to do anything one considers wrong.

Mr Hare tries to work his way out of this paradox (it has been debated by linguistic philosophers for years, being a worse headache than the toothache) by saying that he who does something he considers he ought not to do, does not in fact *choose* at all (*Freedom and Reason*, 5.7). What happens is that he is driven to act against his principles by the overmastering effect of irrational impulse. Far from acting deliberately, he is in fact the mere passive agent of his own passions. As proof of this Mr Hare quotes the poet Ovid:

> "Meanwhile Aeetes' daughter's heart took fire,
> Her struggling Reason could not quell Desire. . . .
> 'This madness how can I resist?' she cried,
> 'No use to fight, some god is on its side . . .
> Urged this way—that—on Love's or Reason's course,
> I see and praise the better, do the worse.'"

and also the Apostle Paul:

> ". . . what I do is the wrong which is against my will; and if what I do is against my will, clearly it is no longer I who am the agent, but sin that has its lodging in me."

He does not add that this unlikely combination of authorities could be quoted in every lawcourt to get the accused off on a plea of "temporary insanity". The Judge might have some caustic remarks to make. Here it is only necessary to say that it involves no logical contradiction to recognise the prescriptions of one's society and at the same time deliberately try to get away with ignoring them.

6. THE SOCIAL NATURE OF MORALITY

The universalisable character of moral judgments, correctly noted by Mr Hare and other linguistic moralists, is a consequence of the essentially social nature of morality. That a moral prescription applies not to anyone in particular but to anyone in like circumstances is simply the result of the fact that such principles are enunciated for the purpose of regulating social life. Similarly, though moral principles are enunciated by individuals (indeed, it is absurd to say that anything is ever enunciated except by individuals), they differ from ordinary "imperatives" or "commands" in that the individual who uses moral words does not suppose himself to be speaking merely for himself.

When, for example, a sergeant-major shouts "Shoulder arms!" it is *him* issuing an order to the squad. But when the C.O., instructing the recruits in their duty, tells them they ought always to polish their buttons and have their hair cut, it is not merely him as an individual issuing an order (though it is an order, and if they disobey it he will put them in the guard house). He is not speaking only for himself. What *is* he speaking for? He is the mouthpiece for enunciating a universal prescription to regulate army life. If he has not studied linguistic philosophy and is prone to category-confusion, he may well maintain, if asked, that he is speaking for The Army, which makes its prescriptions known through the voices of its officers. The Army itself, he may add, is an arm of The State, and The State's prescriptions are derived from God. It is quite easy to see, in such examples, how the prescriptive and universalisable use of words to fulfil certain social requirements generates the illusion that moral principles are laid down for individuals by a supernatural authority. And certainly (whatever Mr Hare may have to say to the contrary), in considering himself subject to moral principles the individual considers himself subject to prescriptions which are not laid down for him by the fiat either of himself or of any other individual.

The authority, however, is not supernatural but social: it is the natural product of the social association of persons.

7. INDIVIDUAL AND SOCIAL QUESTIONS

The key questions to decide in moral argument are, then, not individual questions but social. Before people each try to work out "on what principles should I act?" they should give some consideration to the question "on what principles should we act?"

Grave as may be the individual's moral problems in contemporary society, such as the problem of whether to tell a lie, or sleep with a member of the opposite sex to whom one is not legally contracted for that purpose, or smoke in a "no smoking" compartment, there are nowadays (and there always have been) collective or social problems that are a good deal graver. These are problems about how public affairs should be conducted, and how and to what ends people should work in concert. The individualistic way of posing moral questions (which linguistic moralists seem to think the only way presented in "the actual use of language") assumes that once having worked out principles of what each individual ought to do, all moral questions are by implication answered. For if everyone agrees on the principles on which everyone ought to act, what else remains to decide on? On this assumption Mr Hare concluded that the same principles which work in private life when individuals respect each other's interests are equally applicable in public affairs. But as we have seen, the assumption is false. For the human relationships and conflicts of interests and aims which arise in public life are of a different order from those affecting people in their private lives.

It is indeed for this reason that we are faced in contemporary society (and the same has been true in the past) with the unedifying spectacle of public men who conduct their private lives in the most moral way, and whose indignation knows no bounds whenever their colleagues are caught out in any misdemeanour, making themselves responsible for public policies in which the ruthless pursuit of interests is but barely disguised by a few moral catchphrases. Their personal moral principles need not be questioned, but they simply do not apply in public affairs, and so they conduct the latter in a very different style. At the same time, the moral demand is made that all individuals should learn how to conduct themselves individually on moral principles, regardless of the state of the society in which they have to live. Yet it is a bit hard to expect certain Asians and Africans, for example, to cultivate individually the domestic and civic virtues of British or American suburbanite commuters when they are being bossed by puppet rulers and harried by mercenaries, or to expect the youth of Britain and the United States to behave as models of propriety when their elders are spending so much public money on hydrogen bombs and failing to provide them with decent homes or even playing fields.

There can be no doubt, however, that moral questions—that is to say, questions answered by prescriptive judgments—are raised, and due to the conditions of human existence are bound to be raised, not only about the private behaviour of individuals but about the conduct of public affairs. For example, many people have asked in Britain "Ought the old-age pensioners to be treated like this?" We may also ask such questions as "In modern conditions ought means of production to be privately owned and worked for profit?"

Mr Hare tries, as we have seen, to answer such questions by applying to public affairs the same principles of the reconciliation of interests which he considers fundamental for the conduct of personal life. On the other hand, there are many who would contend that these sorts of questions are not "moral" at all, but are of another kind, namely "political". Morality, it is suggested, is essentially a personal matter, a matter of the conduct of each individual. Though Mr Hare does say that public policies should be decided on moral principles, the fact is that he too continues to regard morals as primarily a personal matter.

Of course, there is a distinction between different types of "ought" questions. The question "Ought the rich to be taxed in order to provide old-age pensions?" is a different type of question from "Ought one to cut down on luxuries in order to support one's aged mother?" But the approach which sees morals as primarily a personal matter in effect separates morals, which is personal, from politics, which is public, and for practical purposes turns morals into a system of exhorting individuals to act on one set of principles while the society on which they depend for their health, education and happiness is managed on quite contrary principles (if, indeed, it is managed on any principles at all).

It is in this sense that most morality, as publicly preached, has always been humbug; and most moral philosophy a mere embellishment of humbug by specious reasoning.

8. SOCIAL ORGANISATION AND PERSONAL BEHAVIOUR

In practice and in logic the answers to questions about the rights and wrongs of personal behaviour depend on the answers to questions about the rights and wrongs of social organisation. To try to consider the former separately and independently can never lead to anything but (to quote Hume) sophistry and illusion.

That this is so in practice is shown by the fact that at all times conceptions of people's duties to one another no less than their duties to themselves have varied with their conceptions of what sort of a social organisation they ought to maintain. For example, conceptions of sexual morality vary with different forms of family organisation. Again, the peculiar virtues of sturdy independence, honest dealing, rendering value for money and, indeed, the degree of submission to arbitration between interests and tolerance of different ideals so eloquently recommended by Mr Hare, belong to a capitalist free-enterprise society, and were not so highly prized in former slave or feudal societies. People who are banded together to defend a threatened regime develop their own peculiar conceptions of loyalty, self-sacrifice and devotion to impersonal symbols such as the Church or the Crown or the Country; while others who combine to resist or overthrow the regime develop conceptions of solidarity and comradeship and giving up everything for the struggle; or if, like the primitive Christians, they think the regime wrong but can do nothing to alter it, they form yet other ideas of how to conduct themselves as a community of saints and martyrs in a wicked world.

Naturally enough, there are some "moral words", such as "theft" and "murder", which almost always imply blame, and others, such as "honesty" and "loyalty", which almost always imply praise (though in different conditions opinions as to what constitutes theft, murder, honesty or loyalty may vary greatly). This is because almost any social organisation must demand some sort of honesty and loyalty from its members and forbid them to murder one another or steal each other's things. Hence the identity of standards of personal behaviour which has always existed amid differences.

And that it is so in logic, that logically conceptions of people's personal duties follow from conceptions of what sort of social organisation they ought to maintain, and not the other way round, follows from the consideration that the use of language to utter moral imperatives is not a use whereby each individual decides for himself how to regulate the action of his own free will, but is a use whereby individuals associated in society state principles for carrying on their social life. That being so, it is evident that to carry on different forms of association entails different moral imperatives.

9. INTERESTS AND REASONS

The universalisability of moral judgments, on which Mr Hare's account of moral reasoning hinges, is a consequence, as I have already noted, of the essentially social nature of morality. Mr Hare, however, treats each individual as if he existed as an individual person independent of society; and then treats moral judgments as if they were prescriptions which each individual decides to make for himself, taking into account that, as it happens, he has to live alongside others of his kind. Consequently the account he gives of the logical property of universalisability, as belonging to moral judgments, is itself not at all complete or adequate; and this in turn affects his account of the logic of moral reasoning.

Mr Hare treats moral reasoning as if it were a matter of each individual making his individual moral judgments consistent. So he concludes that consistent moral principles are such that anyone could consistently wish everyone to act on them. Hence moral principles must always be such as to compromise interests, because everyone must wish that everyone else should reconcile their interests with his; and similarly they must not let ideals be such as to trample on interests, because everyone must wish that no one else's ideals should lead to his own interests being trampled on. Quite apart from the practical impossibility, in existing circumstances, of everyone consistently acting on such principles, this entails, as we have seen, that the existing social set-up on which existing interests depend ought to be preserved and no fundamental social changes ought to be made.

But suppose such changes are socially desirable, and that certain existing vested interests are a barrier to desirable social reorganisation? Are we to conclude that it is logically impossible for there ever to be a valid argument in support of such judgments? There is some mistake in the logic which leads to such a logical consequence, just as there is some mistake in the logic which concludes that it is logically impossible for anyone to choose to do anything he considers wrong.

The primary moral questions, on which all others depend, concern the desirability of different forms of social association. And with these moral reasoning has to begin.

Moralists have formed their ideas of what is socially desirable or undesirable, couched them in grandiose moral language, and given all manner of reasons for them; but what in effect they have generally been doing is to express conflicting social aims corresponding to conflicting class interests. In class-divided society social aims or ideals reflect class interests. And hence to argue rationally about what is socially desirable involves finding reasons or standards by reference to which to judge or evaluate *interests*. Before questions of how far to compromise and reconcile interests can be rationally decided, a decision must be reached on which interests take precedence, which are to be subordinated to which.

Generally speaking, moral judgments reflect interests. And naturally, when there exists a fair amount of agreement on the desirability or otherwise of certain kinds of action (for example, theft, or cruelty, or telling lies; or, in another sphere of activity, starting a nuclear war) that is because those kinds of action appear desirable or undesirable from the standpoint of *all* or at any rate most interests. Such agreement is usually strongest about what is undesirable rather than what is desirable. People tend to agree more readily in being sure of what they should not do than of what they should do. Moral judgments are accordingly arrived at, as is obvious (and as Hume long ago pointed out), not so much by processes of reasoning as by essentially irrational or pre-rational ideological processes. We tend to judge first and then, stimulated especially by our disagreements, to look for reasons. Then, in the light of reasons, we may modify our judgments. In this way moral judgments are generally neither entirely irrational nor entirely rational; reason plays a part in their formation, but rather in moulding what is already proposed than in originally proposing anything.

In moral philosophy, as distinct from social anthropology, we are concerned, as Mr Hare has said, with the sort of reasons that can validate moral judgments. And though he does not say this, it is worth noting that this concern is itself the application of a moral principle. To say that we should try to make our moral judgments such as can be validated by reason, and criticise them and modify them in the light of reason, is itself a moral principle (though far from universally agreed), just as it is to say that we should base our judgments of matter of fact on the honest endeavour to ascertain the facts (and that is not universally agreed either). Both these principles amount to the injunction to submit judgments to certain kinds of criticism and test. Discussion of theoretical questions of ethics, as of the theory of knowledge and scientific method, often fails to take into account the complicating factor that the discussion itself is inescapably a matter of moral controversy which, like all such controversy, reflects conflicting social interests.

How can we reason about questions of social desirability? What else than a factually-based account of society can supply such reasons, yet how can a factually-based account supply them?

Formally, there can be no doubt that Hume was right in insisting that no factual statement or combination of factual statements can entail a prescriptive statement. And so, as Mr Hare points out in *The Language of Morals* (2.5), "No imperative conclusion can be validly drawn from a set of premises which does not contain at least one imperative". But that merely says that no prescriptive judgment can be formally deduced from non-prescriptive judgments. Of course not. As Hume also showed, no scientific generalisation is formally deducible from any set of factual statements; and so it is not surprising that no moral generalisation is deducible either. Hume's principle only shows how not to reason about moral questions— that is to say, not to try to conclude about desirability by formal deduction. But formal deduction is not the only, nor indeed the chief, method of reasoning.

A good or valid reason for judging something desirable is not the same as a cause for certain people desiring it. And if it is a *good* reason, it is not merely a reason "for me" or "for my group" but for anyone who takes into account the objective circumstances which are cited.

It is this last point about moral reasons that constitutes the missing constituent of the logical property of universalisability as applied to moral judgments. A universalisable judgment commits the speaker to the view that reasons supporting it hold good for anyone. The same applies, of course, to factual statements, such as "The train is running late", which, as Mr Hare has said, are universalisable. On the other hand, there may be some doubt as to whether it applies, in all contexts, to such a statement as "This is red". And that, of course, is why it is open to doubt whether "This is red" always states an "objective" fact in the same way as "The train is late". Indeed, the two words "universalisable" and "objective", as applied to judg-ments, are practically synonymous. That a value judgment is univer-salisable means, that it is intended to be objective as distinct from being a mere subjective expression of preference. Thus if I say that something is desirable, I may be merely expressing my personal preference. But if such a statement is put forward as a moral judg-ment, or as a universalisable prescription, I am saying that that thing *is* desirable and that there are reasons for holding it so which are good for anyone. Evidently, then, a judgment which is universalisable or objective should be supported by good reasons; and if such cannot be found, or if such are found for some incompatible judgment, then the truth of the original judgment is open to doubt or is refuted. In this sense, we may speak (as we very generally do) of the "truth" of value judgments, just as we speak of the "truth" of factual judg-ments. It is true that they are not "pictures of facts" in the sense defined by the simpler versions of the correspondence theory of truth; but neither are factual judgments.

The reasoned recommendation of a way of social life cannot, then (and so far Mr Hare would agree), simply cite causes why I or any other particular person or group of persons in fact desire it. To do that is merely to cite particular interests in opposition to others, and to supply no reasons why the former should prevail over the latter.

On the other hand, it is not required that such a reasoned recom-mendation should be universally *applicable* at all times and places, regardless of existing social conditions. For what is practicable must always depend on circumstances, so that what is or is not a rational recommendation must always depend on the actual historically con-ditioned character of the social set-up in which it is made. Nor is it required that whatever is recommended must be equally *acceptable* to everyone. As we have seen, such a requirement is impossible to meet anyhow. Thus because individuals live in historically condi-tioned social relations, and are made what they are to a great extent by social conditioning, it is impossible for any way of life recom-mended as desirable to be even practicable, let alone acceptable to all individuals, in all circumstances; or where people are divided by class interests for it ever to be both practicable and acceptable to them all.

If, then, we are to find good reasons for current judgments about what is socially desirable, and what interests should prevail, this requires, first of all, an accurate description of the current state of society—its economic basis, the interests and conflicts of interest contained within it, the individual and collective needs which people have acquired in it and the ways in which and extent to which the current social relations permit their satisfaction, and the possibilities of maintaining social stability or of effecting social changes.

And it requires, secondly, a scientifically based general theory about man and his social life. It is such a theory that provides the basis for evaluations, the standards of judgment. For it permits a comparison of the actual with the possible which provides insight into the defects of our social relations and mode of social behaviour relative to the objective requirements for the development of social life, and into practical ways of overcoming them. In other words, if only we can work out a scientifically based general theory of man and society, we can do what Hume said was logically impossible, namely, find a way both practical and rational of concluding from what the human situation is to what ought to be done in it, and of finding reasons for what we think ought to be done in the investigation of the human situation.

The chief reason why Hume, and still more his followers, thought that that was logically impossible was that they would never admit that social investigation could do more than record lists of facts— they denied it the right enjoyed by other branches of science to establish a general theory. In actual practice, however, people always do argue from an account of a particular set-up, judged in the light of a general theory (however vague and implicit that general theory may be), to the conclusion that certain things are desirable or undesirable, and ought to be changed or left alone. And those who disagree, argue by denying that the current set-up is as described, or denying the general theory, or denying both. For example, I have yet to meet anyone who admitted the truth of Marxist general theory and of its particular descriptive analysis of capitalism, and at the same time denied the Marxist conclusion of the desirability of replacing capitalism by socialism; they have always found fault with some item of the general theory or of the particular analysis or both.

How Marxism establishes a rational basis for value judgments and for the critique of value judgments I shall try to indicate in the last part of this book. Here it suffices to say that, on questions of social desirability, reasoned judgment is always based, and cannot but be based, on theories about the actual conditions of human existence. And likewise when it comes to questions of the rights and wrongs of individual conduct and personal relations, no reasons can be given without presupposing some such theory. Such theories have tradi-tionally been religious—and hence the widespread idea that morality is inseparable from religion. But there are also all manner of non-religious or lay theories. As we have seen, even Mr Hare has a theory of man, though a very vaguely formulated one—the theory of indi-vidualism. The real point for moral reasoning, then, is first of all to discuss and test such theories, and then to test value judgments in the light of the theories and in the course of practical experience.

10. WANTED—A MATERIALIST PHILOSOPHY OF MAN

The discussion of the linguistic analysis of the language of morals, at least as it is presented by Mr Hare, thus leads us to the same con-clusion as was reached in discussing the more general linguistic theories of language and logic. It is quite untrue that the investigation of the actual uses of language, however useful some of its findings may be for showing how to avoid certain pitfalls of confusion, suffices by itself to instruct us how to think better about either philosophical problems in general or about the more practical problems posed in moral philosophy. To think better about moral or any other questions cannot be done with no other aid than describing the actual uses of language and stating only what everyone admits. To quote Engels for the third time (and now it is a temptation to invoke the Bellman's principle that "what I tell you three times is true"), it requires that we should study "to comprehend the real world as it presents itself to everyone who approaches it free from preconceived idealist fancies" and "relentlessly to sacrifice every idealist fancy which cannot be brought into harmony with the facts conceived in their own and not in a fantastic connection."

Mr Hare set out to show how linguistic analysis of the language of morals would succeed in "helping us to think better about moral questions". But to think better about moral questions requires a philosophical materialist approach applied to the actual social situa-tion of mankind—if you like to put it in such terms, a materialist philosophy of man. Only by such methods can we hope to make moral thinking both practical and rational.

CHAPTER SEVEN

A Place in the Establishment

I. CRITICISM OF LINGUISTIC PHILOSOPHY

HAVING now examined in some detail what I take to be the principal teachings of the contemporary linguistic philosophy, I shall try to reach as balanced an estimate as my preconceptions allow of this philosophy as a whole. This means trying to decide what is acceptable and what is not in its teachings, on their face value, and also trying to see them in their historical setting as representative of opinions and trends in contemporary society.

Like every philosophy, this one took shape in a process of critically considering the views of predecessors and seeking a way out of their difficulties. (That much was true even of the first philosophies that ever existed, for philosophy as a distinctive kind of intellectual exercise did not come into being through the sudden discovery of philosophical problems but rather through a critical attitude directed at earlier pre-philosophical myths and religious ideas.) The linguistic philosophy arose, as I tried to show in the first part of this book, through trying to dispose of problems and get out of difficulties posed by the earlier development of empiricism, and particularly by the application of the method of logical analysis. It is this, rather than any continuity of doctrine, that makes it the continuation of the great empiricist tradition in modern philosophy joined with the tradition begun by the founders of modern symbolic logic. That is how it *arose*, and that is what it *is*. For like a living body, a philosophy is what its genetical constitution makes it.

Linguistic philosophy is a particular way of trying to get out of the difficulties created by the past development of empiricism. And what is most characteristic of this way is its negativity. Problems are solved by showing that they are wrongly formulated, and that there are no such problems. Difficulties are got out of by showing that they arise simply from misunderstanding the uses of words, and that there are no such difficulties. Theories are put to rights by showing that philosophical theory itself is due to misunderstanding, and that there is no need for theories.

This means that characteristic of linguistic philosophy is, amongst other things, a totally unhistorical view of philosophy. It is only a succession of verbal muddles. And this succession is brought to a fortunate stop when linguistic philosophers investigate the actual uses of language. Then, as Wittgenstein said, the solution of the problems of philosophy is seen in the vanishing of the problems. But yet, this solution itself can only be made plausible because the unhistorical approach to past philosophy leads to misunderstanding what philosophers were doing. And it generates its own new myth that "what everyone admits", that is, ordinary factual statement, sets no problems. But when at length linguistic philosophers have decided that the common man is right in denying that a table is a collection of sense-data, all the problems of philosophy are still not disposed of.

Perhaps the best achievement of linguistic philosophy, and its greatest boon to perplexed humanity, is to have at last freed empiricism from the bogey of subjective idealism. But it has done that only at the cost of imposing prohibitions on what we are allowed to say which free us not only of subjective idealism but of any coherent philosophical theory at all, and consequently leave a legacy of incoherence and ambiguity. What is a language game? What is an actual use of language? How demonstrate the logically permissible uses of language, and distinguish them from impermissible ones, if they may be given no foundation? These are among the new difficulties which linguistic philosophy generates in its turn.

Because of its negativity, the criticism of linguistic philosophy must take the form of arguing, not that the kind of theory it puts forward is wrong (for it puts forward no theory), but that the kind of theory it forbids is wrongly forbidden.

Consequently two quite opposite criticisms can be made of linguistic philosophy. These critical points of view face respectively to the past and to the future. On the one hand, it may be criticised for having rejected the whole of what has been called "metaphysics". But on the other hand it may be criticised because, having justifiably rejected metaphysics, it has no theory to put in its place and nowhere to go.

At the end of *My Philosophical Development* (1959) Russell says that "the new philosophy seems to me to have abandoned, without necessity, that grave and important task which philosophy throughout the ages has hitherto pursued. Philosophers from Thales onwards have tried to understand the world . . . I cannot feel that the new philosophy is carrying on this tradition."

What remains far from clear in Russell's account is how this tradition, which the linguistic philosophy has abandoned, is to be carried on. Russell thinks philosophy must be "analytic", and with that no one need quarrel, for the word is vague enough to include almost whatever one wants. But is the analysis which he recommends as contributing to understanding the world still to consist of setting forth the elements of the world to which all true statements refer? In so far as his views at the latter end of his philosophical development remain continuous with those at the beginning, it would seem that he objects to linguistic philosophy because of its rejection of that kind of analysis. Hence he rebuts its criticism of the old logical-analytic method, and considers that the world is eventually to be understood by continuing to apply it. This is to criticise linguistic philosophy on points where a very good case can be made for its being in the right.

Such criticism is always in the end inconsistent and incoherent, for neither Russell nor anyone else has ever been able to say how this kind of philosophical analysis can validate its conclusions. In so far, therefore, as linguistic philosophy is criticised from this point of view, the criticisms fail to hit it.

Criticising the idea that philosophers need only describe the uses of language and not give them any foundation, Mr Ernest Gellner said that "one cannot describe the use-in-the-world of an expression without having a picture of that world first" (*Words and Things*, VII, 3). This remark is true enough, and yet it is incoherent because fundamentally ambiguous. What is this "picture of the world" and how is it to be got? If it is a "picture of the world" of the kind that traditional logical analysis, and before that traditional metaphysics, set out to furnish, then the linguistic philosophers are surely right in proposing to get along without it. Mr Gellner complained that they have contrived a built-in immunity to criticism, because they have always got an answer to everything. But why should they not have an answer to critics whose basic criticism of them is that they refuse to get bogged down in unrewarding problems from the past?

On the other hand, linguistic philosophy may be criticised because, having justifiably said that a critical and analytic approach to the problems of human thinking requires, not metaphysics, but an investigation of the uses of language, it still fails to see that any investigation of the uses of language raises the problem of finding the right approach to the investigation of the life and requirements of people who use language. Having rejected metaphysics, we still require a theory of man, according with and connecting up the different aspects of social life and experience, and demonstrating the foundations for extending and deepening our knowledge, and rationalising and humanising our purposes.

2. THE REVOLUTION IN PHILOSOPHY

Linguistic philosophers claim to be the heirs of a great revolution in philosophy.

This is no new claim. Philosophy has been revolutionised many times since the Church lost its grip on it, but most of the revolutions made little material difference to anyone. There was, indeed, a genuine revolution, not only in ideas but in material life, when the mechanical and chemical sciences started to be a major force of production. And the processes then started must yet compel social changes and changes in ideas more revolutionary than anything seen so far. Associated with this, there was a genuine revolution in philosophy, the main herald of which was Francis Bacon; its completion depends on bringing it home to ideas on man and society. But what of the other revolutions? There was the revolution effected by Locke, which saddled the empirical approach with subjective idealism. There was the so-called copernican revolution effected by Kant, who awoke from his dogmatic slumbers to ask how *a priori* synthetic knowledge was possible. Then there was the revolution which proclaimed that philosophy was logical analysis. And then Wittgenstein in rapid succession led two revolutions, the first setting up the verification principle and the second knocking it down again. At last linguistic philosophers appear as the heirs to revolution, and discover that it all makes no difference at all, and that everything is as everyone except philosophers always thought it was.

Linguistic philosophers have made a thorough clean up of subjective idealism. But what is remarkable is how very little difference they claim this makes to what anyone should say or do. They have taken Berkeley at his word when he said that in philosophy "we are not deprived of any one thing in nature. Whatever we see, feel, hear, or any wise conceive or understand, remains as secure as ever, and is as real as ever . . . That the things I see with my eyes and touch with my hands do exist, really exist, I make not the least question" (*Principles,* 34–5). Hence in the end their only difference from Berkeley is that whereas he said that Matter has no real existence, and only Ideas exist, they say that such statements are unnecessary and meaningless. All that philosophy has ever done, according to them, is to add something puzzling and unacceptable to what everyone admits. Just refrain from doing that, and stick, as Berkeley said he wanted to do, to what everyone admits, and all philosophical puzzles are ended, along with philosophy itself as traditionally practised. This is the final revolution in philosophy—the cleaning up of verbal muddles. The new revolutionary aim of philosophy is simply to cure philosophical confusion.

In the course of its recent development professional philosophy, with its special philosophical problems, has been getting extremely remote from life's problems. Having got so remote, the linguistic philosophers, the most professional of all, discover that all the problems are only muddle and are quite pointless. The outcome for them is to get more remote than ever—simply to devote their professional skill to removing muddles which no one but professional philosophers bothered about anyway. For them philosophical problems arise only from philosophical misuses of words, so that the only problem for philosophers is to clear up one by one the muddles of other philosophers. If that task were to be completed, there would be an end to philosophy as a profession. This is to reduce professional philosophers to the status of those islanders who lived by taking in each other's washing. But fortunately for them, such an activity is self-perpetuating. Their jobs are not in danger. For when they have done with cleaning up their predecessors' confusions, they still find an occupation in cleaning up each other's.

In short, the sequence of revolutions has eventually led to a position where philosophers have no purpose apart from debunking philosophy. They have deprived philosophy of any aim.

Philosophers for some time tried to function as hangers-on of science, seeking to interpret it, to explain what its terms stand for and what its propositions mean. Whatever linguistic philosophy has positively to say is said in the field of logic, where a clarification has been made of the meaning of meaning in the light of investigating the uses of words. This knocked the bottom out of the interpretation schemes of the analytic philosophers—and the linguistic philosophers mistook this for a revolution. In fact, philosophers had been hunting the snark—hunting for what we really mean when we make statements, and for what words really stand for. They had not heeded the warning given to the original snark-hunters:

> "But oh, beamish nephew, beware of the day,
>   If your Snark be a Boojum! For then
>   You will softly and suddenly vanish away,
>   And never be met with again!"

And the end was, of course, that the Snark *was* a Boojum.

So what this revolution amounts to is that an entire line of philosophical speculation has come to nothing. All the real questions of life and of knowledge for life remain, while philosophy has vanished and has nothing to say about them.

3. THEORYLESSNESS

The vanishing which occurred when Wittgenstein discovered the snark makes the linguistic philosophy a puzzle for critics. For what is it? As Mr Gellner complained, it is hard to catch; you may hunt it with thimbles and hunt it with care, but you never quite know what it is you are after. Or as Shakespeare said in a different context, "a man knows not where to have her". As I have tried to show, the linguistic philosophy is not a theory—not even a theory about the uses of language—but a cure or therapy for theories. What is revolutionary (or at least novel) about it is not that it puts forward any new and revolutionary theory about the world and its reflection in human thought, or about man, or about the foundations of human knowledge, or about the purpose of life, or about anything else that has been of interest to those interested in philosophy, but that it denies that any theory is needed on the grounds that none of the questions asked make sense. The end of the line of theorising begun when Locke's critique of "innate ideas" stimulated Berkeley to query "abstract ideas" in general, is the imposition of a general ban on all philosophical theory.

What is distinctive about linguistic philosophy is not what it asserts but what it denies. Its novel and distinctive feature is not that it says that philosophers should investigate the uses of words (which had been said by many philosophers before) but is the adoption of the principle announced by Wittgenstein (and not since argued about, but simply taken as gospel) that the different uses of words have no one thing in common.

From this follows the peculiar methodology of the investigation of the uses of language, which is confined to describing and exemplifying lots of different uses, distinguishing and comparing them, clarifying many particular confusions in the process, and summed up in the precept: only describe, don't try to explain or derive or give any foundation.

This principle and this methodology is what constitutes the therapy for theories and the general ban on theory. For a general theory in any field of inquiry depends on finding something in common. If there is nothing to be found in common, then there can be no theoretical generalisation, no theory but only the description of details and the comparison of cases.

As I have tried to show, there nevertheless *is* something in common to the uses of language. If this is denied, the investigation becomes theoryless, random and aimless, simply creating new problems and confusions of its own, which it cannot deal with, for every old problem or confusion that is removed. But when, in view of this, one seeks to derive the phenomena of language from their source, to explain them, to find their foundation—then one is immediately involved in general theory about man and his relation to nature, the foundations of human consciousness and knowledge, the foundations of human purposes and evaluations—in other words, in questions of philosophical theory involving much more than only describing the uses of words.

There are two opposite approaches to the making and formulation of theory about the human situation and its problems—materialist and idealist. As Engels put it, "The great basic question of all philosophy . . . is that concerning the relation of thinking and being" (*Ludwig Feuerbach*, 2). To explain men's conditions of life and mode of life from their ideas, is idealism; whereas to explain material conditions from material causes, and to regard ideas and aims as arising in response to material conditions, is materialism. Similarly, to consider the world as though created or modelled in conformity to forms and categories of thought, is idealism; whereas to consider the forms and categories of thought as consequential on our need to understand for human purposes the conditions of our existence, is materialism.

Every general theory embodies one or other approach, or an inconsistent mixture of them or effort to reconcile them. And so, as Engels said, "the great basic question" is that of which approach to take. To follow up consistently the approach which is learned from the experience of developing the methods of empirical science, is to take the materialist approach. In the end, the objection to every sort of idealist approach in theory is that it proceeds by false abstraction to conclusions in principle unverifiable. But the objection to the materialist approach is of another kind. It is that it is potentially dangerous to vested interests entrenched behind organised systems of mythology. It is far from true that every anti-establishment movement adopts a standpoint of materialism or that every school of thought which inclines to materialism is anti-establishment; for real life is more complicated than over-simplified definitions of what is "progressive" and "reactionary" would allow. Nevertheless it is true that every establishment has always scented danger in materialism, in case it is carried too far.

Since the modern development of the sciences, most philosophers have been engrosed with making philosophy scientific—but at the same time with avoiding dangerous applications of materialism. This is still true of linguistic philosophy.

Like logical positivism before it, the linguistic philosophy denies or bans the whole question of materialism versus idealism. It is said that such a question "concerning the relation of thinking and being" is a pseudo-question and the product of mere verbal confusion. Like all the brands of recent analytic philosophy, the linguistic philosophy is, in its protestations at any rate, opposed to idealist-type speculations. But it is opposed to materialism as well.

The traditional way of being at once scientific and anti-materialist was established by Berkeley, and consists of saying that statements about material things and material processes really refer to sensations or ideas. But by saying this, empirical philosophers tied themselves up in a knot of solipsism. At length, after they had spent more than two centuries tying themselves up worse and worse in trying to untie themselves, Wittgenstein adopted the expedient of the great Alexander and cut the knot with a single stroke. The therapy for theories did it. The philosophers were now freed from solipsism, but they remained as free from materialism as ever. No wonder they became "engrossed in the exciting work of following up their fresh insights"! It is the distinctive bans against theory—there is no one thing in common between uses of language, don't try to explain anything, don't give anything a foundation—that enabled them to avoid all the traps of solipsism and at the same time to avoid

materialism. But it is these bans, thought up to avoid the old solip-
sistic difficulties while still abjuring materialism, that cause all the
difficulties for linguistic philosophy.

Thoroughly to investigate the uses of language is a good idea for
philosophy. For thought cannot be separated from the uses of
language, so that the most fundamental questions for philosophy are
indeed questions concerning uses of language. It is not the injunction
to investigate uses of language, but the injunction that in so doing
one should "only describe", that is open to criticism as the cause of
all the difficulties and inconsistencies and incoherences which we
have already noted as afflicting the linguistic philosophy. How
distinguish mere superstitions from the products of human acumen?
How relate the ways we use words to the realities we are talking
about? How understand and formulate the logical or formal necessities governing the uses of language, and distinguish them from
the consequences of the grammatical and syntactical rules of particular languages? How understand and formulate the correct ways
of employing categories, and distinguish category-mistakes, which
may be committed in any language, from the mere violation of
idiomatic usages in particular languages? How criticise or find
reasons for moral principles and desirable ends of human association?
These and similar questions are all posed by linguistic analysis, but
the bans on theory forbid their being answered, or suggest answers
which are obviously mere equivocations.

But raise these quite arbitrary bans—and then you open the way to
formulating a general materialist and revolutionary philosophy of
man, totally different from the linguistic philosophy, but at the same
time not contradicting but, on the contrary, incorporating the positive
findings of its detailed investigations.

4. THE LOGIC OF SCIENTIFIC DISCOVERY

The bans against theory imposed by linguistic philosophy are quite
groundless, and the therapy for theories is itself the cause of new
forms of mental derangement.

But the negative ideas that inspire them—the ideas of not looking
for any one thing in common, only describing, not giving any
foundation—do correspond to what has long become the standard
approach, not to the sciences in general, but to the investigation of
human activities. Since to use language is a human activity, it is
quite natural that philosophers who have uncritically imbibed such

an approach to investigating human activities should apply it to
investigating the uses of language.

As Marx observed, the approach developed in economic investigations has consisted of "only describing . . ." As he wrote to Engels
(June 27, 1867), economists became interested in "only the immediate
form in which relationships appear . . . and not their inner connections". And as he wrote in the Afterword to the second German
edition of *Capital* (1873), this enabled some of them to function as
"hired prize-fighters; in place of genuine scientific research, the bad
conscience and the evil intent of apologetic". Similarly in sociology
and history, investigation consists of recording, describing and classifying. Of course, generalisations, even quite bold ones, are allowed
in so far as they simply consist of extrapolating observed correlations
of observable data. But as for fundamental theory such as directs
and unifies the sciences of nature, which not only describes but gives
a foundation, that is not allowed.

Refusal to accept the ban on theory which has for some time been
imposed in the social sciences, and has now been extended by the
linguistic philosophers to philosophy, is supposed to open the door
wide to every sort of unverifiable metaphysical speculation. And
the ban is indeed considered highly expedient, because those who
only describe human affairs keep an open mind about them, whereas
theories close people's minds and turn them into dogmatists and
fanatics. It is alleged that any one thing in common underlying all
human activities must be something invented and unverifiable;
that to explain must be to cook up a fantasy-explanation; and
that to give a foundation must be equivalent to imposing a
dogma.

But why? What is the basis for these allegations?

Scientific method as successfully developed in the natural sciences
always at a certain stage of investigation arrives at conclusions about
something in common, and such conclusions then constitute the
fundamental theories of the sciences. The sciences then leap from the
level of mere description and classification to that of explanation;
from the level of merely recording observations, and correlations of
observations which enable certain predictions to be hazarded, to
that of deeper understanding and control of the phenomena. Thus
the work of such investigators as Galileo and Newton arrived at the
fundamental conclusion that the condition of existence of any body
at any instant is that it has a certain motion of its own and is acted

on by external forces. The fundamental investigations of physics deal with what is common within all chemical and physical change. Since Darwin the biological sciences have proceeded from the fundamental idea that every organism lives by assimilating and adapting itself to an environment. And similarly Marx proposed as the foundation for the social sciences the proposition that men live by associating together to produce their means of subsistence—and for the specialised science of economics, that the one thing all commodities have in common is that they are products of human labour, and that therefore what people are doing when they exchange commodities is to exchange the products of definite quantities of socially-necessary labour-time. What is there unique about human activity which should forbid the same type of fundamental theory being worked out for the social sciences as has been worked out for the natural sciences? And what is there in the simple propositions of Marx which is invented, fantastic or dogmatic, as compared with the fundamental propositions at present found acceptable in other spheres of inquiry?

In *The Logic of Scientific Discovery* Dr K. R. Popper showed that every scientific theory, every scientific generalisation or hypothesis, takes the form of a "conjecture" which is suggested by reflection on experience and practice but has to be *falsifiable*. If it is so framed that nothing could conceivably falsify it, it is not susceptible to any kind of empirical test and so does not belong to the body of science.

For some reason or other, Dr Popper has since concluded that this condition precludes the possibility of any fundamental theory about men and human society. But why such theory should be any more unfalsifiable than similar theories about natural phenomena, he does not tell us. Very fundamental theories become, it is true, very obvious as their consequences get worked out, and no one expects them to be falsified, though conceivably they could be. In that respect, the "fundamental law of motion of human society", which Marx propounded, is in exactly similar case to, for example, the first and second laws of thermodynamics. Various secondary hypotheses about particular things may turn out to be mistaken and have to be corrected, but that does not necessitate the revision of the fundamental theory, nor does this in turn render the fundamental theory unfalsifiable and reduce it to the status of what Dr Popper has called "a reinforced dogmatism". It is not the view that the investi-

gation of human activities should proceed on the basis of fundamental
theory that is dogmatic, but the view that it should not.

In his diatribe *The Poverty of Historicism* Dr Popper recalls that
in section 15 of *Logik der Forschung* he had shown that "every
natural law can be expressed by asserting that such and such a thing
cannot happen"—so that if it does happen, the law is falsified.
"For example, the law of conservation of energy can be expressed
by: 'You cannot build a perpetual motion machine'; and that of
entropy by: 'You cannot build a machine which is a hundred per
cent efficient'." He is certainly right about that. Thus the first and
second laws of thermodynamics make it just too bad for people who
would like to build perpetual motion machines or machines one hundred per cent efficient. And similarly, the fundamental laws governing
the development of social relations make it just too bad for people
who would like to combine full employment, continuous technological advance, a steadily rising standard of living, and a lasting
peace, with maximum profits for employers of labour. If, however,
someone did build a perpetual motion machine, which ran without
fuel, or a machine one hundred per cent efficient, or if somewhere
there did come into existence a society not based on producing the
means of living, or a profit-motivated society without capitalist
contradictions, then the very fundamentals of both thermodynamics and sociology would have to be very thoroughly over-
hauled. Yet nothing of the sort has happened to date, nor is it
likely to.

Evidently, then, there are no grounds for forbidding fundamental
theory concerning human activities. With human affairs and human
activities, as with nature, such theory leads from appearances to
reality, from form to substance, from external relations to inner
connections. These are words horrifying to many empiricist philosophers, and especially linguistic ones. In the past it was thought
advisable to avoid certain words lest we conjure up the Devil. Today
the words just used are abjured lest we conjure up the shade of a
far worse personage, namely Hegel. And yet to do what these words
describe one does not have to become a Hegelian. One does not have
to make anything up, or engage in fantasy or speculation, or
renounce the open mind, or produce unfalsifiable systems of reinforced dogmatism. One does not have to do anything that Newton,
Darwin or Einstein have not taught us to do.

The fact is, that to oppose description to explanation is a totally false antithesis, just as it is to oppose detailed investigation to finding something in common.

Yet the whole basis of the linguistic philosophy lies in posing these false antitheses. Wittgenstein did not make them up, he only borrowed them from what has for long been the official practice of bourgeois social science in opposition to Marxism.

5. PROFESSIONALISM AND SPECIALISATION

A feature of linguistic philosophy, and indeed one of its strong points, is that it has given up the old positivist aim of interpreting the sciences. The sensationism, neutral monism and so forth of the nineteenth century, which was smuggled into the twentieth by labelling it "logical analysis", has been dropped. But by what has it been replaced? By nothing. Linguistic philosophers have had much to say about "scientific language" in its distinction from and relation to "ordinary language", so as to show that there is no contradiction between "scientific" and "common sense" statements —language being used to perform a somewhat different job in the one case from the other. They have also criticised nineteenth-century theories of inductive inference and scientific method, such as were developed out of J. S. Mill's *Logic*. These careful linguistic investigations do show that certain traditional views about the sciences could make their interpretations sound plausible only by misrepresenting actual uses of words. So far, so good. But in its discussion about the sciences linguistic philosophy sets aside any questions of explaining, or justifying or finding the foundation for scientific methods and scientific knowledge. It has no theory, no philosophy of science at all, in the sense of having anything to say about the foundations of the sciences, their interconnections and unity, or their purposes and uses.

Its lack of connection with the sciences is one of the principal indictments against linguistic philosophy made by Bertrand Russell in the last chapter of *My Philosophical Development*. He calls linguistic analysis "triviality" (but this is not the right word, in my opinion), and continues:

"The only reason that I can imagine for the restriction of philosophy to such triviality is the desire to separate it sharply from empirical science. I do not think such a separation can be usefully made. A philosophy which is to have any value should be built upon a wide and firm foundation of knowledge that is not specifically philosophical. Such knowledge is the soil from which the tree of philosophy derives its vigour . . . philosophy cannot be fruitful if divorced from empirical science. And by this I do not mean only that the philosopher should 'get up' some science as a holiday task. I mean something much more intimate: that his imagination should be impregnated with the scientific outlook and that he should feel that science has presented us with a new world, new concepts and new methods, not known in earlier times, but proved by experience fruitful where the older concepts and methods proved barren."

On the other hand, linguistic philosophers usually justify the sharp separation they make between philosophy, as linguistic analysis, and empirical science, on the grounds that professional philosophers are not professionally qualified to discuss scientific questions. Thus Professor Ryle, when delivering the Tarner Lectures, endowed for the discussion of "the Philosophy of the Sciences", excused himself from dealing with the sort of questions dealt with by former lecturers on the grounds that "I am disqualified . . . by the simple bar of technical ignorance . . . I have long since learned to doubt the native sagacity of philosophers when discussing technicalities which they have not learned to handle on the job, as in earlier days I learned to doubt the judgments of those towing-path critics who had never done any rowing" (*Dilemmas*, I). Scientists know their own business, and should be left by philosophers to get on with it.

The old positivist philosophy of science, as I tried to show, got round to justifying the concepts and methods currently used in the social sciences by way of its misinterpretation of the natural sciences. The function of the sciences, it said, could only be to record observations and correlations of observations. Linguistic philosophy, on the other hand, will not thus legislate for the sciences, or mis-interpret them—and very properly not. But the practical outcome remains much the same. Scientific experts know their own business; so the methods adopted in social studies are not to be questioned, and laymen, including philosophers, must accept what the experts tell them. The outcome is that the general practice of "only describe" adopted by experts in social studies is accepted by philosophers and then applied by them to their own speciality of investigating uses of language. Here the practice is turned into a principle, and once that is done it in effect continues to justify the approach to social studies, just as the older positivist philosophy of science did.

That all specialists know their own business is a veritable article of faith in linguistic philosophy. Who is the philosopher to lay down the law for them? And so it turns philosophy itself into another specialised inquiry, an inquiry into the actual uses of language—with its bounds set so as not to overlap with any of the empirical sciences, but within those bounds accepting the same limitations which experts say all studies of human activity should accept.

In this, linguistic philosophy has the feature of carrying the professionalisation of philosophy, which has long been a product of academic life, to an extreme.

This type of professionalism is entirely modern. For such ultra-specialisation is a natural feature of bourgeois society, growing to extremes as technology advances and with it monopoly. The skilled intellectual, formerly a free-lance citizen of the world with his interests flung wide and his fingers in all manner of pies, has more and more become a professional, an employee, a man with a specific job. This has long applied in the sciences, and has intruded into the so-called arts subjects and the humanities, where experts worry each at his own little piece of culture, with as little qualification to scientific judgment as scientists have to artistic or literary or even moral and political judgment. And now the system of specialisation is completed when philosophy becomes strictly specialist.

It is of course true that the development of modern society creates and demands the development of a variety of special skills and special branches of knowledge. But must the specialisation of human skills lead to the specialisation of human individuals? The fate of the individual would become, if this tendency persisted, like that of the unfortunate selenites whom H. G. Wells portrayed as an awful warning to mankind in *The First Men on the Moon*. There some individuals had evolved enormous hands, suited to special types of manual work and to nothing else, and were almost brainless; while others, the intellectuals, had evolved huge heads of various shapes, each with some special part of the brain enlarged while other parts had atrophied. This was to portray how the individual who is trained and confined to one and only one special function is in reality help-lessly subjugated to an impersonal social organisation, for all his individuality. Individuals thus become, as Engels once put it, the subjects and not the masters of their own forces of production and their own social organisation. But rather than accept such a fate it is pertinent to ask ourselves to what ends our social organisation is to be directed by us, and in what ways the special skills and branches of knowledge evolved in social life are to be used for purposes that will enrich the life of each separate individual and of all taken together.—We may ask such questions, but specialist philosophy will not allow them to be answered. The foundations, connections and purposes of human activities are no one's business in the society in which everyone is trained and employed for his own speciality.

6. A CLASS IDEOLOGY

In this context, the characteristic bans on theory of the linguistic philosophy may be studied as a truly classical case of class-conditioned ideology.

In describing the relation of the ideologists of a class to the class they represent, Marx long ago explained that it consists of nothing so simple as that the ideologists are themselves members of the class, or even enthusiastic admirers of it. "According to their education and their individual position," he wrote, "they may be as far apart as heaven from earth." What ties the ideologists to the class they represent is "that in their minds they do not get beyond the limits which the latter do not get beyond in life, that they are consequently driven, theoretically, to the same problems and solutions to which material interests and social position drive the latter practically. This is, in general, the relationship between the political and literary representatives of a class and the class they represent" (*The Eighteenth Brumaire of Louis Bonaparte*, 3).

The owners and managers of monopoly-capitalist economy are concerned in practice with nothing but the expansion and profitability of their own particular branches of industry and commerce, and to this end they hire hands and brains. The linguistic philosophers are certainly not monopoly capitalists and, so far as one can tell, they mostly neither like nor admire monopoly capitalists. Professional philosophers are not capitalists but professional workers employed at universities for specialised purposes of teaching and research, and as such they often show fight on a variety of issues ranging from university grants and salaries to the defence of peace and democratic liberties. Good for them! But what makes them ideologists of monopoly capital is that in their minds they do not transgress the limits which monopoly capital will not go beyond in life.

But of course, there is no irrevocable fate which imposes such limits on the mind of any individual student or teacher of philosophy. As Mr Hare has well said, it is open to everyone to think and to choose as he pleases. Or to use a phrase of William Blake, these limits are merely "mind-forged manacles". It is possible for the mind to break them, if one chooses to try.

The specialism of the linguistic philosophy, and its corresponding idea that everyone knows his own business, accounts for what Russell and many others have felt to be the "triviality" of this philosophy, and also for what Mr Gellner called its "blandness" and "complacency". Blandly and complacently it fiddles away while Rome burns.

It is also because linguistic philosophy has no theory to defend that it is able to defend itself so effortlessly and to answer all comers. It is an extraordinarily self-contained philosophy, as Mr Gellner noted; but it has few possibilities of development. For the same reason, it is simultaneously in a very weak position from which to counter rival philosophies, whether of the right or of the left. Linguistic philosophers are mostly progressively liberal in their practical outlook—the typical standpoint of the professional workers in Britain. Hence on at least some immediate practical questions some of them may tend to keep left, and to place themselves with a foot in the same camp with those whom theoretically they would regard as highly doctrinaire socialists. When it comes to Marxism and Communism, as a theory and as a social policy, they lack argument, and can appeal only to the alleged expertise of anti-Communist specialists and entrench themselves behind rather absurd and crude, though doubtless very honest, misunderstandings of Communist theory and aims. As an example of the latter one might cite Professor Ayer's remarks to the newspapers about dialectical materialism on his return from a visit to the U.S.S.R. However, far more to the point is the feebleness of the linguistic philosophy, as a would-be rationalist, humanist, liberal and empiricist outlook, to deal with all kinds of obscurantist doctrines of the right. All it can say is that these doctrines offend against the logic of language and don't mean anything. This is indeed a feeble barrier to raise against a flood of emotionally-charged preachings and teachings which only too obviously do mean something and use language in a way capable of influencing and directing action.

As a philosophy, the linguistic philosophy is, on all social questions, in relation to all the problems of real life, remarkably quietist, non-partisan and non-militant. It expresses the outlook of would-be enlightened commonsense, getting on with your own speciality to the best of your ability and leaving others to get on with theirs, in the belief that if everyone did so everyone would get on very well in a spirit of mutual good will and compromise. And it is this very outlook which was theoretically adumbrated by Mr Hare as the conclusion of his examination of the language of morals. This is an outlook that has pretty deep social roots in Britain. Over two hundred years ago it was expressed very persuasively by Hume. While Britain ruled the waves and was the workshop of the world it even seemed at times to work very well. It today expresses the very essence of a system of parliamentary democracy in which an elected government is courteously kept in order by a loyal opposition, and no one would dream of seriously challenging anyone's right to make profits out of other people's labour. But those who live by such an outlook have never, for all their professions, been able to stop others from getting away with murder. Indeed, they have been known to get away with it themselves.

7. A PLACE IN THE ESTABLISHMENT

In a capitalist society there are many philosophies which seemingly compete, because they contradict each other, but are socially supplementary. Thus there are religious philosophies and anti-religious ones, rational ones and irrationalist, sceptical doctrines and systems of dogma. There is no such thing as "a bourgeois ideology" which is all of one piece. What is most characteristic of ideology is that it moves amid dilemmas and controversies in which some take one side and some the other. But behind the ever varying disputes of the ideologists there remains in permanence the tough outlook of the men with the power, for whom theories mean nothing except as means of getting their own way or of amusing intellectuals and keeping the masses in order. It is in this context that there has for long been practised what has been harshly called "the treason of the clerks". This is the treason of intellectuals who discuss questions in academic seclusion and put up no challenge to the powerful groups whose interests stand in the way of human progress. Is not this true of many professional philosophers in this age of scientific progress and of mass poverty and barbarous war? What possibilities there are for the advance of the whole of humanity—and how they write them off! This, I think, must be the final judgment on linguistic philosophy. Just now this philosophy is being patronised and encouraged, and is making a clean sweep in British universities. But it cannot possibly satisfy the aspirations and needs of the people, and especially the youth, for theoretical enlightenment and guidance. Nor is it very likely to enjoy its privileged access to university chairs and television screens for very long—any move either to the right or to the left in the balance of British politics would be likely to disturb it.

Yet despite its seclusion and its evasiveness, this philosophy is far from trivial or negligible. In its own very specialised sphere of linguistic investigation it has undoubtedly made discoveries, clarifications and criticisms of lasting value to any philosophy which sets out to comprehend human life and purposes.

The history of philosophy has always been a story of gain and loss. A philosophy earns a permanent place in the body of progressive thought, and achieves ideas not to be erased, by its discoveries, critical analyses and clarifications. The linguistic philosophy has done this, which is more than can be said for some of its contemporary rivals. But at the same time, a philosophy gains only a temporary prestige in so far as it earns for itself a place in the temporary establishment by its expression of the limitations, evasions and prejudices corresponding to the interests and practices of the ruling class.

III

Marxism

CHAPTER ONE

The Dialectical Materialist Approach

I. A CLEAN BREAK

THE fundamental disagreement between Marxism and the linguistic philosophy is not a disagreement between rival systems of philosophical statements—for neither the one nor the other is such a "system". In what, then, does the disagreement consist?

This disagreement does not preclude a measure of agreement on a number of important points. Both agree that knowledge about nature and society, about mankind and the world we inhabit, is to be won only by empirical means, with nothing known *a priori* and everything subject to the tests which scientific method exacts. Both agree in rejecting speculative philosophical theories of the sort which say, as Wittgenstein put it, "it must be like this". And for both there remains nothing of the old types of philosophical investigation which sought to determine "the nature of the world" in advance of the detailed discoveries of the empirical sciences. For both, therefore, the only part which remains of the inquiries philosophers traditionally made independently of the empirical sciences is that which falls within the domain of logic.

The first philosopher to announce this conclusion was Friedrich Engels, who wrote in the first chapter of *Anti-Duhring*: "What still independently survives of all former philosophy is the science of thought and its laws—formal logic and dialectics. Everything else is merged in the positive science of nature and history." It is interesting to compare this statement with what Bertrand Russell was to say a quarter of a century later, in the Tarner Lectures of 1914: "Every philosophical problem, when it is subjected to the necessary analysis and purification, is either found to be not philosophical at all, or else to be . . . logical." By calling a problem "not philosophical at all" he meant that its answer depended on some empirical investigation. And from Russell's saying that logic is "the essence of philosophy" eventually ensued the conclusion drawn by linguistic philosophers that the independent province of philosophy is inquiry into "the logic of our language".

The special character of the linguistic philosophy lies in its specialisation. It continues to regard philosophy as a specialised discipline, that can be pursued independently of every other, with its own special questions and special ways of answering them. These special questions are "logical" ones, which means, among other things, that empirical methods of investigation and test are inappropriate to them—hence philosophy's independence of the empirical sciences. But they are so formulated as to exclude what Engels referred to by using the word "dialectics". Russell began by thinking of special philosophical questions as of the form "What exactly do we mean by so-and-so?" When linguistic philosophers had subjected such questions to "the necessary analysis and purification" they eventually emerged as questions about the actual uses of language.

Philosophy is accordingly pursued with no other aim than simply to settle these very special "logical-philosophical" questions. That is alleged, by some at least, to be a socially very rewarding pursuit. Thus (although he said later that the linguistic philosophers had overdone the specialisation of philosophy) Russell concluded his *History of Western Philosophy* (1946) by claiming: "The habit of careful veracity acquired in the practice of this philosophical method can be extended to the whole sphere of human activity, producing, wherever it exists, a lessening of fanaticism with an increasing capacity of sympathy and mutual understanding. In abandoning a part of its dogmatic pretensions, philosophy does not cease to suggest and inspire a way of life." But this alleged application of specialised logical-philosophical inquiry is entirely extrinsic to the aims of the inquiry itself. And in any case, as the record shows, the actual clarification of the moral and political problems of contemporary society by specialist philosophers has not been impressive.

For Marxism, on the other hand, the aim of philosophy—and for Marxism philosophy is a living activity and not a fossilised doctrine —is to deal with the problems coming up out of our contemporary social life which we, who by now have found out so much by the practice of empirical inquiry, have to face as a result of the advances of science and technology. The aim is to arrive at theoretical clarifications which are of practical value for human life—for formulating human purposes and ways and means of realising them. Such clarifications, of course, cannot be of the finalised or dogmatic variety: they can be arrived at only to be tested in practice as the starting point for further clarifications. For Marxism, in short, the aims of philosophy are out in the wide world, and not enclosed in the study or the lecture room.

It may be said that that means only that Marxism and linguistic philosophers are using the word "philosophy" to stand for different things. The only disagreement is that we each try to do something different but use the same word for it. Such an easy mode of reconciliation will not do, however. For the specialised linguistic philosophy has reached the conclusion that the wider aims of philosophy are formulated only as a result of misunderstanding the logic of our language. Under whatever name they may go, the aims proposed by Marxists for philosophy are said to be illusory ones. And of all the aims those generally called "philosophers" have ever set themselves, the only ones not based on misunderstandings are said to be the specialised ones of investigating the logic of our language. The disagreement is about philosophy and not merely about the use of the word "philosophy". Marxism is not concerned to challenge any particular analytic description of uses of language made by linguistic philosophers. On the contrary, many of these detailed analyses are very accurate. But the linguistic philosophy, with its therapy for theories, opposes Marxism by saying that the sort of philosophy on which Marxism relies, the formulation of the dialectical materialist approach to understanding the world and our place in it, cannot be done at all.

The specialised philosopher's philosophy has become played out. All that is left of it is an investigation of language, producing, as we have seen, some very useful points of logic incapsulated within a great deal of confusion. In specialising in logical questions philosophers forgot the truth of which Russell has reminded them: "A philosophy which is to have any value should be built upon a wide and firm foundation of knowledge that is not specifically philosophical . . . philosophy cannot be fruitful if divorced from empirical sciences." Because logical questions are the only ones conclusions about which do not rely on empirical techniques of investigation, it does not in the least follow that the questions of philosophy are exclusively logical, or that there are not questions of philosophy, distinct from the questions of particular empirical sciences, for which the findings of the sciences are relevant. As Engels so carefully put it, questions of logic (and dialectics) are the only ones surviving from philosophies which tried to decide "the nature of the world" independently of the sciences; but that is not to say that they are the only questions of philosophy.

The attitude of the specialist-philosophy was typified in Wittgenstein's statement that the theory of evolution has no particular relevance to philosophy. "The Darwinian theory has no more to do with philosophy than has any other hypothesis of natural science" (*Tractatus*, 4.1122). But the philosophy for which the discovery of evolution and its mechanism has no particular relevance is, if not completely obscurantist, at least completely irrelevant to human welfare and human understanding.

Jean-Paul Sartre has said that Marxism is "the contemporary philosophy". And that it is, in opposition to both the older philosophy and to the linguistic philosophy which claims to dispose of the older kind. But Marxism cannot be understood, criticised or practised unless one understands that as the contemporary philosophy it works on a new and contemporary conception of philosophy itself. For while there is historical continuity of philosophy, at the same time its questions, aims and relations with other branches of inquiry change, and change profoundly, in the course of historical development, under the influence of the development of technology and the sciences, and of social change.

For Marxism, philosophy is not a separate discipline, it is not a speciality with its own special subject matter or problems or premises. It is not distinguished from other kinds of inquiry by having for its subject matter some particular aspect of things, or by philosophers asking peculiar questions which do not interest other people, or by its making its own startling discoveries (such as that everything is different from what most people have generally believed, or that queer things exist which most people have never dreamed of). But that does not mean that Marxism is content to "leave everything as it is". Very much the contrary!

For Marxism, philosophy is that kind or branch of inquiry which is concerned with criticising, analysing, connecting and making consistent the fundamental concepts employed in different fields of inquiry (concepts of both method and object), with the aim of arriving at a well-founded conception of the human condition and of human potentiality and purpose. Such a philosophy is quite indispensable in the contemporary world, because of the contemporary stage of development of the sciences and technology, and because of the contradictions set up in contemporary social relations and contemporary ideas of life and how to live it. It is indispensable as an element for creating solidarity and common purpose, and waging the struggle for human progress.

Marxists do not agree with confining philosophy to a technical procedure of what Wittgenstein called "the logical clarification of thoughts", or, as he said later on, to describing "the actual use of language". Nor is it a specialised technique with which only specialists are concerned, but an activity which concerns everyone, and of which everyone may judge the results.

The chief evil accruing from the specialisation of philosophy, which culminates with the linguistic philosophy, is that it makes the conception of the human condition and of human purpose at once everyone's business and no one's business. And so it turns thinking on the subject into something alien to and divorced from scientific method and the qualities of scientific rigour and precision. This is then the field for do-gooders and crafty theologians, for impractical idealists and scheming politicians. Philosophy leaves it all to them.

There is need for a clean break, not with any particular line of theorising—for there is no theory left to break with—but with the whole idea of the specialisation of philosophy. There is need to reinstate the old aim of constructing "a world outlook"; but not as a speculation and not as a dogma, not as a theory that "it must be like this", and not only for the sake of satisfying the desire of a few individuals for understanding, but as a social methodology for so understanding human life as to be able to give it a value and purpose for each and for all.

2. A SCIENTIFICALLY BASED VIEW OF MAN

The central achievement of Marx was to apply scientific method to the understanding of man and society. The foundation of the Marxist view of humanity and human relations and purposes lies simply in applying scientific method.

Science, or employment of scientific method, is self-supporting, self-justificatory, autonomous. It does not need any independent philosophical foundation, by reference to any collection of first principles or axioms carrying a supposedly more authoritative assurance with them than belongs to science itself. For the practice of science—that is to say, its whole development as an organised social activity for finding out about what concerns us—is its own justification.

When something has been investigated in a scientific way, then superstitions about it, or merely superficial descriptions, are thereby demonstrated to be superstitions or superficialities. As to how well founded a scientific discovery or conclusion may be, the appeal is to the investigation itself and its applications, and not to any general philosophy, or any collection of general principles, supposedly known independently of and prior to the investigation, by reference to which the investigation itself is to be judged. To be sure, it is always possible to criticise an investigation, or particular steps in it, as being in some way unscientific or not up to standard; and in point of fact, most investigations have to be subjected to such criticism, as a result of which faults are found and fresh investigation is begun. But the standards of criticism are themselves developed in the course of scientific investigation. They may be formulated as principles of scientific method (though no such formulation is ever complete or final); but they are not arrived at independently of the practice of the sciences or introduced into scientific practice from outside.

This, incidentally, is why it is often and notoriously quite difficult to "refute" anyone who maintains such propositions as that the earth is flat, or that species have not evolved, or that social ideas and institutions do not reflect class struggles. For it is very easy to assert such propositions and to quote a lot of familiar experience to support them. But the demonstration that they are erroneous depends on a great deal of painstaking work done by a great many people. Hence even the rudiments of a scientific outlook are the product only of a very long process of social endeavour, and its possession by individuals is the product only of good education.

The growth of the sciences and technology in modern times has discredited the idea that philosophy should tell about the nature of the universe and man's place and purposes in it independently of the investigations of the sciences. For it replaces such speculations by verifiable hypotheses, and compels us to think out our purposes in relation to our real powers and needs.

When the modern development of science and technology began, the feudal philosophy, which at once came under attack, was concerned primarily with tracing and making manifest the design of God, and teaching men to live according to that design. Everything was to be settled on authority competent to reveal the grand design— direct revelation, or the doctrines of earlier philosophers and fathers, or the kind of scholastic logic which laid down that "it must be like this". The eventual culmination and *reductio ad absurdum* of this outlook came when the theologians declined to look through Galileo's telescope, on the grounds that if it showed anything contrary to what theology and philosophy had decided must be the case, then it was the telescope that was at fault and not theology or philosophy.

Bacon proclaimed as a general principle what Galileo acted on, namely, that we can know how things are only by the invention of research techniques to find it out empirically, and not by concluding as to how they are from how they must be. Bacon himself still thought this implied that we should find out bit by bit how God had designed the world to be. But the final implication was that we should not think of the world as created or designed at all.

The notion that whatever is, is made what it is according to a preconceived or pre-existing plan, is one that dies hard. It has certainly long outlived ancient and feudal philosophy and theology. For a long time the notion persisted that the world does and must answer to a design—that it consists of things of such and such kinds moving together and related to one another in such and such ways. The very word "law", as used to denote the invariable rules obeyed by things in interaction, brings in the idea of the enactments of a lawgiver. While mechanics, including "celestial mechanics", was still the premier and model science, this notion continued to be impressed on the sciences. And what Marxists have called "mechanistic" (or better, "metaphysical") materialism consists simply of a generalised formulation of this same notion. It was a plan of creation, the blueprint of the world design—and though Laplace told Napoleon that in his reproduction of the blueprint God was an unnecessary hypothesis, the Emperor, along with more humble and rational people, still found it hard to believe that there should be such a well designed and well regulated creation without any creator.

The advance of the sciences themselves has broken through the conception of design—which no longer survives within the theory of the sciences, but only within philosophy, and popular metaphysics and theology, separated from the sciences. It has become evident in field after field of inquiry that things are not created as they are, but come to be and change in ever varying inter-relationship. There is no master pattern of creation, but the patterns we observe have themselves to be accounted for out of the processes of becoming. The problem of tracing the design of the world, or of finding out the nature of the universe as a whole, or of specifying the essential patterns and forms of things to which particular things must conform, is found to be unanswerable because it rests on a misunderstanding.

The price that has to be paid now for adopting a scientific approach is to exchange revelations about the totality of things, or the nature or design of the universe, for verifiable information about particular things or aspects of the whole. What concerns us is to understand our own conditions of existence, capacities and needs, and other things in relation to them; and it is this that we can do by the methods of the sciences. And such is the approach adopted by Marxism. The core of Marxism is a scientifically based view of man.

A comprehensive theory about man, which is at the same time a way of directing social practice, as Marxism is, is sure to present a dual nature according to how you look at it and how you take it. As what we do changes our circumstances, and so makes us think things out afresh, the guiding theory grows and, like any living thing, changes while remaining recognisably the same. On the other hand, it presents at any time a body of doctrines and policies. You can look at it and take it, therefore, either as a living and growing unity of theory and practice, or as a fixed system of doctrines and policies. Critics of Marxism nearly always look at it in the latter way, and, unfortunately, this is also how some Marxists themselves take it. But a system of dogma cannot be sustained; only a living unity of theory and practice is viable. The view of man which living Marxism works out does not rest on some great and final generalisation about the universe, arrived at by a philosophical argument independent of scientific method, but is itself a case of scientific generalisation.

3. NO FINAL CERTAINTY

No such generalisation can lay claim to that finality and infallibility which it has been hoped would attach to non-scientific or extra-scientific generalisations about the universe as a whole. Of course, the appeal to an infallible person or committee or book or doctrine, whose word will settle any disputed or doubtful question once and for all, is totally foreign to science. The idea that somehow or other we must find an infallible source of truth, because if we have not got certainty and finality we are left in uncertainty, expresses an antithesis which belongs only to pre-scientific ways of thinking. No scientifically based generalisation can be certain and final, because neither the people who made it nor the methods they used are infallible, and because it is subject to test, and so long as it is used the test continues. But that does not mean that it lacks foundation or cannot be relied on for practical purposes. On the contrary, it is supposed final certainties that lack foundation and cannot be relied on.

In the introduction to his *History of Western Philosophy* Russell wrote: "To teach how to live without certainty, and yet without being paralysed by hesitation, is perhaps the chief thing that philosophy, in our age, can still do for those who study it." And that is true enough, for what it comes to is to teach how to judge of the things that concern us, and to frame our purposes, in the light of scientific appraisal. For example, no engineer building a bridge or a dam claims "certainty" for the scientific principles he applies, but he is not "paralysed by hesitation". He manages to design and build the thing, and the principles applied serve also for the detection and correction of mistakes as the work goes along.

However, before the sentence quoted Russell had written: "Science tells us what we can know, but what we can know is little, and if we forget how much we cannot know we become insensitive to many things of very great importance. Theology, on the other hand, induces a dogmatic belief that we have knowledge where in fact we have ignorance, and by doing so generates a kind of impertinent insolence towards the universe." But these statements are very questionable.

The words "little" and "importance" are, as Russell should not need reminding, relative terms. However much we can know, there remains, no doubt, much we cannot know. In other words, relative to what we cannot know what we can know "is little". It does not follow, however, that what we cannot know includes "many things of very great importance". Importance for what? For example, we cannot know anything about galaxies so far away that no signals from them reach us—not even whether or not there are any such galaxies. But are such things "of very great importance" to us? On the other hand, relative to what it is important to know for the sake of human life and happiness, what we can know is not "little" but much. In effect, Russell says that science cannot tell us much of importance about ourselves, for the guidance of our lives—which is simply not true. It is not by forgetting how much we *cannot* know that "we become insensitive to many things of very great importance", but rather by forgetting how much we *can* know.

As for theology, does it induce "a dogmatic belief that we have knowledge where in fact we have ignorance"? We are not *ignorant* of the properties of God as we are ignorant of the properties of objects we are not able to investigate (such as the inhabitants of planets in remote galaxies). What is wrong with theology is not that it claims knowledge where in fact there is ignorance, but that it sets up illusions and calls them knowledge. Russell deplores dogma about God, ultimate reality, the nature of the universe, the totality of things, and so on, on the grounds that it "generates a kind of impertinent insolence towards the universe". To think you know all about everything is certainly, as Russell suggests, deplorable—but not so much because it is impertinent to the universe as because it is a ridiculous illusion of a kind that leads to reckless behaviour.

The objective of the Marxist view of man and formulation of human purposes is to work out something we can continue to live by. And of course, what is ascertainable for such working out is never complete and is never finally certified. There is always work in progress, never work completed. And because human life goes on, and is so varied and variable, the very idea of a complete and rounded off doctrine which would impose a final pattern on to human activities, relations and purposes, is not only in practice an absurdity but a very injurious one at that. It is of the nature of scientifically based ideas to be always under review and revision. So the Marxist world outlook does, indeed, "teach how to live without certainty". And at the same time it teaches how to live "without being paralysed by hesitation". It does not teach that "what we can know is little", or consider it "impertinent insolence towards the universe" to claim that we *can* get to know about whatever is "of very great importance" to us, or when generalisations are pretty well established propose to revise them without good reason. It gets rid of illusions of knowledge and power to increase real knowledge and power—control of natural forces and of our own social use of them.

4. METHODOLOGY

Marxism completes the revolution of philosophy which was begun under the stress of modern science and technology. The advancement of the sciences was facilitated by capitalism and by ideas adapted to capitalist conditions, but its product is communism and communist ideas.

One should say "Marxism" and not "Marxist philosophy", because the latter is a part of Marxism and there is no separable theory of Marxist philosophy. A separable philosophical theory would no more function as Marxist philosophy than a separable head would function as a head. A separable head is only a dummy head, and the same goes for a separable philosophy. Professional academic philosophers, including the linguistic ones, find the absence of any separable Marxist philosophy both puzzling and obnoxious. One can, indeed, write a book expounding Marxist philosophy, but not without bringing into it topics which are not academically recognised parts of "philosophy".

The linguistic philosophers were right in saying that philosophy disappears as a separate theory. But that does not mean that philosophy disappears, but that it finds its place in the organism of integrated and developing materialist theory of man and his place and purpose in the universe. As for the linguistic philosophers, they know that the old philosophy which claimed to operate separately from the sciences has disappeared, but yet they try to keep a separated philosophy going as a very restricted, very specialised discipline. The result is an amazing phenomenon, like the grin of the Cheshire Cat.

Marx called his philosophy "dialectical materialism". This expression does not, however, stand for any set theory of the nature and layout of the universe. And in that respect it is, in its proper use, a quite different kind of expression from, say, "neutral monism" or "logical atomism". The neutral monism of Mach and the logical atomism of Russell were theories about the ultimate elements and structure of the universe. The expression "dialectical materialism", on the other hand, does not stand for any such metaphysical theory, but is descriptive of the approach that is made to forming theories and views about particular matters of interest. The proper use of the expression is, therefore, adjectival rather than substantive. Dialectical materialism is not a philosophical theory about everything, as distinct from scientific theories about particular things or aspects of things. One's theories and views about things are "dialectical materialist", and "dialectical materialism" is not an additional theory.

To make dialectical materialism out to be another theory, distinguished from others by its comprehensiveness, is a "category mistake" of much the same sort as that which makes out that one wears a pair of gloves as well as a glove on each hand. Marxism does not propose a number of theories each about a particular topic, plus dialectical materialism, but all its theory is dialectical materialist. Dialectical materialism is "fundamental" in Marxism in the sense of being the methodology or approach which characterises and unifies all Marxist theory.

Hence it is not a premise from which the rest of Marxism follows by formal deduction. It is not a theory, known somehow *a priori*, which says that the universe "must be like this".

Nor is it a very general generalisation drawn inductively from observation. It does not say anything like: "All things so far examined are material, therefore everything is material", or "All mental processes so far examined are products of material processes, therefore everything mental is a product of material processes", or "All things so far examined contain internal contradictions and are subject to change, therefore everything contains internal contradictions and is subject to change", or "All quantitative changes so far examined have led to qualitative changes, therefore all quantitative changes lead to qualitative changes". It does not formulate super-scientific inductive generalisations, which apply not to particular spheres of being but to being in general.

All these misunderstandings are mere vulgarisations, of a sort that can well, as linguistic philosophers would say, be described as violating the proper uses of language. They derive from the very ancient dogma put forward by Aristotle, that while particular sciences deal with particular departments of being, metaphysics, the supreme science, deals with "being as being". To formulate principles of dialectical materialism is to formulate principles of approach or methodology for making theory, taking into account the relation of human thinking to human existence.

The materialism of this approach consists in its being confined to describing and explaining observable things in verifiable ways (as Engels put it, explaining what happens in the material world from the material world itself), and deriving ideas and purposes from how things are found to be and not, on the contrary, concluding as to how things are from ideas and purposes to which they are supposedly made to conform. And its dialectical character is inseparable from its materialism. Rather than putting forward hard and fast classifications and definitions to which it is supposed everything must necessarily correspond, it takes into account the actual changeability, variability and interconnectedness of things, and regards all classifications, formulas, generalisations and descriptions as provisional, and as relative only to some particular phase or state, or to some particular level of abstraction arrived at in description and explanation.

For the opposite kinds of approach Marxists have customarily reserved the words "idealism" and "metaphysics".

Scientific theory is materialist and dialectical. Or in so far as the theory propounded in any particular branch of science does not bear this character, that is only because that branch has remained at a primitive classificatory and descriptive level, or because of the obtrusion into it of idealist and metaphysical notions surviving from past philosophy. It is no part of the function of dialectical materialism to instruct scientists to make up theory in some way foreign to the sciences. It cannot lay down from first principles the kinds of techniques scientists shall use in their investigations, or the conclusions to which the use of those techniques will lead. On the contrary, its function in relation to particular sciences is to assist in purging their theory of extra-scientific philosophical preconceptions.

For philosophy, the dialectical materialist approach entails that philosophers should not try to arrive at conclusions as to how things are independently of the investigations and findings of the sciences, or to formulate general theories about the nature of the universe going beyond (as such theories are bound to go beyond) what has been scientifically ascertained.

As applied to the conception of man, of the human condition and human purposes, it entails that we should base our conception of what people are, what they depend on and how they live, on trying to find out as much as we can about human relations and how they are constituted and change; and that we should frame our ideas as to how to live and how to conduct our relations, what to do about our conflicts, perplexities and troubles, and what purposes to pursue, on what we have been able to find out about our circumstances, our needs and our possibilities of changing our circumstances in accordance with our needs.

As applied to the conception of the whole environment of man and of man's place in it, it entails that this should become a generalisation from the findings of the separate sciences. The unity of the sciences consists in their all contributing information about man and his environment; and as Engels wrote in the first chapter of *Anti-Duhring*, "As soon as each separate science is required to get clarity as to its position in the great totality of things and of our knowledge

of things, a special science dealing with this totality is superfluous."
Thus the information available already enables us to formulate, as a
basis to go on, provisional general conceptions of the cosmic environment and its evolution, of the origin of life on earth and the evolution
of its forms up to man and human society, and of the development
of chemical processes and relations out of physical ones, of biological
processes and relations out of chemical ones, and of human activities
and relations out of the processes of biological evolution. This is a
conception of man in his environment, derived from the human
practice of searching, changing, understanding and mastering the
material conditions of human life, and reapplicable in that practice.

Finally, there remains for philosophy the independent task of
investigating and formulating the constitutive guiding principles of
human thought itself, which must be observed in assembling information in communicable form and drawing from it conclusions,
evaluations and purposes as a basis for deciding what to believe and
what to do.

Evidently, what Engels called "the science of thought and its laws"
differs from what are generally called empirical inquiries—those of
the special sciences—in as much as it deals with different questions.
The logical character of an inquiry is always definable by that of its
questions; and differences of questions likewise dictate differences in
the methods or procedures appropriate for answering them. The
special or empirical sciences deal with questions of the structure, conditions of existence, interconnections and laws of operation of observed
events (physical, chemical, biological, social, and so on), and their
answers inform our practice in relation to these phenomena. On the
other hand, the "science of thought and its laws, formal logic and
dialectics" deals with questions of how to formulate consistent, concrete, informative statements. "The ideal is nothing else than the
material world reflected in the human mind and translated into
forms of thought", wrote Marx in the Afterword to the second
edition of *Capital*. The "science of thought and its laws" is concerned
with questions of how to make such "reflection" and "translation"
faithful, correct or informative, as distinct from distorting, illusory
or uninformative. Its conclusions, therefore, do not state "matters of
fact" comparable with statements of the special sciences.

Dialectics provides no definite factual information, any more than
formal logic or mathematics. To learn, for instance, that quantitative changes give rise to qualitative changes (a recognised "law

of dialectics") provides no definite information whatever of the sort which can guide practice in any particular context—in contrast, for example, to the laws formulated in chemistry about how the addition of particular atoms in molecular structures gives rise to qualitative chemical changes. And consequently such a "law of dialectics" is not to be established or disestablished by controlled observation and experiment in the way an "empirical law" is. It is, of course, abstracted from observed facts, and exemplified or illustrated in them; but it is not established experimentally. Experiments are required to ascertain just which quantitative changes produce which qualitative changes—but not to establish that these changes are connected, and that a concrete account of phenomena must always connect them.

In this sense, then, the "science of thought and its laws" is, as Engels stated, "independent" of special empirical sciences. But at the same time it is not independent of empirical sciences, if such independence is taken to mean that it could as well be worked out if there were no empirical sciences and without any reference to the conclusions of empirical sciences.

The investigation of the laws of thought has as an important part of its subject matter the actual procedures and work of empirical sciences. We could not first work out a priori how to think, and only afterwards apply the conclusions by thinking like that in the sciences. On the contrary, the practice of the sciences must have been established before we can investigate the principles. Otherwise there would be nothing to investigate. And then the principles can be further applied and developed in the practice. Furthermore, thinking is something people do. It is a performance depending on the human brain functioning as what Pavlov called "the organ of the most complex relations between the animal and its environment" and on the social use of language. An investigation of the laws of thought has, therefore, to start from a conception of people who think, and of what they are doing when they think, and of their use of language; and this conception is properly derived from accumulated findings of empirical sciences and not made up in advance. Otherwise, instead of investigation of the laws of thought there can only be word-spinning about something purely imaginary—thought in the abstract, separated from people using language—as was done, for example, in Hegel's *Science of Logic*.

5. THE CIRCULARITY AND THE TEST OF
DIALECTICAL MATERIALISM

Dialectical materialist philosophy is in its whole procedure essentially circular.

At the start of *The German Ideology* Marx and Engels stated: "The premises from which we begin are not arbitrary ones, not dogmas, but real premises from which abstraction can only be made in the imagination. They are the real individuals, their activity and the material conditions under which they live . . . These premises can thus be verified in a purely empirical way." Starting from "real individuals, their activity and the material conditions under which they live" leads to conclusions about the principles according to which they must think, so as best "to comprehend the real world" and "sacrifice every idealist fancy which cannot be brought into harmony with the facts conceived in their own and not in a fantastic connection". Thinking in that way leads to developing the dialectical materialist conception of man in his environment, of the human condition and human purposes. And this in turn leads round again to a vindication of the starting point, the demonstration that "the premises from which we begin" are indeed "not arbitrary ones, not dogmas, but real premises . . ." and that there is nothing else either to start with or to finish with or to think about on the way.

This circularity of a train of thought which leads back again to where it started (but with a much fuller conception of the starting point adumbrated in the process) does not, however, exemplify the logical fallacy known as "arguing in a circle"—"circularity" or *petitio principii*. A fallaciously circular argument is one which proceeds by formal deduction from premises to a conclusion which is already assumed in the premises. It assumes a conclusion in order to prove it. The dialectical materialist argument, on the other hand, is not a case of formal deduction and makes no claim to prove anything by formal deduction. Its circularity is a demonstration of consistency and completeness. Such circularity is required of a comprehensive philosophy of life.

The objection has been made against Marxism that it is a closed system. And of course it is closed, in the sense that it excludes: it excludes and is meant to exclude "every idealist fancy". But does this make it what Dr Popper has called "a reinforced dogmatism"? According to Dr Popper, a reinforced dogmatism is a system so designed as to be made "secure against any sort of criticism or attack", "a dogmatism which is elastic enough, by using its dialectical method, to evade any attack" (*What is Dialectic?* first published in *Mind*, 1940, and republished in *Conjectures and Refutations*, 1963). His objection against such dogmatism is that it is incapable of any sort of test; for, as he very properly says, a theory can only be tested in so far as circumstances are conceivable which would falsify it.

Marxism has so far proved irrefutable—and that, according to Dr Popper, quite conclusively refutes it. Here he confuses doing well in tests with being untestable. He is like an examiner who disqualifies the candidate on the grounds that he has done so well he must have cheated.

It should be noted, in the first place, that, as Marx and Engels said, "the premises with which we begin . . . can be verified in a purely empirical way". And indeed, "real individuals, their activity, and the material conditions under which they live" are empirically established about as well as anything can be.

As for the general Marxist theory about man and society, it is, as I remarked earlier, far from being in principle or *a priori* unfalsifiable. On the contrary, as with other well founded scientific theories, particular extensions of it do in fact quite often become falsified—but not in such a way as to necessitate completely scrapping the whole theory and starting again, but in such a way as to lead to its correction in detail, amplification and development. As with other well founded and fundamental scientific generalisations, the falsification of the fundamental Marxist generalisations about man and society would be surprising though still not inconceivable.

If there were perpetual motion machines, and the people using them had social relations, institutions and culture functionally unrelated to their way of getting a livelihood, then that would falsify both the laws of thermodynamics and the laws of social development formulated by Marx. That the example is so far-fetched simply shows how well founded and mutually consistent are Marxism and thermodynamics.

But in the second place, it is absurd to demand that the general principles which Marxism applies in making theories should be subject to empirical test in the same way that the resulting theories are. Not even Dr Popper rejects a scientific approach on the grounds that its methodological principles are unfalsifiable. The idealist and metaphysical types of approach to making theories are, indeed, refuted on the grounds that the theories they make are in principle unverifiable. But on the same showing, the dialectical materialist approach is upheld because it rules out every unfalsifiable theory or "idealist fancy". Marxism as a whole is not unfalsifiable; and all it need plead guilty to is that its basic approach has led to the formulation of theories about man and society so well founded as not to be falsified. And these theories themselves lead to the conclusion that that basic approach is the right one to make. What is wrong with that? Where is the reinforced dogmatism? The strength of the theory supports the approach made in making the theory.

We can be as sure as we can ever be sure of anything that we are on the track of the right ideas, when we can formulate laws of thought which lead to thinking about ourselves and our conditions of life in a way that is continually verified and works out in practice, and when those conclusions about ourselves show why those must be the laws of our thought. Marxism is no reinforced dogmatism, but stands or falls by that kind of test. Marxists say it stands, and busy themselves with developing it as a going concern. Let those who say it falls find the evidence and arguments, which they have not found yet, to knock it over.

CHAPTER TWO

The Laws of Thought

I. FORMAL LOGIC

In discussing the linguistic philosophers' investigations of the actual use of language I came to the conclusion that what distinguishes language as a means of communication is its expression of propositions. Language has the unique functions of negating, abstracting and generalising. These, by the way, should not be conceived of as separable or co-exclusive functions—like walking, running and jumping as achieved by moving the legs. For purposes of logical exposition we can, of course, speak about or represent symbolically negation as distinct from generalisation, or generalisation as distinct from abstraction. But all propositions combine negating, abstracting and generalising functions. Every significant sentence negates, abstracts and generalises.

Operations involved in making propositions can be considered purely formally. That is to say, we can investigate the proposition-making operations performed in sentences in abstraction from their meaning. For a *formal* investigation is one which abstracts from meaning. For example, consider such sentences in English as "This rose is red", "This pig has wings", "This triangle is equilateral", and equivalent sentences in English expressed in other idioms (such as "The rose I am calling your attention to has the colour denoted by the word 'red' "), and equivalent sentences in other languages, and then abstract the logical operations exemplified by all those sentences by disregarding the differences of both meaning and verbal construction. To do that is to start a formal investigation of logical operations. This is what is done in formal logic, and to do it the specialised symbolic techniques of formal logic have been worked out (starting from the rather crude and inadequate techniques of Aristotle's *Analytics*, his genius having consisted in inventing a technique but not in perfecting it).

The special business of formal logic is to work out the symbolic techniques of representing logical operations (of key importance was the recent invention of quantification technique); and to construct a logical calculus, with techniques for testing it and demonstrating consistency and completeness. This is a specialised science, allied to mathematics. What it does is to demonstrate how to conduct with consistency logical operations of any degree of complexity.

Those responsible for the great recent advances in formal logic were perhaps motivated mainly by personal interest and curiosity: they wanted to make these demonstrations because they can be made, much as mountaineers wanted to climb Everest "because it is there" (though some, like Russell, were apparently inspired also by a notion that they would achieve a revelation of the ultimate structure of the universe). Certainly, the science that has been achieved is far removed from the paltry practical aim sometimes claimed for formal logic—of being an aid to the art of disputation or catching other people out in logical fallacies. But the fact remains that formal logic, like various branches of mathematics, was not developed until advances of empirical sciences and of technology provided a stimulus and a demand; and though it is not of very much use to human beings as a compendium of instructions on how to think consistently (it is far easier to think consistently than to master such a complicated science as formal logic), it is of the greatest use, and indeed indispensable, for the purpose of programming computers. Machines do not think for themselves, and so a calculus of logical operations has to be available before we can make them think for us.

Formal logic, then, has become a formal science in its own right, with a status like that of mathematics. It is no part of philosophy, but something philosophy has to take into account. In the past, its development was hampered by being treated as a part of philosophy —as a result of which quite different sorts of questions were continually mixed up together and the quite different procedures required for dealing with them were not observed. While Boole, Frege and others were turning formal logic into a science, a whole crop of rival and incompatible philosophical "logics" emerged, ranging from J. S. Mill's to F. H. Bradley's. These can now be written off. But as with other sciences, including mathematics, questions remain about what formal logic does and how it does it, and about its connections with other sciences; and these can properly be regarded as coming within the sphere of philosophical investigation.

2. CATEGORIES

Professor Ryle distinguished what he called the logical investigation of categories from formal logic. While his account of both is open to criticism (and was duly criticised above), the distinction is of profound and far-reaching philosophical importance.

To start investigating categories is to become concerned with meaning, and to depart from purely formal inquiry. For this reason there is not and cannot be anything like a calculus of categories, nor are symbolic techniques like those of formal logic and mathematics applicable. At the same time, while not a formal inquiry, an inquiry about categories is not an empirical inquiry either—for its findings are not subject to empirical test. As Ryle has said, a "category proposition" is a generalisation to contradict which leads to absurdity; and so it is certainly not empirically falsifiable, like an empirical generalisation.

Hume proclaimed that whatever was neither formally certified nor empirically verified should be committed to the flames. But the very fact that he said so showed that he could not have meant what he said, for such a principle is self-destructive. The conclusions he himself arrived at were neither formally certified nor empirically verified, nor could such conclusions be. Hume was, in fact (in a rather unmethodical way, but he deserves perpetual respect as a pioneer), undertaking an investigation of categories—especially in his famous discussions about material objects, minds and causality. There are no good reasons for committing his philosophical writings to the flames, though there are good reasons for concluding that he made mistakes in them.

It is an old prejudice in philosophy that all statements must be either "empirical statements" or else be "known *a priori*", that is, independent of experience. This dichotomy goes back to Hume, and was further fixed in the minds of philosophers by Kant. But it is totally false and misleading, like so many other hard and fast antitheses. Thus mathematical principles are not established empirically like the generalisations of the empirical sciences, but they are certainly derived from experience and not known independently of experience. And this is true also of the principles concerning "categories" which are of primary interest to philosophy.

The systematic or methodical investigation of categories has to do with the word-function of abstraction. Formal logic deals with abstraction only in the way of calculating the logical operations involved in abstracting a conclusion from premises. For instance, from information "All A's that are B are C", plus information that "This A is B", can be abstracted the conclusion "This A is C". This is the sort of abstraction a computer can be programmed to perform. And of course, when very complicated information is fed into it, it can abstract conclusions, as required, which human brains would make very heavy work of abstracting.

But there are procedures of abstraction depending not on the logical form but on the meaning. For instance, from information "This rose is red" may be abstracted "This rose is not white"; and that abstraction does not depend on the logical form of propositions but on meaning. Suppose a rose grower had a computer to tell him how many roses of different colours he had sold, so that for each sale it registered the colour of the rose. It would not work unless in programming it he had been guided by the principle: "These are the colours of roses . . . and a rose of one colour is not of any other colour". But that is not a proposition of formal logic, and is not demonstrable or certifiable by procedures of formal logic. Suitably generalised (for it applies not only to roses), it may be called, after Ryle, a "category proposition".

Propositions stating colour may be termed a category of propositions, distinct from, for example, those stating shape or weight. And obviously, there are principles or rules for abstraction ("category propositions") dealing not only with abstracting one proposition of a given category from another of that category (such as deriving "This is not white" from "This is red"), but also for abstracting propositions of other categories (such as deriving "This has a shape" from "This has a colour"). To go against category rules, or "category propositions", always results in absurdity or non-informativeness—such as saying that "So and so's red roses are white", or "So and so's roses have no shape or size".

Such examples or the conclusions of an investigation of categories may well be regarded as trivial and obvious, so that such an investigation may be thought trivial and unnecessary. However, two points are already worth noting.

The first is that a computer has to deal with definite categories of information, and has to be instructed and programmed according to the rules for those categories. The people who build and instruct computers must know those rules before they can make machines that obey them. Computers themselves could not conclude to such rules by any process of their own mechanisms.—This is an illustration of the fact that human thought, on the one hand, and what computers do and can conceivably be made to do, on the other, are by no means the same. A machine can quite well be made to observe and record observations and generalise and abstract from what it observes. But just as it does not fall in love with other machines and produce little ones, or co-operate with other machines in socially producing and distributing their means of sustenance, so it lacks the capacity of developing for itself the categories of thought and the rules for operating with them. It is not made of the right stuff for doing such things. In an age of automation and computation it is important to work out with great care principles concerning categories as well as a calculus of formal logic.

Secondly, even some of the most apparently trivial category rules are not so obvious as they look. Take colour, for example. Information about how things are coloured includes not only such items as "This is red" but also "This looks red". Thus it can be stated: "This is red, but it looks yellow in this light". Again, how tell the colour of, say, the sunset on Mars, when there is no one there looking at it? Indeed, what does anything look like when no one is looking at it? Such considerations show that it would be mistaken to regard information about colour as information about certain simple qualities which either do or do not belong to things irrespective of their relationships with other things. Propositions specifying colour are evidently *relational* propositions, though this is disguised by the verbal forms in which they are often expressed. Hence there is plenty of room for painstaking investigation of the categories of propositions even in the case of such apparently trivial examples as that of propositions stating colour, and it yields conclusions which are far from obvious at first sight.

This kind of discovery of the not so obvious in the obvious was what originally led to the use of the expression "dialectics". Thus Plato illustrated dialectics by holding up a finger and asking if it was short or long. It was short in relation to longer things, and long in relation to shorter things. From this he reached the important and by no means obvious conclusion (essentially a conclusion about category, though he did not put it in these terms) that propositions specifying length are a category of relational propositions. From this, incidentally, it already becomes evident that there is no sort of incompatibility, as has sometimes been suggested, between dialectics and formal logic. To say, as Plato said, that a finger is short and long—or short and not-short, and long and not-long—does not contravene the formal logical principle of non-contradiction.

Of very great interest are categories of propositions at what may be termed different levels of abstraction, together with the connections between them. For example, to describe and distinguish things in terms of their sensible qualities (such as colour) is to operate at a certain level of abstraction. But information about what produces these sensible differences (for instance, what makes things look one colour rather than another) belongs to another level of abstraction and is formulated in propositions of different category. And the second category of information does not replace the first, but connects with it. Together these different categories of information constitute information about (in the case of colour) how bodies reflect light and how that affects our senses. This kind of connection of propositions at different levels of abstraction and of different category is of great importance in the management of information. For on it depends the proper assembly of relatively abstract items of information into something more concrete—filling in and generalising our conceptions of the matters that concern us.

All information is abstract (how could it not be?). And what I have just called the management of information (which is the practical business of thinking, as distinct from what Engels called "idealist fancy") consists of assembling abstractions. Information is not only negative and positive (for example, "This rose is not white" and "This rose is red"), and more or less generalised ("All roses have thorns" and "All red roses have thorns"), and more or less abstract ("This rose is red" and "This rose is red and sweet-smelling")—all of which are differences of form and are treated in formal logic. It also exemplifies a host of what may be called different modes of abstraction, which are not distinguished in formal logic because they are not formal differences. For example, to talk about colour and to talk about shape, to talk about sensible appearance and to talk about physical-chemical constitution, to talk about internal structure and to talk about interaction and interrelation with other things, and so on, all exemplify different modes of abstraction.

The sense in which the much-abused word "category" is used in the context of a logical investigation of categories is the sense in which category of proposition corresponds to mode of abstraction. In general, different categories of proposition result from different modes of abstraction. To take a very simple example. "This is red" and "This became red in the process of being painted" are propositions of different category—the first exemplifying what one might (in semi-Hegelian language) term a category of "being" or "quality", and the second of "becoming" or "causality". Their connection by way of abstraction is evident, since the first proposition is relatively more abstract than the second, and could be called an abstraction from the second. In both information is assembled, and the assembly of information in the second is such as to render a more concrete account of the same thing of which the first gives a more abstract account.

To investigate differences of category, therefore, is not simply to describe the ways words are permitted to be put together in various languages, as Ryle and other linguistic philosophers have supposed. It is to investigate modes of abstraction and their assembly, which are expressed in the permissibility and impermissibility of combinations of words.

3. DIALECTICS

In his paper on *Categories* Ryle said that "category propositions" describe and distinguish "the logical type" of different expressions used in statements, and so concern "only collocations of symbols". But he added that this does not equate them with "the propositions of philologists, grammarians or lexicographers . . . Nor does it imply that they can say nothing about the 'nature of things'. If a child's perplexity why the Equator can be crossed but not seen, or why the Cheshire Cat could not leave its grin behind it is perplexity about the 'nature of things', then certain category-propositions will give the required information about the nature of things. And the same will hold good of less frivolous type-perplexities."

Because he confined philosophy to describing "collocations of symbols", Ryle may be justly likened to Horatio. At the same time, because he set philosophy the task of formulating category-propositions, and considered that this (especially in its "less frivolous" applications) would throw some light on the "nature of things", it may be said of him that there is more in his philosophy than he dreamed of. For the yield of this investigation is nothing more nor less than the principles of materialist dialectics.

Dialectics, as an investigation and discipline distinct from formal

logic, deals with categories—and so studies and distinguishes modes
of abstraction and assembly of abstractions. Evidently, for the
purposes of managing information there is required not only the
observance of formal consistency, as enjoined by formal logic, but
also the observance of the rules of abstraction and assembly of
abstractions, as enjoined by dialectics. Dialectics comprises the procedures for arriving at less abstract and more generalised working
conceptions of ourselves and our environment by the proper conduct
and assembly of the different modes of abstraction.

Thus, for example, it is generally agreed among Marxists that
dialectics has to do with understanding things in their inter-relations
and changes, as opposed to the "metaphysical" way of considering
things separately, out of relationship and in abstraction from their
changes. Evidently, to get a concrete picture of any phenomenon
we must assemble the available information in a way that adequately
reflects the actual interconnections and motion of things, and thus
understand the separate properties of things, and their temporary
states, as products of processes of interaction and change. The dialectical approach consists in doing this—its "laws" are the laws
for doing it. As Lenin observed, the essence of dialectics is "the
concrete analysis of concrete conditions".

This makes the word "dialectics" a many-purpose one—as it is,
indeed, in common use. Thus one may speak of "dialectics" in
general, as the universal method of procedure of right thinking, and
also of "the dialectics" of any topic one chooses to mention. One
can speak of "the dialectics" of the thought-process in general, as
management of information, and also of "the dialectics" inherent
in the subject matter of thought. But there emerges as of the very
greatest interest and importance the investigation of the most universal modes of abstraction and assembly which are variously
exemplified and applied in dealing with *any* subject matter on which
information may be abstracted and assembled.

Hegel has the credit of being the first to open up this department
of investigation, in his *Science of Logic*. True, he obfuscated the
whole issue by working with a merely mystical conception of
category. But as Marx said of him (in the Afterword to the second
German edition of *Capital*): "The mystification which dialectic
suffers in Hegel's hands by no means prevents him from being the
first to present its general form of working in a comprehensive and
conscious manner. With him it is standing on its head. It must be

turned right side up again, if you would discover the rational kernel within the mystical shell." If only linguistic philosophers could so far overcome their prejudices as to ignore the mystifying misuses of language in Hegel, they might be able to extract the "rational kernel" for themselves, and break out of their own shell. As Engels remarked in the *Dialectics of Nature* : "If we turn the thing round, then everything becomes simple, and the dialectical laws that look so extremely mysterious in idealist philosophy at once become simple and clear as noonday."

To this department of investigation belongs, for example, the investigation of the rules of qualitative and quantitative determination and their connection—the so-called "law of the transformation of quantity into quality". What is subject to qualitative determination is subject to quantitative determination, and *vice versa*; and these are so connected that alteration of the one is not independent of alteration of the other. Again, there belongs too the investigation of the so-called "unity and interpenetration of opposites" and of "dialectical contradiction". To describe processes, motions and operations always involves the deployment of polar oppositions, such as "attraction and repulsion", "increase and decrease", "growth and decay", "addition and subtraction", "forwards and backwards", and so on.

But investigation of universal laws of dialectics remains an open field. It is something that has been projected but not yet systematically done. And the laws that have been written down, following Hegel, still lack both the precision of formulation and the systematic derivation to be expected of anything that can rank as science. The laws of dialectics should be, as Engels claimed, "as simple and clear as noonday". If they are not, and if their interconnection is not evident, that is because not enough work has been done on their formulation. (A case in point is the so-called "law of the negation of negation".)

This may perhaps be thought a great failing. But to work out reliable theory it is not necessary first to work out all the principles which reliable theory exemplifies. On the contrary, no more than you have to work out all the laws of locomotion before you can walk do you have to work out all the laws of thought before you can think. It has been reported that Marx was always meaning to write a systematic treatise on logic and dialectics. But he never did. And even if he had tried, he might not have succeeded. For such an

enterprise calls for a lot of highly specialised work, and most of this
was done afterwards, and some of it by linguistic philosophers. To
deal with dialectics requires a grounding in formal logic. Engels
did make a few remarks about formal logic in his notes for the
Dialectics of Nature, as well as about mathematics in *Anti-Duhring*;
but today these date badly. The well known practicality of Marx
prevented him from writing his treatise on logic and dialectics, not
only because as a practical man he had other things to do, but also
because it is never practical to undertake tasks for the fulfilment of
which the conditions are not ripe. For the same reason he never
tried to work out the detailed principles of socialist planning, which
his followers now have to wrestle with. But what he did work out
provides a secure starting point for socialist planning and socialist
philosophy alike. He did establish the dialectical materialist approach,
leaving it to his successors to work out the abstract principles of its
logic as that becomes necessary for purposes of understanding,
criticism and further development.

4. THE LAWS OF DIALECTICS

I have already remarked that the findings of an investigation of
categories are distinguished from the propositions of formal logic
in that they are not formal, and so are not to be symbolically constructed and tested in the way logical formulas are. But they are not
empirical generalisations, and so are not comparable with even the
most fundamental laws formulated by empirical sciences. For
instance, the laws of thermodynamics deal with transformations of
energy from one form into another. But "the law of the transformation of quantity into quality" is not a comparable law, just
as "transformation of quantity into quality" is not comparable with
"transformation of mechanical motion into heat". These exemplify
different uses of the word "transformation".

In the *Dialectics of Nature* Engels called the laws of dialectics
"the most general laws", and said that they were "abstracted" from
"nature and human society". But if he meant, or is interpreted as
meaning, that laws of dialectics are comparable with, say, laws of
motion as formulated by Newton or Einstein, differing only in being
even more general, then that simply exemplifies confusion in the
use of the words "law" and "general" (admittedly very confusing
words), since the latter are empirical laws and the former are not.
There is not a shred of evidence to suggest that Engels was actually

guilty of any such confusion—that he really thought that, for example, the "law of transformation of quantity into quality" was a transformation law of the same logical type as, say, the first law of thermodynamics. Some of his interpreters did afterwards perpetrate such confusion—but Engels himself simply did not deal with such logical questions, which had not yet been raised at the time he was writing. The point can, if one likes, be put like this—that the difference between these laws is not only a quantitative difference, of degree of generality, but a qualitative difference; they are different *kinds* of law, or exemplify different uses of the word "law".

Perhaps the difference can be most perspicaciously brought out in terms of Dr Popper's criterion for a "scientific" (or empirical) law. Such a law, he said, must be falsifiable. Sure enough, the laws of thermodynamics, for example, are falsifiable, even though never actually falsified. But principles or laws concerning categories, including "the most general" ones, or universal "laws of dialectics", are not falsifiable—or if they are, they are not correctly formulated. For instance, certain scientific or empirical laws stating and forecasting how particular changes happen state and forecast how certain quantitative changes bring about certain qualitative ones. Such laws are subject to empirical test (falsifiability), as to whether the connection of qualitative with quantitative change is always in fact as stated. But that qualitative and quantitative changes are always connected is not similarly subject to test. That they are connected in a particular way in a particular case has to be empirically established or disestablished—but not that they are connected. Thus "the law of the transformation of quantity into quality" is, as Engels said, exemplified in scientific laws, and in that sense it may be said to be "abstracted" from the same factual data as are generalised in scientific laws. But at the same time it is not a more general empirical law, comparable to scientific laws, and the method of arriving at its formulation and of testing its correctness is entirely different.

In his inaugural lecture at Oxford (*Philosophical Arguments*, 1945) Professor Ryle said that "a pattern of argument which is proper and even proprietary to philosophy is the *reductio ad absurdum*". He was evidently referring to those arguments in philosophy which concern, in his phraseology, the logical investigation of categories. Correctly formulated principles concerning category, or "category propositions", are such that their breach results in "absurdity"—and this is the test of such principles. That (I believe) is in principle correct. But he had earlier ended his paper for the Aristotelian Society on *Categories* by asking: "But what are the tests of absurdity?" And this vital question was still not answered. In criticising, above, the linguistic interpretation of category, I suggested the way of answering this question.

The kind of absurdity that results from breach of category principles is not the same thing as violation of the rules of the actual or significant use of given languages. For example, it is no more a violation of those rules to say that quantitative changes can go on and on indefinitely without involving qualitative changes (which Hegel and Marx said should not be said), than it is to assert the independence and immortality of ghosts which temporarily inhabit the machines of our bodies (which Ryle and Marx said should not be said). The "absurdity" of such statements consists rather in what I have called their uninformativeness.

Those very simple and obvious examples of "category mistakes" which linguistic philosophers quote from Lewis Carroll are of this kind. For example, when the White King misunderstood Alice's statement that she "saw nobody on the road" he was expressing the curious view that the person Nobody is the person who is there when no visible or tangible person is there. This raises a laugh; but its "absurdity" is of the same kind as that perpetrated by primitive peoples and theologians who say that your immortal soul is that part of you which thinks and feels and acts when you yourself have ceased to think or feel or act. Of the same order of absurdity is the statement that the Cheshire Cat's grin remained after the Cat had disappeared. Some such absurdities are very easy to recognise, and are funny; and others are not so easy to recognise, and are serious. To the latter class belong those absurdities which result from breach of the general principles of materialism and dialectics. The point of these general principles, and what makes their formulation worthy of being called "the science of thought and its laws", and their observance as essential for right thinking as is observance of the laws of formal logic, is that they are the principles for maintaining informativeness and removing illusion and fantasy.

We can very well speak, if we want to, in violation of laws of dialectics, of things which are not affected by other things and are eternal, indestructible and changeless. Language permits us so to speak, and it involves no grammatical or syntactical error, no violation of principles of formal logic and no logical contradiction. But if we try to describe a world consisting of such things, then we are describing something unrecognisable and unverifiable. For how could we recognise anything or verify its existence unless it affected us in some way? And how can anything which is fixed and changeless and does not interact with anything else possibly so affect us? To speak of such things is to speak of things in principle unverifiable —like, for example, Leibniz's monads. Statements about them are uninformative or, as Engels put it, "fantastic", or as Ryle puts it "absurd".

Similarly with quantitative specifications unconnected with qualitative ones, or with processes free of opposition or dialectical contradiction. For example, we can very well describe a physical system in which the law of gravity did not hold in the form we know it. Thus bodies might attract each other with a force not inversely proportional to the square of their distance; or in the formulation made by general relativity theory, quite different geometries might apply. But what of a physical system in which forces acted between bodies but none of these forces were attractive? It is not very hard to see that such a system is an "absurdity". One can talk of such a system, but it is mere "fantasy". So in *Dialectics of Nature* Engels wrote about the necessary correlation of attraction and repulsion in physical systems, and showed that this was a case of the more general principle of "unity of opposites". Again, one can speak of a system in which quantitative changes did not involve qualitative ones. But how could we recognise or measure any quantitative changes unless there were recognisable qualities connected with them? And how could we formulate generalisations or "laws" governing such changes except in terms of such connection? As Engels put it in *Dialectics of Nature*, "the dialectical laws are really laws of development of nature, and are valid for theoretical natural science". They are "laws of development of nature", and theoretically "valid", because no material system and its laws could be described in concrete terms except in conformity with the dialectical principles. Hence they are always and necessarily found exemplified in natural as well as social science, whenever we undertake "the concrete analysis of concrete conditions". Their formulation is first suggested as a result of observing their occurrences and exemplification (somewhat as mathematics is first arrived at from observation and practical application, and not produced ready-made *a priori* out of people's heads, the concepts of number and measure, just like those of quantity, quality, opposition, and so on, being derived from experience). But at the same time, once they are formulated, the necessity of dialectical laws, and consequently their logical distinction from empirical laws, can be demonstrated, and their formulation be then systematically corrected and made more exact in the procedure of demonstration.

5. DIALECTICS AND MATERIALISM

An important consequence of this account of dialectics is that it renders invalid the separation so often made in expounding Marxist philosophy between materialism and dialectics.

In his little book on *Dialectical Materialism* (which was extracted from the larger *History of the Communist Party of the Soviet Union,* 1938) J. V. Stalin separated materialism from dialectics by saying that the former was "the theory" and the latter "the method". Mechanistic or pre-dialectical materialism is, perhaps, "a theory"— that is to say, a "metaphysical theory" which attempts to state the ultimate constitution and structure of the universe. But dialectical materialism is not "a theory" in that sense, or in any sense of the word in which "theory" may be contrasted with "method". The fact is that the derivation and substantiation of the principles of dialectics is at the same time that of the principles of materialism— they are inseparable and are principles of exactly the same sort, being demonstrated in terms of the correct marshalling of categories in informative discourse.

Thus, for example, Ryle was quite right in calling the idealist theory of "the ghost in the machine" a "category mistake", even if one may disagree with his account of category. And so is it a category mistake to adopt the more general idealist approach that "thinking is prior to being", as it is to adopt such typically "undialectical" ideas as that things are what they are independent of their relations with other things and of their modes of coming into being and ceasing to be, or that qualitative and quantitative changes take place independently, or that processes proceed free of contradiction. To think in a consistently materialist way is to think in a dialectical way and to think in a consistently dialectical way is to think in a materialist way. These ways are the laws of thought, because they are the ways of assembling information, keeping thought within the bounds of informativeness and excluding illusion and fantasy. Materialism is not "a theory" that requires experimental verification and could be falsified, any more than it is a "metaphysical theory" which is somehow established *a priori*; nor are the laws of dialectics laws that require experimental verification and could be falsified; for any verifiable theory is materialist and dialectical.

The "mystification which dialectics suffers in Hegel's hands" was due to the way he separated dialectics from materialism, and tried to base formulation of laws of dialectics on idealist theory. The way Marx began to put this right was by getting rid of "preconceived idealist fancy". Hegel started with a preconceived and absurd idealist theory, to the effect that Thought or The Idea exists timelessly and independently of anyone's thinking, and that the world is created to be as Thought thinks it. Then (supposing himself to have what Ryle and others would now call "privileged access" to The Idea) he tried to write down in a book the sequence of Categories (in this context capital letters are used as a mark of respect for timelessness) in accordance with which the world is created. The result, naturally enough, was "mystification". Marx, on the other hand, did not start with any "preconceived idealist fancy". He started from "real premises from which abstraction can only be made in the imagination . . . the real individuals, their activity and the material conditions under which they live". He started to work out how these real individuals must think and assemble their information in order to inform their practice. That is what he meant by turning dialectics "right side up again".

To work out the laws of thought is to work out the principles in accordance with which we must think in order to inform our practice. It is not, therefore, an *a priori* inquiry of the sort Kant imagined, but it starts, as Marx and Engels said, from "real premises" which are "verified in a purely empirical way".

At the same time, it is by no means the same as stating the laws in accordance with which subjective processes of thought proceed, as contrasted with the laws (studied by empirical sciences) in accordance with which objective processes proceed. Indeed, such a misunderstanding is an absurd one—for thought-processes are just as "objective" as any other processes, and to find out how they proceed requires, as for any other processes, examining the evidences of their occurrence. The generalised principles of materialism and dialectics no more provide information, additional to that obtainable by empirical means, about thought-processes and how they proceed than they do about any other processes and how they proceed. And

they apply equally to both. They are not statements of information
but principles of its assembly. But as such they do serve to correct
erroneous views (those that take the form of illusion and fantasy),
and consequently to specify the category-formation of truthful views.

It is in this sense (and a very important sense it is) that the working
out of the principles of materialism and dialectics may be said, in
Ryle's words, to inform us about the "nature of things", and of
their reflection in human thought; or, as Engels put it (*Ludwig
Feuerbach*, 4), materialist dialectics becomes "the science of the
general laws of motion both of the external world and of human
thought". How things are and move (the forms of interconnection,
the transformations of quantity into quality, the contradictions), and
how this movement is to be reflected in our thought, is the discovery
of materialist dialectics.

Principles of materialist dialectics, then, are expressible in less
negative and "frivolous" terms than Ryle supposed, when he
observed that the conclusion that "the Cheshire Cat could not leave
its grin behind it" enlightened us "about the nature of things". For
what we learn from these principles is of considerably greater and
more general practical importance. Thus, for example, the conclusion
that "it is not the consciousness of men that determines their being,
but their social being that determines their consciousness", or, more
generally, that "being is prior to thinking", is at once more generalised than a principle about cats and their grins, and what we learn
from it is in practice more important for us—since in practice no
one gets led astray by supposing that grins exist independently of
faces, whereas many get led astray by supposing that thinking or
consciousness exists independently of real individuals and their social
being. Similarly with conclusions about the dependence of qualitative changes on quantitative ones, and other "laws of dialectics".

If we consider principles of materialist dialectics, such as those
mentioned as having been first formulated by Marx and Engels,
my contention in this chapter is that they evidently differ from the
generalisations arrived at by the empirical sciences in that they are
not established and tested by the same type of directed observation
and empirical test, and that their applicability in the guidance of
practice is therefore also not of the same sort. Their character and
application is essentially that of "laws of thought", as Engels already
emphasised when he included "dialectics" along with "formal logic"
in "the science of thought and its laws", stressing that it was

demonstrable "independently" of "the positive science of nature and history".

However, this does not entail, as Kant supposed in his fanciful theory of "synthetic *a priori* knowledge", that they are somehow spun out of the inner resources of the mind and imposed by the mind upon "the phenomenal world" which it constructs for itself as its "object". On the contrary, they are indubitably and universally *true* of the processes of the *real* world, which we get to know about, but which proceed in accordance with these "laws" independently of our knowing them. Such a contention can appear paradoxical only to those who are still under the spell of the old antitheses of *a priori* and *a posteriori*, or of "analytic" versus "synthetic" knowledge.

The distinguishing feature of principles of materialism and dialectics is that they concern *categories*. They lay down correct ways of assembling relatively abstract items of information in order to arrive at concrete and informative conclusions. Category principles, considered in their aspect as reflecting objective reality or "the nature of things", are characterised by their absolute generality (corresponding to Aristotle's conception of truths true of "being as being"), in distinction from generalisations of natural or social sciences which deal with particular classes of phenomena. As I have said, this "quantitative difference" of degree of generality marks a "qualitative difference" in the character of the generalisations.

Of course, as Engels often and justifiably insisted, such generalisations, far from being spun out of the mind from its own inner resources independent of all experience (the conception of the mind spinning anything out of itself independent of experience is absurd) are arrived at as a result of experience. And naturally, errors or crudities in their formulation may be detected as a result of contradictions with experience. But the test or demonstration of the correctness or otherwise of such generalisations goes beyond merely ascertaining their empirical confirmation. Their demonstration depends on demonstrating, not as with empirical laws that they are not in fact falsified, but that to imagine their falsification results in "absurdity" or "fancy" in the sense of uninformativeness.

For example, Marx's principle that "social being determines consciousness" was arrived at by studying the facts of human history, and criticising the conclusions reached by historians and sociologists who proceeded on an opposite principle. But in its generalised form, "being is prior to thinking", this principle is one which must necessarily be observed in assembling information, because not to do so is to introduce uninformative fancies in principle unverifiable. In that respect it differs from Marx's formulation of the basic law of development of human society, which dealt with the particular way in which men live by developing a mode of production.

Thus Engels, with complete consistency, said on the one hand that laws of dialectics are "laws of thought", and on the other (in the preface to *Anti-Duhring*) that "there could be no question of building the laws of dialectics into nature, but of discovering them in it and evolving them from it". He went on to say that "the revolution which is being forced on natural science by the mere need to set in order the purely empirical discoveries . . . must bring the dialectical character of natural events more and more to the consciousness even of those empiricists who are most opposed to it . . . It is possible to reach this standpoint because the accumulated facts of natural science compel us to do so; but we reach it more easily if we approach the dialectical character of these facts equipped with the consciousness of the laws of dialectical thought."

CHAPTER THREE

Socialist Humanism

I. MAN AND THE UNIVERSE

THE philosophical family in which both the linguistic philosophy and Marxism are related by common descent is a humanist one. Marxism inherits not only the scientific empiricist tradition but the linked tradition of humanism. This link was first closed in philosophy by Hume, in whose *Treatise of Human Nature* the insistence that "objects become known to us only by those perceptions they occasion", and that philosophy as opposed to superstition "contents itself with . . . the phenomena which appear in the visible world", was linked with the proclamation that "human nature is the only science of man".

The humanist injunction, whose most famous expression was that of Alexander Pope:

"Know then thyself, presume not God to scan,
The proper study of mankind is man."

and which Hume put into effect in philosophy, contrasts with the medieval view that to understand ourselves we must learn what God intended when he created us with the universe around us, and with the ancient view expounded by Plato that we must understand the eternal forms of which the visible world is an imperfect reflection. Humanism takes the view which Plato objected to so strongly when it was first put forward by Protagoras, that "man is the measure of all things". Everything else is to be judged in accordance with how it affects men and can be used by men. Everything men do is to be done for the sake of men and to be judged by its effects on men. Men are not to regard themselves as existing for the service of anything else. Men were not created to serve God, but their purpose is to make other things serve men.

The Copernican hypothesis which removed the earth, the habitation of men, from the centre of the universe, and made it a small planet circling the sun, which in turn was subsequently shown to be a medium-sized star circling around within one among many galaxies, is generally regarded, and was so regarded the moment it was published, as a blow against the then established view of how and why God created man. Intellectually, it delivered a shock which the modern world is still trying to assimilate. It has detracted from the privilege and importance of the human race in the scheme of things, and made men into mere specks of organic matter whose existence and continued existence can be of no importance in relation to the vast concourse of bodies in inter-stellar space. From the point of view of the universe, *sub specie aeternitatis*, men are negligible. And it is extremely likely that in the course of time they will all be destroyed anyhow, leaving no trace behind.

The realisation that we are of no special importance in the universe must bring the realisation that we are nevertheless of supreme importance to ourselves. For mankind, what is important is the development of mankind and of human capacities. And of course, we are now only at the beginning of such development, every step in which means surpassing the bounds of what were previously thought inescapable human limitations. We can enrich our life on earth, and extend our exploration of space—discovering, perhaps, much more about the conditions which not only gave rise to our own existence but to that of analogous forms of intelligent purposive life in other parts of the galaxy or other galaxies; and perhaps not only about the mode of formation of the material world we inhabit, and the life in it, but also about its mode of dissolution. But however great our activity and discovery, it cannot terminate in a comprehensive understanding of the entire infinite universe; such a thing is anyway only a hangover from theology, and it cannot be done. The point is to reach a comprehensive understanding of ourselves and our capacities, and of other things in so far as we depend on them and they affect us and can be related by us to the development of our own purposes—and this we *can* do, by the exercise of science.

This is the basic standpoint of humanism adopted by Marx, and recommended by Marxism. "Man is the highest being for man," he wrote—and added that that implied "the categorical imperative to overthrow all conditions in which man is a humiliated, enslaved, despised and rejected being" (*Critique of Hegel's Philosophy of Law*). And in the *Economic and Philosophical Manuscripts:*

"Natural science will include the science of man in the same way as the science of man will include natural science." In that early work he called his standpoint "humanism" and "naturalism". His humanism was naturalistic because it denied that men were created by or subordinated to any supernatural agency. Its premises were men as they are observed to exist on the earth, as given, as products of natural causes, as organisms living within and living by their interaction with the natural environment, all their needs arising from this mode of life, and their abilities to satisfy them depending on the natural powers of their own bodies. Later he preferred the word "materialism", to mark his opposition to the idealist approaches which produced their own brands of naturalism and humanism. His humanism was materialist because it staked everything on being able to explain whatever concerns us in our lives in terms of processes in space and time and given to our senses. It rejected every theory that was not based on active investigation and could not be tested by empirical methods. It was open-minded as to what might yet be discovered about our environment and our powers, but closed-minded towards theories which transgress the limits of verifiability.

"What is man?" is the key question which men have to answer for themselves, and in terms of it manage their lives. Marxism is essentially an attempt to answer it, and the answer proposed is based on empirical evidences.—As was pointed out above, this produces a circularity in the Marxist train of thought (as there must be in any thinking which does not start from supposedly self-evident first principles), in as much as Marxism demonstrates the material nature of man by first accepting it as given.‾

2. SOCIAL PRODUCTION

Men are distinguished from all other forms of life on earth by their social production of their material means of life. The natural precondition was the evolution of the human hands and brain, which led to men distinguishing themselves from the rest of nature by their social use of tools and speech—by working and speaking, living by labour and, in so doing, developing the capacity to imagine and to think.

Homo sapiens is the product of the evolution of species by natural selection. But with men living by social production a new kind of evolutionary development begins. In general, the evolutionary development of living species amounts to change in means and methods of appropriating the organism's requirements from nature. Prior to man, this has always meant some structural change in organisms themselves; for instance, forms of life which evolved in the sea gave rise to those living on land through the development of lungs. With men, however, the organic structure does not change, but in the course of social production men develop techniques. For instance, men can now fly, not because they have grown wings but because they have built aircraft; and they have acquired remarkable powers of sight, not because the structure of the eyes has changed, but because they have built microscopes and telescopes.

Human evolution is the evolution of techniques. And it is a progress, in as much as, in a most obvious sense, men advance from lower to higher techniques. Further, this progress is, in a sense, predetermined from the very beginning of social production—not that every technique was bound to be discovered by a certain time, or to be discovered at all, but that in the relation of the human organism to nature, though still unexplored by man, is contained the possibility of every technique that can ever be discovered, and the dependence of the more complex and later techniques on the simpler and earlier ones. It is like a short-sighted man finding his way up a staircase. He can never know what the next step will bring until he approaches it (obviously, we can never know what there is to be discovered until we approach its discovery), and he may break his leg at a particular step and never get any further; but the steps from bottom to top are all predetermined in the structure of the staircase.

Living by social production, men develop the tools and implements they use for production, together with the knowledge and skill involved in using them. In short, they develop their forces of production. And to do this, they enter into relations with one another necessary to ensure the performance of labour, the management of the whole productive process and the distribution of the product. In short, they enter into social relations of production. And the progressive development of forces of production brings in turn changes in relations of production and so in the whole structure and character of human society.

The hypothesis which Marx put forward as the fundamental law governing social life (and it has yet to be falsified or replaced by one that fits all the facts better) consisted of positing, first, that people in society have always to bring their relations of production into conformity with their forces of production, and second, that the relations of production condition the character of all human institutions and human activities and purposes. Without production men cannot live as men, and without conformable relations of production they cannot successfully produce. The existence of given relations of production is, then, the basis on which the whole of social life is carried on; and whenever, in the development of social production, relations of production have ceased to conform with the developing forces of production, that is, have ceased to promote their successful use but begun to disrupt it, then they have to be brought back into conformity.

"In the social production of their life," Marx wrote in the summarising Preface to *Critique of Political Economy*, "men enter into definite relations that are indispensable and independent of their will, relations of production which correspond to a definite stage of development of their material productive forces. The sum total of these relations of production constitutes the economic structure of society, the real foundation, on which rises a legal and politcal superstructure and to which correspond definite forms of social consciousness. The mode of production of material life conditions the social, political and intellectual life process in general. It is not the consciousness of men that determines their being, but, on the contrary, their social being that determines their consciousness. At a certain stage of their development, the material productive forces of society come in conflict with the existing relations of production, or—what is but a legal expression of the same thing—with the property relations within which they have been at work hitherto. From forms of development of the productive forces these relations turn into fetters. Then begins an epoch of social revolution. With the change of the economic foundation the entire immense super-structure is more or less rapidly transformed."

3. HUMAN RELATIONS

All human relations develop out of the social production of the material means of life. Indeed, human individuals themselves are so created, since it is only by being brought up a member of society, and so entering into human relations and experiencing human needs, that the organism genetically constituted as *Homo sapiens* becomes a person.

By "human relations" is meant not simply any relation into which human individuals enter, but those relations into which only human individuals, or persons, can enter. For instance, just to sit down together, or to go hunting together, is not a specifically human relation; but to sit down at a meeting or a party, or to go hunting after the manner of a primitive tribe, or with the Pytchley or Quorn, is a human relation—only people could participate in such relationships. The uniqueness of man lies in the social use of tools and speech, the latter being requisite for the former. Human relations develop among tool-using animals, but they are not confined to relations of production and their distinctive mark is the way language enters into them.

The use of language is an essential element in the formation of human relations. They could not exist unless spoken into existence.

Thus Professor Austin was doing more than amuse himself with linguistic subtleties when he gave his lectures on *Doing Things with Words*. It is, as he said, the use of words in the marriage ceremony that marries people; the words serve not merely to state that certain people are married, but to marry them. But quite apart from this specialised performative use of words essential for the conduct of human institutions, the very capacity of language to express propositions means that by using it people bring themselves into relationships which could not hold apart from its use; and these are the uniquely *human* relations.

A certain mystery that has often been attributed to human relations is thus dissipated. They have been supposed to be in some way "transcendental", because they seem to elude any merely naturalistic description of observable facts and material motion. Describe all the manifold physical and chemical motions of human bodies, and you have still said nothing about human relations. But human bodies do not enter into human relations independently of what they say and think, so that language has more to do with these relations than simply to state them as facts. It is only by using language that people enter into them.

Thus if observers from another planet were to carry home any adequate account of what they found people doing, they would have not only to observe and record their behaviour but discover the meaning of human speech.

Indeed, language is an essential means whereby human individuals relate themselves to the external world in ways additional to those of other animals. Men obtain their requirements from nature by the purposive social use of tools and implements, and this they can only do in so far as language serves them for the imaginative conception of their purpose and for organising its realisation. In this process, whatever affects men is translated into terms of human thought, reflected and related to other things in terms of the categories of human thought, and thus becomes an object of human knowledge. By this means men relate themselves to nature in another way than the other animals. And so do they relate themselves to each other. Hence every relation between persons, whether a production relation or not, and whether an institutionalised type of relation or not, owes its existence to the use of language.

Take love, for example. Does this consist simply of mutual feelings, a purely emotional bond which can come into existence independently of people's possessing the use of language? Absolutely dumb sexual attachment would not be human, and it is well known that the whole character of such attachment between persons involves the exercise of imagination and varies with the way they have learned to think of each other. It is not merely that feelings may be expressed in language, but that human feelings are not felt by animals lacking the use of language, since without language they lack imagination and could not enter into human relationships. (This example provides a clue, incidentally, to the role which literature plays in developing human relations; the expression it gives to them and the images it makes of them are factors in making and changing them.)

The use of language owes its origin to social production, since to carry on social production people must speak to one another. And just as social production is the distinctive activity of man, so are relations of production, or property relations, the basic human relations. They are the precondition of all other human relations, which are all conditioned by whatever are the forms of property. All relations into which people enter are so conditioned—how people treat one another, how they regard each other, how they co-operate together and how they fight one another.

Not the least important of the uses of language, then, is to constitute or bring into being the relations of production. Marx already equated these with "property relations", calling the latter "but a legal expression of the same thing". Words are, of course, used to describe property—as when one says that a large part of the land on which London is built is the property of the Duke of Westminster. But the use of words is also requisite to institute property.

Animals which do not *say* "These things are ours", or "This is

mine" and "This is yours", have no property. A dog may guard its
bone and a Duke his land; but the land belongs to the Duke in
another sense than the bone to the dog; property begins with appropriation (collective or individual), but does not end there. Without
their "expression", property relations could not exist at all. Thus the
"legal expression" of relations of production, as property, does not
merely state that people stand in certain relations, as a fact that is
the case whether stated or not, but is requisite for bringing them into
those relations.

Hence the language of property, the "legal expression" of the relations of production, without which those relations fall apart and
vanish and human association would become unworkable, is of
profound importance for the formation of all human relations, of all
relations between persons, without exception.

4. DIVISION OF LABOUR AND PRIVATE PROPERTY

The fact that language is requisite to institute property does not
mean that it is possible, by saying whatever we please, to institute
whatever relations of production we please.

The existence of property means that affairs are regulated by
certain prescriptions, that people assume certain rights and obligations. For this it is required, firstly that certain conditions (often
quite elaborate ones) must be satisfied without which entitlement to
property does not hold good, and secondly that the prescribed rights
and obligations must be enforceable. But what prescriptions as to
property can be effectively instituted and enforced depends on the
circumstances and, above all, on the character of the production process itself. Thus Marx said that people enter into relations of production "independent of their will". How they can and do regulate their
social production does not depend on free choice (they do not all get
together, as was once imagined, and freely institute a "social contract") but on the character of the social production it is required to
regulate.

In their primitive state, possessing only the very crudest and
simplest techniques by which they had first raised themselves above
other animals, people could live only in small groups, jointly appropriating and sharing out such means of life as they could obtain.
They were still completely dependent, like other animals, on the
natural conditions of their habitat and what it provided for them.
After living in such a condition for countless generations, some

people managed to break this dependence by finding out how to cultivate crops and domesticate animals.

The invention of agriculture led to the kinds of human relations with which we are now familiar in recorded history. By breaking their subordination to nature and beginning to subdue nature to human purposes people entered into those relations with each other which led the liberal historian Gibbon to describe history as the record of "the crimes, follies and misfortunes of mankind". Keenly aware of the fact of progress, he yet compared the way people actually treated one another with the kind of relations he would have expected were we really, as some have claimed, rational animals—and so queried the value of the progress made and whether anything any better could ever be achieved by man. The same query still demands an answer today. Progress, in the scientific and technological sense, is a fact, but where is it getting us and what is it worth?

Any technique demands some kind of division of labour, with different people performing different functions in the economy. It seems probable that with very primitive techniques the principal division of labour was based on the natural division of the sexes. The invention of agriculture eventually brought new division of labour of a much more artificial and elaborate sort. It led to a greater multiplicity of jobs in growing crops and looking after animals. Then the discovery of the use of metals led to the differentiation of various industrial crafts from agricultural labour. And as population increased and people lived in bigger communities and more contact was established between different communities, it led to the differentiation of both management and distribution from productive labour. All this in turn altered the relations of the sexes and the structure of the family: women became relegated to the dependent and subordinate position which civilised peoples afterwards came to regard as natural. At the same time, labour began to produce a surplus. Whereas in primitive conditions the most that a human group could do by combined productive efforts was to get enough for them all to live on, those engaged in production now produced more than enough for their own subsistence, so that it became possible for non-producers to be supported on the labour of the producers.

The division of labour, with production of a surplus, meant that people entered into new relations of production, which could no longer be expressed in terms of the primitive ideas of communal property with everything being shared out among the members of a

group. New forms of property had to be instituted, private property,
giving expression to new relations of production within which people
could effectively regulate the division of labour which their techniques involved. For as Marx and Engels observed in *The German
Ideology* (I, 1) "the various stages of development in the division of
labour are just so many different forms of ownership; i.e. the existing
stage in the division of labour determines also the relations of individuals to one another with reference to the materials, instruments
and products of labour".

Thus instead of everything being shared out, products are exchanged. They pass from hand to hand, and have to be regarded as
belonging to the different people who acquire them in the process.
Similarly, different means of production come to be regarded as
belonging to different individuals or groups of individuals.

Property is a socially regulated form of appropriation. And the
most noteworthy feature of private property is that, in acquiring it,
people no longer communally appropriate products of communal
labour, but individuals or groups within the community appropriate
means of production, and articles for use or exchange produced by
other individuals or groups. It means that some people acquire an
entitlement to the products of other people's labour.

Thus the appropriation of objects as private property, both means
of production and means of consumption, consists not simply of a
relation between people and objects but of a relation between people
and people—a relation of social production.

Private property was not instituted by choice but by necessity,
"independent of men's will". Theologians like Aquinas and political
philosophers like Locke supposed it natural for men to acquire
private property. If that were true, then it would have to be admitted
that in civilised communities not only are some people more equal
than others but also more natural. It is true, of course, that the human
mode of life requires that people should always enter into relations of
production, expressed as property relations; but so long as they remained nearest to their natural condition the idea of instituting
private property never entered their heads. Private property came into
existence out of the (very unnatural) division of labour involved in
higher techniques, and it was technological progress which in the
first place made it necessary.

Private property was a condition for the technological progress of
human communities and for the increase of their command over

nature and of their wealth. And it was equally a condition for freeing some people from the drudgery of necessary productive labour and allowing them to develop their intellectual powers, and so for the development and diversification of human interests and human personality, and of culture and the arts. Evidently, it profoundly affected all human relations in a number of ways, making them quite different from the simple and direct person to person relationships characteristic of primitive communities.

Reliable evidence about the historical development of all human communities is, from the nature of the case, rather hard to get, and in many cases not obtainable at all. As Marx's own researches already showed, no simple historical "law" postulating a universal stage-to-stage development for every human community will fit the facts; and while everything people do is conditioned by their social relations of production, not everything they do can be directly attributed to economic causes. In the course of history, as various communities have carried on their social production and adapted their production relations in various ways to their productive forces, diverse formations of property relations (in Marx's phrase, "social-economic formations") have been instituted locally and undergone various metamorphoses. In these, a variety of specific types of human relation arising out of private property have emerged—such as the relation of master and slave, lord and serf, guildmaster and journeyman, capitalist and wage-labourer, and a host of others. But quite apart from such specific relationships established locally, and their effects on all human relations within local communities, it is possible to distinguish certain universal ways in which private property affects human relations, irrespective of the particular form of property.

5. ALIENATION AND THE DEPERSONALISATION OF HUMAN RELATIONS

The principal and universal effect of private property on human relations is to divide people up within communities, in such a way that the labour of some becomes the necessary means which others must subdue to their own purposes in order to get from it the products they desire.

Hence there is introduced into human relations a man-made assymetry distinct from the natural assymetry of the relations of men and women, stronger and weaker, older and younger, parents and children, and so on. This is the assymetry characteristic of domination and exploitation. It means that people are so divided up and estranged that for some of them other people stand in the relation of depersonalised things or objects, to be used as means to ends, without regard to their personality. It means that what people learn to set a value on is not the enjoyment of human activities but the external objects they can manage to appropriate and to possess which they compete with other people and use other people. This estrangement is superimposed on the personal relationships between human beings, in which all are to each other simply other persons with whom one is living in the community, their differences being simply differences of sex, age, ability, character, and so on. It means that persons or, at all events, their inherent personal capacities exerted when they work, become the property of other persons, to be used up as those others direct—as happens, for example, with slaves or serfs or wage-workers. The introduction of man-made assymetry, or inequality, into human relations means their depersonalisation. The unequal or assymetrical relations between persons resulting from division of labour and private property are relations holding between them, not by virtue of their being persons with such and such characteristics, but by virtue of their holding or not holding entitlements to property. Hence these relations are not personal ones, which can be voluntarily adjusted as between persons, but depersonalised or impersonal relations.

The fact that in the regulated system of production and appropriation some people are treated by others as things, and that, in that respect, they or their personal capacities become other people's property, was described by Marx, in the *Economic and Philosophic Manuscripts*, as "self-alienation", meaning that an integral part of their own persons is alienated as the property of others.

This alienation has a depersonalising effect on human relations generally, and not only on those specific relations in which the alienation occurs. Human fellowship is replaced by relations in which people have to use other people, and to see the end or good of their lives not in relations with other people but in things, and in the use of other people to obtain possession of things. It means that everyone is related to everyone else by impersonal relations, depending on property. Naturally, they are all people and can and do enter into personal relations. But personal relations are conditioned and coloured by impersonal ones. For example, a slaveowner or feudal magnate or employer may be keenly aware of the personalities of slaves, serfs or employees, and do his best to treat them accordingly; and they may even respond with respect and affection. But this does not in the least alter the impersonality of the relationship.

The fact that people are for other people objects for use has fundamentally affected the relations between the sexes. Personal sexual relations based on the natural difference between the sexes, the pleasure and support they naturally afford each other, and the rearing of children, are made unequal in the sense that women are subjected to men and treated as objects—means for sexual use, means for the production of children, and amongst the propertied classes means for alliances of properties, for producing heirs and, very often, as items of property themselves. Thus as well as other divisions a division is created cutting right through the human race, in which the natural difference of sex become a difference of status, and in which the personal relations between the sexes in their sexual activity are partially or even wholly depersonalised.

Such alienation effects in human relations are so well known from experience as to be perfectly obvious. They have been for so long familiar as to be simply taken for granted, so that few think there is anything remarkable, still less remediable, in human relations being like this.

The introduction of inequality, alienation and depersonalisation into human relations brings into the human community antagonisms entirely distinct from personal antagonisms—oppositions of interest between whole groups or classes of people arising, not from personal disagreements or quarrels, but from differences in their methods of acquisition. These antagonisms are utterly impersonal, and may cut right across the personal likes or dislikes of people for one another; but willy nilly, people are caught up in them. The history of all communities thus becomes, as was stated in *The Communist Manifesto*, "the history of class struggles". And because people are for other people things for their use, wars of conquest result and, on the other side, wars of liberation, with all the destruction, cruelty and suffering they bring. The social violence and cruelty which has long been characteristic of human behaviour is not the result of the aggressiveness of human individuals (there is, of course, such an aggressiveness, and it is harnessed in class struggles and wars), but of the property relations into which they have entered in the development of social production.

At the same time the divisions within society have a polarising action, in which the toil is concentrated at one pole and its reward at the other. Thus for the masses of producers (and this has always meant primarily agricultural producers) there is unending toil, filling their whole lives, with a bare subsistence to show for it, and ignorance and squalor without opportunity to enjoy the benefits of the sciences and arts, while the reward of this toil in the way of comfort, luxury, education and culture goes to the opposite pole of society, the ruling class and the privileged. Similarly, the masses are able to exert only manual skills and crafts, while the work of the intellect and of artistic creation is monopolised by a privileged few, dependent on and patronised or employed by the ruling class. And similarly, the advances of civilisation are concentrated in towns, while the rural hinterland remains in backwardness. With every advance in technical accomplishment the effects of this polarising action become greater. The greater the sum of social wealth, the greater becomes the inequality between the wealth of the few and the poverty of the many.

The upshot of alienation and the depersonalisation of human relations is that people in their social activity find themselves subject to impersonal forces—which they themselves have unwittingly created but over which they have no control. Thus human relations themselves confront people as an alien power, influencing their actions and the results of their actions, and determining the relations into which individuals can consciously enter with one another. Hence, unlike production in which men produce what they intend to produce, the development of social relations proceeds in directions independent of and often quite contrary to men's intentions, like any natural process the laws of which are independent of men's will.

In another sense of "alienation", men have collectively alienated their own social relations, and not only that but their own means of production, their own products and their own institutions, so that instead of these being under the collective control of men, subordinated to human purposes, men's lives are subordinate to them. People find themselves passively accepting or struggling to get free of their own alienated creations. Thus in developing the means of production people have become individually subordinate to them, so that the peasant is tied to the land and the animals, and the industrial worker to the machine. The means of production are not the man's servant, but he becomes theirs. When products are produced not for the producers' use but to be appropriated by others and exchanged, men lose collective control over them and instead fall under the control of their own products exercised through the impersonal power of money. In the divided condition of humanity state institutions are set up to maintain social order and direct public policy, and then people become subject to the state. The interests of the state are set up, demanding service and sacrifice from persons in precedence to their personal interests.

6. RELIGION

The relations into which people enter with one another in obtaining their means of life are reflected in the way they think about human life in general, and human needs. The alienation and depersonalisation of human relations universal in communities that have advanced beyond primitive techniques accounts for religion becoming so pervasive a feature of men's conscious life in such communities.

Religion is the product of this state of human relations. While a number of very primitive ideas and magical practices have been incorporated into religious rituals (for example, scholars have traced Christian rituals back to primitive magic, and Protestant Churches are still reckoned "high" or "low" according to the extent to which their rituals incorporate it), religion is a phenomenon of human consciousness quite distinct from the magic by which primitive peoples try to subdue nature and strengthen their own hands. Religion presupposes a degree of technical progress. It presupposes that the extreme dependence of men upon nature in primitive communities has been overcome, and that therefore the primitive consciousness of union with nature, expressed in magic and animist ideas, has been overcome too. With religion man conceives of himself as a being apart from nature, taking cognisance of the natural properties of things in order to use them for human ends.

There have been and are a variety of religions practised by different people in different circumstances. Moreover in civilised communities religion is always a two-tier phenomenon. There is religion as understood, obeyed and practised by the uneducated masses, and there is the doctrine and theory adumbrated by officials who direct it from the top. Between these big differences can develop, resulting in mass breakaways. But ignoring the variegated forms of religion, the contradictions among them and the ways in which they are rationalised in religious doctrines, certain fundamental features remain in common. All religions teach a doctrine of the supernatural, according to which the natural world is a dependency of the supernatural, and man is not a merely natural being but has a stake in the supernatural world. And all religions combine this with teachings about the fallen, lost or sinful condition of man in his natural existence, and about the road to salvation. The combination of conceptions of the supernatural with those of sin and salvation is the hallmark of religion (by itself, a doctrine of the supernatural is merely idealist metaphysics, a by-product of the rationalisation of religion by sophisticated leisure classes).

Evidently, the religious conception of the supernatural presupposes a conception of nature to which the supernatural is opposed. And this presupposes a development of technology which has overcome primitive animist ideas, so that natural processes and their laws are conceived as independent of human activites. Thus, for example, a procedure for turning wine into blood would be, according to primitive conceptions, simply a piece of magic, and not a miraculous abrogation of the laws of nature confirming faith in the supernatural. The religious conception of the miracle contradicts the primitive conception of magic, even though it develops out of it, just as the religious opposition of the supernatural to the natural contradicts primitive animism. Religion introduces into men's ideas of their condition a fundamental dualism—the opposition of man to nature, of the supernatural to the natural, of spirit to matter, and of the eternal and changeless to the temporal and changeable.

This dualism constitutes the ideological essence of religion. Thus religious doctrines are not hypotheses invented to explain the phenomena of nature, which are superseded as the sciences develop other types of hypotheses. Many scientists are still religious: that does not mean that they inconsistently support incompatible hypotheses, since religion is not a hypothesis comparable with those of the sciences. It continues alongside and complementary to the development of technology and natural sciences.

With the conception of the supernatural goes that of sin and salvation. Man, conceived as divided from nature by his spiritual attributes, is conceived as in his natural existence a fallen being. But he can win salvation from this state, though it is not to be realised in this earthly life—and all religious teachings, precepts and rituals are concerned with how to do so. Of course, ideas of what salvation consists of, and of what to do to be saved, vary greatly, as do ideas of the fate of those who remain in sin (though this is always unpleasant). The idea of sin is, along with that of the supernatural, a fundamental idea of all religion, and sin is no more to be described in empirical terms than is the supernatural. Thus to say that people are sinful is not the same as to describe typical modes of behaviour and express disapproval. Sin does not consist merely of bad behaviour (though, as Saint Paul made clear, the sinful nature of men results in their bad behaviour). Nor does salvation from sin consist of finding the way to lead a good and happy life on earth.

Religion has been condemned on the grounds that it is a system of illusions propagated by agents of the ruling classes to deceive the masses. Yet it did not arise by being imposed on the masses, but arose from amidst the masses themselves. It has been condemned for serving to support systems of exploitation and to incite to and justify man's inhumanity to man. Yet both oppression and the fight against it, cruelties and the protest against them, individual greed and the ways of altruism and self-sacrifice, savage wars and persecutions and appeals for tolerance and reconciliation have been practised in the name of religion and been apparently inspired by religious ideas and motives. The fact is that religion is not simply a system of doctrines craftily worked out, and it is not itself a primary motive power in society, either for good or ill. It is the reflection in ideas of the alienated human relations within which all men's social action takes place.

The lives of men, the realisation of their intentions, and their relations with each other, are dominated by an impersonal power which has no natural origin or explanation. In the human community man is opposed to man, actuated by something inherent in but alien to himself. These are the objective circumstances reflected in religion —in the religious ideas of supernatural power, and of the lost and sinful condition of men from which we can escape only by seeking a salvation not of this world. These fundamental and universal religious ideas are thus the reflection in human consciousness of the alienation of human relations. The language of religion is the peculiar and universal language in which people come to represent to themselves their condition and their relations with each other and with nature, when they have still found no way of comprehending how they have brought themselves into this condition, or of bringing what they have alienated under their own conscious purposive control.

The universal prevalence of religion is due to the universal occurrence of conditions in which men lack control over the social use of their own means of satisfying their needs. According to religion, men can never satisfy their needs without help—and that help is not the mundane help of other men, nor the help afforded by scientific knowledge, but extra-human supernatural help. In the dualistic religious conception of man and his needs, the nature of man is divided into the material and the spiritual, and his spiritual needs are offset against his material ones. The sorrows of the material deprivation of the masses and the divided condition of mankind are compensated by the spiritual consolations of religion.

Hence, as Marx was already insisting in his *Contribution to the Critique of Hegel's Philosophy of Law* (1843), the criticism of religion is the criticism of the human conditions which give rise to religion, and the criticism of the religious conception of the human condition and of human needs must rest upon the investigation of the actual condition and needs of men, and of how men by their own efforts can satisfy their needs. The people cannot find the way to "their real happiness" so long as they seek "the illusory happiness" provided in religion. "The demand to give up illusions about their condition is the demand to give up a condition that requires illusions . . . The immediate task of philosophy, which is at the service of history, once the other-worldly form of human self-alienation has been unmasked, is to unmask self-alienation in its this-worldly form. Thus the criticism of heaven turns into the criticism of the earth, the criticism of religion into the criticism of rights, and the criticism of theology into the criticism of politics."

7. CAPITALISM AND SOCIALISM

Capitalist property and capitalist production relations, which have been instituted in modern times, represent the extreme limit, and so the final form, of the process described by Marx as human "self-alienation".

With capitalism all products are produced as commodities, and labour-power and, indeed, all human abilities are put up for sale and so alienated by their possessors. The depersonalisation of human relations reaches an extreme in which the subordination of some people to others takes the form of the subordination of them all to completely impersonal organisations. Thus in a feudal society, for example, men were subject to their lord or their king; but in a capitalist society, while some give orders for others to carry out, the employee is equal as a person to his boss and the employer is a corporation—of a peculiar type instituted by monetary statements of entitlement to property. The holdings of capitalist corporations are derived from appropriations of the products of labour, so that, as Marx put it, their sway represents the rule of "dead" over "living" labour. The great capitalist monopolies and trusts, and the capitalist machinery of state, are faceless and impersonal. Of course, a capitalist community, like any other, is nothing but a lot of people doing things together and speaking to each other; but their relations to each other, and how they treat each other, are governed by impersonal profit-making and profit-disposing organisations, and every relationship in which people live and work together is governed by considerations about money, by the impersonal and alien power of money which has the last say in what they can or cannot do together. Personal deprivation takes new forms. Even as extremes of deprivation of material goods become alleviated, people are increasingly turned loose and left to fend for themselves in their personal lives. The individualistic protest which increases under capitalism, and takes all manner of unconventional and on occasion anti-social forms, is the response to this.

At the same time, the polarisation in society continues, acting not only inside each capitalist community but on a world scale. Men are increasingly equalised, as personal privileges of birth and rank disappear. But the more democratisation and equalisation there is, the more marked becomes the division of classes and the more dangerous and intractable become the conflicts on a world scale. The so-called "disappearance of class distinctions" in capitalist democracies, and the formal recognition that all people are equal members of the human race, only serve to reveal in their nakedness the class conflicts and national conflicts as based on nothing but impersonal divisions of interest. And these conflicts are then revealed as human anomalies, due only to the degree of subjection of persons to an impersonal system.

But if capitalism is the extreme of the alienation process in human relations, it also brings into being the conditions to end it.

Capitalist relations are instituted when the development of relatively advanced techniques demands the purchase of labour-power for the purpose of employing a number of people to work together in a single enterprise. And once the capitalist relations are in operation, the drive for profits from which to accumulate more capital, together with the competition of different capitals, leads to the continuous improvement of techniques. The search begins for motive powers other than those of animal and human muscle (water power, steam power, the internal combustion engine, electrical energy, nuclear power), and the development of mass production methods powered by them. Under capitalism there occurs not only a revolution in techniques but, as *The Communist Manifesto* put it, a continuous revolutionising of techniques. Scientific research is developed as itself a new force of production. The sciences do not simply investigate nature but, by their discoveries, change the relationship of man and nature, by equipping men with new powers.

As a result, a stage has been reached when techniques are available completely to satisfy the material needs of the whole human race. The means and knowhow actually exist to provide abundance to a large population, and to do so with a minimum expenditure of muscular energy, without arduous labour or a high proportion of individuals' time being demanded by labour, so that plenty of leisure, with opportunities for education and enjoyment, should be the right of everyone. Despite the existing mass poverty and technological backwardness throughout large areas, the realisation of such a state of affairs could now be technically accomplished quite quickly, within two or three generations. The obstacle is not lack of means but the human relations which prevent people from uniting to deploy the means.

When men have changed their relationship with nature they can also change their relations with each other. As was enunciated in Marx's fundamental proposition about social development, a change in the first always necessitates a change in the second.

The technological development under capitalism changes the character of the labour process and of the division of labour. This change can be expressed in one word by saying that production becomes socialised. Instead of the production of the totality of goods needed by a community being done by a large number of separate individuals and groups, each working independently and each contributing one product which they themselves or others must appropriate, production is more and more concentrated within large-scale enterprises. A large number of people work together according to a production-plan to produce their output jointly or socially.

Although the development of modern technology began by accentuating the earlier effects of division of labour on human personality, by tying individuals to particular parts of the processes of mass production and making them the servants of machines, its long-term demand is for highly educated people with a grasp of the production process as a whole. The use of modern technology demands indi-viduals who are not the servants but the makers and masters of machines, and for whom, moreover, labour is not the dominant factor in their individual lives. This was already stressed by Marx (in *Capital*), but the most recent developments of automation under-line it even more. By the development of technology capitalism set in motion a new development of the division of labour, reversing the old. This is in contradiction to the division of the community into the rulers and the ruled, the educated thinking elite and the ignorant uneducable mass, which nevertheless it is the whole tend-ency of the property relations to retain.

The socialisation of production under capitalism, then, brings into existence conditions in which it is possible to put an end to relations in which the capacities of some are treated as the property of others, with all the effects which ensue from that. But not only is this possible, it is necessary, if the processes of production are not to be continually interrupted by human conflicts and economic breakdown.

The system of private appropriation, which originally developed out of the division of labour, and which survives in capitalist property relations, is no longer in accord with the new socialised form of production. As Engels put it in *Socialism, Utopian and Scientific*, socialised production is "subjected to a form of appropria-tion which presupposes the private production of individuals . . . The mode of production is subjected to this form of appropriation, although it abolishes the conditions upon which the latter rests." Consequently there exists a contradiction between "socialised pro-duction and capitalist appropriation" and "between the organisation of production in the individual workshop and the anarchy of production in society generally . . . The mode of production is in rebellion against the mode of exchange." Socialised production requires to be socially planned in accordance with social resources and needs, and to be matched by social appropriation, in which entitlement to products rests simply on being a person, a member of society, and not on the ownership of property.

Capitalist private property can and must be converted into social property. How can this come about? Unhappily, with the human race divided and estranged from each other as they are, it cannot possibly come about by general agreement. It can only come about, as other revolutionary changes in property relations have done, through class struggle. Wherever class conflicts exist they cannot but be fought to a conclusion, however long it takes and however much some may wish to bring about a reconciliation.

The socialisation of production in the countries of advanced technology accentuates the contradiction of interest between the magnates of capital and the working people of their own and of the under-developed countries. And the result is, as *The Communist Manifesto* showed, that by organising and hastening the development of socialised production "what the bourgeoisie produces, above all, are its own gravediggers". The effect is to bring together and organise in opposition to capital whole populations of working people.

The difference between this conflict and earlier ones between exploited and exploiting classes is that, with the new character of production, the exploited become organised and educated. There is no further need for a privileged class of rulers, to manage public affairs; the working people themselves have become quite capable of providing the personnel for that purpose.

The original cause of the estrangement within human communities was division of labour leading to private property. And property is the issue of every irreconcilable conflict between men. Property relations are not unchangeable. They are instituted by men and can be changed by men. But the reconstitution of property comes about, and this is the only way it can come about, as the outcome of class struggle. The power to preserve property relations or to change them is the power to make and to enforce laws. Consequently the final issue of the struggle against capital is the issue of securing this power. The practical conclusion of Marx about the struggle for socialism was that it is and can only be a political struggle, based on and mobilising the forces of the classes opposed to capital, with the object of obtaining political or state power to institute a radical change in property relations.

8. COMMUNISM

In his Preface to the English edition (1888) of *The Communist Manifesto*, Engels thus summed up the conclusion of Marxist social theory: "The history of class struggles forms a series of evolutions in which, nowadays, a stage has been reached where the exploited and oppressed class cannot attain its emancipation from the sway of the exploiting and ruling class without, at the same time, and once and for all, emancipating society at large from all exploitation, oppression, class distinction and class struggles."

The fundamental law of development of human society discovered by Marx—the law that men must always bring their relations of production into accordance with their forces of production—does not (as I have already remarked) state any preordained sequence of stages of social development through which every human community must inevitably pass. On the contrary, new forces of production are only developed in rather exceptional local circumstances, and many communities have set up social relations incapable of development, in which they have remained stuck until overrun and overcome by the aggression of others. But Marx's discovery leads to three conclusions about the overall course of social development. It may be noted that these conclusions are not statements of what is deterministically inevitable, but take the form proper to scientific conclusions—that is, they delimit possibilities.

To begin with, the development of forces of production could only take place under conditions of private appropriation, the exploitation of labour, the alienation of human capacities and the depersonalisation of human relations, divided communities and class struggles.

In these circumstances, the sequence of technological progress was bound up with the production of products as commodities. The eventual outcome, bound by the working out of probabilities to be arrived at somewhere some time, whatever digressions and deadends particular communities might get into, could only be the formation of capitalist property relations and the socialisation of production.

Now that outcome has been reached, the sequence of class struggles can be brought to an end with the assumption of power by the exploited class and the institution of socialist relations of production.

"The bourgeois relations of production," wrote Marx in the Preface to *The Critique of Political Economy*, "are the last antagonistic form of the social process of production . . . at the same time the productive forces developing in the womb of bourgeois society create the material conditions for the solution of that antagonism. This social formation brings, therefore, the pre-history of human society to a close."

Once power has passed from the hands of the classes whose mode of appropriation is based on private property, it is possible to begin to transform property relations by making the means and products of socialised production public or co-operative property. This begins the reconstitution of the relations of men to men corresponding to the establishment of the new relationship of men to nature in socialised production. It stops the labour-power of some being the property of others, and by ending capitalist appropriation abolishes the exploitation of man by man and the conflicts forced on men by the impersonal antagonistic relations of classes.

On this basis it is possible to plan social production so as steadily to increase the quantity and improve the quality of the goods and services available to each individual. And at the same time, with the scientific development of technology, it is possible progressively to shorten the necessary working day for each individual, and to ensure that the necessity of working, imposed on men by their relationship with nature, becomes a pleasure instead of a burden. It is possible, as Marx claimed (*Capital*, III, 48, 3), that men should carry out the task of necessary work "with the least expenditure of energy and under conditions most favourable to and worthy of their human nature", and that it should serve them as the basis for free personal activity and personal relations—"that development of human energy which is an end in itself".

The basis is then established for conceptions of men and their needs radically different from the prevailing religious ones. Human needs are now understood as arising solely from the human mode of life rooted in social production, and capable of satisfaction through men's efforts alone. Men are not divided into a degraded material and a higher spiritual part, and need no supernatural help or guidance. Yet their needs are not confined to material needs, in the sense of requirements for the biological functioning of human bodies and the continuation of the species. The characteristic human need is for personal relations with other people. People need human companionship, sympathy, assistance and co-operation first of all to produce together the material means of life and then, on that basis, to develop and enjoy the activities and fruits of human culture. While none of this is possible unless elementary material needs are satisfied (so that to preach that material satisfactions are worthless in comparison with "spiritual" ones is utterly repugnant to the development of human relations and human personality), the material needs of men are themselves humanised and transformed into specifically human as distinct from animal needs. Thus people do not simply need food but need it artfully prepared and served, they do not simply need clothing and shelter but fashions and architecture, and they do not simply need sexual intercourse but the art of love and human relations between the sexes. Socialism is not a new religion, but makes all religion pointless. It establishes the conditions in which people can begin purposively to co-operate to make possible for all the satisfaction of their needs.

The first tasks of socialist revolution are political—to change the state from an organisation functioning to protect private appropriation into one functioning to prevent it; to expand the state by instituting organisation for managing socialist production; and to protect socialist property and put down any efforts to subvert it. These are the tasks covered in Marx's famous phrase "the dictatorship of the proletariat".

These political tasks combine with economic ones—to plan production and distribution so as to deploy all available resources, materials, machinery and labour, to produce the goods and services people need and to share them out; and to expand scientific research and education so as to develop the techniques of planned production, lighten labour and make more and better goods and services available.

The goal of socialist politics and socialist planning is, obviously, to produce an absolute abundance of goods and services, so that all that anyone can need is available to him. And, apart from obstacles of external interference, natural calamities and errors of planning, all of which are surmountable, there is no reason why this goal should not be reached.

The eventual and final abolition of shortages constitutes the economic condition for entering upon a communist society. When there is socialised production the products of which are socially appropriated, when science and scientific planning have resulted in the production of absolute abundance, and when labour has been so lightened and organised that all can without sacrifice of personal inclinations contribute their working abilities to the common fund, everyone will receive a share according to his needs. This economic principle of communism was first announced by the English philosopher William Godwin: "From each according to his ability, to each according to his need."

Before communism can come into operation, however, the affairs of socialist society (called by Marx "the first phase of communism", or the "transitional" phase from capitalism to communism) have to be managed on a different principle: "From each according to his ability, to each according to his work."

Evidently, the socialisation of property in means of production does no more than initiate a change in human relations. It makes it possible of completion, but does not complete it. Socialism abolishes the primary condition of self-alienation, in that no person's abilities are any longer appropriated for the use of another person. But in the socialist economy goods and services are still allocated to each person "according to his work", which means, as Marx put it in *The Critique of the Gotha Programme*, the continuation of unequal "bourgeois right". Defects, he said, "are inevitable in the first phase of communist society, as it is when it has just emerged after prolonged birth pangs from capitalist society. Right can never be higher than the economic structure of society and its cultural development conditioned thereby." Once a socialist economy is well established (as it is today, for example, in the U.S.S.R.) all exploitation of man by man is indeed abolished. All are working together now for the benefit of each. Yet some of the effects of the earlier condition of alienation remain—the inequalities of persons (as Marx put it, their "unequal rights for unequal labour"), the depersonalisation of human relations and subjection of persons to impersonal organisations. What each person can offer by way of labour is still appropriated by a public organisation, and his entitlement to recompense depends on the value it places on what it gets from him. People are still related to each other through their individual relations to an impersonal organisation. They have created this organisation for their own benefit, to an increasing extent they democratically control it, but they still make themselves subject to it. And how they can each develop and help or hinder each other depends not alone on each of them personally but on what they have set up over themselves. With socialism, therefore, for a time at least, some of the alienation effects experienced under capitalism may even be accentuated. For the power and scope of impersonal organisation, and its control over and direction of what people do, increases.—This is a point important to understand, for otherwise we may be surprised and dismayed to find that unpleasant things can still happen in socialist society, which we had hoped could never happen there.

But socialist economic development itself removes the causes of these alienation effects and paves the way for men being finally able to get rid of them in communist society.

Having been depersonalised, human relations can be personalised. Having been made indirect and impersonal, they can be made direct and personal. The relations of millions of people, most of whom can never meet, can be made as personal as those of a group of friends, because they are all engaged together in the common enterprise and adventure of human life. Then, as Marx said (*Capital*, I, 1, 4), "the practical relations of everyday life offer to man none but perfectly intelligible and reasonable relations with regard to his fellow men and to nature".

This ending of the depersonalisation of human relations, and making relations between persons personal, "perfectly intelligible and reasonable", involves two main changes.

The division of society into antagonistic classes made necessary the setting up of states, with their apparatus of law-making and enforcement, of administration and coercion, a public power exercised by people but standing over them to make and enforce public policies to ensure that some interests prevail over others. In the first place, therefore, the ending of class divisions and the impersonal conflicts between classes makes this public power a human anomaly. Special organisations to govern people, with armies, police and officials, together with all the political organisations and parties which have been formed with the object of creating a power to influence and direct state power, will no longer be needed and so can be disbanded. The state, as Engels expressed it, can be made to "wither away". For "state interference in social relations becomes, in one domain after another, superfluous, and then dies out of itself; the government of persons is replaced by the administration of things, and by the conduct of processes of production" (*Socialism, Utopian and Scientific*, 3).

In the second place, the organisation of production itself changes. In socialism, the state takes charge of production. The means of production become state-property. And as class antagonisms disappear in a socialist society, the state ceases to have any function of class repression but continues to function as owner and manager (and protector) of public property. There thus exists an organisation which employs people and makes available to them goods and services in accordance with their work. But eventually the conduct of processes of production can be arranged by people simply working together to make use of things to satisfy their needs, instead of being governed by an organisation standing over them and making use of them for the purpose of publicly appropriating and distributing things.

In socialist society the production plan still takes the form of "a law", an act of state, made and enforced by a planning authority. However much democratic consultation goes on, the planners are still the agents of an impersonal authority—an authority for the government of persons as well as for the administration of things. As resources increase and techniques become more powerful, the problems to be solved in a plan become more complex; and, so it would seem, the more necessary becomes the role of a competent planning authority as an organ of government. But this very complexity of the problems also means that no human agency could possibly solve them without mechanical aid, any more than it could move mountains. The advance of techniques includes techniques of data-processing, communication, computing and directing the use of techniques—and would grind to a stop unless these were included. Hence the planning authority, as a manned apparatus of government, becomes, like the rest of the state, superfluous. Planning must itself become automated. People will use automata to plan production and distribution, just as they use machines to make things and transport them. The most complete automation of the action of persons on things in social production is the condition for the most complete humanisation of the relations of persons with persons.

Such a change in human relations means, essentially, that individual personality is no longer subordinated either to the acquisitive use of other persons or to the service and direction of impersonal organisations and powers. There are only the direct and intelligible personal relations of living individuals, each of whom depends on others for the development of his own personality, as well as for the benefit of the techniques which they all employ together for getting their requirements from nature and making them available to each other.

9. THE CONTEMPORARY PHILOSOPHY OF MAN

Central in the Marxist philosophy is the demand for adopting a strictly scientific empirical outlook on all problems of practice—and this is what is formullated in the principals of the dialectical materialist approach to making theories. It is in accordance with this that there is worked out the Marxist general view or theory of human society and of the nature of human personality and human relations. This lays bare the causes and effects of all those intrusive and often deplored phenomena in human life which come under the heading of "alienation", and demonstrates the practical possibility of now getting over them as a result of the development of technology.

Communism does not, of course, mean anything so unlikely as that no one will ever quarrel or disagree with anyone else, or deceive or injure anyone else, or ever be discontented, or that all will be equally wise and high-minded, and human stupidity never again bring human enterprise to grief. It does mean that social injustice, oppression and strife, the insolence of office and the ostentation of wealth, will be ended along with cultural deprivation and material want. When techniques have been developed to the point when the whole of social production and distribution can be rationally planned for the satisfaction of the needs of all, society can become simply an association of equal persons with no other end than to serve the interests of each individual as an end in himself. The interests of no privileged person or group, and no social organisation, can then claim precedence over the individual needs of any single person. Then, as Marx put it, the "pre-history" of human society will have been brought to a close. And instead of social events being explicable only in terms of relations into which people enter independent of their will, of impersonal conflicts in which they find themselves involved and have to fight out, and of consequences of their actions which no one intended, they will be explained in terms of how people judged, chose and decided.

Marxism demonstrates the actualities and possibilities of human existence—and this, surely, is what philosophy should do for us. It should not be, as the linguistic philosophy seeks to make it, nothing but a specialised investigation of logical questions, but a thinking activity of making good use of such a specialised investigation. Marxism cannot and does not despise logical investigations, with their specialised concern about uses of language; but it does seek to make good use of them.

It is the demonstration of practical possibility that is all-important in philosophy; and one of the chief lessons of the study of logic is on how to employ the practical conception of possibility—and desirability—and overcome misunderstandings due to harbouring the theological-fatalistic conception of necessity. The final issue of class struggle under capitalism is the ending of class struggles and of the divisive effects of private property. The conclusion of Marx's analysis was the clarification of the issue, and the intellectual equipment of the struggle to bring it to a finish. The whole point of the scientific definition of human relations under communism is not to predict what must necessarily come about (for such a prediction is entirely foreign to social science), but is to examine the known character of the existing mode of production in order to demonstrate what it is possible to do and to achieve, which alone will enable human progress to continue. Modern technology contains the possibility of a complete change in human relations, the change to communism; and its full development demands that that change be made.

At the same time as demonstrating the possibilities, therefore, Marxist philosophy also makes us aware of the difficulties and dangers of the present time. The future of mankind does not ensue from the present with the same type of causal necessity as day follows night. Day follows night because there is nothing to disturb the regularity of the motions of the solar system; but since the future of men will be made by men themselves, there is much some men may yet do to retard or divert its course. The future of men still depends on the outcome of their conflicts—in short, upon a fight; and the issue of no fight is settled until the last blow is struck.

In his book written in the thirties, *Fascism and Social Revolution*, R. Palme Dutt asked what could happen supposing that fascism were victorious on a world scale, and concluded that in that case there would occur a retrogression to a new phase of barbarism. Fascism was not victorious and this did not happen—but it could have happened. At the present day we have similarly to ask ourselves what could happen supposing that there is a nuclear war on a world scale. Half the human race would certainly be destroyed, and the greater part of the world devastated and polluted by radio-active fall-out. Some socialists have said that in that case the survivors would be rid of capitalism and so would go ahead to build a communist society. But what grounds have we to determine with confidence how survivors would react in such circumstances? All that is certain is that their condition would be far more miserable than that of any previous generation. With their nervous systems deranged by horrors and their reproductive organs by radio-activity, there is no knowing what they would do. Again, it is possible that the great organisations of state control that modern industry engenders might become so powerful and so fixed into a rigid pattern (as has happened before in the history of some communities) that technological progress would be halted and something like the state of affairs envisaged by George Orwell in *1984* would be realised. These disturbing speculations illustrate the principle that men's future is never settled until it becomes their past.

Finally, in thus publishing the contemporary philosophy of man, Marxism derives from the scientifically-based conception of the human condition and its possibilities rational humanist conceptions of human values and aims, which it sets against the present state of affairs, to inspire the struggle to overcome it and not succumb to its difficulties and dangers. That is what people have always looked for in philosophy.

CHAPTER FOUR

Communism and Human Values

I. SCIENCE AND EVALUATION

THE scientific demonstration of what it is possible to make of human life by progress to communism is at the same time a demonstration of its desirability. It establishes *factual* judgments about the actual character and mode of development of forces of production and relations of production; practical or *political* judgments about what has to be done and who has to do it, if human relations are to be developed in conformity with the possibilities and requirements of technological progress; and, finally, *value* judgments about the desirability of the end and the merit of the struggle to reach it.

The scientific ideas of communism about social development and human personality, and likewise its ideas about how to conduct the politics of class struggle, are not derived from moral concepts or value judgments; they are derived from investigation of human relations and experience of class struggle. On the other hand, moral concepts and value judgments are derived from the scientific and political ideas of communism. Thus communism is not founded on principles of morality but, on the other hand, it enunciates foundations for value judgments. Communism does not by a moral argument deduce an ideal of human association and standards of conduct but, on the other hand, by examining the actual conditions and possibilities of human association and the causes and effects of different kinds of conduct it finds the reasons for judging one form of association more desirable than another, and one mode of conduct better than another.

At the same time, the value judgments which the scientific ideas of communism lead to are not in contradiction to those which have been previously evolved during the progressive development of mankind. Communism does not contradict the traditional conceptions of human values exemplified in the condemnation of greed, cruelty and oppression, the assertion of the rights of individuals, the inviolability of human personality and the brotherhood of men; on the contrary, it embraces them, justifies them by sufficient reasons and shows the way to convert them from ideals into realities.

The evaluative significance of the scientific ideas of communism was already shown very clearly in the work of Marx.

Marx's arguments for replacing capitalism by socialism are not "moral" arguments, in the commonly accepted sense. Yet they are arguments in favour of doing something, in support of certain prescriptive judgments of value. Marx did not simply make a prediction: capitalism will in fact be replaced by socialism, because the laws of social development make it inevitable. He did not merely advise people to make a virtue of necessity by voluntarily acting in the way they were compelled by the laws of history to act anyhow. He investigated the actual development of relations of production, and on this he based prescriptive practical judgments to guide action to change them in a desirable way. He never supposed socialism would be brought into being without the prescribed collective action, or that it could not fail. He stated facts; but he did not merely state facts, in stating them he execrated them and, on the other hand, warmly advocated the new conditions that should replace them. And the more clearly, fully and factually he described the existing conditions and what should replace them, the greater was the moral force with which he drove home his condemnation of the one and advocacy of the other.

This mixed descriptive-evaluative character of Marx's social analysis has been remarked on by a number of his readers. Dr Popper drew attention to it in the second volume of *The Open Society and its Enemies*. The latest to remark on it is Dr E. J. Hobsbawm, who says in his Introduction to the English translation of Marx's *Precapitalist Economic Formations* (1964) that Marx's theory is "a model of facts, but, seen from a slightly different angle, the *same* model provides us with value-judgments".

With the development of the sciences in modern times it has become an axiom in some quarters that questions of fact, such as are ascertained by the sciences, are logically unconnected with questions of value. This conclusion of Hume, revived by the logical-analytic philosophy, became the latter's most influential contention. If you are making a scientific inquiry you are unconcerned with questions about values, and if you are engaged in making evaluations you are not engaged in any kind of scientific enquiry. The confusion of both thought and action leading to and resulting from this antimony is extreme. There is confusion about science and also confusion about values; but the root of it is confusion about science.

Of course, the conclusions of science must not be influenced by antecedent valuations, in the sense that a scientific inquiry must always test its conclusions in terms of what is the case and not of what someone thinks ought to be the case. But that does not mean that scientific generalisation, on the one hand, and evaluation on the other, are separate and independent matters.

The setting of them in antithesis results in the first place from taking natural sciences as the model, and ignoring the special character of social science. When a physicist generalises about the behaviour of atoms, his conclusions merely show how atoms in fact behave and have no bearing on how they ought to behave. This is not surprising, since such words as "ought" apply only in prescribing the behaviour of people and have no meaning if applied to atoms. But social science differs from natural science in that it deals with people, and generalisations about people, stating the actual conditions of their lives and effects of their actions, do have some bearing on deciding what people ought to do.

In the second place, the antithesis results from so limiting the scope of social science that it is not permitted to generalise in the way natural sciences do. In accordance with the old positivist philosophy of science, social science is limited to stating particular facts and formulating statistical correlations. Of course, if scientific inquiry is so limited, social science remains on a merely classificatory and descriptive level, and is not permitted to arrive at the sort of generalisation familiar in the natural sciences and which, in social science, does become relevant to the foundation of evaluations. Such generalisations do not merely describe social relations, but show how people can and do change them corresponding to the development of their actual means of satisfying their needs, and therefore how both existing relations and men's aspirations and aims to change them satisfy or fall short of human needs and possibilities of developing human capacities.

The generalisations which Marx established for social science (comparable with those established as the foundations of other departments of science) do provide a basis for evaluations. This means that not only does the Marxist scientific approach to social questions formulate aims for the present, but the same generalisations on which present aims are based is the basis for evaluation of the past. The Marxist historical approach not only tries to explain what happened, but the way it explains it is the basis for evaluating it, for evaluating historical actions, institutions and movements and, in another sense, social, political and moral ideas. Such evaluation is, indeed, inseparable from the scientific approach to history. If the study of history is regarded as nothing but making a record of events, then naturally it is not evaluative—but neither is it scientific. So far from the scientific approach to society and its history being antithetical to evaluation, the approach which fails to evaluate fails as science.

Scientific generalisation about people and society shows that people can live only by co-operating to obtain their requirements from nature, that they depend on each other, and that they can develop their human nature and human powers only by adapting relations of production to forces of production. Consequently, it shows the deprivations they suffer, in relation to human needs and the latent possibilities of human life, while they remain in primitive conditions and while they suffer the effects of self-alienation.

It is only in our present epoch, when, as Marx put it, social relations have developed to the stage which "brings the pre-history of human society to a close", that it is at length possible for these deprivations to be overcome. And it is now, when to end alienation effects has become a practical question in the field of social action, that the corresponding science can be and is worked out in the field of social theory. Science then establishes the sufficient reasons for the practical desirability of the communist reconstitution of human relations, and of everything that can tend to overcome, and can finally remove, the alienation effects in human relations. This value judgment is not founded merely on the sentiments of approbation or pleasure which may be evoked by the image of personal relations free from impersonal conflicts, and of everyone having the opportunity to satisfy his needs—though there does go with it the cultivation of such sentiments. It is founded on the scientific demonstration that this is what people can and must do in order to develop the mode of human co-operation by which they live.

The guiding principle of the scientific materialist communist humanist method of arriving at value judgments is that what is worth while, what is good, what is right, what ought to be aimed at and done in human relations and human behaviour is what

promotes the human mode of existence—or, as Marx put it in the
Economic and Philosophic Manuscripts, "realises the human
essence". It is what promotes that mode of existence in which people
co-operate to obtain what they require, and in which the development of the personality of each is aided by and aids that of others.

This principle does not exemplify the naturalistic fallacy. It is not
a definition of what "good" means (for of course, as linguistic
philosophers have pointed out, universalisable value judgments are
not factual but prescriptive). What it does is to establish, in terms
of human relations, the objective standard by reference to which
value judgments can be based, not on individual and subjective
sentiments and aspirations, or, for that matter, on class interests,
but on sufficient reasons.

For ages and ages the common people, and the representatives of
progressive thought, · have proclaimed these human values and
deplored and condemned whatever goes counter to them, even while
they have accepted the class values and moral codes thrown up by
particular social formations. But they have proclaimed them as
aspirations hardly realisable, or as realisable only by individuals or
sects who separate themselves from the mass of sinful humanity;
as drawn down as revelations from heaven, not as rooted in the
earthly existence of men. What Marxist social theory does is to
discover the foundations for human values—the reasons for them,
the demonstration of their universalisability or objectivity—in the
science of man; and at the same time discover how men, when they
have advanced to the stage where they are able to establish the
science of man, can conduct and win a struggle to make the conditions
for a good life not a dream but an everyday reality. It strips the
idea of a good life of its supernatural glamour, as something to be
earned by the happy elect in another world, and presents it in
commonplace terms as descriptive of ordinary people going about
their worldly business.

2. HUMAN VALUES AND CLASS INTERESTS

In discussing earlier the linguistic analysis of the use of moral
words and the nature of moral reasoning I concluded that the
primary moral questions, on which the answers to others depend,
concern the desirability of forms of human association.

The Marxist approach is to find a reasoned answer to such
questions by examining the actual way in which human society,

on which all individuals depend, is and has to be kept going. It finds the standard of objective value judgment in the fact that people associate to produce their means of life, and that their form of association either helps or hinders the development and social use of their forces of production. The communist aim is for the establishment of those personal relations between people, free of earlier self-alienation and impersonal restraints and conflicts, in which they can develop and use all the resources of technology for the satisfaction of human needs and, on that basis, freely enjoy as individuals "that development of human energy which is an end in itself". Thus Communism does what all humanist philosophies have sought to do—validate value judgments by reference to the conditions of existence of men as men. It does this, however, not by appealing to sentiments and desires, inclinations allegedly inherent in each separate individual, but by ascertaining the necessary conditions of association for utilising those forces of production by which alone people support their social life and create and satisfy their needs.

In the current circumstances of division of class interests, the communist aim corresponds to some class interests in opposition to others, and demands the subordination of the latter to the former and, eventually, their complete elimination. Aims which do not accord with interests cannot be practicable aims—and therefore there is no sense in arguing about their desirability, since desirability entails practicability. Aims only become real aims and desirable aims when they express interests: they are not, as Marx and Engels insisted in *The German Ideology*, conjured up out of some abstract philosophical conception of man and his good, but they are practically conceived and find expression in the actual historical struggles of living people. But yet the reasoning which validates value judgments does not validate the communist aim merely because it accords with particular interests, but rather values those interests and asserts their over-riding claim, because the interests of working people are ever bound up with the development of human co-operation to satisfy human needs (the human way of life), which can at last be practically realised in the communist aim of the modern working-class movement. As Marx and Engels said, the aim of socialism and communism only emerged from the realm of utopia and became a practical aim with the formation of the modern industrial working class, and only the conscious struggle of that class against those whose interests are opposed to it can bring socialism and communism into being. But the reason for the desirability of the social aim, and for the subordination of some interests to others which it entails until such time as it is completely achieved, is not concerned with the particular interests of particular persons or classes but with what has to be done to bring about relations of production within which people can continue to develop the use of the forces of production they have already created. For to bring relations of production into line with forces of production is what people have to do, what men as men have to do, to carry on their human mode of life. As things are, such a requisite change in relations of production is in the interests of some people (the great majority who do the productive work) and not of others. Hence it involves social conflicts based on conflicts of class interests, and the requirement, rooted in the way human life has .actually developed, of subordinating some interests to others.

An argument from class interests, which merely says "We are workers and socialism is in the interests of the working class, therefore we ought to aim at socialism", has some force as an incentive to struggle, but none at all as establishing the universalisability of value judgments. And like much bad logic, it is also in the long run ineffective in practice. It has nothing to say to workers who feel that their personal interests might suffer in the course of any big social change, and who do not see why they should make personal sacrifices for a cause. It has nothing to say to middle-class people and intellectuals. And, since class interest is considered the source of obligation, it implies that while workers ought to strive for socialism, capitalists ought to strive to stop them getting it. In fact, capitalists do so; but a socialist argument which implies that they *ought* to do so is inconsistent and unconvincing. It is proper that in conducting a struggle for socialism which mainly depends on mass working-class economic and political struggle, the appeal should continually be made to the defence and promotion of working-class interests. But in practice much *more* is required than appeals to class interests, and much more is always said in socialist argument. The appeal is always made to conceptions of "humanity"—to the idea that personal or sectional interests ought to be subordinated to the common good, and that socialism is desirable for the sake not merely of the interests of the working class but of the future of humanity. Capitalists pursuing their own profit stand condemned from the human point of view. And workers fighting for their emancipation as a class are justified. What is involved in class struggles is *more* than a clash of interests.

As Engels showed, today the emancipation of the exploited class means "emancipating society at large from all exploitation, oppression, class distinction and class struggles". That is why Lenin, in his address to the Communist youth on *The Tasks of the Youth Leagues* (1920), after saying "Our morality is derived from the interests of the class struggle of the proletariat . . . communist morality is the morality which serves this struggle, which unites the toilers against exploitation . . .", went on to say: "Morality serves the purpose of helping human society to rise to a higher level and to get rid of the exploitation of labour . . . The basis of communist morality is the struggle for the consolidation and completion of communism."

3. ENDS AND MEANS

All considerations of human values—of what is right or just or good or desirable, and of what ought or ought not to be done, and what is praiseworthy and what is blameworthy—involve considerations about ends and means, and the subordination of means to ends. Broadly speaking, in rational moral judgment the end justifies the means. And not only is this true but in practice this truth is almost universally recognised. For example, a war is thought just if it is waged for just ends. The important questions that have to be answered concern the validation of human ends, and what means they exact.

Rational value judgment about ends and means is not at all the same thing as machiavellian calculation. So-called machiavellianism consists of exclusive preoccupation with particular *interests* (or, as often happens, with what are mistakenly imagined to be those interests), and of saying that anything may be done that serves them. Thus, for example, the original machiavellian Prince was advised to practice any cruelty or dirty trick that he could get away with, so long as it enhanced his power. Similarly, it might be said, from a machiavellian point of view, that any standards of good faith or humanity are quite irrelevant to the pursuit of working-class interests, as they are to that of capitalist interests. Keep faith with no one, if advantage is to be got by breaking it. Kill, oppress and torture whenever there is terror to be spread and advantage to be gained by it. The relevant question here concerns what sort of society would actually be built, and what sort of ends attained, if people acted only on such principles.

In practice, the machiavellian point of view is never adopted by masses but only by leaders. Such leaders generally see interests only in the form of power, so that what preoccupies them is the preservation and enlargement of their own power. While they get put into power as representatives of a class, their career often ends by the class having to get rid of them.

A fundamental principle of rational value judgment about ends and means, and the subordination of means to ends, is that only persons are ends, and anything else only means. This is entailed, obviously, by the standard of judging the desirability of forms of association by how they promote the human way of life, that is to say, how they serve the lives of persons and not anything else. Thus objects are used as means, and similarly institutions are set up as means. Objects and institutions are only means, not ends—and to regard them as ends is a logical absurdity and a moral atrocity. It means subordinating living people, who feel and think, to material things and social institutions which do neither. What it amounts to is symbolised in the well-known festival of the juggernaut: living people throw themselves down before and are crushed by the great juggernaut—which is itself built and pushed along by people.

The principal ideological alienation effect of private property consists of thinking of people as means and of objects and institutions as ends. Thus as Marx and Engels observed in *The German Ideology*, "in all ideology men and their circumstances appear upside down". For instead of objects being fashioned and institutions instituted to serve people, it appears that people must devote their lives to seeking values embodied in objects and be bound by institutions which exact service for their own sakes. As Marx and Engels added, "this phenomenon arises just as much from their historical life process as the inversion of objects on the retina does from their physical life process".

With private appropriation goes the development of commodity production, which profoundly affects the way people think of values —as is shown in customary uses of words. Objects made, exchanged and used are called and thought of as "goods" and "values". This use of language and way of thinking expresses the fact that people have to devote themselves to producing and appropriating objects, which are themselves the values they seek after (or their equivalent in money), rather than the enjoyment of human activity itself. Human activity is for the sake of objects, rather than objects being valued for their use in human activity. This is what Marx (*Capital*, I, 1, 4) termed "the fetishism of commodities". And this upside down way of looking at things, in which objects are the goods and values, results in people being valued in the way commodities are. Thus if businessmen are discussing whom to appoint to manage a new factory, they may conclude: "Smith is a good man". They value the man (in terms of both use-value and exchange-value) in the same way as they value the products.

Having adopted a way of living by appropriating and exchanging objects, and having thus made objects into values to the production and acquisition of which human life is devoted, people have to associate themselves into distinct and rival communities, of which the modern nation is the most highly developed example, and institute states and all manner of organisations, in order to enable the mode of production, appropriation and exchange to be carried on. These organisations or institutions then exact service. When objects are turned into values, so that people are subordinated to objects, and value each other like objects, the result is also that people see their obligations as owed, not simply to other people, but to organisations. Organisations and institutions likewise become ends, and not mere means.

On the basis of private property and commodity production, then, from which emerges that way of speaking and thinking for which objects are "goods" and "values", there emerges also the way of speaking and thinking for which particular communities, institutions and organisations have a being of their own, with their own interests and requirements, independent of and superior to that of individual people, and imposing claims on them. This is, indeed, the source of that whole verbal procedure of making abstractions into concrete things (the so-called "hypostatisation" or "reification", that is, "thingification", of abstractions) which is enshrined in religion, developed in metaphysical and idealist ways of thinking in general, and issues in so many very peculiar uses of language to the confounding of linguistic philosophers today.

The entire upside-down world we have made for ourselves needs putting right side up. In practice, this means achieving the communist mode of productive association in which economic activity is planned for providing for the satisfaction of human needs—in which, in the words of *The Communist Manifesto*, "all production is concentrated in the hands of a vast association . . . an association in which the free development of each is the condition for the free development of all". And in ideas, it means arriving at rational value judgments, in which means are not presented as ends, and only persons and their activities are ends.

The whole materialist philosophy, with its principle that "being is prior to thinking", the whole dialectical materialist method for the proper assembly of information, the whole philosophy of man and science of man, is for arriving at rational value judgments and thus discovering how to live together as human beings.

The communist aim of a desirable form of human association is, of course, economic. For what is or is not attainable by people does depend on the economic organisation of society. At the same time, an aim which was exclusively economic, which only consisted in advocating a certain form of economic activity, would obviously be abstract and incomplete, since economic activity is not the whole of life but only its necessary basis, and not an end but a means. In a society in which the use of modern techniques is developed and planned on the basis of communal ownership, productive work ceases to be arduous or time-consuming. In such a society people must make arrangements to provide themselves with all-round education, to equip themselves with knowledge, mental and manual skills and culture, and to provide themselves with all the opportunities and incentives to develop all-round individual abilities and capacity to enjoy leisure and free activity. The communist aim includes all that, and this is the practical content of the slogan "From each according to his abilities, to each according to his needs". Economic activity and economic organisation is for the sake of the development of the personal capacities, relations, needs and satisfactions of needs, and enjoyments, of individual people.

What, then, of that "free development of human energy which is an end in itself"?

In the totality of individual human activities which make up social life each person and his activity is always dependent on and contributory to other persons and their activity, so that while only persons and their activities are ends, no such end is ever exclusively an end in itself but always at the same time a means to other ends. However satisfying any one activity or its results may be to the individual or individuals concerned, it is always, when viewed in relation to the wider field of social life and to other individuals and other activities, done or achieved not only for its own sake but for the sake of something else—just as no single person could ever exist, or any personal activity be enjoyed, unless supported and sustained by other persons and other activities.

But in the communist conception of social ends, the development of the totality of personal activities, as distinct from particular activities within it, is not advocated for the sake of anything else, but for its own sake. And here is the only absolute in human evaluation.

4. FREEDOM, NECESSITY AND OBLIGATION

The communist form of association, made practical and desirable by men's technological progress, is one in which the end of association becomes, in Marx's phrase, the "free development of human energies". The satisfaction of individual needs is a means to this end. For human needs are the needs for human life, and life is activity of individual organisms. The communist aim is, then, for people to associate to supply the needs of each individual, so that in doing so, and as a result of it, each may enjoy along with and in his dependence on others the free exercise and development of his individual human capacities.

This end is expressed, not just as "development", but as "free development", for the simple reason that in so far as people are constrained or coerced in what they do they are being treated as means and their development and enjoyment of life as persons is distorted and frustrated. The word "free", in this context, therefore carries the negative significance of "not coerced or constrained". An activity is freely done when a person chooses to do it and carries it through without external constraint. A person is free in so far as he is not coerced in his choice of activity and is allowed to do what he chooses to do.

On the other hand, those definitions of "freedom" such as that proposed by Hegel in his political philosophy) which suggest that individuals are only free when regimented by the state, represent only a gross misuse of words for the purpose of calling unfreedom by the honorific name of freedom. The usual apology for such definitions is that the individual can truly be said to be free only when directed for his own good in a way that effectively prevents the domination of his behaviour by his own unfree irrational individual impulses. The free person, however, directs his own impulses for himself, and does not need to be himself subjected for his own good to the impulsive behaviour of policemen.

Evidently, freedom is a possession of individuals. Just as every social attribute is derivative from the activities and relations of individuals, so is freedom. A free society is an association providing for individual freedom. And to the extent that individuals lack freedom their society falls short of being a free society.

Freedom exists only in the persons of definite individuals, and then only in their carrying out definite activities. To speak, therefore of freedom in general, as a condition or as an aim, and to say in general terms that people or society are free or not free, is to use words vaguely and ambiguously in a way that may cover up a variety of negations of freedom (and very often does, as in the contemporary expression "the free world"). It is necessary to say which persons are free, and in what respects, and to do what. In the course of social development (in which alone both freedom and unfreedom occur) men have made themselves free in various respects and in various relationships and, at the same time, enslaved one another in other respects and in other relationships.

The scope of human freedom, in the sense of the variety of activities men are capable of successfully undertaking, is always conditioned by the actual physical constitution of the human body but is the product of technological progress. The invention of technological means and the subduing of natural forces for human ends provides the basis, and the greater the technological proficiency of men the greater is the scope of the freedom attainable by individuals. Thus in primitive societies, although within the communal relations men are comparatively free from coercion and subjection to one another, their technological backwardness places them in a comparatively subject position to nature. There is not much any individual can do outside the round of traditional tribal activities they all do together, and consequently the whole idea of their being individuals with rights and interests of their own does not occur to people. The "noble savage" was only thought to be free by bourgeois romantics, he does not think of himself as a free individual. Consciousness, as Marx and Engels put it (*The German Ideology*, I, 1), remains "mere herd-consciousness". On the other hand, as people have developed their technology and mastery over nature they have made themselves subject to each other. Thus there develops a contradiction between the actual scope of freedom made possible by technological development, and the opportunities which their social relations offer to individuals of benefiting from it. Class struggles accordingly take on the conscious aspect of struggles for freedom—not for freedom in general, but for specific freedoms— as people denied opportunities contend for them, and others combine to defend those freedoms, in the form of privileges, which they have got at the expense of the former.

Capitalism, vehicle of revolutionary technological advance, has allowed extended freedom to be won for individuals, as the under-privileged classes have contended for opportunities of enjoyment and advantage. Although up to the present modern industry has tied people to machines, it is by its productivity the agency of freedom. Its fullest development and use provides for fullest individual freedom. The communist form of association, corresponding to the requirements of the unfettered development and use of modern technology, provides the basis for and serves the end of the maximum enlargement of the scope of human freedom and the enjoyment of free activity by all individuals.

The exercise of free activity is subject to necessary conditions, without which it could not take place. For the unfrustrated enjoyment of freedom, therefore, in any conscious activity, people have consciously to submit themselves to its necessary conditions—to know what they are, and to observe them. In any sphere of activity, freedom entails appreciation of necessity. And this necessity is expressed in negative and conditional generalisations, of the form: "So and so never happens, or cannot be done", "So and so never happens, or cannot be done, without so and so".

In the first place, the carrying through of any undertaking depends on the causal properties of the subject of the undertaking and of the instruments used—including, under the latter heading, the human body itself. It was in this connection that Engels (*Anti-Duhring*, chapter 11) originally said that "freedom consists in the control over ourselves and over external nature which is founded on knowledge of natural necessity". His point was that ourselves and everything else being subject to causal determination does not prohibit the possibility of our free action but is its condition. If *anything* could happen, then we could not make anything happen according to our own intentions. And the more we know about the causal laws which we cannot alter, the more free we are to produce the effects we want. When, after more than fifty years, the same point percolated through to bourgeois philosophy, Professor Ryle remarked that the fact that both billiard balls and billiard players are subject to the laws of mechanics does not prohibit the free play of billiards but is its necessary condition.

To win and realise freedom in human activity, therefore, it is in the first place necessary to appreciate that it is in all respects subject to causal law, and to get to know as much about that law as possible. Such knowledge is a condition for enlarging the scope of our freedom. It is in the second place necessary to appreciate the conditions which must be satisfied in the sphere of human relations. For individuals, the necessity of these conditions, when clearly appreciated, takes the form of obligations. The appreciation of necessity in the form of obligations is, then, a condition for extending and universally realising the actual enjoyment of freedom.

The basic obligation of freedom in communist association is simply the obligation to work. For as Marx observed (*Capital*, III, 48, 3), work must be done, and however much labour is lightened and made interesting and attractive, however short the necessary working hours, and however wide the choice of occupation, it "still remains a realm of necessity". It is indeed, as he said elsewhere (*Critique of the Gotha Programme*), "the prime necessity of life".

In order to be able to work, and then to be able to enjoy the advantages and opportunities afforded by the products of work, human individuals are dependent on one another, and upon their complex social association, in a variety of ways. Indeed, no individual can ever do much without the good will of others. In general, then, individuals who are to enjoy freedom of activity must necessarily work together and then, both in their working relations and in all their consequent relations, they must require of each other and give to each other support, sympathy and consideration.

These necessary conditions in the regulation of human behaviour, that is, the behaviour of individuals, which constitute the obligations necessary for the enjoyment of free personal activity, are summed up in the so-called "golden rule"—treat others as you would have them treat you. You would have them work for you, so you must work for them; you would have them minister to your needs, so you must minister to theirs; you would have them be kind, sympathetic and considerate to you, so you must be so to them; you would not have them use you to your disadvantage in order to get something for themselves, so you must not use them in such a way. This rule was attributed to the legendary Christ; it is simply the expression of the experience and practical wisdom of those who work together. But it has never been practised on any wide scale because (as Jesus himself was reported to have pointed out) it is totally impracticable in societies based on private property.

In communist society, when the practical relations between individuals have become "perfectly intelligible and reasonable", social obligation becomes simply what is necessary as the condition for enjoying free activity on the basis of working together. As moral words are now generally used, the words "must" and "must not" are often and unthinkingly used as synonymous for "ought" and "ought not". In communist society "ought" has no other significance than the ordinary conditional "must". Obligations are simply what everyone must accept in order to carry on their associated free activity, just as, in a related sense, they must accept the laws of nature in order to carry on their intercourse with nature. A person who behaves badly has then to be treated as one who has made a mistake (possibly a very serious one, but only a mistake none the less) which others will take it upon themselves to correct in him—just as someone who makes some mistake at work would be corrected by his fellows. Morality altogether ceases to be something socially *imposed* on individuals as a *restriction* of their activity. And as to all those activities which men and women enjoy together as friends and lovers, and which constitute the principal element in their individual happiness—these do not come within "the realm of necessity" but of free activity, made possible by the mutual fulfilment of obligations.

5. MORALITY, INTELLIGIBLE AND UNINTELLIGIBLE

It may be useful at this stage to sum up the argument so far developed about value judgments. I have proceeded from the standpoint (argued earlier in connection with the linguistic analysis of the use of moral words) that the fundamental question concerns the desirability of forms of human association. To argue this otherwise than in terms of personal preferences or class interests (that is, to try to arrive at an objective or universalisable judgment) depends on the scientific investigation of the human mode of life. Men live by the social production of their means of life, and that form of association is universalisably desirable which permits the unfettered co-operative development and use of the most powerful technology —and that is communism. At the stage of technological development we have now reached it is possible both to lay the foundations of the science of man and, guided by it, to actually achieve communism. It has become in conception scientific, and in practice a practicable objective.

The consideration, then, of what the communist form of association, with its principle of "to each according to his needs", actually makes possible for people shows that this consists of "the free development of human energies". It is this, then, the totality of free activities of free individuals, that we find to be an end in itself. In other words, human life is itself the end of human life. The desirability of communism lies in its being the form of association in which people, masters of nature and unfettered by exploitation of one another, live a free life together, in which their personal obligations consist simply of the golden rule of regarding persons as ends and not as means, and everything else as means of human activity and satisfaction. Men's answer to their own accidental and insignificant place in the universe is then to make everything that comes within our ken our object, there for us to make our own in the sense of use and control, and if not control at all events understanding.

It is in the light of these fundamental conclusions, derived from the science of man, that we can judge the past and the present. No desirable form of association has been established, or has in the past been possible, or conceivable except as a utopia. As Marx put it, we have been in the stage of "pre-history". But we can judge the currents of human activity, and the struggles which people have engaged in and are engaging in now, in the light of the scientific principles of communism—and this is the objective standard of value judgment. Up to fairly recently, it was no more possible for men, lacking the knowhow, to reach a comprehensive objective conception of human ends and human values, and consequent standards of judgment, than to reach one of nature and the laws of development of human society. True, conceptions of communism and of human values have been in men's minds since they first began to think in a way that opposes ideals against actualities. But they could only take the form of impracticable fantasy. Now these conceptions, scientifically based, claim the adherence of the organised working people as a practical programme of social reconstruction, in their interests and within their power to realise.

It is, however, one thing to assert the practicability and desirability of communism, the justice of the class struggles through which alone it can be attained, and the human values which it embodies; but quite another to find how to decide what ought to be done in the actual situations in which we find ourselves when living within social relations that fall far short of communism. The questions about which those discussing ethics have mainly puzzled their heads are precisely such questions of what we ought to do individually and collectively in the day-to-day conduct of contemporary life, and on what principles they can be decided.

In a communist society such questions of morality, private and public, would become perfectly intelligible—for questions of "ought" would become questions of "must", and it would be as obvious that we must not set out to violate the golden rule of human relations as that we must not try to violate the laws of nature : in either case we could not get what we wanted. But where people are still divided, having to use one another as means and subject themselves to their own means of production, to their own products and to their own institutions and organisations, moral standards cannot but appear as *impositions* and, moreover, the contradictions in human relations are reflected in contradictions in standards and in obligations. In so far as human relations fall short of intelligibility and rationality, so must human morality.

CHAPTER FIVE

Communism and Morality

1. MORALITY AS AN ALIENATION EFFECT

As hitherto recommended, morality has always been an external imposition on individuals. And that is because, as words are commonly understood, the question "Why ought I to do this?" is distinct from the question "What will I get out of it?" To be guided only by considerations of personal preference and advantage is the negation of morality. And consequently it is always open to the individual to ask "Why should I be moral at all? And if I am, why should I follow this prescription rather than some contrary one?" In conditions when some moral code has been so thoroughly implanted in people that they never question it, such questions, naturally, do not arise. But in the present transitional state of society they are asked by many people and worry them a great deal.

From the time of Thomas Hobbes, those bourgeois moralists who rejected theories of a supernatural origin and supernatural sanctions for morality have in many cases accepted it as an axiom that people are so constituted as always to seek their own advantage, or their own satisfactions, or (as it used to be expressed) pleasures. Obviously, as Hobbes already pointed out, if everyone seeks only his own advantage, without regard to anyone else, the results must be chaotic and to the advantage of nobody. Puzzling this out led to the utilitarian principle, that morality consists of precepts designed to regulate individual actions in such a way as to make for the greatest advantage, or the greatest possible sum of satisfactions, for everyone. Even Mr R. M. Hare, an overt opponent of utilitarianism, arrived at much the same conclusion when he said that morality arbitrates between interests and finds the ways of best satisfying them all.

There is an obvious snag in the utilitarian principle of basing the morality of actions on the advantages or satisfactions to be gained from them. It is that such satisfactions belong only to individuals, not to communities, and in many cases the advantage to be gained by individuals by acting against the precepts of morality is greater than that to be gained by obeying them. Or in Mr Hare's type of arbitration, it is well known that parties who think they can get more without arbitration than by means of it, tend to refuse arbitration. It is not true that it always pays to be good. But if the only basis for morality is the gaining of satisfactions, how persuade the individual to forego satisfactions for the sake of morality, or for the sake of the satisfactions of others, when he knows that many others decline to forego their satisfactions for the sake of his? Recognising this difficulty, Jeremy Bentham (the most practical and consistent and, therefore, also the most objectionable of all bourgeois moralists) made it his life's work to exhort the legislature to devise laws to ensure that bad people should never get what they wanted. People will never be moral unless in some way bullied or frightened into it. Jeremy Bentham thought (and with some justification) that to make working people, for example, forego the pleasures of idleness and shoulder the moral task of industry it would be more efficacious to legislate for starvation and build workhouses than merely to encourage Wesleyan Methodism and threaten them with hell fire.

For even the most naturalistic bourgeois ethics, therefore, morality turns out to be just as much an external imposition on individuals as it is for more spiritual-minded accounts of it. Derive it from material pleasures and satisfactions or from God and the angels—morality is still a thing alien to and imposed on individuals.

This state of affairs is not difficult to account for. Human society is based on the social production of the means of life, and people's association in society, within which alone they become persons, must always assume some definite form, determined by the mode of production and expressed in their property relations. The form of association determines corresponding moral obligations, in as much as its maintenance and development requires standards of how people should live and behave and treat one another. Moral obligations are then what persons owe to each other on account of their social association. This means that obligations entail rights, which are simply the converse of obligations. If each person has duties to others, they have duties to him—and that constitutes his personal claim on them, or his rights. These conceptions develop and change with the development and change of the form of association. And, naturally, in associations in which different persons are considered as having different social status, obligations and rights are not uniform

for all persons (although Mr Hare and others, writing from the point
of view of bourgeois legality, have thought they necessarily must be).
Some persons have more rights and fewer obligations, and others
more obligations and fewer rights.

There is and can be no such thing as human association "in
general" but only particular forms of association, to which different
prescriptive conceptions of obligations and rights correspond. Where
there are class divisions and one class interest is dominant within the
given form of association, the corresponding obligations and rights
express the dominant class interest, and the corresponding moral
code becomes class-biased, not a code of universal but of class-biased
morality. And then where class interests are in conflict, and where
also the private interests of individuals are in conflict with proclaimed
social obligations, it is impossible that any obligations should be
generally fulfilled or rights respected without being in some measure
enforced. Consequently the assertion of obligations and rights, necessary in human association, has to be effected by socially organised
means of moral exhortation, persuasion and pressure backed by
physical coercion and the exaction of penalties.

It may be concluded that so long as private property, with its
divisive effects, continues to form the basis of human association,
morality must always take the form of a moral code socially imposed
on individuals—and moreover of a code which, while claiming
universality, is in reality a disguised expression of class interest. The
whole long effort of bourgeois radicals to make morality acceptable
to all individuals as being in all their interests is itself merely an
ideological product of the bourgeois property relations. For the whole
concept of "advantage", "interest", "satisfaction" and "pleasure",
on which they try to base morality, is generated from private property
—since it makes the good or end something you get or appropriate,
and not something you do. And it founders hopelessly on the divisive
effects of private property. But whatever the theory of ethics, the
moral code never appears under an amiable or sympathetic aspect.
Whether it appears in the starry raiment of Wordsworth's "Stern
Daughter of the Voice of God" or in the more earthy habilaments of
a Benthamite workhouse master, its accent is always stern and its
aspect forbidding.

Not only does morality, as Lucretius said of religion, present an
alien face "glowering at mortal men", but its deliverances are so
contradictory that the person trying to live a moral life often does

not know what to make of them. As well as being presented with contradictions in standards of judgment and assessment of what is praiseworthy or blameworthy, which are inevitable products of a society in which there are basic conflicts of class and sectional interest, there are no standards of judgment and assessment which yield unambiguous instructions. For example, when both thrift and generosity are virtues, and meanness and extravagance vices, how find the path of virtue and avoidance of vice? Or when obeying authority and consideration for others are both duties, what to do when the instructions of authority are inconsiderate or cruel? It is for these reasons that Aristotle said long ago that virtue was "the golden mean", and later Protestant and bourgeois moralists said that each man was responsible to himself and must follow "the monitor within"—and then denounced those whose inner monitors pronounced instructions they objected to. Today existentialist sages conclude that all choices are morally agonising and one has simply to choose.

These and similar moral contradictions arise from the fact that people see their end or good in the appropriation and possession of objects, see their obligations to one another in the form of obligations to institutions, and treat one another as objects and as means to the production and appropriation of objects. The basic contradiction lies in the fact that no one can then regard others in the same way as he regards himself (and this, no doubt, is also a reason why, in the most sophisticated bourgeois philosophy, the existence of other people as persons like oneself becomes problematic). For whereas people—other people—are regarded as objects and mere means, one can never regard oneself like that. The universalisability and consistency of moral judgments entails the application of the golden rule, but so long as people are so associated as to treat each other as things it can never be consistently applied. Thus moral judgments, which are meant to be universalisable, can never in practice be universalised. There are always moral contradictions and conflicts.

At the same time there has continually been asserted the idea that human relations should be governed by human sympathy, in defiance of all property, all authority and all moral codes. The perennial human conflict is between the expression and application of this idea and the demands made upon people by their economic relations and their institutions. This idea arises from amidst the masses of the working people, and has been eloquently expressed through the ages by poets, prophets, artists and philosophers; the conflict occurs in individual life, in the class struggle, in politics, religion, the arts, philosophy and, indeed, in every department of human activity. So long, however, as the contradictions of real life are not scientifically laid bare, the ideal of human relations seems to come "from the heart" rather than from reason, and to be a sentiment and aspiration rather than a practical programme of social reconstruction. But scientific humanism unites the human heart and human reason. The sentiments of the heart are fully expressed by the voice of reason.

Under communism, morality as an externally imposed restraint on free personal activity disappears, along with its ugly sister products of alienation—the state, politics and religion. For then there are no grounds for maintaining a state organisation to govern people, or engaging in politics to assert particular interests in the state. There are no grounds for imagining people to be lost in their material environment and sunk in sin, depending on supernatural agencies for their salvation. And the form of human association corresponds to individual needs and imposes on individuals no obligations that need be enforced on them contrary to the enjoyment of their free activity. When there are no longer conflicts of interest rooted in the ways people appropriate objects for their use, and when consequently there is no contradiction between how one would want others to treat one-self and how it is in one's interests to treat them, then self-knowledge and human sympathy can become the guide in life, and the golden rule of human relations can at last apply.

2. MORALS AND POLITICS OF CLASS STRUGGLE

The social development through which men make their way towards conditions of freedom involves and always has involved consciously conducted struggle, of men against intractable forces of nature and natural obstacles to human desires, and also of men against men. The former have made men adventurous and inured against various forms of hardship, the latter have made them cruel and vengeful and indifferent to the sufferings of others. As a result of developing language and conceptual thought, and so becoming aware of themselves and each other as persons, with common aims and dependent on each other, men have developed those traits of mutual regard and behaviour which are expressed by the word "humanity". And from exactly the same source, conjoined with the socially produced conflicts between them, they have developed the traits of "inhumanity". These are polar opposites emerging in the same process of human development, and the one could not emerge without the other. Thus if love, friendship, laughter and pity, products of human consciousness, are qualities foreign to the rest of the animal world and assume the form of human values, so is man's inhumanity to man a quality foreign to other animals, assuming the form of human evil. In our present epoch, with the advance of socialised co-operative production and the equalisation of persons, the values of humanity have become more prized than ever before, and are given practical expression in such things as the development of medicine, education and the social services. At the same time it has produced, and continues to produce, far more monstrous evidences of inhumanity than any previous epoch. The same technical resources which enable the one to be practised on a large scale do the same for the other.

To pretend, in the arena of human conflicts, that the precepts of humanity can become the universal guide of behaviour, is simply to close one's eyes to the actual human situation. If conflicts are there, it is impossible to contract out of them. And if any good is to come out of them they must be fought to a finish, and that means that men must go on inflicting injury on men. The Christian precept of "meekness" was advice given to poor men in circumstances when there was no visible prospect of their emancipation—but if "the meek shall inherit the earth" they cannot be meek in claiming their inheritance.

Until all exploitation of man by man is ended, morality cannot be based on a generalised human standpoint, expressing a common human point of view and interest, but only on a class standpoint. It either accepts a class-divided society without challenge, and then it is the expression of the point of view and interest of the exploiting classes; or it demands the abolition of class divisions, and then it is alien to exploiting classes and expresses the point of view and interest only of the others. The morality of scientific socialism and communism is class-biased and militant, and calls for a fight of all the working classes to overcome, as is now possible, the old and still present conditions of exploitation and alienation. For them, the practicability and human desirability of the aim demands and justifies the adoption of all those means of organised struggle which are necessary for attaining it. That implies that regard for human values must be made effective by opposition to whoever frustrates their realisation, and love and respect for one's fellows by hatred and contempt for those who live at the expense of others.

Having seen through the illusions of religion, with its conviction of sin and reliance on divine help; having understood the issues at stake in class struggle; having understood the functions of constituted state authority and the ideologies that go with it; and having rejected the imposition of a supposedly universal morality, whether it is based on calculations of maximum satisfaction and reconciliation of interests, or on divine revelation—for them the guide for conduct (as opposed to simple considerations of personal advantage) can only be found in considerations of what is demanded for the emancipation of labour.

For individuals, this still remains an imposition. For it opposes demands of social responsibility against individual interests, satisfactions and enjoyments. At the same time, a way of life in which each would live for the sake of his own satisfactions, simply making such adjustments and compromises as he has to in view of the fact that other people exist as well, cannot in fact satisfy, because it is the negation of people's togetherness and interdependence. In application, it deprives the individual of any aim to be achieved in his relations with others, on which relations, nevertheless, the whole mode of existence of himself and all other individuals depends. Such a deprived individual (common in all classes of contemporary society) has, of course, his personal ambitions: what he will get for himself, and what he will get others to get for him. But in the moral sense he is aimless. And when his ambition fails, and when, in any case, death overtakes him, he suffers complete frustration. As the popular saying says, "You can't take it with you". Each individual does need something besides his own satisfactions to live for, because of the way we have to live together, and something, too, besides his own personal possessions (in which category immediate family ties are included). This desideratum is often expressed by saying that we need to find "the meaning" of life, or to give life "a meaning", where the word "meaning" is used in much the same way as "aim", "end" or "purpose". Communism does serve individuals by giving life a meaning—a meaning derived from considerations of the real conditions of human life—not contradicted by death, and not derived, as with religion, from fantasies that are fast becoming incredible.

Communism, as the contemporary movement uniting the theory and practice of human emancipation, aims at universality in its practical as well as theoretical teaching. Its task is to work out prescriptions alike for collective public activity, in economics, social organisation and politics, and for individual personal conduct, directed to the end of bringing into being the human relations of communism.

3. THE EMPIRICAL FOUNDATION OF MORAL AND POLITICAL JUDGMENT

This whole discussion about value judgments—about desirable ends, and about what we ought to do—has been based on two important points of logic. The first is that scientific generalisation about social action does not demonstrate that any social outcome is in a fatalistic sense inevitable, but deals with possibilities. Confusion on this point has vitiated much discussion on questions of ethics— including discussion by Marxists. For if a certain outcome is inevitable, whatever we may or may not do, there is no point in reasoning about whether it is desirable or not. There is no point in reasoning about desirable ends if the necessary outcome of our actions is in any case predetermined. The second point of logic depends on the first, and is the point made by the linguistic philosophers—that value judgments, agreeing with factual ones in being universalisable, differ from them in their prescriptive character. These points of logic are, indeed, fundamental for any discussion on morals and politics.

From them follows another, which Mr Hare also did the service of stressing, that practical reason is, as he put it, "a kind of exploration". In other words, it is not possible to work out from first principles a whole system of what ought to be done; but just as scientific judgment is formed and tested and frequently modified in a process of exploration arising from practical experience, so it is and must be with the associated practical judgments. This does not entail scepticism and continual suspension of judgment in practical any more than in theoretical concerns. It means rather that the same type of empirical testing of conclusions applies in both. If Marxists disagree with some of the moral conclusions of other philosophers, that is because we seek to apply to value judgments generally rather more rigorous empirical tests than apologists for capitalism seem to think necessary.

The very conception of human ends, on which questions of practical principle turn, is essentially an exploratory one, based on investigating the general conditions of human existence. No *a priori* guarantee of truth attaches to the generalisations from which alone a generalised conception of human ends can be derived. Their foundation can be no more secure than that of any fundamental scientific generalisation—but that is security enough, and it is on such and only on such security that we have to stake the conduct of our lives.

When it comes not to a generalised conception of ends, but to more detailed conceptions of how to order our lives now, the exploratory or experimental character of practical judgment obviously affords less security. As in the sciences we may feel as secure as we can ever be entitled to feel in the fundamental principles, but less so in less universal generalisations, so it is in general prescriptions for conduct. No biologist seriously expects to have to abandon the theory of evolution, but he does expect to have to modify his ideas about particular biological phenomena. Similarly, while we may not expect to have to abandon the idea that men live by adapting their relations of production to their forces of production (the fundamental idea of Marxism), we would be very foolish if we did not expect to have to modify in the light of practical experience many of our first ideas as to how exactly that should in given circumstances be done and on exactly what principles people should conduct themselves in doing it. Such things as these have to be worked out as we go along, by trial and error, in the light of practical experience. To do that requires, moreover, not only experience but (as Mr Hare also said) an exercise of the imagination. This does not mean imagination in the sense of fantasy, but imagination in the sense of visualising possible situations with the aid of memory of how things have worked out in the past.

It is quite untrue, therefore, that from the conception of an end it is feasible to work out, independent of experience, a set of infallible rules for struggling towards it, and for personal and public conduct. On the contrary, such means have to be imaginatively and experimentally worked out. And that at the same time concretises and modifies the conception of the end. From the standpoint which sees the waging of class struggle as the imperative necessity for winning through to a desirable human mode of existence, the right decisions on action in particular situations, both public and private, must depend on so many variables whose values for given cases cannot be exactly determined, that it must always be impossible to devise formulas to programme any kind of moral-political computer to tell us exactly what to do. We always have to improvise, to some extent blindly, whether in personal or public affairs. For the rightness of actions is only finally decided when their consequences are known, so that questions of what exactly is right are often, at the time they are posed, formally undecidable. Memory and conclusions from the past are what we have to go on. But the more steadily we can keep the aims of communism before our eyes, and the more clearly we can understand the basic economic changes and changes in property relations necessary to realise them, the less likely are we to go irremediably wrong. Communism depends on economic reconstruction, and is economically practicable. If, then, as the study of the whole of human history demonstrates, economic factors are in the long run decisive in changing the mode of human life, there are good grounds to expect that the end will be achieved.

The comparatively short experience of communist practice already bears out these points—and the lesson has, indeed, been hard and painful, and is still being learned.

For example, in conditions of dangerous semi-legal or underground struggle, certain personal qualities come to be most highly valued among revolutionaries, qualities of self-sacrifice, devotion and loyalty combined with toughness. But these very qualities can, in some cases, be themselves so developed that self-sacrifice goes with indifference to the suffering of others, devotion to the cause with personal ambition and personal ruthlessness, and loyalty with unscrupulousness. And then, if victory is won, the very virtues which were prized in individuals turn against the realisation of the ends of the struggle. What took place in the Soviet Union during the years of Stalin's personal power bears this out. There highly prized qualities of determination to build and defend from all comers the socialist economy (and these qualities were not prized for nothing, for it was built and defended) were combined with the ruthless assumption of personal power and wholesale elimination not only of possible rivals but of critics as well.—What was happening was not at all obvious to participants at the time, though it is obvious enough now, and was obvious then to a number of not very friendly onlookers. All this was certainly an experience from which can be drawn conclusions not only about the rights and wrongs of socialist policies, but about the rights and wrongs of personal conduct as well. At the same time, more cultivation of the imagination, and less laying down the law from a standpoint of pretended infallibility, could have rendered much of this experience unnecessary.

The divorce which some have made between political questions on the one hand, and moral ones on the other, is totally alien and contradictory to the scientific socialist conception of human ends. This kind of separation, indeed, has no place in socialist political theory, but was made in the political theory of exploiting classes. And wherever it has intruded into political practice, the results have shown that it hinders rather than helps the realisation of socialist and communist aims. The practice of cold political calculation, which regards persons as mere means to be used for political ends, not only repels many who might otherwise be won for socialism, but also disorientates and disorganises the socialist movement itself—quite apart from the fact that such calculations are usually erroneous anyway, since they forget to take into account important human factors.

For scientific socialism and communism, politics is a means and not an end, and moreover a means which, as Marx and Engels stressed in their theory of the state, should be discarded as soon as circumstances permit. The whole point of socialist politics is to work for people to be able to develop their lives freely on the basis of communal ownership of the means of production. It is true that contemporary conditions do impose political obligations on people, since without politics little can be done on a social scale, and measures have therefore to be taken to see that these obligations are fulfilled. But political obligations are themselves tested by experience, and political life itself is thrown into disarray if politics are so conducted that the political obligations people are urged to accept, or coerced into accepting, are in conflict with what they have learned from experience to consider the decencies of personal behaviour and of regard to others. Political affairs ought to be conducted in conformity with the ascertained requirements of the personal and communal life of people in the contemporary condition of society. Those requirements can be ascertained, not simply by looking them up in books or laying them down in advance, but only in the course of the vast interchange of experience, imagination and ideas which takes place (unless artificially prevented) amongst people who are learning to work and struggle together for obtaining their means of life.

For scientific socialism and communism, then, the principles of political action and of personal conduct are neither counterposed one to the other, nor is the one subordinate to the other. Yet in the conditions of alienation, to cope with and to escape from which those principles are intended, the path of their application is still beset with contradictions. These are manifested alike in the spheres of public policy and leadership, and of individual conduct.

There remain contradictions in socialist-communist politics between, for example, the scientific approach, which demands the thorough and impartial investigation of all the factors operative in a social situation, and the practical necessity of taking immediate political decisions and effecting their operation. There are contradictions between the political aim of securing the maximum freedom for individuals on the basis of democratic organisation, and the political necessity of subordinating individuals to the authority of the party and (when in power) the state. There are contradictions between the long-term aim, which is a free society, and the short-term aim of imposing social reconstruction and beating down opposition to it. There are also contradictions between the divergent interests and consequent political judgments of the participants in the movement, both on a national and a world scale—industrial workers, professional workers, small proprietors, peasants, and peoples of relatively advanced and prosperous industrial regions, on the one hand, and of poverty-stricken underdeveloped territories on the other. And there are contradictions between the interests and aims which individual leaders or groups of leaders may sometimes come to acquire in the possession and enlargement of power, and the interests and aims of the movement as a whole. It is not true that, as Lord Acton declared, "all power corrupts", since there are plenty of examples of people uncorrupted by power. But it *is* true that in power lie sources of corruption.

For individuals, there are contradictions between what the party and the cause claim from them in loyalty, work and sacrifice, and not only their personal pleasures but obligations to others arising from personal ties. The party cannot but claim precedence over the individual; at the same time, a popular party is only an expedient for promoting the welfare of individuals, and individuals have to judge it and its actions by how well it serves the ends for which they support it, and be prepared to criticise, to protest and to demand changes at the same time as they preserve discipline and obey the rules. Members who regard themselves as absolutely subordinate to the party fail to serve the end of the party, just as do those who reject elementary party discipline. There are contradictions between individuals' ideas of right and wrong in the treatment of others, and the way political or party decisions at times call on others to be treated—between standards of individual behaviour based on ideas of humanity, and political decisions which are not (and could not be) based only on general humane considerations.

Marxism, the most political of all philosophies, tells the naked truth about politics—that parties and politics are means of imposing some interests on others in conditions where people are still divided. It is necessary to understand the contradictions of political and moral life, and that they can only be finally solved with the ending of all divisions of interest and of all politics. Aristotle, the founder of moral and political philosophy, perhaps understood such matters rather better than most of his successors when he said that the right action was always the mean between extremes. There is no formula for the mean, except continuously to ascertain and test it in the experience of class struggle.

Hence while we are well able, at particular stages in the development of the movement towards communism, to formulate in general terms "codes" of public and individual conduct, such codes have always and necessarily a provisional character, and are subject to be variously interpreted and variously amended in the course of experience.

Taking all the contradictions into account it is perhaps no wonder that in the conduct of class struggle, both in public policies and in individual conduct, there sometimes occur mistakes, disputes and betrayals, disastrous errors of judgment, and actions of a sort that come to be regarded not as errors but crimes. It is a product of the still inhuman conditions of humanity, in which human relations are not yet intelligible and reasonable. For William Morris spoke the simple truth when he stated, at the conclusion of a lecture on *Communism*, "that any other state of society but communism is grievous and disgraceful to all belonging to it", and that action within the present state of society could never altogether escape the taint of its conditions. The communist will not on that account give up the struggle and talk about "the god that failed", but persevere; and continue to say, as Morris said in the same lecture: "Intelligence enough to conceive, courage enough to will, power enough to compel. If our ideas of a new society are anything more than a dream, these three qualities must animate the due effective majority of the working people; and then, I say, the thing will be done."

CHAPTER SIX

Coexistence and Controversy

I. THE CONTEMPORARY WAR OF IDEAS

MARXISM does not regard other philosophies only as sets of statements, in which one must try to decide which statements are true, which false, and which, perhaps, senseless. It regards them as historical phenomena, and criticises them in historical perspective. And the history of philosophy is not treated in abstraction, as though philosophy had, or could have, a history of its own detached from that of material life. "Men are the producers of their conceptions and ideas —real active men, as they are conditioned by a definite development of their productive forces and of the intercourse corresponding to these," wrote Marx and Engels at the beginning of *The German Ideology*. ". . . on the basis of their real life-process we demonstrate the development of the ideological reflexes and echoes of this life-process . . . Morality, religion, metaphysics, all the rest of ideology and their corresponding forms of consciousness thus no longer retain the semblance of independence. They have no (separate) history, no (separate) development; but men, developing their material production and their material intercourse, alter, along with this their real existence, their thinking and the products of their thinking."

Marxism sees itself historically too, in exactly the same way. Thus Marxism, as a distinctive complex of theory and practice produced in the conditions of the rise of the modern working-class movement and of the transition from capitalism to socialism and communism, will disappear like other philosophies; that is, it will cease to exist as a distinctive class ideology, or as a doctrine or "ism" opposed by rival doctrines. Those modes of expression, presentation and argument which correspond to the assertion of one interest and aim opposed to others will cease to be used, leaving only the disinterested demonstration of universal truth.

As Voltaire said in the article on "Sect" in his *Philosophical Dictionary*: "There are no sects in mathematics, in experimental physics.

A man who examines the relations between a cone and a sphere is
not of the sect of Archimedes; he who sees that the square of the
hypotenuse of a right-angled triangle is equal to the square of the
two other sides is not of the sect of Pythagoras. When you say that
the blood circulates, that the air is heavy, that the sun's rays are
pencils of seven refrangible rays, you are not either of the sect of
Harvey, or the sect of Torricelli, or the sect of Newton; you agree
merely with the truth demonstrated by them . . . The more Newton
is revered, the less do people style themselves Newtonians; this word
supposes that there are anti-Newtonians."

Hence the fact that there is a party calling itself Marxist shows
that the disinterested demonstration of truth is not yet feasible in
philosophy, but that the thinking corresponding to one interest is
opposed by that of another. If one wants to maintain the truth that is
demonstrated in Marxism it can only be by its assertion as a partisan
point of view against others differently motivated.

The rivalries in ideology have something in common with the
rivalries between, say, the salesmen for an up-to-date firm of manufacturers and those of a more old-fashioned firm. No doubt it could
be impartially demonstrated that the one product is far better
designed than the other. But the rival claims continue for all that,
because behind them lie not a common interest in designing the best
product but the conflicting interests of competing manufacturers.
Hence if anyone demonstrates the superiority of the one product, he
is thereby working for the one interest against the other.

Today, as in the past, we are engaged in a war of ideas, in which
the interests of competing schools in maintaining and developing
their ideas reflect the interests of conflicting classes in maintaining or
changing property relations and the ways of life based on them.
There are these differences from the past: that first of all, the
working-class party has, in Marxism, become quite clearly aware of
the class-motivated character of its ideas, and this constitutes, indeed,
an important feature of its ideas; and that, secondly, socialism has
ceased to be only an aim of working-class parties and become the
actual system of society which great states exist to defend and
administer, so that the controversy in the realm of ideas becomes
further the controversy between the ruling ideas in the socialist sector
of the world and those in the capitalist sector.

At the present time, capitalism and socialism coexist—and this is a
significant change from the earlier situation in which there were

only socialist movements but no socialist states. Communists, who are in favour of building socialism and eliminating capitalism all over the world, have always, since the first socialist state was established in 1917, regarded it as the duty of socialist states to build socialism and eliminate capitalism in their own territories, to defend themselves against external intervention, and to render aid and comfort to other peoples fighting for emancipation. At the same time, the circumstances of coexistence led Lenin, and the communists who followed him, to conclude that socialist states should not themselves try to intervene in the internal affairs of capitalist states, or take a direct hand in eliminating them by war or any other means. Thus socialist states should seek to trade with capitalist ones, to enter into diplomatic relations, and to settle state differences by negotiations and compromise. These policies have been dictated by the fact that international war in modern conditions is an unmitigated disaster for all, and not least for socialist countries which need peaceful conditions in which to build socialism; and that the most favourable conditions both for consolidating socialism in places where it already exists, and for working for it in others, are those in which the coexistence of socialism with capitalism remains peaceful.

So far as they are guided by such rational considerations, therefore, both socialist states and socialist movements favour, in state relations, policies of negotiations and compromise. This is far from being a passive attitude, since such policies can succeed only by being imposed upon unwilling and arrogant imperialist powers by socialist strength and mass pressure, and the better they succeed the worse does the position of the remaining exploiting classes become.

However, while it is possible and desirable for communists to propose negotiation and compromise in the sphere of state relations, they cannot negotiate or compromise in ideas. Here battle is joined without the possibility of truce. By and large, the more firmly the custom of negotiation can be established between capitalist and socialist states, and the less they menace each other with arms, the more openly and uncompromisingly will battle be joined in the sphere of ideas. Capitalism having been rendered impotent to subvert socialist states, the task is still to win the minds of the people for the democratic mass struggle to bury capitalist power and capitalist relations, and, by building socialist societies in accordance with communist ideas, to demonstrate the superiority of those ideas.

There are, of course, many who are against making an issue out of ideas an entertaining discussion on the T.V. by all means, but they would as soon quarrel with a man over his face as over his opinions, and regard serious controversy as bad form. This idea about ideas is itself one of the ideas which socialists and communists have to combat; it is bred of capitalist conditions and helps guard them from damaging investigation.

How to conduct and win the war of ideas in the conditions of the peaceful coexistence of capitalism and socialism? Essentially, this is not a matter of just having a bash at an opponent, but of building and surpassing—just as the final demonstration of the superiority of socialism is to be achieved, not negatively by pointing to the misfortunes and deprivations which happen to people under capitalism, but positively by building a socialist society in which there is prosperity, brotherhood and freedom, so that its superiority is manifest. Partisanship does not show itself in arrogance and rudeness, which only bespeak lack of confidence and ignorance, but in scientific method and rationality. The ideas of socialism and communism are those of scientific humanism, and the fight for them is the work of their consistent and constructive development as the answer to the human problems of the age of science and the technological revolution.

Antonio Gramsci, founder of the Italian Communist Party, said long ago that a war of ideas differs from a military war in that the way to win it is to engage the enemy where he is strongest, whereas in military war you seek out the weak points to make a breakthrough. It is easy enough to claim victories by knocking down a few incompetent hack-writers; no well-informed person is impressed by such ideological prowess, however loud the huzzahs, and the other side can effectively retaliate by knocking down a few in return. In bourgeois philosophy, literature and art, as in the sciences, there are people at work of competence and integrity, who are not working to please the government or the heads of finance and industry but to try to solve genuine human problems. These people constitute the strength of bourgeois ideology, and it is over their ideas that the war of ideas is waged.

Hence in controversy the job is not only to refute errors and expose prejudices and preconceptions, but to understand the problems that are raised to get down to their origins and analyse their formulations, and to criticise constructively so as to find how to work towards answering the problems. Some have said that to enter into controversy in such a spirit is to compromise with opponents and concede points to them—non-partisan "objectivity". Such controversialists may perhaps establish themselves for a time in their own circle, where they have shouted down contradiction, but they never even enter into contact with a major opponent. To fight is not to call names and to boast of one's infallibility, but to demonstrate the truth and establish the answers, and so win the minds and enlist the political activity of thinking people, and remove their misconceptions and misunderstandings of the socialist and communist position.

Furthermore, the war of ideas is a war in which we learn. We do not enter it knowing all the answers beforehand, but if the answers are to be found they will be found in the course of fighting for them. Thus those who are not ready to learn from opponents can never win but are sure to lose. To reject in advance everything discovered by those with whom one is in disagreement is to adopt a principle that can only discredit one's own ideas.

Negotiations and compromises are unacceptable in the sphere of ideas because agreements that "if you stop thinking this, I will stop thinking that" are unacceptable, and so are compromises which agree on some middle way of thinking. If workers put in a wage demand for two shillings they may well compromise for eighteen pence—but if one party calls black white, while the other calls it black, they cannot negotiate an agreement that they will both call it grey, so long as what they are arguing about is the truth. Compromises in ideas are therefore always in principle unprincipled. But to learn something to the point from other people's inquiries is not compromise. And if Marxists learn from their opponents in the course of controversy, that is not a compromise in which Marxists take something in fair exchange for giving up something else, or appease their opponents by ceding a point, but it is a strengthening of the Marxist position. The strength of that position lies, indeed, in the fact that Marxism can assimilate the discoveries and creative ideas of opponents of Marxism, and incorporate them into its own development—whereas they cannot assimilate the essential truths which Marxism has established without giving up their own positions. And the more this fact can be demonstrated in the theoretical development of Marxism, the stronger will the Marxist position become.

2. COMMUNISM AND THE TECHNOLOGICAL
REVOLUTION

What is it that is now most vital for the constructive development of Marxist theory? The materialist humanist philosophy must become the scientific philosophy of the new technological revolution.

In the B.B.C. Reith Lectures in 1964, on *The Age of Automation*, Sir Leon Bagrit, one of the computer kings of British industry, said that with fully developed automation, equipped with techniques of communication, computation and control, the human being would "become the real master . . . The unnecessary chores have been removed from him. He is exercising his specifically human function . . . automation has only one real purpose, which is to help us to become human beings." Automation can, of course, have no purpose at all apart from that for which people may choose to use it; but that Sir Leon has correctly stated the controlling purpose of the business firms now introducing automation in Britain, the U.S.A. and other capitalist countries is more than doubtful. The purpose of capital investment in automation, as in earlier technical innovations, is profit. And it would drive even the best designed computer to simulate a nervous breakdown, to ask it to work out how to introduce universal automation of production and the use of techniques of communication, computation and control to plan the whole of production for human needs, so that all "become human beings" and everyone becomes a "real master", while retaining capitalist ownership and private appropriation of profits. The present-day technological revolution is creating techniques which cannot be fully used—cannot indeed be more than very partially used in a few departments of the economy—except under the social relations of communism. They could not yet be *fully* used even under socialism, with state ownership of the means of production and exchange, but only under communism. For these techniques bind together people and their instruments into one co-ordinated and inter-communicating system for satisfying human needs.

Far from being the dream of an ideal society, communism has become the statement of the conditions necessary for using and developing modern techniques. Many wiseacres continue to dismiss it as a utopia which could come into being only very far in the future, if at all; they forget the extraordinarily rapid pace of development of modern technology. In the present-day conditions of capitalism communism is no dream—but what to do about the social consequences of applying modern techniques may soon become, for the magnates of capital, a nightmare.

The function of communist theory is to inform and guide communist practice.

Fundamental is the formulation and testing of the theoretical approach—the dialectical materialist method, the statement of which takes the form of category-propositions—the general principles or laws of materialism and dialectics. This is essentially the approach, and these are the principles, which the practice of the sciences teaches. Marxism sets out to apply them in the study of society, contrary to the precepts of bourgeois philosophy and the practice of bourgeois social science. For the latter ignores principles long applied and ratified in establishing the foundations of natural sciences, and in favour of it philosophers have misconstrued the methods of science. Marxism sets out to develop the scientific materialist theory of man and society, comparable in its empirical foundations and testability to other departments of scientific theory, so as at one and the same time to formulate the practicable communist aims, values and purposes and the practical principles of the struggle to realise them.

The material basis of communism is and can only be the development and communal use of the highest techniques men can devise. The theoretical task is to understand these techniques and their potentialities, and to give direction and purpose to the struggle for the new life in which men will be ends for men and not mere means, and human relations intelligible and reasonable. For this task the strictest observance of the canons of scientific method is necessary, the correct principles for the assembly of information, the empirical testing and retesting of every informative generalisation. It can never be done by propagating dogmas, never be done by relying on hunches or guesses dressed up as authoritative statements, but only by relying on accumulated social experience continuously subjected to scientific analysis.

The dialectical materialist method, as set out in philosophical methodological principles, is the science of the laws of thought— and it has to be developed as a science. Hence to let it remain in the form of aphorisms, approximations, the imprecise statement of general laws not systematically connected together, and so on, is not good enough. Undoubtedly that is how it had to start, but that is not how it can be allowed to remain. Nor is it a very practical way of honouring such pioneers as Marx, Engels and Lenin, and appreciating their theoretical genius, to learn what they said by heart and leave it at that. All must be tied together, developed systematically and consistently in strict conformity with the principles of formal logic, and every link tested according to the canons of philosophical demonstration.

Such very rigorous forms of philosophical formulation, comparable to the rigour of analysis and proof in mathematics, were not so needful when the only practical task of materialist philosophy was to combat idealist illusion and present the general outlook to guide and inspire the economic and political class struggle for socialism against capitalism. Hence a high degree of theoretical refinement was apt to be regarded as something of a diversion from the main task. But times have changed rapidly, and the struggle has reached a new level in which socialism is established, in which the forecast technological revolution which provides the basis for communism is actually upon us, and in which, consequently, it is needful to get ready the theoretical equipment for using the new techniques and building communism. It is true that the class struggle is by no means over but is more acute than ever; but where industry is most advanced a younger generation is growing up who are technologically-minded, and for whom a theory as to how and why to fight the boss must be also a theory as to how and why to use the new techniques—so that what was good enough for their grandfathers is not good enough for them.

Automated production with automata to perform functions of communication, computation and control brings into use not only mechanisms which perform, but with greater power and precision, functions of human hands, but mechanisms which perform with greater power and precision functions of human brains—mechanisms that observe, that communicate, that regulate, and that think out problems more complex than any we can think out without them, so as to be capable not only of working *for* us to produce particular products, but of working *with* us to plan production as a whole. Yet to talk about automata observing, regulating and planning is subject to the qualification that they do so only in the sense that the older machines cut things up, shape them and put them together— they only do it by using up the motive power we have directed into them, and in accordance with the specifications to which we have designed them and the methods of operation with which we have equipped and programmed them. A machine can make for us something we could not make with our hands because we know the operations by which that sort of thing may be made, and design the machine accordingly and link it up with a sufficient source of motive power. Similarly, an automaton can think out for us problems more complex than we could think out with our brains because we know the operations by which such problems may be solved and design the automaton to perform them. Such automata are abstracters and assemblers of information for us. I remarked when discussing "the laws of thought" in an earlier chapter, that formal logic and materialist dialectics are concerned with operations of formulation, abstraction and assembly of information. We must get to know the principles of these operations in no rough and ready way but exactly, accurately, precisely—not so much in order to apply them for ourselves, which we can learn to do well enough for practical purposes without so rigorous a theoretical discipline, but in order to use modern technology in the processing of all categories of information.

Materialist dialectics, as communists have succeeded in working it out hitherto, falls far short of such requirements. The dialectical materialist philosophy is still very rough and ready, made in and for the hurly-burly of the class struggle—providing us already with the scientific principles for formulating human ends and seeing what we must do to fight for them, but requiring further refinements as we come nearer to realising them. Militant materialist philosophy must be suited to the age of automation and computation.

Communist theory, then, is not, as it is often misrepresented to be, a vision or prophesy of the millennium and a faith for the toiling masses, but the scientific philosophy for the modern man, the potential master of techniques. As such it must unite the discipline, precision, method and control by verifiable fact of the sciences with the passion, imagination and affirmation of human values of the arts. It goes on the principle that the condition for freedom is the appreciation of necessity. Hence strictness in the scientific appreciation of necessity is the condition for the imaginative development of human energies in the enjoyment of freedom.

Masses who are aroused for the first time to organised political activity, and for the first time are able to see in it the way out of their poverty and humiliation, are apt to seek in politics what they formerly found in religion—the certainty of a faith, the infallibility of a doctrinal authority. Antonio Gramsci remarked that ideas that communism rests on doctrines which must not be questioned and cannot be revised, and reveals what must inevitably take place, are ideas that spring from and cater for masses who are still acting spontaneously and are still under the spell of religion. The notion of infallible doctrine can appeal only to those not yet familiar with scientific ways of practical thinking, and that of historical inevitability to those who have not yet learned to rely fully on their own powers unaided by a supernatural fate. As the mass movement becomes politically mature, and as its members become educated in struggle and appreciate both the complexity of its conditions and the character of its tasks, such ideas are seen as what they are— primitive myths and illusions.

The practice of communism demands that communists should above all remain close to the masses, act as their voice and their champions, learn from them about what needs to be done and help them to learn from their experience. For it is only masses who can now change society by their action; intellectuals, scholars, politicians are powerless to achieve anything on their own. At the same time, it is the task of communism, in the prosecution of mass struggle, to raise the masses, among whom individual personalities are submerged, to the conditions of association of independently-thinking highly-informed individuals working together for a common interest and aim. In this context then, what may be called a cult of the masses, according to which nothing is to be said or done which anonymous masses do not spontaneously propose, understand and approve, is as bad as the so-called cult of the individual. In fact such cults are not different but the same. Spontaneously acting masses have always looked to a saviour, an infallible leader in whom they can put their whole trust; and he who is set up as such a leader can only succeed in so far as he can appear, as it were, the personification of the masses who trust in him. Communism has, as experience shows, to pass through such phases. But yet it can claim no other foundation for its theory and practice than the exercise of reason, and the only cult reason will allow is the cult of reason. That, however, is no cult at all, because it can have no high priests and in the practice of it each individual has to think, decide and judge for himself in association with his fellows.

Marxism, the theory that informs and guides communist practice, cannot be doctrinaire or claim infallibility. Neither can it be developed by promulgating vast and vague generalisations in the style of many would-be humanistic philosophies, nor yet by cultivating arid precision on isolated problems. It is developed by assembling the information vital for human progress, demonstrating and using the method for assembling facts so as to abstract from them human aims and knowledge of means to attain them. It is devoted to the practical aim of making men the masters of their techniques, so that these can serve them as the basis for enjoying together the free exercise of human capacities. Hence its reliance is on neither faith nor dogma, but only on science.

3. MARXISM AND THE LINGUISTIC PHILOSOPHY

If from these considerations about the development of Marxism we now turn back to the contemporary linguistic philosophy and the Marxist controversy with it, what conclusions can we finally draw?

The linguistic philosophy which has been developed in Britain in the mid-twentieth century arose, as I tried to show in examining its precursors and its own development, from trying to solve the difficulties of previous empirical philosophy which had led to subjective idealist metaphysics, solipsism and a tangle of unanswerable questions connected with them, and from trying to assimilate the demonstrably correct methods and findings of modern formal logic. Its achievement was to rid empirical philosophy of subjective idealism, and to establish the philosophical recognition of formal logic as an independent science. But this was done only at the cost of beating a full retreat from any conception of philosophy as a guide to understanding the real world and its laws, and as a guide in practical life. At the same time as the linguistic philosophy attacked the traditional presuppositions of idealism it denied the very possibility of working out the principles of a consistently materialist approach to human problems. Criticising the logical errors made in traditional metaphysical theories, and in traditional positivism, it arrived at the conclusion that what we need is not to discover how to give our theories a good foundation, but a therapy for theories. The disintegration and irrationality of bourgeois society was faithfully reflected in the linguistic idea that the role of philosophy can only be to debunk attempts at a comprehensive understanding of human life and human purpose, and not to establish the foundations for such understanding. Hence this philosophy, for all its accurate analytic description of certain features of the logic of language, has, like others before it, only reached another dead end. Its positive achievements can only be carried forward by completely overturning its basic and essentially negative presuppositions.

In the very character of its achievement, the linguistic philosophy is, after all, only the tailend of the old philosophy which sought to reach its conclusions independently of the sciences. Having recognised the futility of philosophical systems, and also of interpretations or logical analyses of the findings of the sciences based on trying to establish, in Wittgenstein's phrase, that "it must be like this", the linguistic philosophy found in the uses of language the exclusive sphere of philosophical investigation. It then turned this investigation into an ultra-specialised discipline, with no aim outside itself. In relation to the problems, therefore, of trying to understand the bases of human purposes and activities, its role became simply to divert discussion and dodge the issues—and for practice too, merely to accept things as they are.

We should distinguish on the one hand the definite achievement in the treatment of various technical problems of formal logic, scientific method, semantics and analysis of uses of language with which the linguistic philosophy is associated, and, on the other hand, the distinctive contention of this philosophy—to which it owes its description of "linguistic"—that all this amounts to nothing but description of uses of words and that philosophy cannot get further than such description. The former is of positive value, the latter negative. In a similar way it is important to distinguish in contemporary capitalist society on the one hand the achievements in the continued development of science and technology, and on the other the misuse and frustration of these by pressing them into the service of private profit. In general, the theoretical advances in technical problems of logic, scientific method and analysis of language are connected with the practical advances in technology, while the negative features of the linguistic philosophy are but ideological reflections of the inability of the rulers and managers of capitalist society to make good use of them: the philosophers cannot surpass in theory the limits which the practical men cannot surpass in practice.

The basis of the criticism of the linguistic philosophy is that it concerns itself only with the differences between different uses of words, and maintains that it is possible only to describe the actual uses but not to explain them or give them any foundation. This is to renounce the grand aim of philosophy, which is to demonstrate the foundation of what we think and say, or to work out a well-founded world outlook or way of thinking. Linguistic philosophers say that cannot be done. But this criticism does not in the least imply that the distinctions they have drawn between different uses of words, and the descriptions offered of these different uses, are either untrue or trivial.

On the contrary, when we use words in discussing general and abstract problems it is essential to understand what we are doing, in the sense of being able to distinguish and describe the different uses of words: for much confusion and illusion can result from not doing so, and mistaking what words actually do. As Hobbes said years ago, philosophers are for ever becoming "entangled in words". Philosophy is discourse at a very high level of abstraction; and the higher the level of abstraction, the more readily can we get tripped up and misled by words. Hence no philosophical problem can in the end be thoroughly discussed without linguistic analysis.

Whatever other schools of philosophy may have to say about it, Marxists at any rate, who adopt a materialist approach for which thinking and using language are not two things but one, should welcome the contribution made to the detection and sorting out of verbal confusions (ambiguities, false analogies and category-mistakes) and to the clarification of meaning by the method of the paradigm case.

In the exposition and application of a general theory many words and phrases acquire specific, definite and limited meanings, which they are given within the context of the theory, whereas they may have been given different meanings by common usage outside it, and also by other theories. Naturally, such an all-embracing theory as Marxism has many semantic peculiarities. It provides a context within which words are given specific Marxist meanings, and likewise, in its different departments, contexts within which the same words are used in different ways (as the word "contradiction" is used in a different way in talking of, say, "the contradictions of capitalism" from that in which it is used in the context of formal logic). One can therefore never possibly understand Marxist theory, and still less get far in applying and developing it, unless one is prepared to pay careful and explicit attention to the semantic peculiarities of its terminology—the ways it uses words.

Classical Marxism was not confused by language, not because Marx had already solved all the general problems connected with uses of language, nor because his use of words was always formally precise and never ambiguous, but because it was not systematically developed into regions of application where verbal ambiguities become systematically misleading. As distinct from his strictly scientific work in such fields as political economy and history, Marx's philosophical writing was largely aphoristic in style. But the use of words in the truth-bearing aphorism is quite distinct from that in the confused uninformative generalisation. There is ambiguity and lack of precise definition in both. But in the one case the statement is, as it were, rich with meaning (in an analogous way to that often occurring in poetry), in that it may be expanded into a series of complementary, mutually consistent and mutually supporting statements; in the other case it is merely confused, in that it is capable of bearing a number of mutually inconsistent meanings, or uninformative in that it embodies category-mistakes. The working out and application of the philosophical ideas and approach of Marxism demands the most scrupulous attention to uses of words and their distinctions, and professional knowledge of logical techniques—otherwise in place of clarifications and demonstrations there may be offered only confusions and unverifiable assertions.

At the same time, as the record shows, while linguistic analysis can get you out of some muddles it can get you into others. And while it is necessary in philosophy, that is not to say that it is *all* that is necessary, and still less that it *is* philosophy. An aid to doing something, however indispensable, should not be confused with what it is an aid for doing. That is like twirling a walking stick and saying you have been for a walk. Marxists would not propose to study the uses of language as an end in itself, but as a means to developing the science of the laws of thought, and to developing the general theory of human life and human aims, free from idealist illusions and preconceptions.

Index